The Interpretation and Application of the Most-Favored-Nation Clause in Investment Arbitration

World Trade Institute Advanced Studies

VOLUME 12

The titles published in this series are listed at *brill.com/wtia*

The Interpretation and Application of the Most-Favored-Nation Clause in Investment Arbitration

By

Anqi Wang

BRILL
NIJHOFF

LEIDEN | BOSTON

The open access publication of this book has been published with the support of the Swiss National Science Foundation.

The Library of Congress Cataloging-in-Publication Data is available online at https://catalog.loc.gov
LC record available at https://lccn.loc.gov/2022031975

Typeface for the Latin, Greek, and Cyrillic scripts: "Brill". See and download: brill.com/brill-typeface.

ISSN 2405-9331
ISBN 978-90-04-51788-2 (hardback)
ISBN 978-90-04-51789-9 (e-book)

This book is printed on acid-free paper and produced in a sustainable manner

Contents

Acknowledgements

Anqi Wang

This book is based on my doctoral dissertation, which was completed with the financial support of the China Scholarship Council (CSC).

It is a rather emotional moment to write this acknowledgement, and I have many people to thank. First and foremost, I want to thank my parents for their understanding and unconditional love. As I write this, I have not visited them for three years due to the COVID-19 pandemic. Nevertheless, their support has never been absent.

I would like to take this opportunity to thank my supervisors, Prof. Peter Van Den Bossche and Dr. Rodrigo Polanco, for their invaluable advice and continuous support during my doctoral study. Their immense knowledge and enthusiasm for international law have encouraged me throughout my doctoral research.

This work would not be made possible without the support from my beloved friends. I want to express my sincere gratitude to my colleague, my proofreader and my dear friend Dr. Alex Beyleveld, whose friendship, encouragement and interesting opinions on movies have certainly brightened my doctoral life.

With this opportunity, I would like to thank my best friend Yin, without whom my life would be much less enriched. Her continued love and support have helped me overcome many depressions over the years. I would also like to express my appreciation to my dear friend and my colleague Dr. Aylin Yildiz, whose enthusiasm and loving hugs have surely motivated and comforted me in dark times. I also want to take this chance to express my thankfulness to Dr. Iryna Bogdanova and Dr. Zaker Ahmed. Their friendship is one of the most precious memories during my doctoral study. I admire their remarkable insights and great passion for international law, which have inspired me greatly for the past years. I am also grateful for my friendship with Dr. Qingnan Sun, who has been very considerate and supportive for my years in Bern.

With great pleasure I express my thankfulness to Dr. Anil Aksöz, for all the laughs we had and the enjoyable time we spent together. Moments like these gave me great strength to push forward my work.

I am deeply grateful to my dear friend Dr. Jannik Piepenburg and his family. Without their tremendous motivation and encouragement over the past years, it would be impossible for me to complete my study.

This work was finished during the time of the COVID-19 pandemic, throughout which my dear friend Dr. Gu encouraged and accompanied me with her caring words, and I owe great gratitude to her.

Finally, the publication of my doctoral dissertation would be impossible without the help of Brill and the Advanced Studies Series of the World Trade Institute, to whom I owe extraordinary gratitude.

Thank you all, and may the Force be with you.

Abbreviations

BIT	Bilateral Investment Treaty
CETA	Comprehensive Economic and Trade Agreement
FCN	Friendship, Commerce and Navigation Treaties
FTA	Free Trade Agreement
ICSID	International Centre for Settlement of Investment Disputes
IIA	International Investment Agreement
ISDS	Investor-State Dispute Settlement
MFN	Most-Favored-Nation treatment
NAFTA	North American Free Trade Agreement
OECD	Organization for Economic Co-operation and Development
UNCITRAL	United Nations Commission on International Trade Law
UNCTAD	United Nations Conference on Trade and Development
VCLT	Vienna Convention on the Law of Treaties

Introduction

Since its inclusion in the first bilateral investment treaty (Germany-Pakistan BIT), the Most-Favored-Nation (MFN) clause has become a frequently included provision in international investment agreements (IIAs). MFN clause interpretation and application is a controversial topic in international investment law. Debates are mainly concerned with the appropriate scope of the MFN clause in IIAs, especially the extent to which a given clause incorporates substantive and procedural treatment in other IIAs. It has been argued that the MFN clause should be applied as a treaty tool to multilateralize more favorable treatment. If this argument is accepted, an expansive interpretation of a given MFN clause – which extends its application to procedural and/or substantive provisions not contained in the basic treaty – should be preferred.[1] Meanwhile, some scholars insist on a case-by-case examination of MFN clauses without presumptions.[2] This debate has led to inconsistent decisions in Investor-State Dispute Settlement (ISDS). ISDS tribunals have adopted different – and, at times, directly opposing – interpretations of MFN clauses, this despite relying on similar interpretation methods.

This book critically engages with the above discussion in order to propose a more balanced method for interpreting MFN clauses in IIAs. Its arguments are developed over the course of six chapters in total. Chapter 1 traces the use of the MFN clause from a historical perspective: from its beginnings in the 11th century to its inclusion in modern IIAs. It is noted that the prevalence of the MFN clause in international agreements reflects the contemporary status observed in the global economy of given time. It thrives in liberal economic atmospheres and recedes in times of war or times of economic conservatism. The current IIA system is witnessing a paradigm shift whereby treaties are pursuing a more balanced relationship between state interests and investor protection, and the MFN clause plays a key role in the type of IIAs pursued by states.

1 Stephan W Schill, *The Multilateralization of International Investment Law* (Cambridge University Press 2009); Stephan W Schill, 'MFN Clauses as Bilateral Commitments to Multilateralism: A Reply to Simon Batifort and J. Benton Heath' (2017) 111 American Journal of International Law 914.

2 Simon Batifort and J Benton Heath, 'The New Debate on the Interpretation of MFN Clauses in Investment Treaties: Putting the Brakes on Multilateralization' (2018) 111 American Journal of International Law 873.

Chapter 2 discusses the main methods of interpretation applicable to MFN clauses, looking mainly at customary international law and Articles 31 and 32 of the Vienna Convention on the Law of Treaties (VCLT). This chapter shows that tribunals have reached diverging conclusions based on their assumptions about the relationship between the regulatory power of host states and the protection of foreign investments and investors, even when relying on the same interpretive methods.

Chapter 3 continues examining the MFN clause in case law. It focuses on cases in which claimants invoke the MFN clause to obtain a higher standard of substantive treatment. Specifically, two groups of cases are analyzed. The first of these includes cases in which the MFN clause has been used to provide *de facto* more favorable treatment to claimants. The second group includes cases in which the MFN clause has been used to accord higher standards of treaty protection, including the fair and equitable treatment (FET) standard, full protection and security, the protection afforded by umbrella clauses, and stronger protections in relation to expropriation.

The case law concerning the procedural application of MFN clauses will be examined in Chapters 4 and 5. Chapter 4 examines the case law on the application of MFN clauses to avoid procedural preconditions, such as the one contained in Article X(2) of the Spain-Argentina BIT, which requires that disputes be brought before a domestic court of the host state within a certain period of time before any claim can be brought in front of the international tribunal. Chapter 5 deals with cases in which MFN clauses have been invoked to extend the jurisdiction of tribunals. Specific analysis is provided for each case, including in relation to the position adopted by each tribunal and its application of interpretive methods. After examining the case law, Chapter 6 concludes with observations on the changing nature of the formulation of MFN clauses in modern IIAs and considers the manner in which states, as potential disputing parties, may respond to expansive invocations of MFN clauses in ISDS practice.

Throughout the above chapters, it is suggested that the MFN clause plays an essential role in the current trend of IIA renegotiation, and that MFN clauses in IIAs should not as a general proposition be employed as a tool which multilateralizes international obligations. The interpretation and application of MFN clauses should be based on a case-by-case assessment, not on tribunal assumptions. Specifically, interpretation should be guided by the interpretive methods of international law, including Articles 31 and 32 of the VCLT and the *ejusdem generis* principle. In addition, tribunals should consider other seminal parameters to adopt responsible MFN interpretations. These parameters include, for example, the fundamental role of state consent to international arbitration, a proper balance between investment protection and countries' regulatory space, as well as the ongoing IIA reform to strengthen countries' right to regulate on urgent issues such as sustainable development, public health and climate change, among others.

CHAPTER 1

History of the MFN Clause in International Law

The most-favored-nation (MFN) clause has been used in international law for a long time, and its content and modalities have undergone many changes throughout history. Its first appearance can be found in the 11th century in a Charter of Mantua, where the Holy Roman Emperor guaranteed an Italian city all the privileges granted to "any other city."[1] Since then, MFN treatment has been a central pillar of international commercial policy over the centuries.[2]

This chapter focuses on the history of the MFN clause in international law and will be divided into three parts: The first of these introduces the development of the MFN clause in the international trade law milieu; the second part focuses on its inclusion in IIAs; and the third part deals with MFN clause codification efforts. As such, this chapter will mainly examine the development of MFN clause in international trade law through to its development in the more specific field of international investment law at a later stage in time. Based on this examination, it provides a historical perspective of MFN clause interpretation and application.

1 The Evolution of the MFN Clause in International Trade Law

The first part of this chapter begins with the emergence of MFN treatment, which can be traced back to the Middle Ages, or, as Georg Schwarzenberger puts it, "to the dawn of international law."[3] To this end, the following study is conducted in chronological order, including with reference to early appearances of the MFN clause between the 11th and 16th centuries, the conditional MFN clause during the 17th and 19th centuries, and its incorporation into more recent treaty practice in the 20th century.

---

1 See, for example, Stephen Fietta, 'Most Favoured Nation Treatment and Dispute Resolution under Bilateral Investment Treaties: A Turning Point?' (2005) 8 International Arbitration Law Review 131.

2 OECD, 'Most-Favoured-Nation Treatment in International Investment Law' (OECD 2004) OECD Working Papers on International Investment WP 2004/02 <https://www.oecd.org/daf/inv/investment-policy/WP-2004_2.pdf > accessed 20 April 2022.

3 Georg Schwarzenberger, 'The Most-Favoured-Nation Standard in British State Practice' (1945) 22 British Yearbook on International Law 96, 97.

1.1 *The Genesis of the MFN Clause in the Middle Ages: From the 11th to the 16th Century*

The emergence of MFN treatment can be attributed to the liberal attitude of contemporary governments towards trade and competition between European merchants during the Middle Ages.[4] Ongoing trade activities between European countries during medieval times strengthened relations between nations. They readily concluded treaties with each other to guarantee traders freedom and rights in one another's territories.[5] After failed attempts by powerful commercial countries like Italy, France and Spain to monopolize certain markets, merchants from those countries eventually had to be satisfied with being placed on an equal footing with their competitors in the territory of other states.[6] Thus MFN treatment was guaranteed to beneficiaries for specific benefits received by specific third states.[7] An appropriate example of this is the promises given by the Byzantine Emperor to the Genoans that the latter would be afforded a particular standard of treatment, which was subsequently demanded by the Venetians as well.[8] Moreover, MFN treatment served as an efficient treaty tool in the sense that there was no need to overhaul the original treaty.[9]

From the 12th century onwards, MFN guarantees could more often be seen in commercial treaties concluded between states.[10] MFN treatment during the medieval period largely took the form of unilateral preferences granted by Oriental rulers to European municipalities, with the latter intending to establish a trading monopoly abroad.[11] Also, medieval MFN wording explicitly

---

4 Sophus Reinert and Robert Fredona, 'Merchants and the Origins of Capitalism' [2017] Harvard Business School BGIE Unit Working Paper No. 18-021 <http://dx.doi.org/10.2139/ssrn.3037173>.

5 See for example, the Magna Carta of 1215 which gave all merchants the right to sojourn safely and trade in England "quit from all evil tolls". See further: Nussbaum Arthur, *A Concise History of the Law of Nations* (1st edn, Macmillan 1947).

6 In this regard, see Schwarzenberger (n 3).

7 Tony Cole, 'The Boundaries of Most Favored Nation Treatment in International Investment Law' (2012) 33 Michigan Journal of International Law 537, 543.

8 Endre Ustor, 'First Report on the Most-Favoured-Nation Clause, Special Rapporteur' Vol II Yearbook of the International Law Commission (1969), available at <https://legal.un.org/ilc/publications/yearbooks/english/ilc_1969_v2.pdf> accessed 20 April 2022.

9 Richard Carlton Synder, *The Most-Favored-Nation Clause: An Analysis with Particular Reference to Recent Treaty Practice and Tariffs* (King's Crown Press 1948). In this regard, see also: David D Caron and Esme Shirlow, 'Most Favoured Nation Treatment – Substantive Protection in Investment Law' [2015] SSRN Electronic Journal.

10 See generally Nussbaum Arthur, *A Concise History of the Law of Nations* (1st edn, Macmillan 1947).

11 Ustor (n 8) 159. Regarding the unilateral nature of medieval MFN treatment, Nussbaum analyzes this issue from a medieval Islamic perspective, noting that: "… the Muslim rulers

referred to favors already granted to a small, specific group of trading cities in Europe, the names of which appear repeatedly in discourses discussing the development of international law: Venice, Genoa, Pisa, and Barcelona, amongst others. This is because commercial competition in medieval times existed mainly between this specific group of European cities. Through particularly plain treaty provisions, these cities sought to obtain treatment at least as favorable vis-à-vis their potential competitors.[12] Moreover, in contrast to MFN clauses in modern international economic agreements that offer mainly trade and investment protection, MFN treatment in the Middle Ages was granted mainly regarding a merchant's personal rights such as their lodgings, property, and lives while in foreign countries.[13]

A reciprocal MFN clause later appeared in the treaty between England and the Duke of Burgundy and Count of Flanders concluded in 1417, according to which vessels from all contracting parties were entitled to use harbors in the same manner as third countries.[14] By the end of the 15th century, restrictions on MFN clauses, which applied to a limited number of countries, were lifted, and more favorable treatment began to be granted to "any foreign countries."[15]

The end of the Thirty Years' War in 1648 and the Peace of Westphalia advanced the commercial expansion of European countries, in particular France, England, the Netherlands, and Spain.[16] Countries started seeking more liberal trade and closer trade relations with each other and began distinguishing between commercial treaties and political agreements. These developments were foundational to MFN clauses commonly being included in treaties to ensure equal treatment among competitors from different countries.[17]

---

were little interested in obtaining for their subjects reciprocal treatment in the respective European countries" and that "[t]he explanation seems to be that the Mohammedan law forbade the believers to sojourn for any length of time in the lands of the infidels"; thus, "the Oriental rulers helped in building up the unilaterality of the capitulations … ." See Nussbaum (n 10) 30.

12 Schwarzenberger writes "… how much the achievement of this object means to the chancelleries concerned may be gauged from the language of older treaties which, more openly than modern treaties in this sphere, reveal the particular jealousies and the actual competitors whom the contracting parties had very consciously in mind." See Schwarzenberger (n 3) 97. This treaty practice was also described by some writers as having occurred out of "jealousy". See Schwarzenberger (n 3) 99. See also Ustor (n 8) 159.

13 See Cole (n 7) 545.

14 Ustor (n 8) 159–60.

15 See, for example, the 1490 England-Denmark Treaty, cited by Schwarzenberger (n 3) 97.

16 Nussbaum (n 10) 87.

17 For example, the 1679 Nijmegen Treaty between the Netherlands and Sweden. In this regard see Jacob Viner, 'The Most-Favored-Nation Clause in American Commercial Treaties' (1924) 32 Journal of Political Economy 101.

In conclusion, the MFN clause in its early form was developed and formalized in early trade treaties due in large part to the expansion of foreign trade. Although the evolution of early MFN treatment underwent a major shift from restricted and unilateral to unrestricted and bilateral,[18] the standard was nevertheless clearly rooted in the idea of equality ever since its origin.[19] In other words, its early development shows that it was the medieval merchants' desire for equal treatment that gave rise to the idea of MFN treatment. This guaranteed that foreigners would not receive different treatment in the host country purely on the basis of their nationality.

1.2 *The Appearance of Conditional and Unconditional MFN Clauses: The 18th and 19th Centuries*

Europe in the 18th century was characterized by relative stability, civilization and wealth.[20] This implied more open national policies towards trade liberalization. Commercial treaties became more clearly distinct from political conventions and began to be concluded between a greater number of European countries; as did MFN treatment.[21]

In 1778, a conditional form of the MFN clause was introduced by a treaty concluded between France and the U.S. (the 1778 Treaty). This treaty extended MFN treatment to the contracting parties but conditioned on similar concessions being granted by third parties.[22] Although the conditional MFN clause

18 For a classification of early MFN clauses see Synder (n 9) 19.

19 Synder (n 9) 220.

20 Nussbaum (n 10) 127.

21 Nussbaum (n 10) 127–8. The 18th century has also been described by some writers as first having witnessed the "appearance of commercial treaties". See Ustor (n 8) 160. See also: Guiguo Wang, *International Investment Law: A Chinese Perspective* (1st edn, Routledge 2014).

22 Article II of this treaty read as follows: "the Most Christian King and the United States engage mutually not to grant any particular favour to other nations, in respect of commerce and navigation, which shall not immediately become common to the other party, who shall enjoy the same favour, freely, if the concession was freely made, or on allowing the same compensation, if the concession was conditional." See DP Myers, G Charles and WM Malloy, 'Treaties, Conventions, International Acts, Protocols and Agreements between the United States of America and Other Powers, 1776–1909.' United States Government Printing Office 1910. In fact, the wording "freely, if the concession was freely made, or on allowing the same compensation/equivalent, if the concession was conditional" served as a model for nearly all U.S. commercial treaties until 1923. See Ustor (n 8) 161. For more discussions about conditional MFN clause, see Stephan W Schill, *The Multilateralization of International Investment Law* (Cambridge University Press 2009). See also Surya P Subedi, *International Investment Law: Reconciling Policy and Principle* (Fourth edition, Hart Publishing 2020).

was originally inserted at the insistence of France, it nonetheless suited with U.S. trade policy at the time and was extensively applied thereafter by the U.S. government in its treaty relations with other countries for over a century.[23]

Critics of the conditional MFN clause believe that the concession required by the conditional MFN clause is a *de facto* "purchase" rather than an equal basis for international trade as provided for by the unconditional MFN clause. Under the conditional MFN clause, beneficiary states were obligated to lower tariffs in exchange for better privileges than those originally granted by the basic treaty. In this way, "the conditional clause [did] not grant equality, but the opportunity to purchase equality."[24] Apart from this, the difficulty of identifying the specific concessions granted in each agreement made it impossible to determine the equivalent a country should provide to purchase the equality required by the conditional MFN clause.[25] The constant negotiation of concessions for each country turned into a heavy burden in practice. It explicitly contravened the purpose of the MFN clause, the aim of which was to reduce the negotiation costs associated with concluding new treaties and to facilitate more favorable trading conditions.[26] Even if concessions could be identified and determined, another question was how "equivalent" other countries' concessions would be for the purpose of the conditional MFN clause. Ultimately, conditional MFN will inevitably lead to inequality, as countries would be placed in either a more or a less favorable position.[27] Since the underlying principle of the MFN clause is to treat countries equally, conditional MFN treatment only leads to the very discrimination against which it was supposed to compensate.[28] In this sense, the concept of conditional MFN clause was deployed as a protectionist tool masquerading as a liberalizing device.[29]

---

23 Vernon G Setser, 'Did Americans Originate the Conditional Most-Favored-Nation Clause?' (1933) 5 The Journal of Modern History 319, 319–313. It was said that the conditional MFN was in line with the interest of the U.S. as long as it was a net importer and prioritized industry protection. Under the conditional MFN clause, a country has to grant lower tariffs to imported U.S. products in order to enjoy more favorable tariffs imposed on its products exported to the U.S. See Schill (n 22) 131, footnote 31; Synder (n 9) 243.

24 Synder (n 9) 215.

25 Because it was impossible for identical trade relations to exist between two countries, the equivalent concessions under conditional MFN may lead to constant negotiations and substantive discrimination. See Synder (n 9) 213.

26 See Caron and Shirlow (n 9).

27 Synder (n 9) 215.

28 In this regard, Synder's comments are apposite. He provides as follows: [E]quality of treatment ... involves more than two nations. Its premise is that any third nation shall not be discriminated against. Equality of treatment is not the exchange of satisfactory concession between two nations. See Synder (n 9) 215.

29 Synder (n 9) 216.

Despite the above drawbacks, conditional MFN clauses were nonetheless widespread during the early 19th century and maintained their dominance between 1825 and 1860, with nearly ninety percent of MFN clauses included in treaties during this period using the conditional form.[30]

After a long period of fluctuation between conditional and unconditional MFN treatment, Europe experienced a decline in mercantilism and a revival of liberal trade policies at the beginning of the second half of the 19th century.[31] The 1860 Cobden-Chevalier Treaty between Great Britain and France included promises regarding substantial tariff reductions and the lifting of import bans, coupled with fully-fledged unconditional MFN treatment.[32] The Cobden-Chevalier Treaty indicated a move away from the conditional MFN clause in European treaty practice. On the other hand, the U.S. retained conditional MFN treatment for trade facilitation until 1923.

The practice of including conditional MFN clauses in treaties waned as the U.S. shifted to pushing unconditional MFN clauses in its treaty practice in the wake of World War I. According to a statistical study by Synder with respect to the MFN clauses negotiated between 1920 and 1940, only nine out of over six hundred MFN clauses included in treaties were conditional in form.[33] In fact, the unconditional form of the MFN clause remained dominant from 1860 until World War I, after which the conditional variant never regained prominence.

1.3 *The Status of the MFN Clause during an Unstable Period for World Trade: The 20th Century Onward*

The development of MFN clause during the 20th century can be categorized into four phases, with the two World Wars acting as helpful signposts: from the beginning of the century until the end of World War I (1900–1919), the 'inter-war' period (1919–1929), the period leading up to World War II until the War

30 Ustor (n 8) 162, footnote 28. See also Bryan Coutain, 'The Unconditional Most-Favored-Nation Clause and the Maintenance of the Liberal Trade Regime in the Postwar 1870s' (2009) 63 International Organization 139.

31 Synder (n 9) 212.

32 Article XIX of the Treaty reads as follows: Each of the two High Contracting Powers engages to confer on the other any favour, privilege, or reduction in the tariff of duties of importation on the articles mentioned in the present Treaty, which the said power may concede to any third Power. They further engage not to enforce one against the other any prohibition of importation or exportation which shall not at the same time be applicable to all other nations. See Foreign Office, *British and Foreign State Papers*, vol 50 (William Ridgway 1860) 24–5.

33 Synder (n 9) 242.

came to an end (1931–1945), and the postwar period, which led to the development of modern variants of the MFN clause (from 1945 on).

The build up to and eventual outbreak of World War I dealt a severe blow to international trade in general and the MFN principle in particular, with the application of the latter suffering a temporary setback. The reason for this was predominantly the fact that extending MFN treatment, especially to maritime adversaries, was disapproved of by states against the backdrop of geopolitical tensions and looming aggression.[34] Thus, at the Allied Economic Conference in 1916, it was agreed that "systematic discrimination in economic matters" should be imposed on the adversaries of the Allied Powers.[35]

In the wake of World War I, MFN clauses were largely formulated unilaterally and served primarily to consolidate unbalanced trade relations. The type of unilateral MFN clause contained in these treaties differed from earlier variants such as those from the Middle Ages and, in practice, served as instruments of trade discrimination – the intent behind deploying 'MFN' clauses of this kind was thus the polar opposite of equal treatment.

World War I ushered in a number of years of worldwide economic decline and trade restrictions. Nationalist and protectionist ideologies tempered the inclusion of MFN clauses.[36] Over the years, however, unconditional MFN clauses again began to find prominence in treaty practice, as countries such as Italy, the United Kingdom and Germany advocated for it.[37]

In May 1927, the International Economic Conference was held in Geneva under the auspices of the League of Nations. In an effort to curb increasing trade barriers, the Conference was attended by the major trading countries, amongst others. The Conference stressed the importance of equal treatment as a general principle and urged that "the widest and most unconditional interpretation should be given to the most-favored-nation clause."[38] The conference ended with a trade agreement seen as a precursor to the 1947 General Agreement on Tariffs and Trade (GATT). Although the agreement was not binding, it did underpin the consensus of free trade between nations and, importantly, promoted unfettered application of the MFN principle. During

34 Ustor (n 8) 162.

35 Ustor (n 8) 162.

36 Ustor (n 8) 163, footnote 42. France has undergone several changes pertaining to its MFN policy, and has on several occasions taken a conservative position towards the MFN clause. For more on this score see Synder (n 9) 243.

37 Synder (n 9) 163.

38 League of Nations, Report and Proceedings of the World Economic Conference, Vol 1 (League of Nations 1927), Document C.356.M.129.1927.II (C.E.I.46) 43.

this time, liberal trade had apparently succeeded, and unconditional MFN treatment resumed. This all changed, however, with the onset of the Great Depression in 1929.

The onset of the depression brought renewed international trade tensions, with countries beginning to raise customs duties, employing import quotas and even imposing import prohibitions and implementing exchange controls, amongst other measures. As a result, MFN treatment came under attack and suffered from a resurgence of protectionist measures. According to a survey by Synder, out of approximately five hundred bilateral treaties concluded between 1931 and 1939, only about 40 percent of them included an MFN clause, while the same survey showed that ninety percent of treaties contained an MFN clause before 1931.[39]

The end of World War II brought the free trade ideology back to the center of the international stage.[40] In 1944, the Bretton Woods Conference recognized that the need to rebuild political relations and the economy in the postwar world require MFN treatment as a bridge to bring states together in a more unified and stable legal framework.[41] Following this, the U.S. proposed negotiations on a multilateral trade agreement to its wartime allies. On this basis, a preparatory committee was formed, which met for the first time in 1946 to negotiate a charter for an international trade organization (ITO). The negotiations ended in 1948 with the Havana Charter. Via the Havana Charter, countries attempted to build a multilateral legal framework pertaining to both trade and investment issues. However, the Havana Charter lacked adequate protection to foreign investors from capital-exporting countries and never came into force.[42]

In the meantime, ongoing negotiations on the General Agreement on Tariffs and Trade (GATT) made good progress. This agreement was aimed at substantially reducing tariffs and other barriers to trade, including through eliminating

39 Synder (n 9) 132.

40 Larry Neal, Rondo E Cameron and Rondo E Cameron, *A Concise Economic History of the World: From Paleolithic Times to the Present* (5th edn, Oxford University Press 2016); Bernard M Hoekman and MM Kostecki, *The Political Economy of the World Trading System: The WTO and Beyond* (2nd edn, Oxford University Press 2001).

41 This has been conceptualized by Stephan Schill as the "multilateralizing" function of MFN treatment. See Schill (n 22)134.

42 Tanjina Sharmin, *Application of Most-Favoured-Nation Clauses by Investor-State Arbitral Tribunals: Implications for the Developing Countries* (Springer 2020) 34, which refers to: Interim Commission for the International Trade Organization, Final Act and Related Documents, United Nations Conference on Trade and Employment (New York, 1948). <https://www.wto.org/english/docs_e/legal_e/havana_e.pdf> accessed 20 April 2022; Hoekman and Kostecki (n 40) 12–13.

discriminatory treatment. Because of the countries' strong desire to immediately bring the GATT into force, a protocol on provisional application of the GATT was agreed to on October 30, 1947, by eight of the 23 negotiating countries, including the U.S. and the United Kingdom, two of the major leaders on this issue.[43]

Given the purpose of this agreement, Article of GATT imposed a general unconditional MFN clause which stated that: "... any advantage, [favor], privilege or immunity granted by any contracting party to any product originating in or destined for any other country shall be accorded immediately and unconditionally to the like product originating in or destined for the territories of all other contracting parties."[44] The text of this MFN clause took its wording from predecessor clauses in bilateral trade agreements; only this time, it became enshrined in a multilateral trade agreement. This meant the MFN clause was no longer limited to bilateral trade relations but had been adopted as part of a more extensive and comprehensive international legal agreement. It provided a legal basis for equal treatment and trade liberalization and contributed both economically and politically to postwar reconstruction.[45]

GATT 1947 was later incorporated into GATT 1994, a component of the World Trade Organization (WTO) Agreement. In the meantime, countries continued to pursue the elimination of tariffs and the general liberalization of trade.[46] The importance of the MFN clause in the WTO system can be seen in its ubiquity in WTO instruments. It has been provided for in basically all trade-related areas: trade in goods (GATT 1994, Article I), trade in services (General Agreement on Trade in Services (GATS), Article II), trade-related aspects of intellectual property rights (WTO Agreement on Trade-Related Aspects of Intellectual Property Rights (TRIPS), Article 4), and technical barriers (Agreement on Technical Barriers to Trade (TBT), Article 5). As perhaps the

43 See, for example, John Howard Jackson, *The World Trade Organization: Constitution and Jurisprudence* (Royal Institute of International Affairs 1998) 15–16; Kanu Agrawal, 'Bilateral Investment Treaties: A Developing History' (2016) 7 Jindal Global Law Review 175; Hoekman and Kostecki (n 40) 12–13.

44 Article I of the GATT, available at <https://www.wto.org/english /docs_e/legal_e/gatt47 _01_e.htm> accessed 20 April 2022.

45 The Director of GATT Trade Policy delivered a lecture in 1956 to the Bologna Center of the School of Advanced International Studies of John Hopkins University. This lecture is cited in the third chapter of Gerard Curzon, *Multilateral Commercial Diplomacy: The General Agreement on Tariffs and Trade, and Its Impact on National Commercial Policies and Techniques* (Michael Joseph ed, 1965).

46 'WTO: Understanding the WTO-The GATT Years: From Havana to Marrakesh' <https://www.wto.org/english/thewto_e/whatis_e/tif_e/fact4_e.htm> accessed 20 April 2022.

most important nondiscrimination obligation, MFN treatment helps maintain a rule-based system for states and has been called a cornerstone and "one of the pillars of the WTO trading system."[47]

This section has attempted to illustrate the role and function of the MFN clause within the world trading system since it first appeared. Because of the fierce competition between merchants from different city-states, it originally appeared in the form of promises made by Oriental emperors to foreign merchants. Since then, the mode of MFN treatment has changed several times throughout its evolution, as demonstrated above.

A review of history shows that the development and application of MFN principles largely coincided with the contemporary ideologies of countries and is closely linked to the political and economic situation of a particular era. Thus, MFN treatment has tended to be welcomed and embraced by countries during periods of economic stability and the consequent adoption of liberal policies, usually by powerful countries, while it has been curtailed or even abandoned during periods of economic decline and political tension. As Synder has clarified:

> ... The clause, because it inter-relates the economic policies of nations, fares best when there is general monetary and economic stability and the absence of quantitative restrictions on international trade. When the world economy suffers far-reaching dislocation, or when individual nations experience economic or financial difficulties, the clause is usually abandoned or modified.[48]

2 Incorporation and Development of the MFN Clause in International Investment Law

Following the above overview of the development of the MFN clause in international trade law, this section discusses its incorporation into international investment law, as well as its subsequent development. As a treaty-based obligation, the MFN clause has developed in tandem with modern investment treaties. In other words, the trends relating to the formulation of MFN clauses

---

47 See, for example, Appellate Body Report, *European Communities – Conditions for the Granting of Tariff Preferences to Developing Countries* (*EC – Tariff Preferences*), WT/DS246/AB/R [101].

48 Synder (n 9) 241.

tend to reflect the contemporary global economic environment and investment treaty practice.

In her article 'A Brief History of International Investment Agreement', Vandevelde divides the history of IIAs into three phases, i.e., the Colonial Era (from inception until War II), during which friendship, commerce and navigation treaties (FCN treaties) were dominant as the progenitor of modern IIAs; the Post-Colonial Era, which spanned from 1945 to the collapse of the Soviet Union in 1989, and during which period the BIT became the predominant instrument containing international rules on foreign investment, thriving as it did so; and the Global Era, which kicked off in the late 1980s and during which the number of BITs concluded around the globe surged quite dramatically.[49] According to the United Nations Conference on Trade and Development (UNCTAD), from 2008 onwards an additional paradigm shift has been observed in respect of IIAs, whereby domestic interests of host states and sustainable development have been given more weight vis-à-vis investment protection, i.e., a 'rebalancing' or 'renegotiation' period has ensued.[50] The remainder of this section draws on the timeline offered by Vandevelde and UNCTAD's proposition in relation to the post-2008 position to sketch a history of the MFN clause from the perspective of international investment law.

2.1 *The MFN Clause in the Colonial Era*

In the Colonial Era, the MFN clause was mainly included in FCN treaties. FCN treaties were commercial treaties initially negotiated and concluded in the late 18th and 19th centuries between newly independent states and their former colonial masters, usually so that the latter could obtain market access for their own goods.[51] These treaties were not restricted to trade and contained investment-related issues like the treatment of foreign nationals and navigation during war time. In this sense, FCNs were originally designed to regulate a wide range of legal issues in a single instrument, including, *inter alia*,

49 Kenneth J Vandevelde, 'A Brief History of International Investment Agreements' in Karl p. Sauvant and Lisa Sachs (eds), *The Effect of Treaties on Foreign Direct Investment: Bilateral Investment Treaties, Double Taxation Treaties, and Investment Flows* (Oxford University Press 2009) 3.

50 UNCTAD, *Word Investment Report 2015: Reforming International Investment Governance* (United Nations 2015) 124.

51 See Christopher F Dugan and others, *Investor-State Arbitration* (Oxford University Press 2012) 37. See also Kenneth J Vandevelde, *Bilateral Investment Treaties: History, Policy, and Interpretation* (Oxford University Press 2010) 22 and John F Coyle, 'The Treaty of Friendship, Commerce and Navigation in the Modem Era' (2012) 51 Colombia Journal of Transnational Law 302.

navigation rights, trading rights, rights of entry and establishment, human rights, and, occasionally, the payment of compensation for expropriation.[52] In view of their apparent investment-related nature and their principles that were later adopted by modern international investment law, FCNs have been considered the predecessors of modern BITs.[53]

The FCN project was particularly supportive of what was then contemporary U.S. commercial policy.[54] As a newly independent state during the Colonial Era, the U.S. was the main proponent of this approach with the intention of building stronger commercial ties with the rest of the world.[55] During this period, FCN treaties focused largely on trade relations.[56] MFN treatment was guaranteed in FCN treaties with a view to accord protection to foreign nationals specifically related to trade issues.[57] Although investment protection was included in these treaties, these provisions tended to embody incidental content.[58]

52 Herman Walker Jr, 'Modern Treaties of Friendship, Commerce and Navigation' (1958) 42 Minnesota Law Review. 1491. See also Coyle (n 93); M Sornarajah, *The International Law on Foreign Investment* (4th edn, Cambridge University Press 2017); Vandevelde (n 51) 159.

53 Sharmin (n 42) 30; Sornarajah (n 52) 180. See also Kenneth J Vandevelde, 'The BIT Program: A Fifteen-Year Appraisal' (1988) 82 Proceedings of the ASIL Annual Meeting 532.

54 See, for example, Samuel Flagg Bemis, 'A Diplomatic History of the United States. Pp. Xii, 881.' [1936] New York: Henry Holt & Co.

55 For example, U.S. entered into FCN treaties with the Netherlands (1782), Sweden (1783) and Prussia (1785). Through which the U.S. set a precedent for bilateral commercial treaty relations with western Europe, followed by similar treaty relations with Latin America, then with Asia and Africa. See Kenneth J Vandevelde, 'The Bilateral Investment Treaty Program of the United States' (1988) 21 Cornell International Law Journal 201, 203–6. See also Sornarajah (n 52). On the United States' treaty policy, see Austin T Foster, 'Some Aspects of the Commercial Treaty Program of the United States – Past and Present' (1946) 11 Law and Contemporary Problems 647.Walker (n 52); Robert R Wilson, *US Commercial Treaties and International Law* (Hauser Press 1960); Vandevelde (n 49) 161.

56 Todd S Shenkin, 'Trade-Related Investment Measures in Bilateral Investment Treaties and the Gatt: Moving Toward a Multilateral Investment Treaty Comment' (1993) 55 University of Pittsburgh Law Review 541, 570.

57 In this regard, see Article 2 of the 1778 Treaty. For more discussion about the investment-related provisions of this treaty, see specifically Kenneth J Vandevelde, *United States Investment Treaties: Policy and Practice* (Kluwer Law and Taxation 1992).

58 Investment protection in these FCN treaties was mainly confined to alien treatment accorded to foreign individuals who came to the host state for business purposes. These protections included, *inter alia*, freedom of worship and travel, due process, and procedural rights in the case of arrest and criminal trial. The inclusion of investment protection was therefore deemed by some as the "link" between trade and investment. See Sornarajah (n 52).

In the mid-19th century, multinational enterprises (multinationals) emerged as the main vehicle for foreign direct investment.[59] From the 1830s on, multinationals embarked on overseas business by building up affiliates in the territory of host states abroad and investing in sectors such as manufacturing and mining. This expansion of foreign investment activity was reflected in contemporary treaty practice. First, treaties began to provide protection for "property" as a more general proposition, replacing the traditional concepts such as the "vessels, cargoes, merchandise and effects" of foreign nationals. Second, protection against discrimination was established as a common principle in FCN treaties and was more frequently related to the right of establishment concerning industrial engagement, especially in FCN treaties concluded by the U.S.[60] Third, industrial activities included in treaties were mostly direct investment activities, including in manufacturing and mineral extraction in host states.

The scope of MFN treatment contained in these FCN treaties changed accordingly. Towards the middle of the 19th century, MFN treatment in these treaties had been extended to cover investment-related issues as they pertained to not only natural persons, but also corporations.[61]

2.2 *The MFN Clause in the Post-colonial Era*

The end of World War II gave rise to decolonialization and newly independent countries. These countries were former colonies and were particularly sensitive about foreign investment. They considered foreign investment as a form of neocolonialism because these investments were controlled by foreigners, and often by former colonizers.[62] In the meantime, the emergence of the Socialist Bloc led by the Soviet Union encouraged developing countries to boost economic development by tightening domestic regulations instead of via the free market.[63] Additionally, Latin American countries reaffirmed the Calvo

59 Geoffrey Jones, *Multinationals and Global Capitalism: From the Nineteenth to the Twenty-First Century* (Oxford University Press 2005).

60 See, for example, Article VII of the Treaty of Friendship, Commerce and Navigation concluded between the U.S. and Japan in 1953, a copy of which is available at <https://tcc.export.gov/Trade_Agreements/All_Trade_Agreements/exp_005539.asp> accessed 20 April 2022.

61 See, for example, Article IV of the Treaty of Amity, Commerce and Navigation concluded between Denmark and Liberia (1860). See also Vandevelde (n 93) 50.

62 Dean M Hanink, *The International Economy: A Geographical Perspective* (J Wiley 1994) 234; Robert Gilpin and Jean M Gilpin, *The Political Economy of International Relations* (Princeton University Press 1987) 247–248.

63 E Wayne Nafziger, *The Economics of Developing Countries* (3rd ed, Prentice Hall 1997) 106–08.

Doctrine, which emphasized the application of domestic regulations to investment disputes and excluded the possibility of diplomatic protection being asserted by home states.[64] As a result, a number of developing countries began closing their economies and expropriating existing foreign investment.[65] In light of this, the just compensation standard for expropriation came to be contained in the contemporary FCN treaties to protect foreign property.[66]

During the same period, several attempts were made to build a multilateral investment protection system. As was previously noted, the attempt to build a liberal investment regime for both trade and investment under the Havana Charter failed. In 1948, the International Law Commission (ILC) released two draft statutes related to an arbitration tribunal for foreign investments and a foreign investment court respectively.[67] In 1949, the International Chamber of Commerce (ICC) published the International Code of Fair Treatment for Foreign Investment, which included provisions on non-discriminatory treatment, free transfer of investment-related payments, fair compensation for the expropriation of investments, and ICC arbitration on investment disputes.[68]

The Abs-Shawcross Draft Convention on Investment Abroad in 1959 is another example of these attempts. It contained provisions on fair and equitable treatment (FET), a prohibition on unreasonable or discriminatory measures and uncompensated expropriations, as well as provisions relating to the resolution of state-state and investor-state disputes. In 1961, Professors Louis Sohn and Richard Baxter published the Draft Convention on the International Responsibility of States for Injuries to Aliens (also known as the

---

64 Jorge E Viñuales and Magnus Jesko Langer, 'Foreign Investment in Latin America: Between Love and Hatred' in Claude Auroi and Aline Helg, *Latin America 1810–2010* (Imperial College Press 2011); Rodrigo Polanco Lazo, 'The No of Tokyo Revisited: Or How Developed Countries Learned to Start Worrying and Love the Calvo Doctrine' (2015) 30 ICSID Review 172, 172; Robert Freeman Smith, 'Latin America, The United States and the European Powers, 1830–1930' in Leslie Bethell (ed), *The Cambridge History of Latin America: Volume 4: c.1870 to 1930*, vol 4 (Cambridge University Press 1986); Donald R Shea, *The Calvo Clause* (NED-New edition, University of Minnesota Press 1955).

65 Vandevelde (n 49) footnote 52.

66 Vandevelde (n 49) 163.

67 Reprinted in UNCTAD, 'International Investment Instruments: A Compendium' (United Nations 1996) Volume I, multilateral instruments. UNCTAD/DTCI/30(Vol.I), available at: <https://unctad.org/system/files/official-document/dtci30vol1_en.pdf> accessed 20 April 2022.

68 Andrew Paul Newcombe and Lluís Paradell, *Law and Practice of Investment Treaties: Standards of Treatment* (Wolters Kluwer Law & Business; Kluwer Law International; Sold and distributed in North, Central and South America by Aspen Publishers 2009) 16–17.

1961 Harvard Draft).[69] In 1967, the Organisation for Economic Co-operation and Development (OECD) released its Draft Convention on the Protection of Foreign Property. Although these proposals were never adopted as binding instruments, the principles contained therein can nonetheless be found in later bilateral investment treaties.[70]

Realizing that a legal framework for multilateral investment would be impossible in the near future, countries began to conclude bilateral investment treaties (BITS) in parallel with the FCN program.[71] The BIT process began when Germany and Pakistan concluded the first BIT in 1959. This treaty included a post-establishment MFN clause, with Article 3(3) of the Germany-Pakistan BIT providing MFN treatment concerning compensation in the event of war, armed conflict, or revolution.[72] Germany's practice was immediately followed by other Western European countries. MFN treatment was maintained as the major form of investment protection against discrimination in early BITS, particularly in relation to expropriation by host states.

During their formative years, BITS were mainly negotiated and concluded between developed and developing countries and their main purpose was foreign investment protection.[73] The MFN clause gradually became prevalent in investment treaties. The wording of MFN clauses during this period tended to be general and with few limitations. For example, Article 2(2) of the 1960 Germany-Malaysia BIT provided that:[74]

---

69 See Louis B Sohn and RR Baxter, 'Responsibility of States for Injuries to the Economic Interests of Aliens: II. Draft Convention on the International Responsibility of States for Injuries to Aliens' (1961) 55 American Journal of International Law 545, 548.

70 For research on the attempts to establish a multilateral investment legal framework, see Franziska Tschofen, 'Multilateral Approaches to the Treatment of Foreign Investment' (1992) 7 ICSID Review – Foreign Investment Law Journal 384.

71 For a history of BITS, Jeswald W Salacuse, *The Law of Investment Treaties* (Second edition, Oxford University Press 2015) 97–103; Jeswald W Salacuse, 'BIT by BIT: The Growth of Bilateral Investment Treaties and Their Impact on Foreign Investment in Developing Countries' (1990) 24 The International Lawyer 655; Rudolf Dolzer and Christoph Schreuer, *Principles of International Investment Law* (Second edition, Oxford University Press 2012) 4–11; Agrawal (n 43); Vandevelde (n 49) 39; Andrew Guzman, 'Why LDCS Sign Treaties That Hurt Them: Explaining the Popularity of Bilateral Investment Treaties' (1998) 38 Virginia Journal of International Law 639, 601; Joshua Robbins, 'The Emergence Of Positive Obligations In Bilateral Investment Treaties' (2006) 13 University of Miami International and Comparative Law Review 72.

72 Germany – Pakistan BIT (1959). A copy of which is available at <https://treaties.un.org/doc/Publication/ UNTS/Volume%20457/volume-457-I-6575-English.pdf> accessed 20 April 2022.

73 Guzman (n 71) 642.

74 Germany – Malaysia BIT (1960), a copy of which is available at <https://jusmundi.com/en/document/treaty/en-germany-malaysia-bit-1960-germany-malaysia-bit-1960-thursday-22nd-december-1960> accessed 20 April 2022. It has also been argued that MFN clauses

> Unless specific stipulations made in the document of admission provide otherwise, investments by nationals or companies of either Contracting Party in the territory of the other Contracting Party, shall not be subjected to treatment less [favorable] than that accorded to … investments by nationals or companies of any third party …[75]

On the other hand, efforts by developing and socialist countries led to the recognition of expropriation of foreign investment without payment of market value. In December 1962, The United Nations General Assembly (General Assembly) adopted Resolution 1803 () concerning permanent sovereignty over natural resources. Resolution 1803 recognized the right of host states to expropriate with "appropriate compensation," which was required to be governed by domestic and international law. According to Resolution 1803, in the event of disputes regarding the determination of such compensation, the domestic courts of host state would take priority unless an agreement had been reached for the submission of such disputes to international adjudication.[76] In 1974, the General Assembly adopted, by a substantial majority, the Declaration of the New International Economic Order (NIEO). Under the NIEO, states would still have "full permanent sovereignty" over economic activities and the nationalization of foreign investment would fall under state sovereignty.[77] On 12 December 1974, the General Assembly adopted the Charter of Economic Rights and Duties of States (CERDS), declaring that states had the right to nationalize, expropriate or transfer ownership of foreign property with appropriate compensation, taking into account relevant laws and regulations and all other circumstances considered pertinent by the state.[78]

---

saved countries from lengthy renegotiation of treaties for higher standard of investment protection. See Cole (n 7) 554; OECD (n 2) 142.

75 See also: Article 2 of the Germany – Turkey BIT (1962). A copy of which is available at <https://edit.wti.org/document/show/543454ef-ac83-4282-a446-5fe011272f22?textBlockId =80fc84f7-8b92-4c44-ac98-39a71187e996&page=1> accessed 20 April 2022; Article 2 of the Germany – Liberia bit (1961). A copy of which is available at <https://edit.wti.org/document/show/e196d23b-49a9-4144-9964-3802399ae3ba> accessed 20 April 2022.

76 General Assembly Resolution 1803 (xvii) of 14 December 1962, 'Permanent Sovereignty over Natural Resources', available at <https://www.ohchr.org/Documents/ProfessionalInterest/resources.pdf> accessed 20 April 2022.

77 UN General Assembly, 'Declaration on the Establishment of a New International Economic Order (1974)'.

78 Article 2.2 (c) of the Charter of Economic Rights and Duties of States, Contained in General Assembly Resolution. 3281(Xxix), UN GAOR, 29th Sess., Supp. No. 31 (1974) 50, a copy of which is available at <https://investmentpolicy.unctad.org/international-investment-agreements/treaty-files/2778/download> accessed 20 April 2022.

In response to the risk of undercompensated expropriation, the number of BITs kept growing throughout the 1970s. The United Kingdom signed its first BIT in 1975, while the U.S. inaugurated its BIT program in 1977. During this time, BITs were still largely North-South agreements, i.e., signed between developed and developing countries, with different motivations on each side. While developed countries sought investment protection, especially against expropriation, developing countries attempted to attract foreign investment to boost their domestic economy.[79] MFN clauses were frequently included as substantive standard in these BITs.[80] In 1966, the Convention on the Settlement of Investment Disputes between States and Nationals of Other States (ICSID Convention) came into force. In 1968, Investor-State Dispute Settlement (ISDS) was first included in a BIT between the Netherlands and Indonesia, Article of which required the submission of "any dispute that may arise in connection with the investment" to ISDS.[81] Several characteristics of MFN clauses during this period reflected the leading BIT paradigm. First, they were drafted in general terms without exceptions.[82] In BITs that did contain MFN exceptions, these exceptions were mainly limited to treaty privileges in regional economic integration organization (REIO) and taxation treaties. An MFN exception was initially adopted in the U.S. BITs. Article of the U.S.-Panama BIT, for example, provided MFN treatment with exceptions in the Annex to that treaty for the purpose of protecting state regulatory interests.[83] Afterwards, MFN exceptions drafted in general terms gradually became popular practice.[84]

---

79 Kenneth J Vandevelde and others, 'Bilateral Investment Treaties in the Mid-1990s.' (United Nations 1998) UNCTAD/ITE/IIT/7 5. See also Richard Baldwin, '21st Century Regionalism: Filling the Gap between 21st Century Trade and 20th Century Trade Rules' [2011] World Trade Organization, Economic Research and Statistics Division 39.

80 Cole (n 7) 557.

81 Article 5(2) of the Netherlands – Indonesia BIT (1968). A copy of which is available at: <https://investmentpolicy.unctad.org/international-investment-agreements/treaty-files/3329/download> accessed 20 April 2022, provided, prior to its termination, an MFN clause in relation to "investment, goods, rights and interests." This was the first time that the Netherlands included an MFN clause in its BITs.

82 See, for example, Article 3(1) of the Japan – Egypt BIT (1977). A copy of which is available at <https://investmentpolicy.unctad.org/international-investment-agreements/treaty-files/1083/download> accessed 20 April 2022.

83 U.S. – Panama BIT (1982). A copy of which is available at <https://investmentpolicy.unctad.org/international-investment-agreements/treaty-files/3353/download> accessed 20 April 2022.

84 See, for example, Article 3(3) of the Germany – Montenegro BIT (1989). A copy of which is available at <https://investmentpolicy.unctad.org/international-investment-agreements/treaty-files/4743/download> accessed 20 April 2022.

Second, considering the looming risk of expropriation, MFN clauses were often agreed to as specific guarantees for fair, treaty-based compensation. For example, the UK-Haiti BIT included a paragraph on expropriation in Article 3 that reads as follows:

> Nationals or companies of either Contracting Party who suffer investment losses as a result of war or other armed conflict, revolution, national emergency or civil unrest in the territory of the other Contracting Party shall be accorded by that Party treatment no less favourable than that granted to its own nationals or companies in respect of restitution, indemnities, compensation or other forms of repara- tion. All such payments shall be freely transferable.[85]

Some countries, like the Netherlands, started drafting MFN clauses with reference to other substantive treatment. For example, Article 5 of the 1968 Netherlands-Indonesia BIT included MFN treatment as a ground for the "same security and protection" accorded to foreign investors.[86] A clear reference to FET or full protection and security in the MFN clause later became a frequent practice of the Netherlands.[87]

Third, the scope of MFN clauses was largely limited to the post-establishment phase, with the U.S. BITs as an exception. As noted above, it had been a practice of American FCNs to accord MFN treatment with respect to both the establishment and admission of foreign investment.

The 1980s saw over two hundred newly concluded BITs in total, more than doubling the number concluded in the previous decade.[88] In 1987, the first treaty-based ISDS case was filed by Asian Agricultural Products Limited

---

85 Article 3(3) of the Germany – Haiti BIT (1973). A copy of which is available at: <https://investmentpolicy.unctad.org/international-investment-agreements/treaty-files/1337/download> accessed 20 April 2022.

86 Article 5 of the 1968 Netherlands – Indonesia BIT (n 81) read as follows: (1) Each Contracting Party shall ensure fair and equitable treatment to the investments, goods, rights and interests of nationals of the other Contracting Party and shall not impair, by unjustified or discriminatory measures, the management, maintenance, use, enjoyment or disposal thereof by those nationals; (2) More particularly, each Contracting Party shall accord to such investments, goods, rights and interests the same security and protection as it accords either to those of its own nationals or to those of nationals of third States, whichever is more favourable to the investor.

87 See, for example, Articles 4 and 5 of the Netherlands – Sri Lanka BIT (1984). A copy of which is available at <https://investmentpolicy.unctad.org/international-investment-agreements/treaty-files/2083/download> accessed 20 April 2022.

88 Vandevelde and others (n 79) 9.

(AAPL) against Sri Lanka in terms of the United Kingdom-Sri Lanka BIT.[89] This case was the beginning of a new chapter in investment law.

2.3 *The MFN Clause in the Global Era*

The Global Era began at the end of the 1980s. This period witnessed profound changes to the IIA landscape.[90] First of all, the number of BITs concluded increased rapidly.[91] BITs were no longer negotiated exclusively between developed and developing countries, but also began to be concluded between developing countries as well.[92] During this period, BITs also mainly addressed the issue of investment protection, although their focus shifted from regulating expropriation to facilitating investment liberalization.[93]

The year 1992 marked the failure of an attempt to establish a Multilateral Agreement on Investment (MAI) due to developed countries' differences around the core principles of investment law.[94] The fragmentation of investment law continued. With the introduction of GATS and the Agreement on Trade-Related Investment Measures (TRIMS Agreement) in 1994, the WTO succeeded for the first time in including trade in services and restricting investment measures capable of hindering trade within the multilateral international trade framework. As a result, investment provisions were increasingly included in regional trade agreements (RTAs) to regulate, protect, and liberalize investment.

Regional and multilateral economic integration increased. The inclusion of investment provisions did not take hold until the North American Free Trade Agreement (NAFTA) was concluded in 1994.[95] This agreement was concluded between the U.S., Canada and Mexico, two developed countries, and one developing country. Chapter 11 of NAFTA provided a template for investment

89 *Asian Agricultural Products Ltd (AAPL) v Republic of Sri Lanka, Award dated 27 June 1990*, ICSID Case No. ARB/87/3.

90 Kenneth J Vandevelde, 'Sustainable Liberalism and the International Investment Regime' (1998) 19 Michigan Journal of International Law 373.

91 UNCTAD, 'Recent Developments in International Investment Agreements' IIA Monitor No. 2 (2005). UNCTAD/WEB/ITE/IIT/2005/1, a copy of which is available at: <https://unctad.org/system/files/official-document/webiteiit20051_en.pdf> accessed 20 April 2022.

92 For a study on how developing nations changed their attitudes and roles regarding BITs, see Vandevelde (n 49). See also Michael Burgess, 'The World Bank – the East Asian Miracle' (1995) 18 Asian Studies Review 147.

93 Vandevelde (n 49) 183.

94 UNCTAD (n 50) 123. See also Edward M Graham, *Fighting the Wrong Enemy: Antiglobal Activists and Multinational Enterprises* (Institute for International Economics 2000).

95 Philip Zelikow, Maxwell A Cameron and Brian W Tomlin, 'The Making of NAFTA: How the Deal Was Done' (2001) 80 Foreign Affairs 176.

protection and dispute settlement, as Article 1103 adopted the North American method and required pre-establishment MFN treatment of foreign investors and investments "in like circumstances."[96] NAFTA ushered in a period where IIAs were concluded as part of regional integration strategy.[97] The number of FTAs including investment provisions increased after the conclusion of NAFTA. By 2005, at least 215 FTAs containing investment provisions had been concluded, many of which provide protections against discrimination such as national treatment and MFN treatment.[98]

Another notable change during the Global Era occurred in relation to the use of dispute settlement mechanisms. Following *AAPL v Sri Lanka*, investors began utilizing ISDS mechanisms far more extensively, especially from the late 1990s onwards. At the time, respondent states were mostly developing countries.[99] In 1997, Canada became the first developed country acting as a respondent state before an arbitral tribunal.[100] In 1998, the U.S. also received a request for arbitration from a Canadian investor.[101] BITs began to have impacts deleterious to the interests of developed countries as well. The 2000 *Maffezini v Spain* case was groundbreaking in that it was the first time a tribunal applied the MFN clause to incorporate more favorable procedural treatment from a different source than the BIT on which the claim in question was based, which contained a broadly drafted MFN clause that referred to "all matters relating to investment."[102]

The *Maffezini* decision led to countries around the world reconsidering MFN formulations in their IIAs. Prior to *Maffezini*, the interpretation of the MFN

96 Article 1103 of North American Free Trade Agreement between Canada, The United States and Mexico (NAFTA) . A copy of which is available at <https://investmentpolicy.unctad.org/international-investment-agreements/treaty-files/2412/download> accessed 20 April 2022.

97 Baldwin (n 79) 22.

98 See Jo-Ann Crawford and Barbara Kotschwar, 'Investment Provisions in Preferential Trade Agreements: Evolution and Current Trends' (2018) WTO Staff Working Paper ERSD-2018-14. Available at: <https://www.wto.org/english/res_e/reser_e/ersd201814_e.pdf> accessed 20 April 2022, where the authors calculate the number of MFN clauses incorporated in PTAs.

99 UNCTAD (n 50) 123.

100 The case of *Ethyl Corporation v The Government of Canada* (ICSID), which was eventually settled. All pertinent documents relating to this case are available at: <https://jusmundi.com/en/document/decision/en-ethyl-corporation-v-the-government-of-canada-award-on-jurisdiction-wednesday-24th-june-1998> accessed 20 April 2022.

101 *Loewen Group, Inc and Raymond L Loewen v United States of America*, ICSID Case No.ARB(AF)/98/3 71.

102 *Emilio Agustín Maffezini v The Kingdom of Spain, Decision of the Tribunal on Objections to Jurisdiction dated 25 January 2000*, ICSID Case No. ARB/97/7.

clause by arbitral tribunals was of no concern to treatymakers. However, the unexpected interpretation and application of the MFN clause by the *Maffezini* tribunal raised concerns among states regarding the unintended extension of investment protection, especially in relation to the extent to which these types of interpretations and applications by tribunals could conceivably constrain regulatory policy space. As a result, some countries responded by including declarative notes alongside their MFN clauses. For example, the 2003 Draft Free Trade Agreement of the Americas (FTAA) included a note directly in response to the *Maffezini* decision. It declared in clear terms that:

> The Parties note the recent decision of the arbitral tribunal in the Maffezini (Arg.) v. Kingdom of Spain, which found an unusually broad most favored nation clause in an Argentina-Spain agreement to encompass international dispute resolution procedures … By contrast, the Most-Favored-Nation Article of this Agreement is expressly limited in its scope to matters "with respect to the establishment, acquisition, expansion, management, conduct, operation, and sale or other disposition of investments." The Parties share the understanding and intent that this clause does not encompass international dispute resolution mechanisms such as those contained in Section C.2.b (Dispute Settlement between a Party and an Investor of Another Party) of this Chapter, and therefore could not reasonably lead to a conclusion similar to that of the Maffezini case.[103]

Although the note was deleted from the official treaty text, "*Maffezini* Notes" were adopted by many treaties in an attempt to unambiguously delineate the scope of application of MFN clauses. Additionally, the 21st century saw more detailed and refined MFN clauses in BITs. Take Germany for example. Article 3 of the 2002 Germany-Thailand BIT provides for MFN treatment but specifies certain types of treatment that should be considered "less favorable," which includes "unequal treatment in the case of restrictions on the purchase of raw or auxiliary materials, of energy or fuel or of means of production or operation of any kind, unequal treatment in the case of impeding the marketing of products inside or outside the country, as well as any other measures having similar effects." It also explicitly excludes measures related to the public

103 UNCTAD, '*Most-Favoured-Nation Treatment: A Sequel,* UNCTAD Series on Issues in International Investment Agreements II' (United Nations 2010), a copy of which is available at: <https://unctad.org/system/files/official-document/diaeia20101_en.pdf> accessed 20 April 2022.

interest.[104] This type of specification was included in the 2008 German Model BIT,[105] and has been incorporated in many BITs signed by Germany during the Global Era.[106]

In view of its experience as a respondent state in ISDS proceedings, the U.S. introduced a new Model BIT in 2004 to clarify the scope and meaning of investment obligations.[107] The 2004 Model BIT continued using traditional MFN texts, but also provided a detailed list of non-conforming measures under the MFN clause in order to reserve contracting parties' regulatory power on key domestic issues.[108]

2.4 *The MFN Clause in the Rebalancing Era*

Several factors contributed to the re-orientation of old generation IIAs, the first of which was the increasing number of ISDS cases. This was closely linked to the legitimacy crisis of contemporary ISDS mechanisms which resulted in inconsistent and contradictory interpretations of MFN clauses by tribunals, which in turn became a highly debated issue. As a result, up to 33 percent of BITs concluded between 2012 and 2014 explicitly rendered dispute settlement inapplicable in relation to the MFN clause, compared to

104 Article 3 of Germany – Thailand BIT (2002). A copy of which is available at: <https://investmentpolicy.unctad.org/international-investment-agreements/treaty-files/1428/download> accessed 20 April 2022.

105 Article 3 of the 2008 Germany Model BIT. A copy of which is available at: <https://investmentpolicy.unctad.org/international-investment-agreements/treaty-files/2865/download> accessed 20 April 2022.

106 See, for example, Article 3 of the Germany – Iran BIT (2002). A copy of which is available at <https://investmentpolicy.unctad.org/international-investment-agreements/treaty-files/3501/download> accessed 20 April 2022; Article 3 of the Germany – Guatemala BIT (2003). A copy of which is available at <https://investmentpolicy.unctad.org/international-investment-agreements/treaty-files/1330/download> accessed 20 April 2022; Article 3 of the Germany – Egypt BIT (2005). A copy of which is available at <https://investmentpolicy.unctad.org/international-investment-agreements/treaty-files/1072/download> accessed 20 April 2022; Article 4 of the Germany – Trinidad and Tobago BIT (2006), available at <https://investmentpolicy.unctad.org/international-investment-agreements/treaty-files/1434/download> accessed 20 April 2022; Article 3 of the Germany – Oman BIT (2007). A copy of which is available at <https://investmentpolicy.unctad.org/international-investment-agreements/treaty-files/1383/download> accessed 20 April 2022.

107 UNCTAD (n 50) 124.

108 See Article 14 of the 2004 U.S. Model BIT. A copy of which is available at: <https://investmentpolicy.unctad.org/international-investment-agreements/treaty-files/2872/download> accessed 20 April 2022.

only 3 percent from the 1950s to 2011.[109] In this regard, some countries took even more radical steps: some terminated their existing IIAs; some deleted the MFN clause from treaty texts; and some even withdrew from the ICSID Convention.[110]

The 2008 economic crisis was also a catalyst for countries to recognize the importance of regulatory power in the pursuit of key domestic agendas such as sustainable development.[111] As mentioned above, developed countries like the U.S. and Canada refined their Model BITs to gain greater regulatory power over domestic issues such as health, safety, the environment and the promotion of internationally recognized labor rights, amongst other things.[112] Last but not least, developed states gradually became capital-importing countries (in addition to being capital-exporting countries), with developing countries achieving economic success during this period. In other words, "the old distinction between capital-exporting developed countries and capital-importing countries was blurring."[113]

This shift in roles led to a rethinking of the relationship between investment protection and state regulatory powers. Countries began realizing the imbalance of old generation IIAs and attempted to revise their existing investment treaties, thus developing a new generation of IIAs which sought to expand the regulatory policy space available to host states.[114] As a result, investment protection has gradually been 'rebalanced' as the perceived need for greater regulatory discretion on the part of countries has grown. In view of the changing paradigm in the investment regime, UNCTAD has identified five areas in its road map for IIA reform. These include safeguarding states' right to regulate while providing investment protection, ISDS reform, investment promotion and facilitation, ensuring responsible investment and enhancing systemic consistency. Essential policy agendas in IIA reform include

---

109 UNCTAD, 'Taking Stock of IIA Reform.' IIA Issues Note 1 (2016). Available at: <https://unctad.org/system/files/official-document/webdiaepcb2016d3_en.pdf> accessed 20 April 2022.

110 UNCTAD, '*World Investment Report 2010: Investing in a Low-Carbon Economy*' (United Nations 2010). See also UNCTAD (n 109) 14.

111 UNCTAD (n 50) 125.

112 UNCTAD (n 50) 124. In view of broadly drafted standards of protection and the risk of investment disputes, countries have notably begun to review their investment policies with the help of international organizations like UNCTAD.

113 Vandevelde (n 49) 182.

114 Catharine Titi, *The Right to Regulate in International Investment Law* (1st edn, Nomos 2014) 72.

Sustainable Development Goals (SDGs), Corporate Social Responsibility (CSR), public health (in particular in relation to countries' response to COVID-19 pandemic) and gender equality, amongst others.[115]

The MFN clause is of obvious importance to this re-orientation process. A detailed and specific MFN clause will prevent foreign investors from seeking more favorable treatment in other IIAs concluded by the host state, helping countries make their policies effective.[116] In this regard, a 2010 UNCTAD report on the MFN clause suggested options for more detailed, carefully drafted MFN clauses for countries to consider.[117] These options included, *inter alia,* drawing clear distinctions between investors and investments,[118] including systemic exceptions,[119] and clearly specifying the scope of MFN clauses, amongst other things.[120]

With the importance of the MFN clause in the IIA re-orientation process in mind, countries have implemented measures which clarify the scope of MFN clauses. In the 2019 Slovakia Model BIT, for example, Article 6 explicitly excluded ISDS from the scope of MFN treatment and national treatment.[121] Another example is the 2019 U.S.-South Korea FTA. The original 2012 U.S.-South Korea FTA included a general MFN clause in its investment chapter, mandating MFN treatment for foreign investors and their investments.[122] In 2018, the U.S. and Korea renegotiated their FTA and concluded a revised agreement with a different approach to MFN treatment. Article 11.4 in the investment chapter provides *ex post* MFN treatment that excludes treatment from treaties concluded prior to the basic treaty from the scope of the MFN clause.[123] Moreover,

---

115 UNCTAD, 'International Investment Agreements Reform Accelerator' (2020). UNCTAD/DIAE/PCB/INF/2020/8. A copy of which is available at: <https://unctad.org/system/files/official-document/diaepcbinf2020d8_en.pdf> accessed 20 April 2022.

116 Sharmin (n 42) 55.

117 UNCTAD (n 103).

118 UNCTAD (n 103) 104.

119 UNCTAD (n 103) 104.

120 UNCTAD (n 103).

121 Slovakia Model BIT (2019), a copy of which is available at: <https://investmentpolicy.unctad.org/international-investment-agreements/treaty-files/5917/download> accessed 20 April 2022.

122 Article 11.4 of U.S. – Korea FTA (2007). A copy of which is available at <https://ustr.gov/sites/def ault/files/uploads/Countries%20Regions/africa/agreements/pdfs/FTAs/South%20Korea%20FULL.pdf> accessed 20 April 2022.

123 For a better understanding of the *ex ante* and *ex post* MFN clause concepts, see Chapter 3 of this book.

an additional paragraph was added which excluded dispute settlement provisions from other treaties being incorporated through MFN protection.[124]

Another notable trend in the rebalancing period is the rising number of megaregional agreements that contain investment provisions or investment chapters. These agreements usually contain reform-oriented investment provisions with cautiously drafted MFN clauses.[125] For example, in November 2018, NAFTA was replaced by a new free trade agreement, the United States-Mexico-Canada Agreement (USMCA).[126] The USMCA guarantees MFN treatment to the investors and investments of another Party "in like circumstances" in Article 14.5 of its investment chapter, with text that is largely similar to its predecessor in NAFTA. Building on this, Article 14.5 provides explicit explanation of the term "in like circumstances," which should be considered in light of the totality of the circumstances, particularly when the favorable treatment is based on a legitimate public interest.[127]

In addition, USMCA explicitly excludes the application of MFN treatment to ISDS with an interpretative footnote to Article 14-D.3.[128] This has limited the application of MFN treatment to certain types of substantive protection provided in other treaties. Moreover, a footnote to Article 14-D.3 also restricts the definition of "treatment" under Article 14.5 to exclude provisions in third-party treaties that "impose substantive obligations," and, as such, the term only encompasses "measures in connection with the implementation of substantive obligations."[129] This discourages the practice of invoking treatment not provided for in the basic treaty, which could impose unintended international obligations on the respondent state via the MFN clause.[130]

124 A new paragraph 3 was inserted via the 2018 amendment to the FTA, a copy of which is available at: <https://investmentpolicy.unctad.org/international-investment-agreements/treaty-files/5792/download> accessed 20 April 2022.

125 UNCTAD, 'Recent developments in the international investment agreement regime: Accelerating IIA reform', IIA Issues Note No. 3 (2021), available at: <https://unctad.org/system/files/official-document/diaepcbinf2021d6_en.pdf> accessed 20 April 2022.

126 U.S.-Mexico-Canada Agreement (USMCA, 2018). A copy of the full text of the agreement is available at <https://investmentpolicy.unctad.org/international-investment-agreements/treaty-files/6008/download> accessed 20 April 2022.

127 Article 14.5.4 of the USMCA (n 126).

128 Footnote 22 of USMCA (n 126) provides that "[f]or the purposes of this paragraph: (i) the 'treatment' referred to in Article 14.5 (Most-Favored-Nation Treatment) excludes provisions in other international trade or investment agreements that establish international dispute resolution procedures or impose substantive obligations ..."

129 Footnote 22 of USMCA (n 126).

130 See, for example: Alejandro Faya Rodriguez, 'The Most-Favored-Nation Clause in International Investment: Agreements A Tool for Treaty Shopping?' (2008) 25 Journal

Investment law is a rather fragmented regime. Since World War II, almost all attempts to multilateralize investment law have failed, creating a complex "spaghetti bowl" situation which consists of over three thousand intertwined IIAs.[131] Nonetheless, clear paradigmatical trends have emerged within the fragmented IIA system that have driven the formulation of MFN clauses in treaties. During the FCN years, treaties were mainly concluded for the purpose of investment protection for Western countries. The MFN clause was therefore included to provide a guarantee against discrimination for Western foreign investors. As a result, MFN clauses tended to be drafted in general terms without effective exceptions during the Colonial Era. During the Post-Colonial Era, countries began concluding BITs in response to expropriation by newly independent countries. MFN clauses were therefore often linked to losses from expropriation, or war, as well as compensation stemming from military conflicts. In the Global Era, ideological distinctions between developing and developed countries became blurry, and the dominant IIA paradigm at this time was investment liberalization rather than investment protection. The wording of MFN clauses became more specific, often including detailed exceptions, in order to reflect this shift. This feature continues in the still ongoing Rebalancing Era. During this time, states have begun to redirect dominant IIA paradigms towards a more balanced approach which takes greater cognizance of regulatory policy space, with investment protection playing an increasingly less consequential role (albeit that it still plays a very significant role). As a result, MFN clauses in contemporary IIAs have been drafted in an attempt to ensure the rebalancing desire by states. As such, the MFN clause is not used purely as a device that promotes multilateralism; it is increasingly applied delicately as part an effort to balance the regulatory policy space demanded by states and their people with investment protection.

3 Codification Efforts by the International Law Commission

The MFN clause has been a treaty-based obligation rather than a norm of customary international law.[132] That is to say, states' obligation to accord MFN treatment only exists when included in a treaty.[133] Nonetheless, in view of its

of International Arbitration 89. Regarding the trend of megaregional IIAs, see: UNCTAD (n 125).

131 UNCTAD (n 50) 161.

132 Sharmin (n 42) 42; Cole (n 7) 540; Schwarzenberger (n 3) 103.

133 OECD (n 2) 129.

importance, efforts have been made to codify MFN treatment at the multilateral level. In this regard, the following discussion will focus on the MFN Draft Articles compiled by the International Law Commission. The codification process initiated by the ILC is the most recent systematic attempt to compile the MFN clause into international law. ILC codification efforts can be divided into two periods, the first from 1967 to 1978 and the second from 2006 to 2015.

In 1967, the MFN clause was included in the Commission's work schedule focusing on treaty law during the 19th session of the ILC under the heading "the most-favored-nation clause in the law of treaties." The Commission appointed Mr. Endre Ustor as Special Rapporteur for this topic. In 1968, the 20th session of ILC deemed it necessary to clarify the scope and effect of the clause as a legal institution in all aspects of its practical application. The first report on the MFN clause by the Special Rapporteur was submitted in 1969. This report mainly covered the history of the MFN clause, including its application in trade relations since the 11th century and codification endeavors after the World War I. At its 28th session in 1976, the Commission submitted the first reading of the draft articles to the governments of Member States for observations. The final text with thirty draft articles on the MFN clause (with commentaries) was finally adopted at the 30th session in 1978.[134] It was then recommended to the General Assembly for the purpose of concluding a convention on this issue. At the 46th session of the General Assembly in 1991, the subject was listed on its provisional agenda and given further consideration. After considering all the material at hand, the General Assembly decided to bring the MFN draft articles to the attention of Member States and interested intergovernmental organizations for consideration in relevant cases and to the extent they deemed consideration appropriate.[135]

The 1978 draft articles on MFN clauses contains thirty articles with commentaries under each provision. They dealt with issues of, *inter alia*, the definition of MFN treatment, its legal basis, scope, and the operation thereof. To this end, the ILC referred extensively to relevant international public law disputes in its commentaries and brought up illustrative opinions on important rationales and principles underpinning MFN treatment. The cases and instruments relied

134 See International Law Commission, 'Draft Articles on Most-Favoured-Nation Clauses with Commentaries', *Yearbook of the International Law Commission*, vol II:2 (1978). A copy of which is available at <https://legal.un.org/ilc/texts/instruments/english/commentaries/1_3_1978.pdf> accessed 20 April 2022.

135 See International Law Commission, 'Summaries of the Work of the International Law Commission: Most-Favoured-Nation Clause (Part One)' <http://legal.un.org/ilc/summaries/1_3.shtml#a10> accessed 20 April 2022.

on by the ILC arguably seem obsolete and far-fetched from a current international investment law perspective,[136] and for these reasons serve a limited function for the purpose of this book. Nonetheless, these draft articles manage to conceptualize MFN treatment within the context of international law and provide it with a clear outline to facilitate future interpretation. As such, the draft articles and commentaries will serve as a foundation and often revisited guideline for further analysis of MFN treatment in the remainder of this book.

Thirty years after the final text of the MFN draft articles, the Commission decided, at its 60th session in 2008, to put the topic on its agenda again. At its 61st session in 2009, the Commission set up a study group on the MFN clause and prepared a framework for future work in this regard.[137] At its 62nd session in 2010, the Commission reviewed various papers based on the aforementioned framework defined in 2009. These papers included, *inter alia*, a catalogue of MFN provisions and papers on the 1978 draft articles, GATT and WTO practice, and OECD and UNCTAD analyses of the MFN clause, amongst other things. The Commission also took note of the *Maffezini* case in view of the application of the MFN clause in arbitral practice.[138] In 2011, the Study Group set out a future work agenda at its 63rd session, drawing on the working paper on the interpretation and application of the MFN clause in IIAs, which constituted a skeleton of pending questions with an overview of the work done by the Study Group on this topic thus far, and recent arbitration decisions, amongst other things. The final report (the final report of 2015) on the Study Group's work was then submitted in 2015 at its 67th session. The ILC recommended that this final report be brought to the attention of the General Assembly and suggested that it be disseminated widely.[139]

In denying the utility of revising the 1978 draft articles, the final report of 2015 was more of a summary of the development of the MFN clause than a codification instrument. It especially focused on the development of international investment law over time from the perspective of the often-tangled interpretation and application of MFN clauses by arbitral tribunals and attempted to provide a solution within the context of treaty interpretation as embodied in the VCLT.

---

136 Especially in light of the innovative interpretation of MFN treatment in BITs by *ad hoc* arbitration tribunals.

137 See International Law Commission, 'Summaries of the Work of the International Law Commission: Most-Favoured-Nation Clause (Part Two)' <https://legal.un.org/ilc/summaries/1_3_part_two.shtml> accessed 20 April 2022.

138 *Maffezini* (n 102).

139 See International Law Commission (n 135).

4 Conclusion

This chapter has presented the evolution of MFN treatment from trade agreements in the 11th century to its inclusion in modern international trade and investment treaties. The history of MFN treatment in international trade law suggests that, although it has been applied in different scenarios with different wordings, its rationale nonetheless remains consistent. As one of the main instruments guarding against discriminatory treatment as between foreign competitors, MFN treatment has, since its origins, been utilized by countries to guarantee a level-playing field for foreign traders. However, the historical approach taken by this chapter suggests that the prevalence and coverage of MFN treatment changes alongside the trade policy preferences of states, which largely reflects the contemporary economic situation they find themselves in at a given moment in time. In other words, MFN treatment has a wider scope (e.g., as embodied by the unconditional approach to MFN treatment) in times during which trade liberalism is dominant economic paradigm globally (or at least semi-globally), while its scope appears more restricted (e.g., as embodied by the conditional approach to MFN treatment) or even completely removed due to protectionism in times of geopolitical tension and war.

The situation is slightly different for MFN clauses in investment law. As discussed in this chapter, MFN treatment has been used in BITs in different eras for different purposes. Indeed, in Colonial Era FCN treaties, treaties were concluded to protect overseas investment. A broadly drafted MFN clause was typical at that time. In the Post-Colonial Era, treaties were concluded between developed and developing countries to protect and attract investment, respectively. This made the MFN clause largely a treaty promise from host states, especially in relation to compensation in respect of expropriation. In the Global Era, countries concluded IIAs as part of liberalization efforts and the MFN clause was mostly used to facilitate investment flows. The situation changed drastically during the Rebalancing Era, during which countries began to rethink the IIA system, revising, renegotiating, and terminating current IIAs. IIAs are considered an essential part of the 21st century regionalism,[140] and the role of the MFN clause has changed alongside changes to the global economic situation. It is no longer merely included as a treaty obligation by countries seeking to attract foreign investment. Rather, it is now a key issue

140 Heng Wang and Lu Wang, 'China's Bilateral Investment Treaties' in Julien Chaisse, Leïla Choukroune and Sufian Jusoh (eds), *Handbook of International Investment Law and Policy* (Springer Singapore 2020) 2.; Baldwin (n 79).

for negotiators when attempting to contain the effect of new generation IIAs. This suggests that a cautious or circumspect approach to the interpretation and application of MFN clauses is necessary insofar as the practice of contemporary international investment law is concerned.

CHAPTER 2

Interpretation of the MFN Clause

Following the last chapter on the historical development of the most-favored-nation (MFN) clause, this chapter examines the various methods adopted in investor-state dispute settlement (ISDS) fora in order to interpret MFN clauses. The discussion will mainly focus on three distinct sources of interpretive methods: (i) customary international law; (ii) the interpretive principles enshrined in Articles 31 and 32 of the Vienna Convention on the Law of Treaties (VCLT); and (iii) the arbitral precedents in this regard. The interpretative practice of other international courts like the International Court of Justice (ICJ) and WTO Appellate Body will also be analyzed where relevant.

1 Customary International Law

In view of ISDS tribunals' frequent reference to customary international law in their interpretations of MFN clauses, this part starts by examining the customary international law principles that have most frequently been relied on by tribunals: (i) *expressio unius est exclusio alterius*; (ii) *ejusdem generis*; (iii) the contemporaneity principle.

1.1 *The* Expressio Unius est Exclusio Alterius *Principle*

Expressio unius est exclusio alterius indicates that the explicit mention of one thing suggests the exclusion of another. It is, however, more a rule of logic than of law.[1] It is often relied on by disputing parties and tribunals in ISDS in their efforts to delineate the scope of MFN clauses. In *National Grid*, the tribunal decided that since dispute settlement was not among the list of exceptions referred to in the MFN clause at issue in the basic treaty, it was implicit that dispute settlement provisions from other instruments could be incorporated via the clause in the basic treaty: it applied the *expressio unius est exclusio alterius* principle.[2]

1 Christoph Schreuer, 'Diversity And Harmonization Of Treaty Interpretation In Investment Arbitration' in Malgosia Fitzmaurice, Olufemi Elias and Panos Merkouris (eds), *Treaty Interpretation and the Vienna Convention on the Law of Treaties: 30 Years on* (Brill | Nijhoff 2010) 6.

2 *National Grid PLC v The Argentine Republic, Decision on Jurisdiction dated June 2006*, UNCITRAL Arbitration [82].

Similarly, in *RosInvest*, the tribunal relied on the fact that dispute settlement was not one of the expressly listed exceptions in the basic treaty to incorporate the dispute settlement provisions in a different instrument which, unlike the basic treaty, permitted claims to be brought in respect of expropriations.[3]

On the contrary, in *Plama*, the tribunal took account of, *inter alia*, the ordinary meaning of the MFN clause in question, and the context and negotiating history of the Cyprus-Bulgaria Bilateral Investment Treaty (BIT) and favored a different conclusion than the one reached by applying the *expressio unius est exclusio alterius* principle, the result of which would have been to widen the scope of the MFN clause.[4]

Although widely relied on by tribunals, the *expressio unius est exclusio alterius* principle should perhaps be applied with caution because, as illustrated above, tribunals sometimes reach diverging conclusions when relying on it.[5] Best, perhaps, would be to use the principle as a secondary tool in support of an argument primarily premised on a different interpretive method, which is an approach that a number of tribunals have followed in practice.[6]

1.2 *The* Ejusdem Generis *Principle*

"*Ejusdem generis*" is Latin for "of the same kind." It is a principle captured in Articles 9 and 10 of the Draft Articles as a rule under which an MFN beneficiary "acquires, for itself or for the benefit of persons or things in a determined relationship with it, *only those rights which fall within the limits of the subject-matter of the clause*."[7] According to the ILC, *ejusdem generis* is a principle of interpretation recognized under customary international law and is generally applied by international tribunals and national courts.[8]

The *ejusdem generis* principle played a central role in the *Ambatielos* case. This case concerned a contract for the purchase of nine ships concluded between a Greek national, Mr. Nicolas Eustache Ambatielos (Ambatielos), and the government of the United Kingdom (UK). When sued by the UK government in the British courts for payment delays that allegedly amounted to

3 *RosInvestCo UK Ltd. v The Russian Federation, Award on Jurisdiction dated October 2007*, SCC Case No. 079/2005 [135].

4 *Plama Consortium Limited v Republic of Bulgaria, Decision on Jurisdiction, 8th February 2005*, ICSID Case No. ARB/03/24 [191].

5 Schreuer, (n 1) 6–7.

6 See, for example, *RosInvest v Russia* (n 3) [135].

7 International Law Commission, 'Draft Articles on Most-Favoured-Nation Clauses with Commentaries', *Yearbook of the International Law Commission*, vol II:2 (1978), Article 9 (1). Emphasis added.

8 International Law Commission (n 7).

breach of contract, Ambatielos raised a number of counterclaims, arguing that there was a delay in delivery by the UK government and that he was owed compensation for the losses he suffered due to this delay.[9] After losing his case in court of first instance, Ambatielos appealed to the British Court of Appeals and attempted to present new evidence. Relying on British procedural rules, the Court of Appeals rejected this attempt since the evidence in question was supposed to be presented by Ambatielos in the court of first instance.[10]

After losing in the Court of Appeals, Ambatielos turned to the Greek government for diplomatic protection, which resulted in it bringing to an international arbitration commission on his behalf. The Greek government invoked the MFN clause in a Greece-UK treaty, claiming that Ambatielos was entitled to the same treatments afforded by the UK to nationals from other countries. Specifically, Greece alleged that Ambatielos was entitled to a particular standard of treatment as per the treaty, as well as generally in terms of the "rules of international law, justice, right, and equity applicable thereto."[11] In Greece's view, the Court of Appeals, by refusing to admit the new evidence, violated the standards in question.[12] In response, the UK contended that the MFN clause is only capable of importing standards of treatment applicable to the same category of subject to which the clause itself related. Since the MFN clause at issue referred only to "matters relating to commerce and navigation," it did not cover the issue of "administration of justice" germane to the case before the commission.[13]

The *Ambatielos* commission agreed with the UK that the MFN clause could only import treatment from other instruments in respect of the same category of subject as that to which the clause itself related.[14] The tribunal further stated, however, that the protection of the rights of traders naturally finds a place among the matters dealt with by treaties of commerce and navigation. In this sense, the "administration of justice" was not something that was to be excluded from the guarantee of equal treatment in relation to "commerce and navigation." As a result, the commission decided that treatment that related to the administration of justice was covered by the MFN clause in question and could thus be incorporated by the basic treaty from elsewhere.[15]

9 *The Ambatielos Claim (Greece, United Kingdom of Great Britain and Northern Ireland), Arbitral Award of the Commission of Arbitration in 1956*, 91–94.
10 *The Ambatielos Claim* (n 9) 94.
11 *The Ambatielos Claim* (n 9) 106.
12 *The Ambatielos Claim* (n 9) 105–106.
13 *The Ambatielos Claim* (n 9) 106.
14 *The Ambatielos Claim* (n 9) 107.
15 *The Ambatielos Claim* (n 9) 107.

For Cole, the significance of the *Ambatielos* decision is that it endorsed the essential role of the *ejusdem generis* principle in the interpretation of MFN clauses.[16] As the following chapters in the book reveal, however, the importance of the *ejusdem generis* principle was not fully recognized in subsequent dispute settlement proceedings. At times, tribunals misconstrue the principle and reach contradictory conclusions in relation to the interpretation of MFN clauses. For example, in *Maffezini*, the tribunal notably decided that procedural treatment formed part of the list of areas in respect of which MFN treatment was supposed to be accorded and therefore that the *ejusdem generis* principle could not be relied on in order to prevent the incorporation of more favorable treatment contained in a treaty other than the basic treaty in question.[17] On the contrary, in *Salini*, the tribunal applied the *ejusdem generis* principle and reached the opposite conclusion. It referred to the *Maffezini* decision and decided that the case *in casu* was markedly different from that in *Maffezini*. As such, the tribunal decided that the MFN clause in the basic BIT could not be relied on in order to incorporate a more favorable dispute settlement procedure.[18]

Application of the *ejusdem generis* principle, as a general proposition, entails a number of pre-conditions. First, the alleged more favorable treatment seeking to be incorporated from outside of the basic treaty should fall within the scope delineated by the MFN clause in the basic treaty itself. Moreover, the party seeking to incorporate more favorable treatment should be in similar relationship with the host state. In its Draft Articles, the ILC explains that states cannot be regarded as being bound beyond the obligations they have undertaken.[19] The stance taken in this book, which is justified in subsequent chapters, is that the *ejusdem generis* principle should be given more weight by tribunals and should be applied in a manner which leads to an appropriately balanced interpretation of MFN clauses.

1.3 *The Contemporaneity Principle*

The principle of contemporaneity requires that the terms of a treaty "be interpreted according to the meaning which they possessed, or which would have

16 Tony Cole, 'The Boundaries of Most Favored Nation Treatment in International Investment Law' (2012) 33 Michigan Journal of International Law 537, 567.

17 *Emilio Agustín Maffezini v The Kingdom of Spain, Decision of the Tribunal on Objections to Jurisdiction dated 25 January 2000*, ICSID Case No. ARB/97/7 [56].

18 *Salini Costruttori S.pA and Italstrade S.pA v Hashemite Kingdom of Jordan, Decision on Jurisdiction dated 9 November 2004*, ICSID Case No. ARB/02/13 [117–118].

19 International Law Commission (n 7) 30, para 11.

been attributed to them, and in the light of current linguistic usage, at the time when the treaty was originally concluded."[20] The principle of contemporaneity is based on the idea that the purpose of treaty interpretation is to determine the intention of contracting states and that the text of the treaty, as the main record of this intention, should be construed pursuant to the meaning the parties intended to give to its terms. In other words, the interpretation of a treaty must be based on the meaning of its terms at the time the treaty was concluded.[21]

The principle of contemporaneity has been applied by a number of tribunals in ISDS practice. For example, the tribunals in *Daimler* and *ICS (I)* applied this principle in order to ascertain the meaning of the term "treatment" in the MFN clauses respectively at issue.[22] In *Daimler*, the tribunal first sought to determine the definition of the term "treatment" as a general concept as used in the MFN clause in question. Despite a lack of submissions on the treaty's drafting history demonstrating an understanding of the term "treatment" shared by Germany and Argentina at the time of its conclusion, the tribunal applied the rule of contemporaneity and sought to understand the meaning generally ascribed to the term by the broader international community of states at the time of the conclusion of the treaty.[23] For this purpose, the tribunal relied especially on the 1992 World Bank Guidelines on the Treatment of Foreign Direct Investment (Guidelines).[24] Part of the Guidelines was devoted to the term "treatment" and did not mention dispute settlement mechanisms. The tribunal noted that although the Guideline was a soft law instrument, it nevertheless represented an "indication of the prevailing view among the community of states during the period contemporaneous to the adoption of the Germany-Argentina BIT."[25] As such, the fact that an international dispute mechanism was not contained in the Guideline led the tribunal conclude that

20 Fitzmaurice, G. G., 'The Law and Procedure of the International Court of Justice 1951-4: Treaty Interpretation and Other Treaty Points' (1957) 33 British Yearbook of International Law 203, 203.

21 Roberto Castro de Figueiredo, 'Evolving Meaning: The Interpretation of Investment Treaties and Temporal Variations' (*Kluwer Arbitration Blog*, 2015).

22 *Daimler Financial Services AG v Argentine Republic, Award Dated 22 August 2012*, ICSID Case No. ARB/05/1; *ICS Inspection and Control Services Limited v The Argentine Republic (I), Award on Jurisdiction dated 10 February 2012*, PCA Case No. 2010–9.

23 *Daimler v Argentina* (n 22) [220].

24 'Report to the Development Committee and Guidelines on the Treatment of Foreign Direct Investment' (World Bank 1992). A copy of which is available at: <https://documents1.worldbank.org/curated/en/955221468766167766/pdf/multi-page.pdf> accessed 20 April 2022.

25 World Bank (n 24) [224].

the term "treatment" as understood by Germany and Argentina at the time of the conclusion of the BIT referred merely to the host state's *direct* treatment of investments and not to the conducting of any international arbitration arising out of that treatment.[26]

In *ICS (I)*, the tribunal considered that the meaning ascribable to the term "treatment" was a key issue in determining whether the MFN clause in that case was intended by the relevant contracting states to substitute for the consent provided in the text of the treaty that required it.[27] Given that neither disputing party submitted direct evidence as to the particular meaning of the term "treatment" at the time of the conclusion of the treaty, the tribunal, as in the *Daimler* case, turned to the principle of contemporaneity for an answer. Again following the approach taken by the *Daimler* tribunal, the Guidelines were relied on as a "valuable indication of the prevailing view among the community of States during the period leading up to the adoption of the UK-Argentina BIT."[28] Here, too, the tribunal came to the conclusion that the term "treatment" as understood by the parties at the time of the conclusion of the BIT referred merely to the host state's *direct* treatment of investments and not to the conducting of any international arbitration arising out of that treatment. Therefore, the contracting parties could not have anticipated that a type of dispute settlement mechanism could fall within the scope of treatment contemplated by the MFN clause when they negotiated the treaty.[29]

2 Articles 31 and 32 of the VCLT

Articles 31 and 32 of the VCLT constitute a codification of the customary international law on interpretation and are frequently referred to by arbitral tribunals.[30] A hierarchy exists between the two provisions.[31] This is evident from the text of the respective provisions. Article 31 is titled "general rule of

26 *Daimler v Argentina* (n 22) [224].
27 *ICS Inspection v Argentina* (n 22) [285].
28 *ICS Inspection v Argentina* (n 22) [295].
29 *ICS Inspection v Argentina* (n 22) [313].
30 Tarcisio Gazzini, *Interpretation of International Investment Treaties* (First Edition, Hart Publishing 2016) 112; Tanjina Sharmin, *Application of Most-Favoured-Nation Clauses by Investor-State Arbitral Tribunals: Implications for the Developing Countries* (Springer 2020) 73.
31 For the different views on the interpretation of Article 31 and 32 themselves, see M Waibel, 'Demystifying the Art of Interpretation' (2011) 22 European Journal of International Law 571.

interpretation" and drafted in mandatory terms. It provides that "a treaty shall be interpreted in good faith in accordance with the ordinary meaning to be given to the terms of the treaty in their context and in the light of its object and purpose." Article 32, on the other hand, is titled "supplementary means of interpretation," which includes looking into the preparatory work that led to the conclusion of a particular treaty as well as the circumstances in which it was concluded.[32] This part examines these two provisions more closely, with a specific focus on: (i) the elements of Articles 31 and 32; (ii) their application by international courts and tribunals; and (iii) their application by arbitral tribunals in the specific context of interpreting MFN clauses.

2.1 *Article 31 of the VCLT as Containing the Core Principles of Treaty Interpretation*

Article 31 of the VCLT requires that treaty interpretation be approached with reference to a combination of considerations, including good faith, the ordinary meaning of language deployed, the context in which the treaty was concluded, and its object and purpose. According to the ILC, these elements should be considered together in interpreting a treaty text with a view to applying them as one, uniform and integrated rule.[33] The text of Article 31 reads as follows:

1. A treaty shall be interpreted in good faith in accordance with the ordinary meaning to be given to the terms of the treaty in their context and in the light of its object and purpose.
2. The context for the purpose of the interpretation of a treaty shall comprise, in addition to the text, including its preamble and annexes:
   (a) any agreement relating to the treaty which was made between all the parties in connection with the conclusion of the treaty;
   (b) any instrument which was made by one or more parties in connection with the conclusion of the treaty and accepted by the other parties as an instrument related to the treaty.
3. There shall be taken into account, together with the context:
   (a) any subsequent agreement between the parties regarding the interpretation of the treaty or the application of its provisions;

32 Vienna Convention on the Law of Treaties (1969). A copy of which is available at: <https://legal.un.org/ilc/texts/instruments/english/conventions/1_1_1969.pdf> accessed 20 April 2022.

33 United Nations Conference on the Law of Treaties, First and Second Session, Documents of the Conference (1971) A/ CONF.39/1 l/Add.2, 39. Available at: <https://treaties.un.org/doc/source/docs/A_CONF.39_11_Add.2-E.pdf> accssed 20 April 2022.

(b) any subsequent practice in the application of the treaty which establishes the agreement of the parties regarding its interpretation;

(c) any relevant rules of international law applicable in the relations between the parties.

4. A special meaning shall be given to a term if it is established that the parties so intended.[34]

Article 31(1) makes reference to four crucial principles of treaty interpretation and is frequently regarded as the "golden rule" of VCLT treaty interpretation.[35] Empirical research by Fauchald provides support for this proposition.[36] He examines the interpretive methods adopted by arbitral tribunals in their awards and decisions, showing that among 35 International Centre for Settlement of Investment Disputes (ICSID) decisions that relied on the VCLT in order to interpret treaties, only around half of them (16) made reference to rules and principles not alluded to in Article 31(1).[37] The same trend is visible in research by Weeramantry, who finds that out of a total collection of 258 arbitral awards and decisions, Article 31(1) was comfortably the most frequently relied on provision in the VCLT (it was referred to in 136 cases). This is followed by general references to Article 31(79 cases), references to Article 32 (67 cases), and then by references to Article 31(2) (49 cases), Article 31(3) (12 cases), and Article 31(4) (2 cases).[38]

This brings us back to the point that there was no anticipated hierarchy among the principles contained in Article 31(1) itself. As mentioned above, the ILC intended for these principles to be applied in combination, and to be "thrown into the crucible" in the hope that "their interaction would give the legally relevant interpretation."[39] Therefore, while international courts and

34 Vienna Convention on the Law of Treaties (1969) (n 32) 31.

35 Eduardo Jiménez De Aréchaga, 'International Law in the Past Third of a Century (Volume 159) Collected Courses of the Hague Academy Intl L 1' 43. Jan Peter Sasse also argued that, the 'starting point for most tribunal is Article 31 of the Vienna Convention on the Law of Treaties.' See Jan Peter Sasse, *An Economic Analysis of Bilateral Investment Treaties* (Gabler 2011).

36 OK Fauchald, 'The Legal Reasoning of ICSID Tribunals – An Empirical Analysis' (2008) 19 European Journal of International Law 301.

37 Fauchald (n 36) 314.

38 J Romesh Weeramantry, *Treaty Interpretation in Investment Arbitration* (1st ed, Oxford University Press 2012) 222 Appendix I, table 3. It should be noted that tribunals often rely on more than one interpretive method and that one case may accordingly be linked to more than one provision of the VCLT.

39 United Nations Conference on the Law of Treaties, First and Second Session, Documents of the Conference (1971) A/ CONF.39/1 l/Add.2 (n 33) 39.

tribunals often begin with the ordinary meaning of treaty provisions as a starting point, they do not stop there.[40] In WTO case law, Appellate Body has largely relied on dictionaries for ordinary meanings, which have been considered of limit function and need to be determined in a contextualized method.[41] For example, in *EC – Asbestos*, the Appellate Body observed the limited function of dictioinaries for the interpretation of the term "like products" in Article III:4 of the GATT 1994 and opined that it had to be "interpreted in light of the context, and of the object and purpose, of the provision at issue, and of the object and purpose of the covered agreement in which the provison appears."[42]

The necessity of a combination of interpretive methods is largely due to the inadequacy of the ordinary meaning of words as a self-standing method and its often inextricable link to the context in which the words were used. This is borne out by WTO Appellate Body in the *US – Continued Zeroing* case, where the Appellate Body explained that:

> A word or term may have more than one meaning or shade of meaning ... a treaty interpreter is required to have recourse to context and object and purpose to elucidate the relevant meaning of the word or term ... it should be kept in mind that treaty interpretation is an integrated operation, where interpretative rules or principles must be understood and applied as connected and mutually reinforcing components of a holistic exercise.[43]

---

40 Isabelle Van Damme, 'Treaty Interpretation by the WTO Appellate Body'(2010) 21 The European Journal of International Law 3 605, 620. For an example in this regard, see *B-Mex and others v Mexico*, whereby the respondent-appointed arbitrator Raúl E. Vinuesa expressed in the dissenting opinion that "Any good faith interpretation of a treaty rule starts with the analysis of the ordinary meaning to be given to the terms thereof." *Deana Anthone, Neil Ayervais, Douglas Black and others v United Mexican States, Partial Award dated 19 July 2019, Partial Dissenting Opinion by Raúl E. Vinuesa,* ICSID Case No. ARB(AF)/16/3 [34].

41 Van Damme (n 40).

42 Appellate Body Report, *European Communities – Measures Affecting Asbestos and Asbestos-Containing Products* (*EC – Asbestos*), WT/DS135/AB/R [88]. In a similar vein, the Appellate Body in *US – Gambling* explained that "dictionaries alone are not necessarily capable of resolving complex questions of interpretation, as they typically aim to catalogue all meanings of words – be those meanings common or rare, universal or specialized". See: Appellate Body Report, *United States – Measures Affecting the Cross-Border Supply of Gambling and Betting Services* (*US – Gambling*), WT/DS285/AB/R [164].

43 WTO Appellate Body Report, *United States – Continued Existence and Application of Zeroing Methodology,* WT/DS350/AB/R [268].

Similarly, in ISDS, Weeramantry has observed that when noting the importance of the text of a given treaty as the starting point of treaty interpretation, tribunals seldom limit themselves to the ordinary meaning of treaty terms in performing their interpretative duties. According to Weeramantry, this implies that tribunals' understanding of treaty texts for the most part include the ordinary meaning of the language used together as well as the context, object and purpose of the text.[44] This proposition is also supported by the scholarship on point. Gardiner, for example, believes that ordinary meaning cannot be divorced from context since it is "immediately and intimately linked with context and to be taken in conjunction with all other relevant elements of the Vienna rules."[45] By the same token, Van Damme argues that "all interpretation is contextual," and that it is the prerogative of the interpreter to decide how context is to be applied.[46]

A similar approach has been endorsed by Gardiner, who proposes that the inclusion of context as a principle in Article 31 has a dual purpose. The first is to assist in qualifying the meaning of terms with a view to preventing an over-literal interpretation or selecting an ordinary meaning where more than one meaning exists, and the second is to identify the materials to be considered when deciding what constitutes "context."[47] In Weeramantry's monograph, he claims that "the criteria of ordinary meaning and context are fused and applied as one rule."[48] JG Merrills further argues that a given text might have more than one ordinary meaning and that, without more, one does not have criteria for choosing between different ordinary meanings. As such, an interpreter is "directed in Article 31 towards a variety of contextual matters with the object of assisting him to choose between the alternatives offered."[49] Similarly, according to Andrea Bianchi, "what makes the meaning of a word 'plain', 'clear' or 'unambiguous' is not any linguistic property the word may have, but rather the context in which it is used and the code used for communication in a particular situation by a certain community."[50] Finally, as Sir Sinclair has explained in relation to the interactions between these principles,

44 Weeramantry (n 38) 51.

45 Richard K Gardiner, *Treaty Interpretation* (Oxford University Press 2008) 165–76.

46 Isabelle Van Damme, *Treaty Interpretation by the WTO Appellate Body* (Oxford University Press 2009) 213.

47 Gardiner (n 45) 177.

48 Weeramantry (n 38) 63.

49 JG Merrills, 'Two Approaches to Treaty Interpretation' (1971) 4 The Australian Year Book of International Law 55, 59.

50 Andrea Bianchi, 'Textual Interpretation and (International) Law Reading: The Myth of (in)Determinacy and the Genealogy of Meaning' in Pieter HF Bekker, Rudolf Dolzer and

> reference to the object and purpose of the treaty is, as it were, a secondary or ancillary process in the application of the general rule on interpretation. The initial search is for the 'ordinary meaning' to be given to the terms of the treaty in their 'context'; it is in the light of the object and purpose of the treaty that the initial and preliminary conclusion must be tested and either confirmed or modified.[51]

The ILC has placed primacy to the treaty text as "the basis for the interpretation of a treaty."[52] It considers the treaty text as the authentic expression of the intentions of treaty parties, and clarification of the meaning of treaty text as the starting point of treaty interpretation.[53] This emphasis on textual interpretation is also visible in the negotiating history of the VCLT, which indicates that most member states preferred a steadfast focus on the words of the treaty with extraneous evidence of intended meaning relegated to a secondary role.[54]

As the literature and case law referred to above suggest, the application of Article 31(1) should entail cautious navigation between the interpretive principles it contains, based on a careful examination of the textual circumstances that led to the particular words of a treaty being selected. However, Article 31(1) provides interpreters general principles to be followed without clarifying how much weight should be given to each principle it contains. As a result, this has provided tribunals with fairly broad discretion in according a weight to each principle.[55] One implication of this is that it is possible for an interpreter to accord different weights to each of the factors in order to reach a preferred

---

Michael Waibel (eds), *Making Transnational Law Work in the Global Economy* (Cambridge University Press 2010) 40.

51 Sir Ian Sinclair, *The Vienna Convention on the Law of Treaties* (Melland Schill Monographs in International Law 1984) 130. On the interaction of Article 31(1) elements in the course of treaty interpretation, see also Weeramantry (n 38).

52 United Nations, 'Yearbook of the International Law Commission, Vol II. Documents of the Second Part of the Seventeenth Session and of the Eighteenth Session Including the Reports of the Commission to the General Assembly' (UN 1967) A/CN.4/SER. A/1966/Add. 1. <https://legal.un.org/ilc/publications/yearbooks/english/ilc_1966_v2.pdf> accessed 20 April 2022.

53 United Nations (n 52).

54 Merrills (n 49) 55.

55 According to Waibel, '...on account of the limited number of substantive rules, the interpreters are left with considerable room for maneuver'. See: Waibel (n 31) 575. Ian Brownlie described these principles as "the comparatively general principles which appear to constitute general rules for the interpretation of treaties." See Ian Brownlie, *Principles of Public International Law* (7th ed, Oxford University Press 2008) 35; Joost Pauwelyn and Manfred Elsig, 'The Politics of Treaty Interpretation: Variations and Explanations Across International Tribunals' in Jeffery L. Dunoff and Mark A Pollack (eds), *Interdisciplinary*

outcome.[56] This implication has caused the "general, question-begging and contradictory" issue in international investment arbitration which concerns Brownlie. That is, tribunals' differential applications of Article 31(1), particularly as it relates to MFN clauses, have led to a debate concerning whether tribunals should adopt a textual or teleological approach when interpreting treaty texts. These approaches are discussed in the subsection below.

2.1.1 Should Interpreters Follow the Textual or Teleological Approach to Treaty Interpretation?

The textual and teleological approaches to the interpretation of MFN clauses both refer to Article 31(1) of the VCLT.[57] While the textual approach focuses on the specific wording of a given MFN clause on a case-by-case basis, teleological interpretation entails giving more weight to the object and purpose of treaties and the MFN clauses they contain.

The textual approach has been adopted by a number of tribunals, including the *İçkale*, *Salini*, *Plama*, *Telenor* and *HICEE* tribunals, amongst others.[58] This approach features a detailed textual examination of MFN clauses whereby tribunals tend to conduct a systematic application of Article 31(1) of the VCLT.

Perspectives on International Law and International Relations: The State of the Art (New York: Cambridge University Press 2011) 450.

56 See also Gardiner (n 42) 45, where the author, after analyzing the *Ceskoslovenska Obschodni Banka (Jurisdiction)* arbitral decision, concluded that '[t]here was not, however, a systematic application of each part of the general rule, followed by assessment of whether to refer to supplementary means of interpretation. The tribunal applied such of the rules as were appropriate, including reference to accounts of the preparatory work at an early stage of its interpretation on one point. This is consistent with the practice adopted in many courts and tribunals, even if not with a narrow reading of the Vienna Convention.'

57 On the conventional wisdom of MFN interpretation, see Simon Batifort and J Benton Heath, 'The New Debate on the Interpretation of MFN Clauses in Investment Treaties: Putting the Brakes on Multilateralization' (2018) 111 American Journal of International Law 873; Martins Paparinskis, 'MFN Clauses and Substantive Treatment: A Law of Treaties Perspective of the "Conventional Wisdom"' (2018) 112 American Journal of International Law (Unbound) 49.

58 *İçkale İnşaat Limited Şirketi v Turkmenistan, Award dated 8 March 2016*, ICSID Case No. ARB/10/24; *Salini Costruttori S.p.A. and Italstrade S.p.A. v Hashemite Kingdom of Jordan, Decision on Jurisdiction dated 9 November, 2004* ICSID Case No. ARB/02/13; *Plama Consortium Limited v Republic of Bulgaria, Decision on Jurisdiction dated 8th February 2005*, ICSID Case No. ARB/03/24; *Telenor Mobile Communications AS v Republic of Hungary, Award dated 13 September 2006*, ICSID Case No. ARB/04/15; *HICEE BV v The Slovak Republic, Partial Award dated 23 May 2011*, PCA Case No. 2009–11. For more detailed discussion of the cases, see infra Chapters III, IV and V.

For example, in *Plama*, the tribunal adopted a textual examination pursuant to Article 31(1) in considering whether to allow the claimant to incorporate ICSID arbitration provisions from a third-party BIT through an MFN clause contained in the basic treaty.[59] It considered, *inter alia*, the ordinary meaning of the term "treatment," the context, object and purpose of various provisions, and subsequent practice (including treaties concluded between the contracting parties and third parties, and subsequent negotiations between the contracting parties after entering into the subject BIT), as well as the "special meaning" principle contained in Article 31(4), which the tribunal ultimately found to be inapplicable in relation to disposing of the case at hand. In this regard, the tribunal cited Sir Sinclair's warning about the potential results of adopting a teleological interpretation via undue emphasis on the object and purpose of a treaty, the extreme forms of which may "even deny the relevance of [the] ... intentions of parties."[60]

In *Salini*, the tribunal also denied the investors' attempt to incorporate a more favorable dispute settlement clause through the MFN clause contained in the Jordan-Italy BIT in order to submit its contractual dispute to ICSID arbitration instead of Jordan's domestic court system. In reaching this conclusion, the tribunal examined the wording carefully and declared that the MFN clause at issue did not include any textual indications suggesting that its scope of application included procedural issues. Subsequently, the tribunal proceeded to compare the specific wording of the MFN clause in question with the wording of the MFN clause at issue in *Maffezini*. It concluded that the MFN clause at issue in the dispute before it "[did] not envisage 'all rights or all matters covered by the agreement' [as was the case in *Maffezini*]."[61] In addition, the tribunal looked at the context of the basic treaty with reference to its Article 9 and explained that "the Claimants [had] submitted nothing from which it might be established that the common intention of the Parties was to have the most-favored-nation clause apply to dispute settlement," on the contrary, for the tribunal, "the intention as expressed in Article 9(2) (dispute settlement provision) of the BIT was to exclude from ICSID jurisdiction contractual

59 The MFN provision set forth in Article 3 of the Cyprus – Bulgaria BIT reads as follows: 1. Each Contracting Party shall apply to the investments in its territory by investors of the other Contracting Party a treatment which is not less [favorable] than that accorded to investments by investors of third states. 2. This treatment shall not be applied to the privileges which either Contracting Party accords to investors from third countries in virtue of their participation in economic communities and unions, a customs union or a free trade area.

60 Sinclair (n 51) 130.

61 *Salini v Jordan* (n 58) [118].

disputes between an investor and an entity of a State Party in order that such disputes might be settled in accordance with the procedures set forth in the investment agreements."[62]

Last but not least, the tribunal in *HICEE* refused to accept the claimant's attempt to import less restrictive *ratione personae* requirements from third treaties through the MFN clause in the basic treaty. It explained that it "endorse[d] the approach adopted by other investment tribunals that each most-[favored]-nation clause is to be interpreted according to its own terms."[63]

On the other hand, the teleological approach tends to be rooted in the object and purpose of basic treaties, resulting in broad – and at times pro-investor – interpretations of MFN clauses. For example, the *Maffezini* tribunal explained that the MFN clause in Argentina-Spain BIT should be interpreted in the light of the treaty's object and purpose, which the tribunal saw as being "the protection of foreign investors." Therefore, for the tribunal, "[n]otwithstanding the fact that the basic treaty containing the clause [did] not refer expressly to dispute settlement as covered by most favored nation clause, tribunal considers that there are good reasons to conclude that today dispute settlement arrangements are inextricably related to the protection of foreign investors, as they are related to the protection of rights of traders under treaties of commerce."[64]

Later, the *Siemens* tribunal aligned itself with the position of the *Maffezini* tribunal on the same issue. In *Siemens*, the claimant invoked the MFN clause to eschew the eighteen-month period for local remedies in the basic treaty without applying the fork-in-the-road provision in the third-party treaty.[65] The tribunal upheld this claim, and drew on the preamble of the basic treaty, stating as it did that it "provides that the parties have agreed to the provisions of the Treaty for the purpose of creating favorable conditions for the investments of nations or companies of one of the two States in the territory of the other

---

62 *Salini v Jordan* (n 58) [118].

63 *HICEE v Slovakia* (n 58) [149].

64 *Maffezini v Spain* (n 17) [54].

65 *Siemens AG v The Argentine Republic, Decision on Jurisdiction dated 3 August 2004*, ICSID Case No. ARB/02/8. The MFN clause in the Argentina – Germany BIT is worded as follows: "(1) Neither Contracting Party shall subject investments in its territory by or with the participation of nationals or companies of the other Contracting Party to treatment less [favorable] than it accords to investments of its own nationals or companies or to investments of nationals or companies of any third State.

(2) Neither Contracting Party shall subject nationals or companies of the other Contracting Party, as regards their activity in connection with investments in its territory, to treatment less [favorable] than it accords to its own nationals or companies or to nationals or companies of any third State."

State." For the tribunal, "[t]he intention of the parties [was] clear," that is, it was "to create favorable conditions for investments and to stimulate private initiative."[66] Similarly, the *SGS* tribunal also referred to the preamble of the subject BIT in support of a broad interpretation of the MFN clause at issue in that dispute, stating "the BIT is a treaty for the promotion and reciprocal protection of investments" and that "[a]ccording to the preamble it is intended 'to create and maintain [favorable] conditions for investments by investors of one Contracting Party in the territory of the other.'"[67] The tribunal accordingly reached the conclusion that "it is legitimate to resolve uncertainties in its interpretation so as to [favor] the protection of covered investments."[68]

On this point, the decision of the *RosInvest* tribunal is also noteworthy for its broad interpretation of the MFN clause central to that dispute, which rested on a teleological approach.[69] After contemplating whether the MFN clause in the UK-Soviet BIT extended to arbitration procedures, the tribunal answered the question in the affirmative on the grounds that "this [was] a normal result of the application of MFN clauses, the very character and intention of which is that protection not accepted in one treaty is widened by transferring the protection accorded in another treaty" and continued to note that "[i]f this effect is generally accepted in the context of substantive protection, the Tribunal sees no reason not to accept it in the context of procedural clauses such as arbitration clauses."[70]

The textual-teleological distinction reveals certain presumptions of tribunals in relation to the interpretation of MFN clauses. Some tribunals have interpreted MFN clauses on a preexisting understanding of the investor-state relationship in a given BIT, as opposed to on a more rigid reliance of principles contained in the VCLT. This suggests that they select VCLT principles and the weights they should ascribed in a given situation *ex post* in order to support their conclusions. This will almost inevitably lead to conflicting interpretations, even where a given MFN clause in one case is virtually word-for-word verbatim to a different clause in a different case. These preferences of ISDS

66 *Siemens v Argentina* (n 65) [81].

67 *SGS Société Générale de Surveillance SA v Philippines, Decision on Jurisdiction 29 January 2004*, ICSID Case No. ARB/02/6 [116]. The MFN clause in Switzerland-Philippines provides as follows: Each Contracting Party shall in its territory accord investments or returns of investors of the other Contracting Party treatment not less [favorable] 'than that which it accords to investments or returns of, its own investors or to investments or returns of investors of any third State, whichever is more [favorable] to the investor concerned.'

68 SGS v *Philippines* (n 67) [116].

69 *RosInvest v Russia* (n 3).

70 *RosInvest v Russia* (n 3) [131–132].

tribunals above for particular interpretive methods have led to the development of the so-called textual and teleological schools of thought.[71]

This book takes the view that the textual approach is more aligned with interpretive principles enshrined in Article 31 of the VCLT. This is because the textual school takes into account all the elements of Article 31 in an integrated way. On the other hand, the teleological school weights a treaty's object and purpose disproportionately. As such, the WTO Appellate Body in *Japan – Alcoholic Beverages II* found that the "object and purpose" contained in Aritcle 31 is only instrumental in confirming and justifying interpretations and should not be applied as "an independent basis for interpretation."[72] In addition, by adopting the teleological approach, tribunals tend to extract and rely on the object and purpose of a given treaty from its preamble, which is problematic for a number of reasons. First, because the object and purpose of treaties may not necessarily be included in the preamble of a treaty, which means that focusing on the preamble alone will lead to tribunals losing sight of the rationale of the MFN clause as a treaty provision.[73] Second, international agreements usually have multiple purposes other than investment protection. This is particularly outlined by WTO Appellate Body in the case of *US – Shrimp*, where it considered that "most treaties have no single, undiluted object and purpose but rather a variety of different, and possibly conflicting, objects and purposes."[74] This is even more often the case in contemporary era of rebalancing, during which, as explained in Chapter 1 of this book, States have increasingly been concluding IIAs that dilute the pro-investor approach. All of this leads to the conclusion

---

71 Batifort and Heath (n 57).

72 Appellate Body Report, *Japan – Taxes on Alcoholic Beverages* (*Japan – Alcoholic Beverages II*), WT/DS8/AB/R, WT/DS10/AB/R, WT/DS11/AB/R, footnote 20.

73 Sharmin (n 30), citing Pr Thulasidhass, 'Most-Favoured-Nation Treatment in International Investment Law: Ascertaining the Limits through Interpretative Principles' (2015) 7 Amsterdam Law Forum 3, 14–24. Although the Appellate Body of *EC – Chicken Cuts* helds a different opinion by stating that the term "its object and purpose" makes it clear that the starting point for ascertaining "object and purpose" should be the treaty itself in its entirety, the Appellate Body nevertheless also admitted that "Article 31(1) does not exclude taking into account the object and purpose of particular treaty terms, if doing so assists the interpreter in determining the treaty's object and purpose on the whole. We do not see why it would be necessary to divorce a treaty's object and purpose from the object and purpose of specific treaty provisions, or vice versa." See: Appellate Body Report, *European Communities – Customs Classification of Frozen Boneless Chicken Cuts* (*EC-Chicken Cuts*), WT/DS269/AB/R, WT/DS286/AB/R, WT/DS269/AB/R/Corr.1, WT/DS286/AB/R/Corr.1, 238–240.

74 Appellate Body Report, *United States – Import Prohibition of Certain Shrimp and Shrimp Products* (*US – Shrimp*), WT/DS58/AB/R, 17.

that in order for the interpretation of MFN clauses to properly reflect the objectives of the VCLT, a more textual approach is necessary; to take an alternative approach would defeat the rightful attempt by states to rebalance their IIAs. As Chukwumerije correctly points out:

> It is important that tribunals not allow their understanding of the purpose of BITs to supplant the ordinary meaning and context of the treaty provisions. Rather than allowing a focus on the purpose of BITs and MFN clauses to drive their interpretation of these MFN clauses, tribunals should remain true to the philosophy of the Vienna Convention by emphasizing the ordinary meaning of MFN clauses, interpreted against the background of both the context and the purpose of the treaty in which they are contained.[75]

Third, a treaty inevitably results from compromise. There are many tradeoffs, both perceived and actual, in relation to investment protection and its implications. These tradeoffs are often carefully navigated by states when negotiating with one another on which provisions to include in a treaty. In other words, a treaty is a package deal. As Cole has described, treaty negotiation is an "interrelated enterprise, with substantively unconnected elements of the treaty often being used as [tradeoffs]: one party getting its preferred language in the first clause in exchange for the other party getting its preferred language in the second clause."[76] Nondiscrimination is but one of the provisions contained in this treaty package. Teleological interpretations often lose sight of this fact. For Cole, teleological approach "risk[s] allowing the goal of market equalization to override the operation of the MFN clause itself."[77]

2.1.2 Subsequent Agreements and Practices

Article 31(3) of the VCLT anticipated the consideration of subsequent agreements and practices alongside the consideration of treaty context. Article 31(3) reads as follows:

> There shall be taken into account, together with the context:
> (a) any subsequent agreement between the parties regarding the interpretation of the treaty or the application of its provisions;

75 Okezic Chukwumerije, 'Interpreting Most-Favoured-Nation Clauses in Investment Treaty Arbitrations' (2007) 8 The Journal of World Investment & Trade 597, 615.

76 Cole (n 16) 579.

77 Cole (n 16) 541.

(b) any subsequent practice in the application of the treaty which establishes the agreement of the parties regarding its interpretation.

Some authors have conflated paragraph (a) and (b) since they can be hard to distinguish from each other, and also because the subsequent practice element is less frequently applied.[78] In what follows below, "subsequent agreement" and "subsequent practice" will first be examined separately as two different interpretative methods sometimes applicable to MFN clause. Thereafter, they will be analyzed together to illustrate what they collectively imply.

2.1.2.1 *Subsequent Agreements*

Fauchald notes the difference between the two forms of agreements in Article 31 of the VCLT. The first is an agreement concluded *in connection* with the conclusion of the treaty, as included in Article 31(2) as part of treaty context. The second is a subsequent agreement regarding the interpretation of the treaty which, according to Article 31(3)(a), should be examined "together with" the context.[79] In view of the two forms, practice relating to the interpretation of MFN clauses shows that most of the discussion is centered on Article 31(3)(a).

As such, in its commentary on the Draft Articles on the Law of Treaties, The ILC considers subsequent agreement under Article 31(3)(a) as "a further authentic element of interpretation to be taken into account together with the context."[80] As can be seen from its wording, Article 31(3)(a) is not clear about the form an instrument should take in order to be considered a "subsequent agreement." In the case of *EC – Bananas III,* the WTO Appellate Body construed ILC's "authentic interpretation" as those bearing specifically upon the interpretation of a treaty.[81] Moreover, the Appellate Body delineated that

---

78 In this regard, Weeramantry held that: "rather than arranging this section into cases that fall either under Article 31(3)(a) or (b), it will proceed to discuss the two provisions *together*. This approach is due largely to the difficulty in classifying the conduct of the treaty parties as an agreement (which, as discussed later, need not be in writing) under Article 31(3)(a) or as an instance of article 31(3)(b) practice establishing an agreement." See Weeramantry (n 38) 82.

79 Fauchald (n 36) 328.

80 International Law Commission 'Draft Articles on the Law of Treaties with commentaries', (1966) Yearbook of the International Law Commission, 1966, vol. II.

81 Appellate Body report, *European Communities – Regime for the Importation, Sale and Distribution of Bananas* (*EC-Bananas III*), (*Article 21.5 – Ecuador II*)/ (*Article 21.5 – US*), WT/DS27/AB/RW2/ECU, WT/DS27/AB/RW/USA, WT/DS27/AB/RW2/ECU/Corr.1, WT/DS27/AB/RW/USA/Corr.1, 390–391.

the term "application" in Article 31(3)(a) should relate to the situation where an agreement specifies how existing rules or obligations in force are to be "applied."[82] Therefore, subsequent agreement should not connote the creation of new or the extension of existing treaty obligations.[83]

Given the absence of a formality requirement for subsequent agreement in Article 31(3)(a) of the Vienna Convention, the WTO Appellate Body considers the establishment of subsequent agreement to be a matter of substance, rather than form.[84] That said, the following discussion will include the formality of subsequent agreement as it is a highly debated issue in ISDS practice. In addition, as will be demonstrated below, the form, time and substance of contracting parties' documents subsequent to the conclusion of a treaty is rather crucial to determine the exisence of subsequent agreement, in particular in a fragmented system as international investment regime. Regarding this, according to Gazzini, the core feature of a "subsequent agreement" should be any common intention expressed by the contracting parties, which could be captured in the form of diplomatic notes, an exchange of letters, notes verbales, joint minutes, agreed statements, or any other instrument that conveys the joint intention of the parties.[85] This is discussed more fully below.

2.1.2.1.1 Joint Interpretation Authorized by Treaty Texts as Subsequent Agreements

Polanco has categorized joint interpretations in Article 31(3)(a) into two categories: the first being abstract interpretations, either arrived at by the contracting parties themselves or by a treaty body, for example the Free Trade Committee (FTC) that was established by Article 2001 of the North Atlantic Free Trade Agreement (NAFTA);[86] and the second being intra-arbitration interpretations which support tribunals in a pending case within a strict timeframe, either regarding general issues of interpretation, or specific provisions.[87] The NAFTA

82 *EC-Bananas III* (n 81).

83 *EC-Bananas III* (n 81).

84 Appellate Body report, *United States – Measures Affecting the Production and Sale of Clove Cigarettes (Clove Cigarettes)*, WT/DS406/AB/R, 267.

85 Gazzini (n 30) 286.

86 This is the so-called "institutionalized authoritative interpretations," see Rodrigo Polanco, *The Return of the Home State to Investor-State Disputes: Bringing Back Diplomatic Protection?* (1st edn, Cambridge University Press 2019) 106. See also: North American Free Trade Agreement between Canada, The United States and Mexico (NAFTA). A copy of which is available at <http://www.sice.oas.org/trade/nafta/naftatce.asp> accessed 20 April 2022.

87 Polanco (n 86) 106.

model has been reproduced in IIAs concluded between NAFTA members and other countries. The abstract joint interpretations included in these treaties are formulated as part of the governing law of the treaty, and are therefore binding on tribunals.[88] For example, Article X(6) of Canada-Czech Republic BIT authorizes an interpretation of the treaty between contracting parties to "be binding on a Tribunal established under this Article."[89] Similarly, Article 155 of the New Zealand-China FTA requires the tribunal, upon the request of a contracting party, to request a joint interpretation from the contracting parties. Once made, such interpretation will be binding on the tribunal.[90]

Joint interpretations have been respected by courts and tribunals as well, mostly as an "authoritative statement" of the governing law of the treaty.[91] For example, in the *Kasikili* Case, the International Court of Justice (ICJ) cited earlier work from the ILC and stated that "an agreement as to the interpretation of a provision reached after the conclusion of the treaty represents an authentic interpretation by the parties which must be read into the treaty for purpose of its interpretation."[92]

However, one cannot guarantee that a subsequent agreement on interpretation will always be observed by tribunals.[93] Take the FTC created by NAFTA for example. It consists of representatives from all three NAFTA contracting parties and is tasked with "[resolving] disputes that may arise regarding its interpretation or application."[94] In accordance with NAFTA Articles 1131 and 1132, interpretations issued by the FTC was supposed to be binding on NAFTA tribunals.[95] In July 2001, the FTC released an interpretation concerning, *inter*

88 With only a few exceptions, see: Polanco (n 86) 107.

89 Canada – Czech BIT (2009). A copy of which is available at <https://investmentpolicy.unctad.org/international-investment-agreements/treaty-files/606/download> accessed 20 April 2022. See also Article 16 of the Greece – Mexico BIT (2000) and Article 17(2) of the UK – Mexico BIT (2006).

90 China – New Zealand FTA (2008). A copy of which is available at <https://investmentpolicy.unctad.org/international-investment-agreements/treaty-files/2564/download> accessed 20 April 2022.

91 Polanco (n 86) 121.

92 Kasikili/Sedudu Island (Botswana/Namibia), Judgment of 13 December 1999 34 [49], citing: 'Yearbook of the International Law Commission, 1966' (221AD) II United Nations 221 [14].

93 Polanco (n 86) 119.

94 Article 2011(2) of NAFTA (n 86).

95 Article 1131(2) provided that: An interpretation by the Commission of a provision of this Agreement shall be binding on a Tribunal established under this Section; Article 1132(2) provides that: Further to Article 1131(2), a Commission interpretation submitted under paragraph 1 shall be binding on the Tribunal. If the Commission fails to submit an interpretation within 60 days, the Tribunal shall decide the issue. See NAFTA (n 86).

alia, the minimum standard of treatment in NAFTA Article 1105.[96] Since the interpretative note was issued during a time when several NAFTA arbitrations were still pending, its nature became a highly debated issue.[97] The *Pope&Talbot* tribunal, for example, criticized the FTC interpretation as an amendment disguised as an interpretation.[98] On the other hand, some tribunals are more careful in classifying the 2001 interpretation, and treated it as binding. For example, the *ADF* tribunal refused to view the interpretation as an amendment. It accordingly applied the interpretation because, in its view, there was "[n]o more authentic and authoritative source of instruction on what the Parties intended to convey in a particular provision of NAFTA."[99] Similarly, in *Methanex*, the tribunal determined that the 2001 FTC interpretation constituted a subsequent agreement, and therefore had to be considered in the light of Article 31(3)(a) of the VCLT.[100] The binding nature of FTC interpretations was also confirmed by the tribunals in *Loewen* and *Glamis*.[101]

---

96 NAFTA Free Trade Commission, 'NAFTA Notes of Interpretation of Certain Chapter 11 Provisions on July 31, 2001'. A copy of which is available at <http://www.sice.oas.org/tpd/nafta/commission/ch11understanding_e.asp> accessed 20 April 2022.

97 See in general: Polanco (n 86), 132–38; Guillermo Aguilar Alvarez and William W Park, 'The New Face of Investment Arbitration: NAFTA Chapter 11' (2003) 28 Yale Journal of International Law 3; Stefan Matiation, 'Arbitration with Two Twists: Loewen v. United States and Free Trade Commission Intervention in NAFTA Chapter 11 Disputes' [2003] University of Pennsylvania Journal of International Law 451; Christoph Schreuer, 'Fair and Equitable Treatment in Arbitral Practice' (2005) 6 The Journal of World Investment & Trade 32; Gabrielle Kaufmann-Kohler, 'Interpretive Powers of the Free Trade Commission and the Rule of Law' in Emmanuel Gaillard and Frédéric Bachand (eds), *Fifteen Years of NAFTA Chapter 11 Arbitration* (JurisNet, LLC 2011); Charles H Brower II, 'Investor-State Disputes under NAFTA: The Empire Strikes Back' (2001) 40 Colombia Journal of Transnational Law 43; Charles N Brower and Lee A Steven, 'Who Then Should Judge? Developing the International Rule of Law under NAFTA Chapter 11' 2 Chicago Journal of International Law 193; T Ishikawa, 'Keeping Interpretation in Investment Treaty Arbitration 'on Track': The Role of States Parties' (2014) 11 Transnational Dispute Management (TDM) 115 <https://www.transnational-dispute-management.com/article.asp?key=2048> accessed 20 April 2022; Catharine Titi, 'The Timing of Treaty Party Interpretations' (*EJIL: Talk!*, 18 August 2020) <https://www.ejiltalk.org/the-timing-of-treaty-party-interpretations/> accessed 20 April 2022.

98 *Pope&talbot v Canada, award on the Merits of Phase 2 dated 10 April 2001,* UNCITRAL Arbitration [47]. It nevertheless reached similar conclusion with the Interpretation in its partial award, despite denying the relevance of the interpretation with the case at issue.

99 *ADF Group Inc v United States, Award dated 9 January 2003,* ICSID Case No. ARB(AF)/00/1 [177].

100 *Methanex v United States, final Award of the Tribunal on Jurisdiction and Merits dated 3 August 2005,* UNCITRAL Arbitration [21].

101 *Glamis Gold, Ltd v United States* 362 (ICSID) [599]; *Loewen Group, Inc and Raymond L Loewen v United States of America,* ICSID Case No.ARB(AF)/98/3 71 [126–128].

2.1.2.1.2 Other Forms of Joint Interpretation

There are other forms of subsequent agreements in addition to the types of interpretations authorized by treaty texts as described above. After the decision on jurisdiction by the *Siemens* tribunal,[102] the governments of Argentina and Panama exchanged diplomatic notes and released an "interpretive declaration" of the MFN clause in the 1966 Argentina-Panama BIT. The declaration explicitly excluded dispute settlement from the scope of the relevant MFN clause and clarified that it had always been the contracting parties' intention to do so.[103] However, the status of declaration was disputed and the *Daimler* tribunal refused to take it into consideration, stating that "an interpretive declaration issued by a State after a treaty-based interpretive dispute has already arisen cannot be considered as a definitive guide to the State's original intentions, particularly when the declaration relates to a different treaty – nevertheless the fact that Argentina and Panama had distanced themselves from the understanding endorsed by an earlier tribunal was indicative of their mutual disapproval of that holding."[104]

Gazzini disapproved of the reasoning of *Daimler* tribunal. He argued that the underlying reason for two contracting states issuing any joint interpretation should be irrelevant. On the contrary, states would conclude a subsequent agreement "precisely because they consider that arbitral tribunals have misinterpreted the treaty." In this sense, subsequent agreement should serve a double purpose, i.e., to protect the contracting parties from distorted interpretations and to clarify the meaning of the treaty.[105]

2.1.2.1.3 Non-disputing Party Submissions

Another issue that is challenging for ISDS tribunals to resolve is whether non-disputing parties' (NDPS) submissions during arbitration proceedings could, by definition and in terms of their practice, be identified as subsequent agreements. In NAFTA cases, for example, contracting parties have consistently referred to Article 1128 and consciously confined their Article 1128 submissions to legal issues instead of facts of specific cases. In this way, they attempt to reach a common intention and subsequent agreement. Such attempt can be traced

102 *Siemens A.G. v Argentina* (n 65).

103 For discussions about the declaration, see: *National Grid v Argentina* (n 2) [85]. See also Gazzini (n 30); Y Radi, 'The Application of the Most-Favoured-Nation Clause to the Dispute Settlement Provisions of Bilateral Investment Treaties: Domesticating the "Trojan Horse"' (2007) 18 European Journal of International Law 757, 769.

104 *Daimler v Argentina* (n 22) [272].

105 Gazzini (n 30).

by their disclaimers in these submissions. For example, in *Mobil v. Canada (II)*, Mexico disclaimed in its Article 1128 submission that "Mexico takes no position on the facts of this dispute. The fact that a question of interpretation arising in the proceeding is not addressed in this submission should not be taken to constitute Mexico's concurrence or disagreement with a position taken by either of the disputing parties."[106] Similarly, in *Methanex*, Canada submitted in its Article 1128 statement that "[t]his submission is not intended to address all interpretative issues that may arise in this proceeding" and that "Canada takes no position on any particular issue of fact or on how the interpretation it submits below apply to the facts of this case."[107] These disclaimers represent NAFTA parties' attempt to distinguish between arguments made in a specific case from submissions that reflect a common intention for the purpose of a subsequent agreement.[108]

For instance, in *Canadian Cattlemen*, the U.S. claimed that the "combination" of its own statement, the non-disputing party submission by Mexico in the present case, and the submission of Canada in another case (*SD Myers*),[109] was tantamount to a subsequent agreement as envisioned in Article 31(3)(a) of the VCLT. It was nonetheless rejected by the tribunal on the ground that only submissions made in the same case could constitute subsequent agreement for the purpose of Article 31(3)(a) of the VCLT.[110]

In *Telefónica*, Argentina argued that both parties to the basic treaty had interpreted the MFN clause as excluding dispute settlement from its scope. To establish a subsequent agreement, Argentina relied on certain submissions in *Siemens*, *Gas Natural* and *Maffezini* which followed a similar line of argumentation. To this end, Argentina claimed that these submissions constituted a

106 *Mobil Investments Canada Inc. v Canada (II)* ICSID Case No. ARB/15/6, submission of Mexico Pursuant to NAFTA Article 1128. The U.S. made a similar disclaimer in its Article 1128 submission of this case. See: <https://www.italaw.com/sites/default/files/case-documents/italaw9779.PDF> accessed 20 April 2022.

107 *Methanex v United States* (n 100). Second Submission by Canada, 30 April 2001. Mexico has also adopted such a disclaimer using similar rhetoric. In *Apotex*, Mexico disclaimed in its Article 1128 submission that "Mexico takes no position on the facts of this dispute." See: *Apotex Holdings Inc and Apotex Inc v United States of America (III)*, ICSID Case No. ARB(AF)/12/1, Submission by Mexico dated 8 February 2013.

108 For more examples, see *Resolute Forest Products Inc. v Canada*, PCA Case No. 2016–13, Article 1128 Submissions on Jurisdiction from the U.S. and Mexico. Both documents are availble at <https://www.italaw.com/cases/4369> accessed 20 April 2022.

109 *SD Myers, Inc v Government of Canada*, UNCITRAL Arbitration, Canada Counter-Memorial, 5 October 1999.

110 *Canadian Cattlemen v US, Award on Jurisdiction dated 28 January 2008*, UNCITRAL Arbitration [187].

subsequent act which "indicate[s] their agreement as regards the interpretation of a given provision" and should be binding upon the tribunal insofar as its interpretations were concerned.[111] The tribunal refused to accept this argument. It determined that distinct, independent positions were taken by the two contracting states as respondents in different arbitral proceedings concerning different basic treaties. Therefore, they could not amount to an "agreement" between the two parties for the purpose of treaty interpretation.[112] Gazzini supports this approach as he considers common intention or "a meeting of their minds of intent" a crucial prerequisite for subsequent agreements to exist and argues that "the position taken in proceedings relating to different treaties cannot amount to subsequent agreement, even if the relevant provisions are identical."[113]

That said, some have approved the interpretative value of NDPs' submissions. For example, in *B-Mex and others v Mexico*, the respondent-appointed arbitrator Raúl E. Vinuesa argued that NAFTA Article 1128 submissions are "of a recommendatory nature," if not mandatory, as they will help a tribunal confirm whether the meaning the contracting parties gave, or sought to give, to the rules subject to interpretation.[114] Therefore, such submissions should not be ignored by tribunals especially when they reassert and unanimously confirm a recurrent trend to interpret certain provisions of the treaty.[115]

To conclude, it is at least arguable that through joint interpretations, contracting parties manage to retain some interpretative power at their disposal subsequent to the conclusion of a particular treaty. Given that ISDS cases involve respondent states as one of the contracting parties, a subsequent interpretation should be examined with skepticism if made with an attempt to influence a specific ongoing dispute. According to Polanco, for the purpose of reaching a subsequent agreement in the Article 31(3)(a) sense, it is essential that joint interpretations be timed properly.[116] He notes that interpretations made during a pending dispute are less likely to be considered by the tribunal, since it could be a reaction to the specificities of the case at hand and might

111 *Telefónica SA v Argentine Republic, Decision on Jurisdiction dated 25 May 2006,* ICSID Case No. ARB/03/20 [109].
112 *Telefónica v Argentina* (n 111) [111].
113 Gazzini (n 30) 290. For a different opinion, Titi has stated that "NDP submissions, as well as submissions by the Respondent State, may be relied upon later in other disputes to establish the Parties' subsequent agreement on interpretation". See Titi (n 97) 3.
114 *B-Mex and others v Mexico* (n 40) [95].
115 *B-Mex and others v Mexico* (n 40) [96–97].
116 Polanco (n 97) 137.

not reflect the common intention of the contracting states.[117] As Titi notes, moreover, this also relates to disputing parties' equality of arms and, more importantly, the issue of due process.[118] For Gazzini, this issue is still a matter of common intention. For a common intention to exist, form is irrelevant. All that matters is whether a "common intention" between contracting parties can be established. As a result, non-disputing parties' submissions made by contracting parties should be "directed towards each other."[119] Therefore, the submissions need to at least address the same treaty provision for the purpose of establishing a subsequent agreement as envisioned by Article 31(3)(a) of the VCLT.

2.1.2.2 *Subsequent Practices*

Subsequent practice is another factor included in Article 31(3) of the VCLT which is to be taken into account together with the context. Such practice should "establish the agreement of the parties regarding [the] interpretation [of a particular provision]" in order for them to be considered by tribunals.[120] However, the distinction between subsequent agreements and subsequent practices is not always clear.[121]

In ISDS, the submissions or interpretative documents of contracting parties are claimed either as subsequent agreements or subsequent practices. For example, in *Methanex,* the U.S. asserted that concordant submissions by NAFTA countries concerning the interpretation of the treaty constitute a subsequent agreement or subsequent practice.[122] In *Canadian Cattlemen,* the tribunal held that the sequence of acts and statements before it could not be considered as forming a subsequent agreement for purposes of Article 31(3)(a) of the Vienna Convention, but nonetheless amounted to a subsequent practice under Article 31(3)(b).[123]

According to Gazzini, subsequent agreement and subsequent practice are in a continuum and share the same relevance for the interpretative process.[124]

---

117 Polanco (n 97) 137.

118 Titi (n 97) 2–3.

119 Gazzini (n 30) 290.

120 Vienna Convention on the Law of Treaties (1969) (n 32).

121 International Law Commission (ILC), *Second Report on Subsequent Agreements and Subsequent Practice in Relation to the Interpretation of Treaties,* United Nations General Assembly A/CN.4/671. (2014). A copy of which is available at: <https://documents-dds-ny.un.org/doc/UNDOC/GEN/N14/278/52/PDF/N1427852.pdf?OpenElement> accessed 20 April 2022.

122 *Methanex v United States* (n 100). See also Weeramantry (n 38) 84.

123 *Canadian Cattlemen v United States* (n 110) [181–189].

124 Gazzini (n 30) 294.

The distinction between these two notions lies mainly in their form. While subsequent agreement presupposes formal documents, subsequent practice is less obvious and more flexible.[125] Polanco has noted that under general international law, joint interpretations could also be rendered without explicit authoritative treaty provisions. However, the value of these interpretations is at risk of being questioned since they do not take the form of a common understanding between contracting parties.[126] In this regard, Fauchald argues that the mere coincidence of unilateral statements by contracting parties cannot constitute a joint interpretation "unless the statements relate to each other and there is evidence that the parties intended them to constitute an agreement."[127]

The determination of subsequent practice has been elaborated on by the WTO Appellate Body, where the Appellate Body cited Sir Ian Sinclair and relied on the "concordant, common and consistent" criterion in the following terms:

> [A] 'concordant, common and consistent' sequence of acts or pronouncements which is sufficient to establish a discernible pattern implying the agreement of the parties [to a treaty] regarding its interpretation.[128]

Requirements such as these have been endorsed by ISDS tribunals. For example, the *Canada Cattlemen* tribunal held that the practice of a sequence of facts and acts that amounts to 'concordant, common and consistent' should be considered as 'subsequent practice' for the purpose of Article 31(3)(b) of the VCLT.[129]

Although the "concordant, common and consistent" test is not a binding principle,[130] it nevertheless indicates that the existence of subsequent practice is particularly a matter of evidence. In other words, the establishment of subsequent practice involves not only ascertaining the interpretative practice of contracting states, but also quantifying such practice with criteria like concordant, common and consistent. Therefore, it is at the tribunals' discretion to

125 International Law Commission (n 121).
126 Polanco (n 86) 129.
127 Fauchald (n 36) 328.
128 WTO Appellate Body Report, *Japan – Taxes on Alcoholic Beverages* (n 72) 13.
129 *Canadian Cattlemen v U.S.* (n 110) [189].
130 Nolte (n 121) 22 [47].

ascertain and evaluate whether a subsequent practice has been established in terms of Article 31(3)(b) of VCLT.[131]

This position finds support in the decision of the *Aguas del Tunari* tribunal, where the existence of a subsequent practice as between the Netherlands and Bolivia was denied. The tribunal concluded that the mere coincidence of several statements among contracting parties did not make them a joint interpretation.[132] It took a firm stand on the position concerning its jurisdiction, reaffirming as it did the *kompetenz-kompetenz* principle, and held that even a seemingly plausible concordance of views between the contracting parties did not suffice to decide whether the tribunal had jurisdiction or not, which is still something that fell within the overriding discretion of the tribunal.[133] The above practice is further reflected in the *National Grid, Plama* and *Telefónica* decisions.

In *National Grid*, the tribunal rejected the existence of a subsequent practice between the contracting parties concerning the interpretation of the MFN clause in question due to a lack of sufficient evidence showing a "concordant, common and consist ent" sequence of acts or pronouncements thereof. The tribunal stated as follows:

> While it is possible to conclude from the UK investment treaty practice contemporaneous with the conclusion of the Treaty that the UK understood the MFN clause to extend to dispute resolution, no definite conclusion can be reached regarding the Argentine Republic's position at that time. Therefore, the review of the treaty practice of the State parties to the Treaty with regard to their common intent is inconclusive.[134]

The *National Grid* tribunal reached the right conclusion, even though it mistakenly took into account treaty practice of the UK and Argentina with *third parties*. It erred in this regard because the main requirement for the establishment of a subsequent practice under Article 31(3)(b) of the VCLT is a "'concordant, common and consistent' sequence of acts or pronouncements" between the *contracting* parties i.e. between the UK and Argentina *inter se*.[135]

---

131 Gazzini (n 30) 293. Where the author explicitly refer to tribunals as "interpreter": "under the circumstances, a good deal of discretion is left to the interpreter who is called to assess the subsequent practice of the parties both in qualitative and quantitative terms."

132 *Aguas del Tunari SA v Republic of Bolivia, Decision on Jurisdiction dated 21 October 2005*, ICSID Case No. ARB/02/3 [253–254].

133 *Aguas del Tunari v Bolivia* (n 132) [263]; Weeramantry (n 38) 88.

134 *National Grid v Argentina* (n 2) [85].

135 Gazzini (n 30) 296.

On the other hand, the *Plama* tribunal correctly disposed of a similar issue. The tribunal rejected the relevance of Bulgaria's subsequent treaties signed with third countries because "subsequent negotiations between Bulgaria and Cyprus indicate that these Contracting Parties did not intend the MFN provision to have the meaning that otherwise might be inferred from Bulgaria's subsequent treaty practice."[136] On this point, the tribunal referred to the failed attempts between the two countries to revise the basic treaty. It concluded that "it [could] be inferred from these negotiations that the Contracting Parties to the BIT themselves did not consider that the MFN provision [extended] to dispute settlement provisions in other BITs."[137] This approach was categorized by Gazzini as a "risky exercise" since the attempt at revision failed and no agreement was reached. It was further suggested that the exchange of letters between Bulgaria and Cyprus contributed to the negotiation and possibly sufficed as evidence of the establishment of a subsequent practice under Article 31(3)(b) of the VCLT.[138]

The tribunal in *Telefónica* was more pointed on this issue. It firstly rejected that the defensive submissions of contracting parties made in ISDS amounted to a "practice" of a state. Then it rejected the notion that such submissions were even relevant for the purposes of Article 31(3)(b) of the VCLT since they were "not directed towards each other," and therefore "[did] not evidence an 'agreement', a meeting of their minds or intent as required by the same [Article] 31(3)(b)."[139]

The position adopted by the *Telefónica* tribunal was criticized by Gazzini as being overly formalistic.[140] After all, subsequent practice does not require for a direct agreement to be established. Rather, it requires states to reach an agreement during the application of the treaty, which by definition includes submissions and position papers filed during ISDS arbitration. In other words, subsequent practice is an incremental process based on the concordant, common and consistent interpretation of contracting states.[141] Tribunals come to play a main role in this regard as they have to ascertain and determine subsequent practice based on submitted evidence.[142]

136 *Plama v Bulgaria* (n 4) [195].

137 *Plama v Bulgaria* (n 4) [195].

138 Gazzini (n 30) 296.

139 *Telefónica v Argentina* (n 111) [112–113].

140 Gazzini (n 30) 297.

141 Gazzini (n 30) 297.

142 On this point, the author argued that: "... as a matter of both legal predictability and logic, an arbitral tribunal interpreting the treaty in good faith has to respect the concordant interpretation contained in the relevant statements consistently submitted by all parties to the treaty, provided that (a) such an interpretation is couched in sufficiently clear and

Oppenheim has commented that contracting parties may foresee the potential difficulties of interpretation and may define certain terms before, during, or after the conclusion of the treaty. Such authentic interpretation may be either informal or formal and should override general rules of interpretation.[143] As can be seen from the aforementioned ISDS cases, tribunals tend to set a high threshold for the establishment of a valid interpretation which relies on less formal documents. Moreover, tribunals' interpretations relying on such documents take place on a case-by-case basis. Since tribunals' opinions are not binding on those of subsequent tribunals on the same issue, states have to risk having their submissions overturned in a new case in front of a new tribunal. On the contrary, formal interpretive agreements represent *a priori* the treaty text and are accorded greater deference by tribunals.

In the academic literature, the discussion about the nature and effect of joint interpretations by contracting parties is also conducted at the substantive level.[144] In this connection, concerns have been put forward about downplaying investment protection standards through country interpretation and thus creating biased situations in favor of host states,[145] or that joint interpretations could be amendments in disguise instead of interpretation in a strict sense.[146] On the other hand, supporting voices have pointed out the more positive role contracting parties could take via joint interpretation. For example, according to Roberts, reaching a subsequent agreement or establishing a subsequent practice between treaty members is a way for states to take an active role in interpreting their IIAs and facilitates the ongoing "dialogue" between states and tribunals.[147]

---

general terms; and (b) there are no compelling arguments imposing a different interpretation. As mentioned above, this is not to say that the tribunal must necessarily conform itself to the interpretation espoused in these statements, but rather that the statements become part of the interpretative process. Assuming that the parties to a treaty officially, consistently and persistently express identical positions on the interpretation of the very same treaty, no apparent reasons would prevent the interpreter from taking it into account under Article 31(3)(b)." See: Gazzini (n 30) 298.

143 L Oppenheim and others, Oppenheim's International Law. Vol. 1: Peace (9th ed, Longman 1996) 630.

144 Polanco (n 86) 132.

145 Christoph Schreuer and Matthew Weiniger, *A Doctrine of Precedent?* (Oxford University Press 2008) 1201. Michael Ewing-Chow and Junianto James Losari, 'Which Is to Be the Master? Extra-Arbitral Interpretative Procedures for IIAs' in Jean E Kalicki and Anna Joubin-Bret (eds), *Reshaping the Investor-State Dispute Settlement System* (Brill | Nijhoff 2015) 14.

146 Ewing-Chow and James Losari (n 145) 16.

147 Anthea Roberts, 'Power and Persuasion in Investment Treaty Interpretation: The Dual Role of States' 104 The American Journal of International Law 47, 185, 194.

In conclusion, investment arbitration is a hybrid product consisting of part public international law, part commercial arbitration. This illustrates the dual role of respondent states as anticipated by Roberts. On one hand, they attend the arbitration as sovereign countries and international law-makers (especially considering that most of the investment arbitral cases are treaty-based). On the other hand, they are also in equal position with private investors as disputing parties and subject to awards rendered by tribunals. As such, it is posited in this book that for treaty members to have more interpretive power concerning MFN clauses, it would be optimal for these clauses to be preemptive and well-structured. It is also advisable for them to render interpretations of MFN clauses in an official and formal way, instead of via a retrospective joint interpretation which tribunals may reject as evidence of a subsequent agreement or practice. Finally, as mentioned above, case-by-case submissions have limited legal value and relying on these poses significant risks for states.

2.1.3 Good Faith Principle

Article 31 of the VCLT requires treaty interpretation to be conducted in good faith.[148] Good faith is a fundamental principle of every legal obligation, a general application of which is required in the practice of international economic law.[149] By the same token, Article 26 of the VCLT on *pacta sunt servanda* also provides that "every treaty in force is binding upon the parties to it and must be performed by them in good faith."[150]

Good faith is a rather wide and vague principle in general international law. As noted by Kotzur, the concept of good faith is "ambiguous if not amorphous or elusive."[151] Cheng agrees that the exact implications of good faith as a principle are hard to define.[152] And for Schill and Bray, this notion is inherently ambiguous, difficult to define, and challenging to contextualize.[153]

---

148 Vienna Convention on the Law of Treaties (1969) (n 32).

149 Andrew D Mitchell, M Sornarajah and Tania Voon (eds), *Good Faith and International Economic Law* (First edition, Oxford University Press 2015); Woo Pei Yee, 'Protecting Parties' Reasonable Expectations: A General Principle of Good Faith' (2001) 1 Oxford University Commonwealth Law Journal 195.

150 Vienna Convention on the Law of Treaties (1969) (n 32).

151 Markus Kotzur, 'Good Faith (Bona Fides)' [2009] Max Planck Encyclopedia of Public International Law.

152 Bin Cheng, *General Principles of Law as Applied by International Courts and Tribunals* (Digitally printed 1st pbk version, Cambridge University Press 2006) 105.

153 The authors opined that: 'The mere mention of the term "good faith" can befuddle even the most seasoned adjudicator, as it conjures abstract and elusive ideals of morality, ethical imperatives, and ideas of fairness, justice, honesty and trustworthiness.' See: Stephan W Schill and Heather L Bray, 'Good Faith Limitations on Protected Investments and

According to WTO Appellate Body, good faith in Article 31 of the VCLT requires that the terms of a treaty should not be interpreted based on the assumption that one party is seeking to evade its obligations and to exercise its rights so as to cause injury to the other party.[154] In investment arbitration, the good faith principle involves arbitrators reading treaty texts in a balanced and objective manner.[155] According to Sharmin, the good faith principle requires tribunals to avoid rendering expansive treaty interpretations that may have negative implications for treaty parties.[156] For Reinhold, the good faith principle in treaty interpretation requires tribunals to clear up ambiguous wording, but in a manner that avoids gap-filling which creates new obligations.[157] Interpreting MFN clauses in good faith requires tribunals to defer to the intention of contracting parties as conveyed through the treaty text. An expansive interpretation of an MFN clause may go against the good faith principle and brings about concerns such as treaty shopping and abuse of process.[158] Therefore, the good faith principle requires that MFN clauses not be interpreted in an expansive way that creates unintended obligations for treaty parties.[159]

The good faith principle has been applied by ISDS tribunals in relation to issues arising from the interpretation of MFN clauses. For example, in the *SPP* case, the tribunal was determined to interpret the MFN clause in question "neither restrictively nor expansively but rather objectively and in good faith,"[160] and in accordance with the interpretation rules embodied in Article 31 and 32 of the VCLT. On this point, it noted that:

> [J]urisdictional instruments are to be interpreted neither restrictively nor expansively, but rather objectively and in good faith, and jurisdiction will be found to exist if – but only if – the force of the arguments militating in favor of it is preponderant.[161]

Corporate Structuring' in Andrew D Mitchell, M Sornarajah and Tania Voon (eds), *Good Faith and International Economic Law* (Oxford University Press 2015) 1.

154 Appellate Body reports, *United States – Definitive Anti-Dumping and Countervailing Duties on Certain Products from China (US – Anti-Dumping and Countervailing Duties (China))*, WT/DS379/AB/R, 326–327.

155 Sharmin (n 30) 96.

156 Sharmin (n 30) 96.

157 Steven Reinhold, 'Good Faith in International Law' (2013) 2 UCL Jurisprudence Review 40, 62.

158 Sharmin (n 30) 98.

159 Sharmin (n 30) 98.

160 *Southern Pacific Properties (Middle East) Limited v Arab Republic of Egypt, Decision on Jurisdiction II, 27th April 1985*, ICSID No. ARB/84/3.

161 *SPP v Egypt* (n 160) [63].

According to the ILC, the good faith principle in Article 31(1) also implicitly incorporates the *effet utile* principle from general international law.[162] *Effet utile*, or "effective interpretation," requires international courts or tribunals to interpret treaty provisions "so as to give them their fullest weight and effect consistent with the normal sense of the words and with other parts of the text and in such a way that a reason and a meaning can be attributed to every part of the text."[163]

Effet utile is an internationally established interpretative principle adopted by international courts and tribunals. For example, in *Korea – Dairy* case, the WTO Appellate Body explained that *effet utile* renders treaty interpreters the duty to "read all applicable provisions of a treaty in a way that gives meaning to all of them, harmoniously."[164] *Effet utile* is also practiced by ISDS tribunals. In *ICS (I)*, the tribunal considered subsequent treaties concluded by Argentina in the context of applying the *effet utile* principle. It determined that accepting the claimant's assertions concerning the MFN clause in question would render certain procedural prerequisites contained in the treaty void *ab initio*, which would violate the *effet utile* principle. The *ICS (I)* tribunal held as follows:

> [T]he MFN clause should not be interpreted in a way that deprives … the dispute resolution clause of any meaning without a clear intention to achieve that result. The principle of contemporaneity avoids this incongruity by preferring the interpretation consistent with Argentina's demonstrated treaty practice – namely, that Argentina did not in 1990 understand the term 'treatment' to include the BIT's international arbitration procedures.[165]

Effet utile was also one of the interpretation rules applied by the *AAPL* tribunal, which noted as follows:

> Rule (E): Nothing is better settled, as a canon of interpretation in all systems of law than that a clause must be so interpreted as to give it a meaning rather than so as to deprive it of meaning.[166]

---

162 Makane Moïse Mbengue, 'Rules of Interpretation (Article 32 of the Vienna Convention on the Law of Treaties)' (2016) 31 ICSID Review 388, 394.

163 Gardiner (n 45) 149.

164 Appellate Body reports, *Korea – Definitive Safeguard Measure on Imports of Certain Dairy Products (Korea-Dairy)*, WT/DS98/AB/R [81].

165 *Korea-Dairy* (n 164) [317].

166 *Asian Agricultural Products Ltd.* (AAPL) *v Republic of Sri Lanka, Award dated 27 June 1990*, ICSID Case No. ARB/87/3 [40].

Additionally, the good faith principle also relates to the legal concept of abuse of rights.[167] In *Phoenix Action*, the tribunal explained as follows:

> The principle of good faith … requires parties 'to deal honestly and fairly with each other, to represent their motives and purposes truthfully, and to refrain from taking unfair advantage …' Nobody shall abuse the rights granted by treaties, and more generally, every rule of law includes an implied clause that it should not be abused.[168]

For Gaillard, abuse of rights indicates that "a party may have a right, including a procedural right, and yet exercise it in an abnormal, excessive or abusive way, with the sole purpose of causing injury to another or for the purpose of evading a rule of law, so as to forfeit its entitlement to rely upon it."[169] According to Brabandere, abuse of process is a particular form of abuse of rights because the alleged right is procedural.[170] Specifically, abuse of process relates to challenging tribunals' jurisdiction.[171] Abuse of process can lead to significant prejudice to the party against whom it is aimed and can undermine the fair and orderly resolution of disputes by way of international arbitration.[172] In the context of the application of MFN clauses, abuse of rights and abuse of process relate to the expansive interpretation of these clauses that accords foreign investors more favorable – or, at times, *far* more favorable – treatment which was not anticipated by the contracting parties when the treaty was concluded.

In view of the onset of the Rebalancing Era in the age of a new generation of IIAs as discussed in Chapter 1, the good faith principle requires tribunals to respect the shifting intention of state parties in relation to the conclusion of new IIAs and/or revision of existing IIAs. In this regard, MFN clauses should

167 About abuse of process, see also: John P Gaffney, 'Abuse of Process in Investment Treaty Arbitration' (2010) 11 Journal of World Investment & Trade 515; Some also stated that: 'abuse of process is a concept that is derived from, and for that reason narrower than the principle of "good faith" in general international law.' See: E De Brabandere, '"Good Faith," "Abuse of Process" and the Initiation of Investment Treaty Claims' (2012) 3 Journal of International Dispute Settlement 609, 11.

168 *Phoenix Action Ltd v Czech Republic, Award dated15 April 2009*, ICSID Case No. ARB/06/5 [107], referring to Anthony D'Amato, 'Good faith', in Rudolf. Bernhardt (ed), *Encyclopedia of Public International Law* (1984) 7, 107.

169 Emmanuel Gaillard, 'Abuse of Process in International Arbitration' (2017) 32 ICSID Review 17, 16.

170 De Brabandere (n 167) 12.

171 Hervé Ascensio, 'Abuse of Process in International Investment Arbitration' (2014) 13 Chinese Journal of International Law 763, 764.

172 Gaillard (n 169) 2.

be interpreted in light of their wording and context in accordance with the VCLT. States should opt for narrower, more detailed MFN clauses and tribunals should carefully examine these clauses in order to properly give effect to the shifting intentions of contracting states.

2.2 *Article 32 of the VCLT as Containing Supplementary Methods of Treaty Interpretation*

Unlike Article 31 of the VCLT, which speaks to the "general rule of interpretation," Article 32 provides for "supplementary means of interpretation" and reads as follows:

> Recourse may be had to supplementary means of interpretation, including the preparatory work of the treaty and the circumstances of its conclusion, in order to confirm the meaning resulting from the application of article 31, or to determine the meaning when the interpretation according to article 31:
> (a) leaves the meaning ambiguous or obscure; or
> (b) leads to a result which is manifestly absurd or unreasonable.[173]

As its wording makes clear, the VCLT relegates the *travaux préparatoires* and the circumstances of treaties' conclusion to an auxiliary status vis-à-vis the treaty text.[174] For ILC, Article 32 is to be consulted at a later stage than the application of the general rule of Article 31(1) VCLT and is supposed to be used with an already taken view at ordinary language, context or object and purpose.[175] According to Mbengue, Article 32 of the VCLT apply as a facultative and contingent interpretive rule in international law. By stating that "recourse may be had to supplementary means," it is established that Article 32 provides interpreters with "a mere option."[176] This is supported by the 1950 Advisory

173 Vienna Convention on the Law of Treaties (1969) (n 32).

174 For the negotiating history of Vienna Convention in this regard, see Jan Klabbers, 'International Legal Histories: The Declining Importance of Travaux Préparatoires in Treaty Interpretation?' (2003) 50 Netherlands International Law Review 267; Julian Davis Mortenson, 'The Travaux of Travaux: Is the Vienna Convention Hostile to Drafting History?' (2013) 107 The American Journal of International Law 780 <http://www.jstor.org/stable/10.5305/amerjintelaw.107.4.0780> accessed 20 April 2022; Ulf Linderfalk, 'Is the Hierarchical Structure of Article 31 and 32 of the Vienna Convention Real or Not? Interpreting the Rules of Interpretation' (2007) 54 Netherlands International Law Review 133; Jiménez De Aréchaga (n 35) 46–8.

175 ILC (n 80), 21–29.

176 Mbengue (n 162) 399.

Opinion on the *Competence of the General Assembly for the Admission of a State to the United Nations* by the ICJ, where the Court explained that –

> the first duty of a tribunal which is called upon to interpret and apply the provision of a treaty, is to [endeavor] to give effect to them in their natural and ordinary meaning in the context in which they occur. If the relevant words in their natural and ordinary meaning make sense in their context, that is an end of the matter.[177]

Article 32 does not define either the scope of *travaux préparatoires*, or what is meant by the phrase "circumstances of its conclusion," nor does it provide an exhaustive list of supplementary measures for interpreters to rely on.[178] Mbengue notes that *travaux préparatoires* includes all the written documents that were produced in the process leading up to the conclusion of a treaty.[179] These documents include *inter alia* the successive drafts of the treaty, the negotiation records, the diplomatic exchanges between the parties and the interpretative statements made by the chairman of a drafting committee.[180] As for circumstances of conclusion, Mbengue notes that it mainly refers to the historical background against which the treaty has been negotiated and concluded, which includes political, economic, social and cultural factors, amongst others.[181] With respect to international investment law, an essential issue to be considered in this regard is the economic policy considerations.[182]

In interpreting MFN clauses, tribunals have frequently relied on Article 32 in spite of the fact that it is a supplementary means of interpretation. For example, in *Plama*, one of the reasons the tribunal decided that the scope of the MFN clause in question could not be extended to include procedural issues was the political and economic situations the two contracting parties found themselves in at the time of the conclusion of the basic treaty. In particular, the tribunal noted that the communist regime of Bulgaria favored limited investment protection and dispute resolution provisions in its IIAs.[183] In *Garanti*

177 Competence of Assembly Regarding Admission to the United Nations (Advisory Opinion) [1950] ICJ Rep 4.

178 Mbengue (n 162) 394, referring to Mustafa Kamil Yasseen, 'L'interprétation Des Traités d'après La Convention de Vienne Sur Le Droit Des Traités (Volume 151)' [1976] Collected Courses of the Hague Academy of International Law 79.

179 Mbengue (n 162) 389.

180 Mbengue (n 162) 389.

181 Mbengue (n 162) 392; Sinclair (n 51) 126.

182 Mbengue (n 162) 393.

183 *Plama v Bulgaria* (n 4) [196].

Koza, the tribunal took the UK Model BIT into account when applying Article 32 to interpret the dispute settlement provision in the basic treaty at issue. It explained that "the model BIT from which the parties evidently derived the text of Article 8(2) would be among the circumstances of the conclusion of the U.K.-Turkmenistan BIT that could be considered in interpreting that article."[184]

Article 32 of the VCLT is an important interpretive tool. However, its application serves limited purposes, which is either to confirm the meaning resulting from the application of Article 31, or to determine the meaning when recourse to Article 31 yields an ambiguous, obscure or manifestly unreasonable meaning.[185] As Mbengue rightly observes, the relevance of Article 32 depends on its ability to shed light on the common intentions of the parties.[186] In other words, it is still the treaty text that should be the priority of interpreters, not the negotiation history or the circumstances of the treaty's conclusion.[187]

3 The Role of Arbitral Precedents

There is no formal *stare decisis* doctrine in international law. Decisions made by former courts or tribunals do not have a precedential status as that in common law.[188] This is explicitly provided for in the Statute of the ICJ and also included in instruments such as the Convention on the Settlement of Investment Disputes Between States and Nationals of Other States (ICSID Convention) and UNCITRAL Arbitration Rules.[189] However, international

184 *Garanti Koza LLP v Turkmenistan, Decision on the Objection to Jurisdiction for Lack of Consent dated 3 July 2013*, ICSID Case No. ARB/11/20 271 36. For the use of model BITs during the negotiation of investment treaties, see: Schreuer (n 1) 8.

185 Vienna Convention on the Law of Treaties (1969) (n 32).

186 Mbengue (n 162) 392.

187 There are discussions about whether preparatory work could overturn the ordinary meaning of the treaty text. See for example Weeramantry (n 38) 99–110.

188 G Guillaume, 'The Use of Precedent by International Judges and Arbitrators' (2011) 2 Journal of International Dispute Settlement 5, 16. See also: *Wintershall Aktiengesellschaft v Argentine Republic, Award dated 8 December 2008*, ICSID Case No. ARB/04/14 124 [178].

189 Article 59 of Statute of the International Court of Justice reads as follows: 'The decision of the Court has no binding force except between the parties and in respect of that particular case.' \ Article 53(1) of the ICSID Convention provides that 'The award shall be binding on the parties and shall not be sub- ject to any appeal or to any other remedy except those provided for in this Convention.' Similarly, Article 34(2) of UNCITRAL Arbitration Rules 2010 states that 'All awards shall be made in writing and shall be final and binding on the parties. The parties shall carry out all awards without delay.' See also: European Convention on Human Rights. Article 46(1) of which provides that: 'The High Contracting

courts and tribunals have frequently referred to decisions by earlier adjudicatory bodies in their own decisions. In fact, it has been argued that international courts and tribunals at times treat prior decisions by the same court or tribunal as binding on them, even if they do not explicitly indicate as such. The WTO Appellate Body, for example, has clearly applied a version of *stare decisis* in fulfilling its dispute settlement function.[190] According to the Appellate Body, the GATT and WTO panel reports, and equally adopted Appellate Body reports, "create legitimate expectations among WTO Members. As a result, they should be taken into account where they are relevant to any dispute."[191]

In this context, ISDS tribunals usually first emphasize the non-binding character of the previous decisions before clarifying their own authority of relying on these decisions to support, *inter alia*, their interpretive arguments.[192] For example, in *Mesa Power*, the tribunal decided to elaborate on the relevance of precedent before entering into the merits, as the disputing parties relied heavily on previous decisions and awards. The tribunal stated as follows:

> The Tribunal is not bound by the decisions of other arbitral tribunals. At the same time however, the Tribunal does believe that it should pay due respect to such decisions. Unless there are reasons to the contrary, the Tribunal will adopt the approaches established in a series of consistent cases comparable to the case at hand, subject, of course, to the specifics of the NAFTA and to the circumstances of the actual case. By doing so, the Tribunal believes it will meet its duty to contribute to the harmonious development of investment law and thereby to meet the legitimate expectations of the community of States and investors towards legal certainty and the rule of law.[193]

Parties undertake to abide by the final judgment of the Court in any case to which they are parties.'

190 For relevant discussion regarding this, see: Raj Bhala, 'The Myth About Stare Decisis and International Trade Law (Part One of a Trilogy)' 14 American University International Law Review 845.

191 Appellate Body Report, *US – Shrimp (Article 21.5 – Malaysia)* (n 74), 109; Appellate Body Report, *Japan – Alcoholic Beverages II* (n 72), 107–108.

192 See, for example: Schreuer (n 1); Kaufmann-Kohler (n 97); Guillaume (n 188); Jeffery Commission, 'Precedent in Investment Treaty Arbitration-A Citation Analysis of a Developing Jurisprudence' (2007) 2 Journal of International Arbitration 129.

193 *Mesa Power Group LLC v Government of Canada, Award dated 24 March 2016,* PCA Case No. 2012–17 [221].

Similar practice can be observed in the decisions of ISDS tribunals which were called upon to interpret MFN clauses. For example, in *Convial*, the tribunal rejected the claim that the MFN principle had been violated on account of the absence of discrimination on the part of the respondent state. Prior to reaching its conclusion, the tribunal first cited the decision in *Parkerings* to support its position that "the violation of the MFN clause will only take place if 'the existence of a different treatment accorded to another foreign investor in a similar situation' is verified."[194] In *Sanum*, the tribunal made observations about other cases that were prominently referred to by the parties (especially *RosInvest* and *Tza Yap Shum*) before conducting its analysis on MFN treatment. Here the tribunal explained that it is "not obliged to follow any particular prior decision but it cannot ignore the arguments of the Parties and the decisions they have used to support them."[195]

The consistent interpretation of the "in like circumstances" element contained in NAFTA Articles 1102 and 1103 by a line of NAFTA tribunals through notable reliance on precedent is certainly illustrative of the point that precedent does in fact play a role in investment arbitration. In *S.D. Myers*, for example, the tribunal was requested to examine whether the claimant and domestic investors were "in like circumstances" in order to establish whether the host state had breached Article 1102. The tribunal stated that "[i]n considering the meaning of 'like circumstances' under Article 1102 of the NAFTA, it is similarly necessary to keep in mind the overall legal context in which the phrase appears."[196]

Later, in *Pope&Talbot*, the tribunal agreed with the SD *Myers* tribunal and formulated a test in the following terms:

> Differences in treatment will presumptively violate Article 1102(2), unless they have a reasonable nexus to rational government policies that (1) do not distinguish, on their face or de facto, between foreign-owned and domestic companies, and (2) do not otherwise unduly undermine the investment liberalizing objectives of NAFTA.[197]

194 *Convial Callao SA and CCI – Compañía de Concesiones de Infraestructura SA v Republic of Peru, Final Award dated 21 May 2013,* ICSID Case No. ARB/10/2 [162].

195 *Sanum Investments v Lao People's Democratic Republic (I), Award on Jurisdiction dated 13 December 2013,* PCA Case No 2013–13 [349].

196 *SD Myers v Canada* (n 109) [245]. The tribunal reached to this conclusion through canvassing decisions of WTO appellate body and Canadian domestic court.

197 *Pope&talbot v Canada* (n 82) [98].

The tribunal further concluded that when interpreting the phrase "in like circumstance," there should be an evaluation as to "whether there is a reasonable nexus between the measure and a rational, non-discriminatory government policy, whether those policies are embodied in statute, regulation or international agreement."[198]

In the wake of *Pope&Talbot*, several other NAFTA tribunals were faced with similar claims under Articles 1102 and 1103. In *Feldman,* the tribunal found a group of third-state investors to be comparators for the purposes of establishing whether an Article 1103 had occurred on account of their being subjected to the same legal requirements as the claimant.[199] NAFTA tribunals in the *Methanex*, *ADF* and *UPS* disputes are also among those that follow this method.[200] In *Grand River*, the tribunal canvassed the decisions of prior tribunals and stated as follows:

> While each case involved its own facts, tribunals have assigned important weight to 'like legal requirements' in determining whether there were 'like circumstances' … The reasoning of these cases shows the identity of the legal regime(s) applicable to a claimant and its purported comparators to be a compelling factor in assessing whether like is indeed being compared to like for purposes of Articles 1102 and 1103.[201]

In the end in *Apotex*, the tribunal emphasized the importance of the same legal regime and regulatory requirements in deciding "in like circumstances," referring to the *Grand River* tribunal and its examination of the role of precedent on this issue.[202]

From the aforementioned line of decisions, it can be seen that the invocation of precedent by tribunals usually comes into play as a supportive argument. In turn, earlier decisions are reinforced and given more precedential value each time they are relied on by later tribunals. Therefore, despite significant variance in the interpretation of MFN clauses by tribunals, precedent still

198 *Pope&talbot v Canada* (n 82) [93].

199 *Marvin Feldman v Mexico, Award dated 16 December 2002, ICSID Case No. ARB(AF)/99/1* [171–172].

200 *Methanex v U.S.* (n 100); *ADF v U.S.*, (n 99); *United Parcel Service of America Inc v Government of Canada, Award on the Merits dated 24 May 2007,* ICSID Case No. UNCT/02/1.

201 *Grand River Enterprises Six Nations, Ltd, et.al v United States of America,* UNCITRAL Arbitration [166–167].

202 *Apotex Holdings Inc and Apotex Inc v United States of America (III), Award dated 25 August 2014,* ICSID Case No. ARB(AF)/12/1.

plays a remarkable role in ensuring relative consistency of interpretation in respect of some less controversial issues.

4 Conclusion

Treaty interpretation is a process aimed at revealing contracting parties' intentions when they concluded a treaty.[203] It should be carried out in a way that promotes harmonization and stability of the international legal order. This is particularly essential for a fragmented regime like investment law, where disputes are decided on an *ad hoc* basis by tribunals with reference to different bilateral, or at times plurilateral, investment treaties. On this point, a balanced approach to the interpretative principles enshrined in customary international law and in the VCLT is key. When the interpretive methods discussed above do not lead to an unambiguous interpretation, a responsible tribunal should take into account other factors in order to help reveal states' intentions. These factors include the fact that international investment law is characterized by fragmentation and the fact that the Rebalancing Era has taken place and remains ongoing as discussed in Chapter 1. This indicates that MFN clauses should not be interpreted as being a tool which aims to multilateralize investment rules. Second, ISDS cases usually involve regulations undertaken by host states in pursuit of the public interest and tribunals should be aware of this as background context, especially because this is what the principle of good faith demands. Third, the fundamental importance of state sovereignty in international law should not be forgotten. As will be elaborated in Chapter 5, state consent emanates from state sovereignty and constitutes the basis of tribunals' jurisdiction. Without explicit treaty language granting tribunals jurisdiction in relation to claims which are based on an MFN clause, asserting jurisdiction via expansive MFN clause interpretation constitutes an abuse of process.

In light of the above discussion, the following chapters will unpack the interpretation of MFN clauses by ISDS tribunals in greater detail.

203 For discussions about the subjective and objective approach of treaty interpretation, see Stefan Kadelbach, 'The International Law Commission and role of subsequent practice as a means of interpretation under Articles 31 and 32 VCLT' (2018) Zoom-in 46 Questions of International Law Journal 5–18.

CHAPTER 3

Applying the MFN Clause for Higher Substantive Treatment

This chapter examines the most-favored-nation (MFN) clause as a treaty provision against the backdrop of the history of the clause as well as the methods used to interpret it as discussed in the previous two chapters. The first part focuses on the scope of MFN clauses. Its structure follows the structure of Article 5 of International Law Commission's (ILC) *Draft Articles on most-favoured-nation clause* (Draft Articles), which provides that "MFN treatment is the treatment accorded by the granting State to the beneficiary State or to persons or things having a particular relationship with that State, which is no less favorable than the treatment accorded by the granting State to a third State or to persons or things having the same relationship with that third State."[1] Accordingly, this part examines various elements of MFN clause, including: (i) its beneficiaries (*ratione personae*); (ii) its temporal element (*ratione temporis*); (iii) its subject matter (*ratione materiae*). It also examines various exceptions to MFN clauses in a separate forth section.

The second part analyzes the application of the MFN clause as a treaty provision. It does from two perspectives: (i) claims of a *de facto* violation of an MFN clause; and (ii) invocation of an MFN clause in pursuit of obtaining more favorable treatment via an instrument external to the basic international investment agreement (IIA) at issue in a given case. The chapter ultimately argues that interpretation of MFN clauses should not be based on presumptions, but rather on the specific text of the basic IIA at issue and a proper application of the *ejusdem generis* principle.

1 The Scope of Treatment Covered by MFN Clauses in IIAs

This part of the chapter focuses on the scope of treatment covered by MFN clauses in IIAs. It follows a structure based on Article 5 of the Draft Articles as

1 International Law Commission International Law Commission, 'Draft Articles on Most-Favoured-Nation Clauses with Commentaries', *Yearbook of the International Law Commission*, vol II:2 (1978) Available at: <https://legal.un.org/ilc/texts/instruments/english/commentaries/1_3_1978.pdf> accessed 20 April 2022.

© ANQI WANG, 2022 | DOI:10.1163/9789004517899_005

elaborated above and specifically examines attempts by claimants to expand the type of treatment included as part of the scope of MFN clauses in various IIAs.

The treaty obligation to accord MFN treatment comes into being with certain limitations.[2] Specifically, the standard should be applied in accordance with the precise wording of the basic treaty and the MFN clause it contains, as well as the treatment contained in the third-party treaty, which is alleged to be more favorable, with due reference to established principles of treaty interpretation, especially the *ejusdem generis* principle. For Cole, these limitations are inherent boundaries constructed by MFN clauses that should be examined carefully by tribunals in order to avoid taking an overbroad teleological approach to interpretation.[3] Cole uses three cases to illustrate the general boundaries constructed by MFN clauses: The 1952 *Anglo-Iranian Oil Co* case, the 1956 *Ambatielos Claim* and the 1962 *Rights of Nationals of the United States of America in Morocco* case.[4] These cases will be referred to below where appropriate.

1.1 *The Beneficiary of MFN Treatment (Ratione Personae)*

In Article 5 of the Draft Articles, the ILC explains that MFN treatment concerns, amongst other things, "persons or things in a determined relationship" with the host state, i.e., the beneficiaries or *ratione personae* of MFN treatment.

Most IIAs refer to both investors and investments in their MFN clauses, while some clauses refer to either investors or investments.[5] There has been some debate in this regard. On the one hand, it has been argued that the inclusion of both investors and investments tends to broaden the scope of treatment covered by MFN clauses.[6] For Newcombe and Paradell, references to both investors and investments aid claimants seeking to rely on a broader definition of investment contained in third-party treaties.[7] According to a 2010 United

2 Tony Cole, 'The Boundaries of Most Favored Nation Treatment in International Investment Law' (2012) 33 Michigan Journal of International Law 537, 559.

3 Cole (n 2) 560.

4 *Anglo-Iranian Oil Co (United Kingdom v Iran)* (ICJ); *The Ambatielos Claim* (Greece, United Kingdom of Great Britain and Northern Ireland), Arbitral Award of the Commission of Arbitration in 1956; *Rights of Nationals of the United States of America in Morocco (France v United States of America)* 255 (ICJ); For the discussion about these cases, see Cole (n 2), 560.

5 Kenneth J Vandevelde, *Bilateral Investment Treaties: History, Policy, and Interpretation* (Oxford University Press 2010) 339. Andrew Paul Newcombe and Lluís Paradell, *Law and Practice of Investment Treaties: Standards of Treatment* (Wolters Kluwer Law & Business 2009) 223.

6 Vandevelde (n 5) 339–340; Newcombe and Paradell (n 5) 223; UNCTAD (ed), *Most-Favoured-Nation Treatment: A Sequel* (United Nations 2010) 44–45.

7 Newcombe and Paradell (n 5) 223.

Nations Conference on Trade and Development (UNCTAD) report, restricting the *ratione personae* scope of MFN clauses to cover only investments could limit the set of MFN beneficiaries to local vehicles established in the host state, thereby denying categories of foreign investors the opportunity to benefit from MFN treatment.[8] On the other hand, some tribunals have denied the significance of this issue. These tribunals appear to be of the view that investors and investments coexist, i.e. that "investors will not claim access to international arbitration by way of MFN treatment in the abstract," that "they will assert a breach and harm in connection with a qualifying investment under the relevant [bilateral investment treaty],"[9] and that "the subjective element is ... a matter of emphasis, not of exclusion."[10]

The absence of a reference to investors in the wording of the MFN clause at issue in *MNSS and RCA* was raised by the respondent in relation to the claimant's *locus standi*.[11] In this case, the Dutch claimant invested into a local vehicle (ZN) through purchasing equity and providing loans. The claimant sought to hold the host state liable for breaching its MFN obligation on the basis that it had allegedly accorded less favorable treatment to ZN than to other investors from third states. According to the North Macedonia-Netherlands bilateral investment treaty (BIT), the MFN treatment in Article 3(2) could only be extended *ratione personae* to "the investments of nationals of the other Contracting State."[12] The respondent state argued that the MFN clause in the

8 Here, the concern raised by UNCTAD was that limiting MFN treatment to foreign investments would 'have the consequence of excluding foreign individuals or companies from MFN treatment and limiting it to the locally established juridical person constituted in the Host State or assets acquired under the legislation of the Host State.' See UNCTAD (n 6).

9 *Quasar de Valores SICAV SA, Orgor de Valores SICAV SA, GBI 9000 SICAV SA and ALOS 34 SL v The Russian Federation, Award on Preliminary Objections dated 20 March 2009*, SCC Case No. 24/2007 [101]. Article 4(2) of the basic BIT between Russia and Spain guarantees MFN treatment to foreign investments.

10 *Siemens AG v The Argentine Republic, Decision on Jurisdiction dated 3 August 2004*, ICSID Case No. ARB/02/8 [92].

11 *MNSS BV and Recupero Credito Acciaio NV v Montenegro, Award on 4 May 2016*, ICSID Case No. ARB(AF)/12/8.

12 Article 3(1) and (2) of the BIT read as: 1) Each Contracting State shall ensure fair and equitable treatment of the investments of nationals of the other Contracting State and shall not impair, by unreasonable or discriminatory measures, the operation, management, maintenance, use, enjoyment or disposal thereof by those nationals. Each Contracting State shall accord to such investments full physical security and protection.

2) More particularly, each Contracting State shall accord to such investments treatment which in any case shall not be less [favorable] than that accorded either to investments of its own nationals or to investments of nationals of any third State, whichever is more [favorable] to the national concerned. See: North Macedonia – Netherlands BIT

basic treaty applied only to foreign investments, but not to foreign investors. As the local vehicle, ZN, the investor – and not the claimant's investment – was the subject that directly suffered the discriminatory treatment.[13] Therefore, the claimant was not entitled to rely on the MFN clause. The tribunal did not agree with this argument. It held that since the claimant operated its investment through ZN, the treatment accorded to the "investment" included the manner in which ZN, the investor, was treated.[14]

The precise wording used in different treaties is capable of narrowing the set of beneficiaries entitled to MFN treatment. For example, Article 5 of the Australia-Uruguay BIT accords MFN treatment only to "investments in [a contracting party's] own territory." The absence of reference to an investor in an MFN clause could, however, be remedied by a broad definition of "investor" and "investment" in Article 1 of the same BIT. Article 1(c) defines "investor" as "a natural person of a Party or a company of a Party who has made an investment in the territory of the other Party."[15] Therefore, although investors are not explicitly included in the MFN clause, they are still entitled to MFN treatment through their investment in the host state. Moreover, the difference in the scope of beneficiaries of the MFN clause is of limited importance for ISDS purposes, at least from the perspective of jurisdiction. Of the 117 cases contained on UNCTAD's website in which an MFN violation was alleged, the claimant was not denied *locus standi* by the tribunals in question on even one occasion merely because of an absence of any reference to "investor" or "investment" in the MFN clause at issue.[16] The reason may lie in the fundamental relationship between foreign investors and their investment in the host state. A treaty violation in respect of a foreign investment will always affect an investor, whether it be a natural or juristic person, in the sense that investment must be carried out by a person.[17] According to the *Daimler* tribunal:

(1998). A copy of which is available at: <https://investmentpolicy.unctad.org/international-investment-agreements/treaty-files/1936/download> accessed 20 April 2022.

13 *MNSS v Montenegro* (n 11) [359].

14 *MNSS v Montenegro* (n 11) [360].

15 Australia – Uruguay BIT (2022). A copy of which is available at: <https://investmentpolicy.unctad.org/international-investment-agreements/treaty-files/5853/download> accessed 20 April 2022.

16 UNCTAD Advanced search of ISDS cases according to IIA alleges breach and found: most-favoured-nation treatment, <https://investmentpolicy.unctad.org/international-investment-agreements/treaty-files/5853/download> accessed 20 April 2022.

17 *Siemens v Argentine* (n 10) [92]; *Renta 4 v Russia* (n 9) [101].

> The parallel breadth of these definitions suggests that the (basic) Treaty's grant of MFN treatment to both investors and investments was intended to be complementary and not differential. The MFN guarantees offered to the two categories might even be co-extensive, for it is difficult to imagine a type of MFN treatment enjoyed by an investment that could not correspondingly be claimed by a qualifying investor in connection with that investment.[18]

However, it is arguable that reference to both investors and investment in an MFN clause will indeed broaden the possible beneficiaries covered by the clause, especially insofar as the foreign investment's life cycle is concerned. When a post-establishment approach is taken and the MFN clause in question refers to both investors and investments, investors will enjoy MFN treatment even when their investments in the host state have come to the end of their life cycle. When a pre-establishment approach is taken and the MFN clause in question refers to both investors and investments, the entitlement on the part of an investor to MFN treatment may kick in even before an investment has been made, and "if the investor is not a beneficiary of the standard, then any commitment of MFN treatment with respect to establishment may be lost as a practical matter."[19] This issue will be discussed further below.

1.2 *The Temporal Dimension of MFN Treatment (Ratione Temporis)*

This section discusses the temporal scope of MFN clauses. There are two parts to this discussion: the temporal scope of the MFN clause itself, and the temporal scope of the relevant treaties as a whole (both the basic treaty and the third-country treaty). Temporal restrictions are built in to MFN clauses in order to delineate when they do and do not apply and they cannot simply be overridden through reference to an external legal instrument.[20]

1.2.1 The Temporal Scope of the MFN Clause

This subsection will conduct a two-pronged analysis concerning the temporal scope of the MFN clause *per se*. This includes looking at MFN clauses that are formulated prospectively, as well as at the pre/post-establishment aspects of MFN clauses.

---

18 *Daimler Financial Services AG v Argentine Republic, Award Dated 22 August 2012*, ICSID Case No. ARB/05/1 [232].

19 Vandevelde (n 5) 339.

20 See infra: *CMS Gas Transmission Company v The Argentine Republic, Award dated 12 May 2005*, ICSID Case No. ARB/01/8 147.

1.2.1.1 *Prospective Formulation of MFN Clauses*

Some treaties explicitly limit claiming MFN treatment in relation to treaties that are yet to be concluded. Such restrictions usually appear as exceptions to a given MFN clause. For example, in the 2019 Belgium-Luxembourg Economic Union (BLEU) Model BIT, Article 6(4)(a) excludes the possibility of demanding MFN treatment "under any bilateral or multilateral international agreement in force or signed by the Contracting Party prior to the date of entry into force of this Agreement."[21] The prospective formulation limits the temporal scope of the MFN clause.[22] Under such a formulation, beneficiaries may only demand more favorable treatment accorded in treaties coming into force after the conclusion of the basic treaty. This kind of wording brings with it some predictability for the contracting states since the MFN clause in the basic treaty will not require them to accord more favorable treatment intended for specific countries in the past, thus preventing "cherry-picking" of treatment on a retrospective basis.[23]

Some more recent Canadian IIAs have combined the prospective approach with a list of measures in respect of which MFN treatment cannot be demanded – thus applying the so-called ratchet mechanism, which entails limiting the scope of treatment in respect of which MFN principles apply to treatment granted in yet to be concluded third-party treaties, as well as *a priori* limiting the scope of measure to which MFN treatment applies.

Several questions arise about the rationale for taking a prospective approach to MFN treatment. The first, which has become a central discussion point since the controversial *Maffezini* case,[24] is to what extent temporal limitations are actually capable of preventing "cherry-picking" of treatment. Permitting "cherry-picking" is an inherent part of MFN treatment, even if MFN treatment was designed as a tool to level the playing field for foreign investors

---

21 Belgium – Luxembourg Economic Union (BLEU) Model BIT (2019). A copy of which is available at: <https://investmentpolicy.unctad.org/international-investment-agreements/treaty-files/5854/download> accessed 20 April 2022.

22 As an example, see Mira Suleimenova, *MFN Standard as Substantive Treatment* (Nomos Verlagsgesellschaft mbH & Co KG, 2019).

23 Suleimenova (n 22) 74. See also: Catherine Walsh and Michael G. Woods, 'The Canada-China Foreign Investment Protection And Promotion Agreement: A Comparative Analysis To Canada's Model FIPA – Government, Public Sector – Canada' Mondaq, <https://www.mondaq.com/canada/inward-foreign-investment/213340/the-canada-china-foreign-investment-protection-and-promotion-agreement-a-comparative-analysis-to-canadas-model-fipa> accessed 20 April 2022.

24 *Emilio Agustín Maffezini v The Kingdom of Spain, Decision of the Tribunal on Objections to Jurisdiction dated 25 January 2000*, ICSID Case No. ARB/97/7.

and investments. It is therefore fair to conclude that once MFN treatment is accorded to particular foreign investor, they are entitled to cherry-pick. Even though the type of temporal restriction imposed through taking a prospective approach closes the door for foreign investors to cherry-pick better treatment from treaties that already exist, it leaves the door open for cherry-picking in respect of more favorable treatment accorded in the future. Therefore, the issue of cherry-picking *per se* is not necessarily a problem. Instead, the problem concerns the intention of contracting states and whether they meant for one set of investors to be afforded the same level of treatment as another set of investors.[25]

Secondly, one might also question whether any temporal restriction is necessary in the first place. The difference between a temporal restriction and other subject-matter-specific exceptions, such as taxation agreements, customs unions, and free trade zones, is that a temporal restriction applies more generally without distinguishing between different subject matters. It may thus be less efficient compared with simply limiting the scope of MFN clauses on the basis of subject-matter-specific exceptions.

Given that we are in the Rebalancing Era as discussed in Chapter 1, taking a prospective approach to MFN clauses may be attractive to contracting parties who wish to tactically and incrementally accord foreign investors and investments better treatment on a non-discriminatory basis vis-à-vis other foreign investors and investments.

1.2.1.2 *Pre/Post-establishment Approaches to MFN Clauses*

Investment treaties traditionally include post-establishment MFN clauses whereby foreign investors and investments are permitted at the discretion of host states, i.e., the "admission model" or "investment-control model," and only once admitted does an investor or investment qualify for MFN treatment.[26] This is the main approach adopted in investment treaties, especially those concluded by European countries.

For example, in the Germany-Jordan BIT, Article 2 on "Promotion and Admission" of foreign investments provides as follows:

25 Andrew Newcombe, 'Canada's New Model Foreign Investment Protection Agreement' (2005) 1 Transnational Dispute Management (TDM), <https://www.transnational-dispute-management.com/article.asp?key=361> accessed 20 April 2022.

26 Anna Joubin-Bret, 'Admission and Establishment in the Context of Investment Protection' in August Reinisch (ed), *Standards of Investment Protection* (Oxford University Press 2008), <https://oxford.universitypressscholarship.com/view/10.1093/acprof:oso/9780199547432.001.0001/acprof-9780199547432-chapter-2> accessed 20 April 2022.

> Each Contracting Party shall in its territory promote as far as possible the investment by investors of the other Contracting Party and admit such investments in accordance with its legislation.

In conjunction with Article 2, Article 3 of the Germany-Jordan BIT extends MFN treatment to "investments owned or controlled by investors of the other Contracting Party" (paragraph 1) and "investors of the other Contracting Party, as regards their activity in connection with investments" (paragraph 2).[27]

From the 1990s onwards, some states also started adopting the "pre-establishment" approach, whereby FTAs included pre-establishment MFN clauses in investment chapters so as to further facilitate the liberalization of foreign investment.[28] Under the pre-establishment approach, MFN treatment also applies to the "preparatory" phase leading up to a foreign investment. MFN clauses which include expressions such as "establishment," "admission," and in some cases, "expansion," tend to follow the pre-establishment approach.[29] The pioneer in this regard was Article 1103 of the North American Free Trade Agreement (NAFTA), which provided MFN treatment to investment "with respect to the establishment, acquisition, expansion, management, conduct, operation, and sale or other disposition of investments."[30] Canada, the United States (U.S.), and the European Union have adopted this approach, and there is currently an increasing trend towards taking such an approach in IIAs.[31]

---

27 Germany – Jordan BIT (2007). A copy of which is available at: <https://investmentpolicy.unctad.org/international-investment-agreements/treaty-files/1347/download> accessed 20 April 2022.

28 Suzy H. Nikièma, 'The Most-Favoured-Nation Clause in Investment Treaties' (2017) IISD Best Practices Series 7; Joubin-Bret (n 26) 11.

29 Joubin-Bret (n 26) 13. In this regard, whether the term "expansion" covers both pre- and post-establishment phases remains controversial. It is arguable that it refers to both phases depending on the case at issue. For example, Article 6.3 of the Canada – China BIT (2012) provides that: 'The concept of 'expansion' in this Article applies only with respect to sectors not subject to a prior approval process under the relevant sectoral guidelines and applicable laws, regulations and rules in force at the time of expansion. The expansion may be subject to prescribed formalities and other information requirements.' Canada – China BIT (2012), available at <https://investmentpolicy.unctad.org/international-investment-agreements/treaty-files/3476/download> accessed 20 April 2022. See further: Nikièma (n 28) 7, footnote 22.

30 Article 1103 of NAFTA, the text of which is available at: <https://www.nafta-sec-alena.org/Home/Texts-of-the-Agreement/North-American-Free-Trade-Agreement?mvid=1&secid=539c50ef-51c1-489b-808b-9e20c9872d25> accessed 20 April 2022.

31 Catharine Titi, 'The Evolution of Substantive Investment Protections in Recent Trade and Investment Treaties' (2018) Inter-American Development Bank (IDB) & International Centre for Trade and Sustainable Development (ICTSD) – RTA Exchange Think Piece, Available at <SSRN: https://ssrn.com/abstract=3281574> accessed 20 April 2022. Some

Although covering the entire life cycle of investments, the scope of treatment to which MFN principles are applied in pre-establishment agreements is often limited by systematic exceptions, i.e., by making provision for specific types of measures that fall outside the scope of a particular MFN clause. There are generally two approaches to MFN exclusions: the so-called negative and post list approaches.

The measures on a negative list are excluded from the scope of the MFN clause. An example a of negative list approach is Article 1108 of NAFTA, which establishes explicit exceptions to the MFN treatment granted by Article 1103. In conjunction with Article 1108, NAFTA Annexes I and II provide a detailed list of the non-conforming measures excluded from MFN protection.

While in a positive list, measures not expressly included do not qualify for MFN treatment. An example of this approach is apparent from the General Agreement on Trade in Services (GATS), where each World Trade Organization (WTO) member makes specific commitments in respect of which types of measures it is required to accord MFN treatment.[32] Where a member does not expressly list a measure, it does not have to accord MFN treatment to that type of measure.

Some states also take a hybrid approach in that they at times combine the pre-establishment approach with the admission-model. An example of this can be found in Article 2 of the Bangladesh-Japan BIT, which accords MFN treatment in respect of the admission of foreign investments under domestic law:

1 Each Contracting Party shall, subject to its rights to exercise powers in accordance with the applicable laws and regulations, encourage and create favorable conditions for investors of the other Contracting Party to make investment in its territory, and, subject to the same rights, shall admit such investment;

2 Investors of either Contracting Party shall within the territory of the other Contracting Party be accorded treatment no less favorable than that accorded to investors of any third country in respect of matters relating to the admission of investment.[33]

---

recent Chinese BITs also adopt the pre-establishment model. See Heng Wang and Lu Wang, 'China's Bilateral Investment Treaties' in Julien Chaisse, Leïla Choukroune and Sufian Jusoh (eds), *Handbook of International Investment Law and Policy* (Springer Singapore 2020) 14.

32 Nikièma (n 28) 8.

33 Article 2 of the Japan – Bangladesh BIT (1999). A copy of which is available at: <https://investmentpolicy.unctad.org/international-investment-agreements/treaty-files/269/download> accessed 20 April 2022.

1.2.2 The Temporal Scope of Treaties

In this subsection, the *ratione temporis* of treaties is discussed: first in relation to basic treaties and then in relation to third-party treaties.

1.2.2.1 Ratione Temporis *and the Basic Treaty*

Ratione temporis relates to the question of whether a given treaty applies retroactively. An MFN clause's temporal application is limited by its basic treaty, including through the temporal scope of its dispute settlement provision, which serves as necessary treaty context for interpreting the MFN clause in question. In other words, claims that allege that a given MFN clause has been violated can only be brought for as long as the basic treaty remains extant.

This idea is illustrated well by the *Anglo-Iranian Oil Co* case, which was heard by the International Court of Justice (ICJ) after Iran consented to the jurisdiction of the ICJ on September 19, 1932, but confined its consent to disputes arising "in regard to situations or facts relating directly or indirectly to the application of treaties ... subsequent to the ratification of this Declaration."[34] The United Kingdom (UK) attempted to rely on the MFN clauses in treaties concluded between it and Iran, in1857 and 1903 respectively, in order to obtain the more favorable treatment accorded in similar treaties concluded between Iran and Turkey, as well as Iran and Denmark.[35] The ICJ rejected this attempt because the treaties on which the UK relied were concluded before, not after, Iran submitted to the Court's jurisdiction in 1932. More specifically, the Court held that –

> in order that the United Kingdom may enjoy the benefit of any treaty concluded by Iran with a third party by virtue of a most-[favored]-nation clause contained in a treaty concluded by the United Kingdom with Iran, the United Kingdom must be in a position to invoke the latter treaty. The treaty containing the most-[favored]-nation clause is the basic treaty upon which the United Kingdom must rely. It is this treaty which establishes the juridical link between the United Kingdom and a third-party treaty and confers upon that State the rights enjoyed by the third party. A third-party treaty, independent of and isolated from the basic treaty, cannot produce any legal effect as between the United Kingdom and Iran: it is res inter alios acta.[36]

---

34 *Anglo-Iranian Oil Co* (n 4) [107].

35 UK-Persia Treaty (1857); UK-Persia Treaty (1903); Iran-Denmark Treaty of Friendship, Establishment and Commerce (1934); Iran-Turkey Establishment Convention (1937).

36 *Anglo-Iranian Oil Co* (n 4).

In doing so, the Court clarified an essential point in relation to the application of MFN clauses. That is, the extent to which an MFN clause can be relied on to found a claim at a given point in time is determined by the extent to which the basic treaty is extant at that same point in time. If the basic treaty is no longer in effect, neither is the MFN clause in the basic treaty. If a state does not give retroactive consent in the treaty relied on to bring a dispute, then the MFN clause in that treaty cannot incorporate more favorable treatment from treaties concluded in the past. Or, as Cole rightly points out, unless the more favorable treatment can "in some way be incorporated into the treaty in which the MFN clause is contained, it is simply unavailable to the beneficiary of the MFN clause, whether it is indeed more favorable or not."[37]

In *TECMED*, the claimant attempted to incorporate a more favorable time frame within which to bring a claim from a third-party BIT. Specifically, Title Two of the Appendix in the Spain-Mexico BIT required investors to submit claims no later than three years from the date the investors became aware of or should have become aware of the alleged violation. The Austria-Mexico BIT, meanwhile, allowed investors four years to bring a claim.[38] The tribunal did not permit the claimant to incorporate the seemingly more favorable treatment through reliance on the MFN clause in the basic treaty. It explained its reasoning as follows:

> [T]he Arbitral Tribunal is of the view that Title II (4) and (5) of the Appendix to the Agreement contains requirements relating to the substantive admissibility of claims by the foreign investor, i.e. its access to the substantive protection regime contemplated under the Agreement. Consequently, such requirements are necessarily a part of the essential core of negotiations of the Contracting Parties; it should therefore be presumed that they would not have entered into the Agreement in the absence of such provisions. Such provisions, in the opinion of the

37 Cole (n 2) 563.

38 See: Appendix, title II (5) of the Mexico – Spain BIT (1995), available at: <https://investmentpolicy.unctad.org/international-investment-agreements/treaty-files/5618/download> accessed 20 April 2022. See also: Article 11(3) of the Austria – Mexico BIT (1998), which requires a period "not later than 4 years from the date the investor first acquired or should have acquired knowledge of the events which gave rise to the dispute," a copy of which is available at: <https://investmentpolicy.unctad.org/international-investment-agreements/treaty-files/204/download> accessed 20 April 2022.

> Arbitral Tribunal, therefore fall outside the scope of the most-favored-nation-clause contained in Article 8(1) of the Agreement.[39]

Commentators have raised concerns about the *TECMED* tribunal's reasoning, albeit that it rightly denied the extension of the time period as requested by the claimant.[40] The reason the extension attempt should have been rejected does not lie in the fact that the provisions, in the view of the tribunal, formed part of an "essential core of the negotiations." Nor was it necessary to distinguish between substantive and procedural treatment in this regard. Instead, the reasoning lies in the very nature of MFN clauses. The interpretation of an MFN clause must always take place in proper context, which necessarily includes considering the basic treaty of which the MFN clause forms a part. That is, the basic treaty provides a legitimate basis for applying the MFN clause in the first place. In *TECMED*, the basic treaty simply could not be relied on to bring a claim once three years had elapsed.[41] As a result of the claimant being unable to rely on the basic treaty to bring its claim, the MFN clause, which formed a part of that basic treaty, could not be relied on to ground a claim either.

Similar issues were addressed by tribunals of *M.C.I.* and *Impregilo*.[42] In both cases, the tribunals were faced with an attempt by a claimant to invoke the MFN clause in the basic treaty (the U.S.-Ecuador and Italy-Argentina BITs, respectively). Like the tribunal in *TECMED*, the *M.C.I.* and *Impregilo* tribunals rejected the idea that the MFN clause in the basic treaty could be invoked in order to expand the temporal scope of the basic treaty through incorporating more favorable treatment in a third-party treaty.

1.2.2.2 Ratione Temporis *and the Third-Party Treaty*

The temporal scope of third-party treaties was mainly discussed in the *Rights of Nationals of the United States of America in Morocco* (France v U.S.) decision

---

39 *Técnicas Medioambientales Tecmed, SA v The United Mexican States, Award dated 29 May 2003*, ICSID Case No. ARB (AF)/00/2 [74].

40 R Dolzer and T Myers, 'After Tecmed: Most-Favored-Nation Clauses in Investment Protection Agreements' (2004) 19 ICSID Review 49, 59. See also: Yas Banifatemi, 'The Emerging Jurisprudence on the Most-Favoured-Nation Treatment in Investment Arbitration,' in Andrea K. Bjorklund, Ian A. Laird, Sergey Ripinsky (eds), *Investment Treaty Law: Current Issues III* (BIICL, 2009) 241, 269.

41 *Tecmed, S.A. v The United Mexican States, ICSID Case No. ARB (AF)/00/2* (n 39) [74].

42 *MCI Power Group, LC and New Turbine, Inc v Republic of Ecuador, Award dated 31 July 2007*, ICSID Case No. ARB/03/6; *Impregilo S.pA v Argentine Republic (I), Award dated 21 June 2011*, ICSID Case No. ARB/07/17.

by the ICJ.[43] This case concerned the consular jurisdiction in French Morocco and, specifically, whether it included only civil disputes or extended to criminal issues as well. In furtherance of its arguments, the U.S. relied on the MFN clause in the Treaty of 1836 between Morocco and the U.S.[44] It tried to incorporate a broader consular jurisdiction from treaties that France had concluded with Spain,[45] as well as the UK.[46]

However, neither third-party treaty was in force at that time because of the renunciation of consular privileges by Spain in 1914 and by the UK in 1937.[47] To this end, the U.S. claimed the MFN clause in the basic treaty as "a form of drafting by reference."[48] According to the U.S., the incorporation of rights or privileges through the MFN clause was intended to be permanent and to be invocable even after the third-party treaties had been terminated.[49] The ICJ rejected this stance because it was inconsistent with the contracting parties' intention at the time that they concluded the treaties at issue insofar as their MFN clauses were concerned, which was to "establish and to maintain at all times fundamental equality without discrimination among all of the countries concerned."[50]

What this indicates is that an MFN clause should be applied with a number of temporal factors in mind. For the MFN clause to be successfully invoked, temporal limitations of the clause itself, as well as the limitation of the basic treaty (and potentially third-party treaties) should be properly taken into account.

1.3 *The Subject Matter of MFN Treatment (Ratione Materiae)*

This section examines the subject matter requirement of MFN clauses, i.e., what is meant by "treatment no less favorable." It is an essential issue in this book because it concerns the type and scope of protection that could be

43 *Rights of Nationals of the United States of America in Morocco (France v United States of America)* (n 4).

44 *Rights of Nationals of the United States of America in Morocco (France v United States of America)* (n 4) 176.

45 The General Treaty between France and Great Britain of 1856.

46 The Treaty of Commerce and Navigation between France and Spain of 1861.

47 *Rights of Nationals of the United States of America in Morocco (France v United States of America)* (n 4) 184.

48 *Rights of Nationals of the United States of America in Morocco (France v United States of America)* (n 4)191.

49 *Rights of Nationals of the United States of America in Morocco (France v United States of America)* (n 4) 191.

50 *Rights of Nationals of the United States of America in Morocco (France v United States of America)* (n 4) 191.

incorporated through an MFN clause.[51] In this regard, MFN clauses serve as a bridge or, according to Schwarzenberger, an "empty shell" inserted into the basic treaty and that the investor can load with treatment from third-party treaties.[52]

Article 5 of the Draft Articles defines MFN treatment as treatment "not less [favorable] than treatment extended by the granting State to a third State or to persons or things in the same relationship with that third State,"[53] and leaves the definition of the term "treatment" open. The term "treatment" is generally not defined in IIAs either.[54]

Scholars and ISDS tribunals have examined the term "treatment" (or "standard of treatment") contained in IIAs from the perspective of its ordinary meaning. They have often understood "treatment" as forming part of the contractual obligations undertaken by the parties to a given treaty.[55] "Treatment" entails domestic measures taken by the host state *vis-à-vis* foreign investors, the abuse of which constitutes a violation of a treaty obligation. For example, Salacuse draws on the dictionary meaning of the term, which is "actions and conduct of one person toward another," and defines treatment as a promise by parties to a treaty about their actions and conduct toward investments and investors of the other party. In his view, the goal of investment treatment is to discipline the governance of host states.[56]

Similarly, the *Suez and Interagua* tribunal placed the term "treatment" in the context of its ordinary meaning, defining it as "the rights and privileges granted and the obligations and burdens imposed by a Contracting State on investments made by investors covered by the treaty."[57] Similarly, the *Siemens*

51 Banifatemi (n 40) 256. See also: M Valenti, 'The Most Favoured Nation Clause in BITs as a Basis for Jurisdiction in Foreign Investor – Host State Arbitration' (2008) 24 Arbitration International 447, 448.

52 Georg Schwarzenberger, 'The Most-Favoured-Nation Standard in British State Practice' (1945) 22 British Yearbook on International Law 96.

53 International Law Commission (n 1).

54 Facundo Pérez-Aznar, 'The Use of Most-Favoured-Nation Clauses to Import Substantive Treaty Provisions in International Investment Agreements' (2017) 20 Journal of International Economic Law 777, 799.

55 In this regard, see Relja Radović, 'Between Rights and Remedies: The Access to Investment Treaty Arbitration as a Substantive Right of Foreign Investors' (2019) 10 Journal of International Dispute Settlement 42, 8–9. The author discussed about the legal status of foreign investors in IIAs, and the characteristic of treatment in this sense.

56 Jeswald W Salacuse, *The Law of Investment Treaties* (Second edition, Oxford University Press 2015) 228.

57 *Suez, Sociedad General de Aguas de Barcelona, SA and Interagua Servicios Integrales de Agua, SA v Argentine Republic, Decision on Jurisdiction dated 16 May 2006,* ICSID Case No. ARB/03/17 [55].

tribunal defined treatment as "[behavior] in respect of an entity or a person" and held that this should be read in conjunction with the parameter "no less favorable."[58]

In *Daimler*, the tribunal stated that "treatment" deals with "the actual behavior of the Host States towards a foreign private investment as measured against the international obligations binding upon the state based on treaty law and general international law," and by "actual behavior," it referred mainly to the manner in which a given host state "regulates, protects, or otherwise interacts with specified actors."[59]

The general lack of an explicit definition of "treatment" in international investment law draws particular attention to whether and to what extent MFN clauses are capable of incorporating procedural rules from third-party treaties.[60] In view of this, the next part discusses various attempts by claimants to expand the substantive and procedural scope of MFN treatment and tribunals' decisions in this regard.

1.4 *Exceptions to MFN Clauses*

It is typical for MFN clauses to contain restrictions and exceptions that preclude MFN application in certain areas.[61] Such limitations reflect parties' desire to maintain control over foreign investors or their preference for step-by-step rather than immediate liberalization.[62] MFN exceptions are embodied in Article XX of the General Agreement on Tariffs and Trade of 1994 (GATT), as well as Article XIV of the GATS, in terms of which WTO members could adopt and maintain trade-restrictive measures that are inconsistent with GATT or GATS rules.

MFN exceptions have traditionally included substantive treatment extended through regional economic integration organization (REIO) agreements and tax treaties, as well as country-specific exemptions, where economic sectors or

58 *Siemens. v Argentina* (n 10) [85].

59 *Daimler v Argentina* (n 18) [218].

60 Y Radi, 'The Application of the Most-Favoured-Nation Clause to the Dispute Settlement Provisions of Bilateral Investment Treaties: Domesticating the "Trojan Horse"' (2007) 18 European Journal of International Law 757, 766.

61 OECD, 'Most-Favoured-Nation Treatment in International Investment Law' (OECD 2004) OECD Working Papers on International Investment WP 2004/02; Nikièma (n 28); UNCTAD (n 6); David Collins, *An Introduction to International Investment Law* (Cambridge University Press 2017).

62 Pia Acconci, 'Most-Favoured-Nation Treatment', *The Oxford Handbook of International Investment Law* (Peter T Muchlinski, Federico Ortino, Christoph Schreuer, Oxford University Press 2008) 372.

non-compliant measures have been excluded from MFN treatment. For example, in the Argentina-U.S. BIT, Article II(9) provides as follows:

> The most favored nation provisions of this Article shall not apply to advantages accorded by either Party to nationals or companies of any third country by virtue of that Party's binding obligations that derive from full membership in a regional customs union or free trade area, whether such an arrangement is designated as a customs union, free trade area, common market or otherwise.[63]

In response to case law having rendered seemingly conflicting awards in relation to scope of MFN clauses, contracting parties started including more specific and extensive exceptions in their MFN clauses.[64] Since 1990, Canada and the U.S. have been concluding agreements containing country-specific MFN exceptions. These exceptions or restrictions appear as non-conforming measures (NCMs) in the annexes of these agreements. A key example is Article 1108 of NAFTA as discussed above (which has subsequently been replaced by Article 14.12 in the recently concluded United States-Mexico-Canada Agreement (USMCA). Article 1108 of NAFTA provides an extensive list of MFN exceptions, including *inter alia* country-specific NCMs,[65] and intellectual property rights.[66] In addition to the above exceptions, Annex IV of NAFTA explicitly indicated exceptions to MFN treatment regarding time and sectors, i.e., to exclude treatment accorded under all prior bilateral or multilateral international agreements and for the treatment accorded under all such future agreements concerning specific sectors only.[67] Among these exceptions, government procurement has been brought up several times in NAFTA cases. The claimant and the respondent state have disputed whether specific government actions are styled as constituting "procurement" in an attempt to preclude the application of MFN treatment.[68]

---

63 Article II(9) of the Argentina – United States of America BIT (1991). A copy of which is available at: <https://investmentpolicy.unctad.org/international-investment-agreements/treaty-files/127/download> accessed 20 April 2022.

64 Suleimenova (n 22).

65 NAFTA (n 30), Article 1108(1) and (2). After the entry into force of USMCA, the above paragraphs have been replaced by USMCA Article 14.12(1) and (2). The text of USMCA is available at: <https://ustr.gov/trade-agreements/free-trade-agreements/united-states-mexico-canada-agreement/agreement-between> accessed 20 April 2022.

66 Article 1108(5) of NAFTA (n 30).

67 OECD (n 61) 7.

68 See, for example, *ADF Group Inc v United States of America, Award dated 9 January 2003*, ICSID Case No. ARB(AF)/00/1.

Given the debate regarding the extent to which MFN clauses are capable of incorporating procedural treatment, some IIAs adopted exceptions explicitly excluding dispute settlement from the scope of MFN treatment. India has very explicitly adopted this approach. For example, Article 4.3 of the India-Colombia BIT provides that MFN treatment in the treaty "does not encompass mechanisms for the settlement of investment disputes."[69] A more recent instance is the EU-Canada Comprehensive Economic and Trade Agreement (CETA), Article 8.7(4) of which provides that the "treatment" contemplated in its MFN clause does not include *inter alia* "procedures for the resolution of investment disputes between investors and states provided for in other international investment treaties and other trade agreements."[70]

2 MFN Clauses and Substantive Treatment

Following the first part on the scope of MFN clauses, the analysis in this part turns to discuss attempts by claimants to expand the scope of treaty protection offered by MFN clauses in ISDS practice. This chapter limits itself to the application of MFN clauses in relation to incorporation of *substantive* treatment. Attempts at incorporating procedural treatment are addressed in the next chapter.

According to an empirical study of cases by Shirlow and Caron, claimants invoke MFN clauses in pursuit of more favorable substantive treatment in one of two ways: Either they claim a *de facto* violation of an MFN clause by a host

69 Article 4(3) of the Colombia – India BIT (2009). A copy of which is available at: <https://investmentpolicy.unctad.org/international-investment-agreements/treaty-files/796/download> accessed 20 April 2022.

70 'CETA Chapter by Chapter' (*Trade – European Commission*), a copy of which is available at: <https://ec.europa.eu/trade/policy/in-focus/ceta/ceta-chapter-by-chapter/index_en.htm> accessed 20 April 2022. In their discussions on MFN exceptions, some scholars also include those MFN clauses that explicitly refer to certain specific clauses in the basic treaty and categorize these as exceptions. For example, Collins categorizes Article 3(3) of the UK – Barbados BIT (1993), which intentionally include articles providing treatment such as FET, full protection and security, expropriation, repatriation, etc., under the coverage of MFN, as a form of MFN exception since it did not mention other articles in the same treaty. It is doubtful, however, whether such instances properly constitute MFN exceptions. After all, claimants will still be able to assert that they are entitled to MFN treatment in relation to other types of treatment. As such, these instances are not considered as constituting MFN exceptions for the purposes of this book. See: Collins (n 61) 113.

state in respect of domestic actions (a comparator practice),[71] or they attempt to incorporate a higher standard of treatment from third-party treaties (a comparator treaty).[72] This section is accordingly divided into two subsections, each dealing with one of these two categories.

2.1 De Facto *Breaches of MFN Clauses*

In the case of *de facto* MFN breaches, investors rely on MFN clauses in the basic treaty to allege less favorable treatment at the hands of the host state vis-à-vis treatment received by third-party foreign investors. ISDS tribunals do not often come to the conclusion that a *de facto* breach of an MFN clause has taken place.[73] According to Shirlow and Caron, out of 50 cases they identified which pertain to substantive MFN claims in one way or another, only 13 cases dealt with *de facto* MFN violations that involved the host state allegedly providing more favorable treatment *in practice* to comparable third-state investors, while 37 dealt with attempts to incorporate a higher standard of treatment contained in a comparator treaty.[74] MFN clauses in these cases were usually not drafted to form part of fair and equitable treatment or full protection and security obligations. Instead, they mostly create independent substantive treatment obligations, as in the case of Article 1103 of NAFTA. Such MFN clauses are therefore often referred to as bringing a standalone standard of treatment into existence.[75]

Establishment of a *de facto* MFN violation is a fact-intensive enquiry that needs to take into account the holistic circumstances of the investors in question. For example, the *Mercer* tribunal stated that establishing a violation of MFN treatment would require fact-specific examinations. Specifically, the tribunal thought it necessary to examine whether the foreign claimant was in a similar situation to the identified foreign investors and received less favorable treatment than that accorded to those identified foreign investors.[76] Similarly, according to the *Vento* tribunal:

71 David D Caron and Esme Shirlow, 'Most Favoured Nation Treatment – Substantive Protection in Investment Law' (2015) King's College London Law School Research Paper No. 2015–23, Available at SSRN: <https://ssrn.com/abstract=2590557> accessed 20 April 2022.

72 Caron and Shirlow (n 71).

73 Caron and Shirlow (n 71).

74 Caron and Shirlow (n 71), footnote 7.

75 Suleimenova (n 22).

76 *Mercer International Inc. v Government of Canada, Award dated 6 March 2018*, ICSID Case No. ARB(AF)/12/3 [7.6].

> … neither the treatment nor the similarities or differences between the relevant circumstances can be considered in isolation. What is important are the circumstances as they relate to the alleged treatment accorded to the investors or investments in question[77]

The fact-specific examination of the *de facto* MFN violation focuses on the essential operative terms contained in most MFN clauses, i.e., "in like circumstances" and "less favorable treatment."[78] At times, it may involve examining to what extent host states had discriminatory intent, as well as the burden of proof in arbitration.

2.1.1 "In Like Circumstances"

Although the "in like circumstances" criterion is not included in every MFN clause of the investment treaties, MFN treatment nevertheless inherently entails some sense of likeness in the sense that like treatment is owed to like actors in like circumstances.[79] MFN clauses' likeness requirements relates to the *ejusdem generis* principle codified in Article 9 and 10 of the Draft Articles.[80] Article 10(2) expressly provides that foreign investors should be in the same position as most-favored third-party comparators in order for them to enjoy MFN treatment. The likeness criterion is arguably a threshold issue when it comes to establishing a *de facto* MFN breach, and the failure to make out a case on the issue of likeness has been one of the main reasons for tribunals to reject claims of a *de facto* MFN breach. Given that MFN and national treatment are both relative treaty standards, ISDS tribunals have often addressed the likeness element of MFN clauses in conjunction with that contained in the relevant national treatment clause.[81] In this regard, the *Pope & Talbot* tribunal's method to ascertain the likeness of foreign investors and their domestic comparators in

77 *Vento Motorcycles, Inc. v United Mexican States, Award dated 6 July 2020,* ICSID Case No. ARB(AF)/17/3 [240].

78 AR Ziegler, 'Is the MFN Principle in International Investment Law Ripe for Multilateralization or Codification?' in Andrea K Bjorklund and August Reinisch (eds), *International Investment Law and Soft Law* (2012) 248.

79 Suleimenova (n 22) 151; Andreas Ziegler, 'Most-Favoured-Nation (MFN) Treatment' in Reinisch August (ed), *Standards of Investment Protection* (Oxford University Press 2008) 75; Pérez-Aznar (n 54) 800; Ziegler (n 78) 250.

80 International Law Commission (n 1). Some researches nevertheless do not consider the 'in like circumstances' requirement under the context of *ejusdem generis*. for example, see Caron and Shirlow (n 71). While other researches equate the "in like circumstances" requirement and the *ejusdem generis* principle. See Ziegler (n 78) 250.

81 *Bayindir Insaat Turizm Ticaret Ve Sanayi AS v Islamic Republic of Pakistan, Award dated 27 August 2009,* ICSID Case No. ARB/03/29 [416].

order to establish a breach of Article 1102 of NAFTA on national treatment has generally been accepted by tribunals.

In *Pope & Talbot*, the tribunal was faced with an Article 1102 NAFTA claim brought against Canada for imposing export fees on softwood lumber under the U.S.-Canada Softwood Lumber Agreement (SLA), which allegedly limited the claimant's ability to export and sell softwood lumber to the U.S.[82] The tribunal determined that discrimination could not arise if the foreign and domestic investors were not in like circumstances, even if the two categories of investors were treated differently.[83] The meaning of "like circumstances" is dependent on the legal context and the facts of each case. Following this, the tribunal agreed with the legal context perceived by the claimant as "the trade and investment-liberalizing objectives of the NAFTA," and by Canada as "the entire background of its disputes with the U.S. concerning softwood lumber trade between the two countries."[84] The tribunal put forward what has become an oft-relied-upon test in the following terms:

> Difference in treatment will presumptively violate Article 1102(2), unless they have a reasonable nexus to rational government policies that (1) do not distinguish, on their face or de facto, between foreign-owned and domestic companies, and (2) do not otherwise unduly undermine the investment liberalizing objectives of NAFTA.[85]

In other words, the tribunal found that coming to a conclusion on the existence of "like circumstances" required an examination of different treatment in appearance, the justification of which lay in a reasonable relationship to rational policies "not motivated by preference of domestic over foreign owned investments."[86] This test led the tribunal to reject the claim that Article 1102 of NAFTA had been breached since none of the domestic comparators were in like circumstances with the claimant.

The *Windstream Energy* case involved a moratorium aimed at the indefinite suspension of offshore wind farms by the Government of Ontario, which allegedly froze the feed-in-tariff (FIT) contract between the claimant (Windstream) and the Government of Ontario, thereby allegedly jeopardizing

82 *Pope & Talbot v Government of Canada, Award on the Merits of Phase 2 dated 10 April 2001,* UNCITRAL Arbitration [74].
83 *Pope & Talbot v Canada* (n 82)[79].
84 *Pope & Talbot v Canada* (n 82) [78].
85 *Pope & Talbot v Canada* (n 82) [78].
86 *Pope & Talbot v Canada* (n 82) [79].

a Windstream investment project in Canada.[87] The claimant alleged that the Canadian Government breached the obligation to provide MFN treatment under Article 1103 of NAFTA because it accorded less favorable treatment to the claimant vis-à-vis identifiable comparators. The claimant argued that the moratorium prevented it from pursuing its regulatory process for its investment in Canada, while all other developers of large wind projects were not affected by the moratorium.

In support of its claim, the claimant identified Samsung, a South Korean company that allegedly received better treatment than the claimant. The claimant asserted that it was in a similar situation to Samsung because both were potential recipients of contracts for the development of solar projects. While Ontario offered Samsung a contract for the solar project, no such deal was offered to the claimant, even if it applied for the same solar project after the moratorium. The respondent argued that the claimant misidentified the third-party comparators. For the respondent, the claimant should have realized that the proper comparator was other offshore wind project developers, and not Samsung. According to the respondent, the claimant was offered better treatment than other offshore wind proponents under the moratorium because it was the only one retained while arrangement with all others in like circumstances were in fact canceled.[88]

In its submission on Article 1128 of NAFTA, the U.S. argued that "circumstances" should mean the "conditions or facts that accompany treatment as opposed to the treatment itself." Consequently, Article 1103 required tribunals to take into account host states' regulatory frameworks and policy objectives, as well as the relevant sector of the economy to which these applied. As a result, the claimant and third-party comparators "in like circumstances" must be the same "in all relevant respects but for nationality of ownership."[89]

The tribunal sided with the respondent state in the final award, finding that Samsung was not "in like circumstances" with the claimant. Specifically, the tribunal found that Samsung was subject to a different legal context in comparison to the claimant because it had a separate contract with the Canadian government. It was accordingly understandable that Samsung was not affected by the moratorium. For the tribunal, qualified comparators were other prospective offshore wind project developers to which the moratorium applied. Only to the extent that the claimant was accorded less favorable treatment

87 *Windstream Energy LLC v The Government of Canada, Award dated 27 September 2016*, PCA Case No. 2013–22.

88 *Windstream Energy v Canada (n 87)* [124, 401].

89 *Windstream Energy v Canada (n 87)* [404].

vis-à-vis the properly established comparator could the tribunal conclude that there had been a *de facto* MFN violation. The tribunal found that the claimant was, in fact, rendered better treatment than these comparators because it was the only company that was offered a FIT contract and survived after the moratorium came into place.[90]

In *Apotex* (*III*), the Canadian investor Apotex alleged that the U.S. government breached Article 1103 of NAFTA by issuing an import alert issued to two of the claimant's Canadian manufacturing facilities (Etobicoke and Signet) for violations of the Current Good Manufacturing Practices (cGMP) regulations issued by the U.S. government. To this end, the claimant identified that two foreign companies, Sandoz and Teva, received better treatment as foreign comparators in like circumstances. Specifically, the claimant argued that although Sandoz and Teva were also found to be in violation of the cGMP regulations, they merely received warning letters. This treatment is materially less severe than the import alert issued in respect of the claimant.[91]

The disputing parties notably agreed that the determination of "in like circumstances" required an intensively fact-specific inquiry. Essential factors in this regard should have included whether the claimant and potential comparators belong to the same economic or business sector, were in a competitive relationship with respect to particular goods or services, or were subject to a comparable legal regime or regulatory requirements, among other things.[92] With respect to the identification of the proper comparators, however, the disputing parties disagreed.

The respondent contended that Teva and Sandoz did not qualify as proper comparators because they were not "in like circumstances." This was because different factors were allegedly considered by the U.S. Food and Drug Administration (FDA) when deciding to issue the import alerts in question. It held that one could not expect the U.S. government to take the same enforcement action in relation to alleged violations of the cGMP regulations "regardless of the specific nature of the violations and any factors weighing for and against such action with respect to the particular facility and drugs concerned." Expert testimony also confirmed that the FDA's policy consideration of a "risk-based approach" took into account, among other things, the seriousness of the violations, its public health risks, the company's history and response, including

90 *Windstream Energy v Canada* (*n 87*) [414–416].

91 *Apotex Holdings Inc and Apotex Inc v United States of America* (*III*), *Award dated 25 August 2014*, ICSID Case No. ARB(AF)/12/1 [8.27–8.28].

92 *Apotex v U.S.* (*III*) (n 91) [8.15].

voluntary corrective actions, and whether drugs are medically necessary or in short supply.[93]

After a lengthy review of the facts, particularly the experts' testimony, the tribunal sided with the respondent state and dismissed the MFN claim due to the fact that the claimant was not "in like circumstances" with the comparators it had identified. The tribunal explained that the different treatment was due to two differences in circumstances. First, there was a shortage of key drugs in the U.S. which were produced by Teva's and Sandoz's foreign facilities. This led to different treatment by the FDA. Second, the claimant's failure to take more extensive voluntary actions in response to the FDA's notification of violations of the cGMP regulations at its two facilities, which also led to the FDA's treating the claimant and the comparators differently.[94]

Another NAFTA case that relied on expert testimony is *Mercer*. This case involved a Canadian regulatory agency's alleged failure to provide uniform treatment to pulp mills operated by Mercer, which had the ability to generate its own power, vis-à-vis other customers who were also able to produce their own power. Mercer argued that by denying its Canadian subsidiary (Mercer Mill) the benefits of its foreign comparator (Tembec), Canada breached *inter alia* the MFN obligation contained in Article 1103 of NAFTA.[95] The tribunal was presented with divergent testimony from different experts on whether Mercer Mill was in like circumstances with Tembec. In the end, the tribunal decided to adopt the respondent state's experts' testimony. It confirmed that the differential treatment resulted from a consistent application of domestic policy by the Canadian authority, which to a degree took into account other investors' individual circumstances.[96] Building on this, the tribunal decided that the different treatment did not constitute "discriminatory treatment," and that the investors were in distinct circumstances resulting from Canada's consistent application of its domestic policy.

In *Cargill*, the U.S. claimant alleged that Mexico's adoption in 2002 of a tax on beverages containing high fructose corn syrup (HFCS) affected the claimants' investments in the high fructose corn syrup industry in Mexico.[97] The dispute related to a decree published by Mexico's executive on December 31,

93 *Apotex v U.S. (III)* (n 91) [8.69–8.70].

94 *Apotex v U.S. (III)* (n 91), Part III: The Principal Facts.

95 For a summary of the case, see: <https://investmentpolicy.unctad.org/investment-dispute-settlement/cases/457/mercer-v-canada> accessed 20 April 2022.

96 *Mercer International v Canada* (n 76) [7.31–32].

97 *Cargill, Incorporated v United Mexican States, Award dated 18 September 2009*, ICSID Case No. ARB(AF)/05/2.

2001, which established new tariff rates for the importation of goods for 2002. The decree required an import permit for the claimant to import HFCS from the U.S. to Mexico. The absence of this requirement would have led to the MFN tariff under the 2001 decree being applied to U.S. HFCS imports, which tariff would be much higher than the NAFTA tariff.[98] Therefore, the claimant alleged that Mexico had violated the MFN clause in Article 1103 of NAFTA by imposing import permit requirement only in relation to HFCS imported from the U.S.

In furtherance of its argument, the claimant compared itself with Caso, a Canadian subsidiary of Corn Products International (CPI) that allegedly exported HFCS from Canada to Mexico without the need for an import permit. The respondent doubted that Caso was an appropriate comparator because it is a Canadian subsidiary of CPI and did not have an investment in Mexico's territory. Therefore, it did not count as a foreign investor within the meaning of Article 1103 of NAFTA. The tribunal sided with the respondent. It concluded that to be a comparator company, Caso had to operate its own investment in Mexico's territory. Ultimately, the tribunal dismissed the claim that there had been an MFN violation on the basis that the foreign comparators or investments were not "in like circumstances" vis-à-vis Cargill.

The *Grand River* case involved a 1998 settlement agreement between several states' Attorneys General and major tobacco companies in the U.S. to settle litigation brought by various U.S. states against some U.S. cigarette manufacturers for causing certain tobacco-related illnesses. Certain state legislation partially implemented some of these agreements.[99] The tribunal adopted the method established by prior NAFTA tribunals, which examined whether the particular entities in question faced like legal regimes.[100]

The tribunal held that the reasoning of prior tribunals showed that "the identity of the legal regimes applicable to a claimant and its purported comparators to be a compelling factor in assessing whether like is indeed being compared to like for purposes of Article 1102 and 1103."[101] On this basis, the tribunal believed that qualified comparators, in that case, should have been the firms that also engaged in the wholesale distribution of cigarettes in the territory of the U.S. and who were potentially subject to enforcement actions under the states' complementary legislation.[102] In the end, the tribunal dismissed the MFN claim because Grand River failed to identify a qualified comparator.

98 *Cargill v Mexico* (n 97) [117].

99 *Grand River Enterprises Six Nations, Ltd., et.al. v United States of America, Award dated 12 January 2011,* UNCITRAL Arbitration [8].

100 *Grand River v U.S.* (n 99) [166].

101 *Grand River v U.S.* (n 99) [167].

102 *Grand River v U.S.* (n 99) [165].

Non-NAFTA cases have also examined the likeness issues, even though most BITs applicable in those cases did not contain an explicit likeness requirement in their MFN clauses.[103] In *MNSS*, the claimant alleged that the respondent state interfered with the operation and management of a steel production facility invested in by the claimant (ZN), thus causing its bankruptcy. The claimant asserted that a *de facto* MFN breach had taken place at the instance of the respondent state, for which it proposed KAP, a Cypriot company, as a foreign comparator.

The disputing parties made arguments as to whether ZN was in comparable circumstances to KAP. The claimant argued that ZN and KAP were in comparable circumstances since both were affected by the economic crisis and were involved in bankruptcy proceedings. Therefore, the respondent had breached the MFN clause by granting KAP better treatment. This included allowing KAP to discharge its employees, assuming €22 million in liabilities, and not intervening in negotiations between management and employees, amongst other things.[104]

According to the respondent, KAP was not a qualified comparator because it was in a different economic sector from ZN. Although operating in distinct economic sectors, the tribunal agreed that KAP and ZN could be comparable because they were both jeopardized by the economic crisis as the two largest employers in the respondent state. Both were going through bankruptcy proceedings, as the claimant alleged. However, the different treatment could be explained by *inter alia* the distinct circumstances of KAP and ZN concerning essential aspects like labor-management issues and substantial governmental support before the bankruptcy proceedings kicked off.[105]

In *Parkerings-Compagniet*, the Norwegian claimant incorporated a Lithuanian subsidiary (BP) to carry out contracting operations in Lithuania. It claimed that Lithuania had violated Article IV of the Lithuania-Norway BIT, which pertained to MFN treatment. Such breach allegedly consisted in the

---

103 With the exception of *Occidental*, where Article 2(1) of the Ecuador – U.S. BIT (1993) was drafted in the following terms: '1. Each Party shall permit and treat investment, and activities associated therewith, on a basis no less favorable than that accorded in like situations to investment or associated activities of its own nationals or companies, or of nationals or companies of any third country, whichever is the most favorable, subject to the right of each Party to make or maintain exceptions falling within one of the sectors or matters listed in the Protocol to this Treaty.' See: Ecuador – U.S. BIT (1993). A copy of which is available at: <https://investmentpolicy.unctad.org/international-investment-agreements/treaty-files/1065/download> accessed 20 April 2022.

104 *MNSS v Montenegro* (n 11) [361].

105 *MNSS v Montenegro* (n 11) [362].

Lithuanian Municipality of Vilnius' repudiation of an agreement concerning the creation, development, maintenance, and enforcement of a public parking system or the so-called multi-story car parking project (MSCP project).[106]

In this regard, the claimant referred to a Dutch company called Pinus Proprius as a third-party investor that received better treatment than BP. The claimant alleged that Lithuania violated its MFN obligation in relation to the proposed projects at two different sites in Vilnius, namely Gedimino and Pergales, on several grounds. First, the City of Vilnius refused the Gedimino MSCP project proposed by BP and instead authorized Pinus Proprius to construct the same MSCP on the same site in Gedimino. Second, the City of Vilnius refused to sign a joint activity agreement (JAA) with BP for the Gedimino and Pergales MSCP projects but signed a JAA with Pinus Proprius. Third, after the JAA with Pinus Proprius was declared unlawful under Lithuanian domestic claw, the City of Vilnius converted it into a cooperation agreement while refusing to conclude a similar cooperation agreement with BP as a substitute.[107]

The tribunal rejected the claim that Lithuania had violated its MFN obligations in respect of both the Gedimino and Pergales MSCP projects. It found that BP and Pinus Proprius were not in the same situation. The tribunal began its reasoning by stating that to establish a *de facto* MFN breach, the discrimination "must be unreasonable or lacking proportionality … be inapposite or excessive to achieve an otherwise legitimate objective of the State," that "[a]n objective justification may justify differentiated treatments of similar cases," and that "[i]t would be necessary, in each case, to evaluate the exact circumstances and the context."[108]

The tribunal further rejected the MFN claim on the basis that BP and Pinus Proprius were not in the same situation insofar as the JAA on Pergales MSCP project was concerned for two overarching reasons.[109] First, the tribunal found that BP and Pinus Proprius were subject to different contractual obligations. While Pinus Proprius was obligated to sell the MSCP to the City of Vilnius upon completion, no such obligation existed for BP. BP was allowed to retain ownership of the MSCP and lease or purchase the publicly owned land upon completion. The second difference related to the first. Specifically, the tribunal found that the City of Vilnius entered into a cooperation agreement with Pinus Proprius because the JAA's validity was challenged by the representative

106 *Parkerings-Compagniet AS v Republic of Lithuania, Award dated 11 September 2007,* ICSID Case No. ARB/05/8.

107 *Parkerings v Lithuania* (n 106) [363].

108 *Parkerings v Lithuania* (n 106) [368].

109 *Parkerings v Lithuania* (n 106) [412].

of the government of Vilnius. The subsequent cooperation agreement merely entailed an amendment to the title of the old JAA. Therefore, the tribunal found that the existence or non-existence of a signed JAA with Pinus Proprius and BP, respectively, should play a crucial role in its analysis. Ultimately, the tribunal dismissed the MFN claim because BP and Pinus Proprius were in different circumstances.

Concerning the Gedimino multi-story car parking (MSCP) project, the *Parkerings* tribunal also rejected one of the MFN claims after examining the historical, archaeological, and environmental situation of the Old Town in Vilnius as defined by UNESCO. Recognizing the different treatment between BP and Pinus Proprius, the tribunal agreed with Lithuania and decided that the historical, archaeological, and environmental preservation in this area served as a justification for Lithuania's rejection of the BP project. In particular, the tribunal considered that BP's MSCP project in Gedimino was larger than that of Pinus Proprius, which extended further into the UNESCO-defined Old Town, especially near the historic area of the Cathedral. Therefore, BP's MSCP project in Gedimino could potentially impair the Old Town's culturally sensitive area. Evidence was presented to demonstrate that various domestic bodies had objected to the BP project. On the other hand, the MSCP project proposed by Pinus Proprius in Gedimino was much smaller in size and not as controversial as the BP project. In this regard, the tribunal concluded that BP and Pinus Proprius were not in a similar situation as investors in Gedimino and that Lithuania had legitimate reasons to differentiate between the BP and Pinus Prius projects.[110]

Another pertinent case is *GEA*. This case concerned bankruptcy proceedings in front of the Ukrainian domestic courts. The Ukrainian courts dismissed the proceedings on the basis of a failure on the part of GEA to comply with certain time limitations; GEA was time-barred from bringing its claim. However, in similar proceedings involving a third-party investor from the Seychelles (Regent Co), the claimant succeeded in bringing its dispute, which originated during the same period, despite it not having complied with the same time limitation. The tribunal refused to find that a *de facto* MFN breach had occurred because the claimant and the proposed comparator were not in a similar situation. It stated that –

> with respect to the purported unequal treatment between the Claimant and the Seychelles company, the Tribunal is not convinced that the

110 *Parkerings v Lithuania* (n 106) [397].

> situation of the Seychelles Company is comparable to that of GEA. In the Tribunal's view, the simple fact that claim of the Seychelles Company was not time-barred does not, in and of itself, mean anything, in particular taking into account the differences in the procedural posture between that case and the one at hand.[111]

By far the most controversial decision on this score was rendered in *Occidental*. This case involved the Ecuadorian tax authority's denial of Occidental's request for a refund of value-added tax (VAT). Occidental demanded reimbursement of amounts previously refunded in connection with a participation contract that it had entered into with Petroecuador, an Ecuadorian state-owned company, to carry out oil exploration and production in Ecuador.[112]

The tribunal agreed with the claimant and adopted a relatively broad approach to determining what constituted "in like circumstances." It considered that the expression "in like situations" could not be interpreted in a narrow sense, since the purpose of national and MFN treatment was to ensure that foreign investors were to be treated equally, which could not be achieved by focusing exclusively on the sector to which the comparator investors belonged. As such, the tribunal took into account how domestic companies from other sectors were treated and found that they received VAT refunds, i.e., they were treated more favorably than the claimant.[113] The *Occidental* tribunal was criticized for its broad interpretation of "in like circumstances," which subsequent tribunals have not followed.[114]

All but one of the above ISDS cases were dismissed due to the claimants in question not being considered to be "in like circumstances" vis-à-vis their third-party comparators.[115] It is notable, in fact, that these investment treaties' MFN clauses did not include the likeness criterion until the conclusion of NAFTA. As the case law shows, however, ISDS tribunals consistently requested a certain degree of likeness between foreign and/or domestic comparators even without an explicit likeness requirement in the basic treaties. This jurisprudence

111 *GEA Group Aktiengesellschaft v Ukraine, Award dated 31 March 2011,* ICSID Case No. ARB/08/16 [342].

112 *Occidental Exploration and Production Company v Republic of Ecuador (I), Award dated 1 July 2004,* LCIA Case No. UN3467.

113 *Occidental v Ecuador* (n 112).

114 Jürgen Kurtz, 'The Most Favoured Nation Standard and Foreign Investment: An Uneasy Fit?' (2005) 5 The Journal of World Investment & Trade 861, 871, footnote 39.

115 Ziegler (n 79) 75.

suggests that tribunals have applied the "in like circumstances" element as an inherent feature of MFN clauses.

In this respect, tribunals would primarily consider whether investors face similar legal circumstances, including in terms of *inter alia* the aim and content of investment contracts (*Parkerings*), specific economic circumstances (*MNSS*), and the extent to which a competitive relationship exists (*Grand River*). An exception in this regard was the *Occidental* decision, where the tribunal extraordinarily broadened the scope of likeness to include third-party investors from virtually all sectors. The *Occidental* tribunal adopted a teleological approach. It based its interpretation of national and MFN treatment primarily on the objectives of the IIA in question, i.e., eliminating nationality-based discrimination, rather than on principles of treaty interpretation as embodied in the Vienna Convention on the Law of Treaties (VCLT) and customary international law, particularly the *ejusdem generis* principle.

NAFTA tribunals have been more consistent insofar as the "in like circumstances" criterion is concerned, typically looking at whether investors faced similar legal and regulatory regimes in order to determine whether they were in similar circumstances. This approach is narrower and more balanced compared to the approach taken in *Occidental*. In addition, the NAFTA approach takes the individual circumstances of investors into account as another decisive factor. Even if the legal regime's likeness is established, the enquiry does not end there: under the NAFTA approach, it is still possible that in such circumstances it is insufficient to meet the likeness criterion for the purposes of establishing a breach of the NAFTA MFN obligation. The difference in treatment might, for example, be justified by the different domestic situations faced by host state investors (such as in *Apotex*).

Determining whether investors are in like circumstances is a fact-intense and sometimes highly technical process. As can be seen above, tribunals are prone to give considerable weight to evidence such as the testimony of expert witnesses and government documents. In this regard, respondent states have an advantage when it comes to submitting evidence due to greater accessibility to the types of documents needed to illustrate the existence (or rather non-existence) of "like circumstances."

In summary, the recognition of likeness is the core issue of *de facto* MFN violation and is fact-specific. According to Kurtz, likeness "allows a possible mechanism in which to clearly sort out protectionist measures from those with merely incidental effect on foreign investors."[116] In determining whether

116 Kurtz (n 114) 886.

investors or investments are “in like circumstances,” account must be given to the applicable legal system, as well as the individual situation of the investors in question. As such, according to the Organisation for Economic Co-operation and Development (OECD), legitimate public welfare objectives should be an essential parameter for the identification of the likeness of investors and their circumstances:

> More general considerations, such as the policy objectives of Member countries, could be taken into account to define the circumstances in which comparison between foreign-controlled and domestic enterprises is permissible inasmuch as those objectives are not contrary to the principle of national treatment.[117]

Nevertheless, it remains a challenging task for a tribunal to ascertain the legitimate public welfare objectives of a host state. Other problems are the burden of proof and whether the host states would disguise discriminatory measures as measures taken in the legitimate public welfare.[118] Also, given that evidential materials usually lie in the hands of respondent governments, it turns out to be rather challenging for claimants to meet the burden of proof insofar as likeness is concerned.

Given the possible expansive interpretations by ISDS tribunals, countries have included clarifications regarding “in like circumstances” contained in the MFN clause and national treatment. For example, Article 14.5.4 of the United States-Mexico-Canada Agreement (USMCA) explicitly states that:

> For greater certainty, whether treatment is accorded in “like circumstances” under this Article depends on the totality of the circumstances, including whether the relevant treatment distinguishes between investors or investments on the basis of legitimate public welfare objectives.[119]

---

117 OECD, ‘National Treatment for Foreign-Controlled Enterprises, Including Adhering Country Exceptions to National Treatment’ (2017) 106. A copy of which is available at: <https://www.oecd.org/daf/inv/investment-policy/national-treatment-instrument-english.pdf> accessed 20 April 2022.

118 Tanjina Sharmin, *Application of Most-Favoured-Nation Clauses by Investor-State Arbitral Tribunals: Implications for the Developing Countries* (Springer 2020) 269.

119 USMCA (n 65). For more discussion on the current trend of treaty drafting in this regard, see infra Chapter 6.

2.1.2 "Less Favorable Treatment"

Once it has been established that comparator investors are "in like circumstances," less favorable treatment must be shown for claimants seeking to establish a *de facto* violation of an MFN obligation. Similar to the "in like circumstances" criterion, a finding of "less favorable treatment" is fact-specific determination when it comes to claims of *de facto* MFN violations. This issue is particularly controversial in cases where claimants seek to incorporate a higher substantive or procedural standard of protection, as will be discussed below.

Tribunals have taken different approaches to determining whether treatment accorded to a foreign comparator is more favorable. In this regard, "more favorable" has been equated with "equal," "same," or "the best." The Draft Articles deliberately avoided any reference to "equal" or "identical" in its wording. The ILC acknowledged that the term "equal treatment" is closely related to the operation of the MFN clause, while "identical" is relatively rigid and "similar" is vague. The ILC explained the reason for choosing the term "more favorable" over "same" as follows:

> [A]lthough a most-[favored]-nation pledge does not oblige the granting State to accord to the beneficiary State treatment more [favorable] than that extended to the third State, it does not exclude the possibility that the granting State may accord to the beneficiary State additional advantages beyond those extended to extended to the most-[favored] third State ... Consequently, the treatment accorded to the beneficiary State and that accorded to the third State are not necessarily 'equal'.[120]

ISDS tribunals tend to view "less favorable treatment" as requiring states to provide only the "best in jurisdiction" treatment, though not necessarily the same regime. In *Mercer*, for example, the tribunal agreed with the claimant that it was entitled to the "best in jurisdiction" treatment under Articles 1102 and 1103 of NAFTA.[121] In *Apotex*, the tribunal found that the challenged treatment "must have some not-insignificant practical negative impact" for the claimant to be considered as having received less favorable treatment.[122]

Moreover, tribunals seem to be aware of the relationship between different treatment and foreign investors' circumstances. That is, the latter might justify the former, rather than the other way around. For example, the *Mercer* tribunal held that Celgar was treated differently from two other foreign comparators.

120 International Law Commission (n 1) 23.
121 *Mercer International v Canada* (n 76) [7.37].
122 *Apotex v U.S. (III)* (n 91) [8.21].

But the different treatment "[could] best be explained on the basis of their individual circumstances" under the consistent policy adopted by Canada.[123]

In this regard, the reasoning of *Parkerings* tribunal was somewhat confusing. When addressing the difference in treatment asserted by the claimant, the tribunal noted that "an objective justification may justify differentiated treatments of similar cases,"[124] and that "the situation of the two investors will not be in like circumstances if a justification of the different treatment is established."[125] In a later paragraph analyzing the case's facts, the tribunal stated two significant differences between the claimant and the most-favored foreign comparator, which justified the different treatment they received.[126] It appears that the tribunal equated the distinct individual circumstances with justification for less favorable treatment, which in turn constitutes a decisive element for investors to be in particular circumstances.

This decision raises the question of whether there is some logical connection between "different treatment" and "in like circumstances" in relation to claims of *de facto* MFN obligation violations, especially given the variety of analytical steps adopted by tribunals in this regard. These steps start with whether investors are in like circumstances and end with whether the claimant is treated less favorably.[127] Indeed, a finding of an MFN breach requires that the claimant was treated *less favorably* than other foreign investors *in like circumstances*. Under this formulation, less favorable treatment and in like circumstances are two independent and parallel requirements, and the absence of either is not sufficient to establish an MFN violation.

In summary, "less favorable treatment" and "in like circumstances" are two crucial constitutive elements of MFN clauses. Seemingly different treatment can be justified on the basis that different investors in fact find themselves in different circumstances, whether legal or factual. In this regard, the "in like circumstances" criterion could be broadly applied because these circumstances may include scenarios such as when the respondent state claims to have carried out a governmental policy in a consistent and non-discriminatory manner,[128] or the investor has not proven to be a qualifying investor in the territory of the host state.[129] However, claimants must overcome a significant technical

123 *Mercer International v Canada* (n 76) [7.45].
124 *Parkerings v Lithuania* (n 106) [368].
125 *Parkerings v Lithuania* (n 106) [375].
126 *Parkerings v Lithuania* (n 106) [410].
127 *Grand River v U.S.* (n 99) [163]; *Bayindir v Pakistan* (n 81) [416]; *Cargill v Mexico* (n 97) [228].
128 *Mercer v Canada* (n 76).
129 *Cargill v Mexico* (n 97).

threshold to establish a *de facto* MFN violation: that is, providing the evidence to support it.

2.1.3 Burden of Proof

The Latin maxim *actori incumbit (onus) probandi* means the one who alleges a thing must prove that thing; that is, it is the party who presents a particular version of the facts of a case who must establish the existence of such facts.[130] It is a legal principle in relation to evidence that is widely accepted in most jurisdictions, including in arbitration rules. For example, Article 27(1) of the United Nations Commission on International Trade Law (UNCITRAL) Arbitration Rules (UNCITRAL rules) provides that:

> Each party shall have the burden of proving the facts relied on to support its claim or [defense].[131]

In ISDS practice, claimants' failure to meet their burden of proof is a significant reason for tribunals to reject *de facto* MFN claims. According to the *Apotex* tribunal, for example, the legal burden of proof should be distinguished from the evidential burden of proof. The former stays with the claimant, while the latter shifts during the proceedings.[132] Therefore, the claimant and the respondent state must each prove their respective positive cases.[133] Notably, the

130 *Pulp Mills on the River Uruguay (Argentina v Uruguay), Judgment of 20 April 2010*, ICJ [162]. See also: Aaron X Fellmeth and Maurice Horwitz, *Guide to Latin in International Law* (Oxford University Press 2009).

131 UNCITRAL Arbitration Rules. A copy of which is available at: <https://uncitral.un.org/sites/uncitral.un.org/files/media-documents/uncitral/en/uncitral-arbitration-rules-2013-e.pdf> accessed 20 April 2022.

132 *Apotex v U.S. (III)* (n 91) [8.7].

133 *Apotex v U.S. (III)* (n 91) [8.8]. Similar position was held in *Marvin v Mexico*, whereby the tribunal quoted and emphasized the statement of the WTO Appellate Body in *U.S. – Wool Shirts and Blouses*, where it was stated that: 'Various international tribunals, including the International Court of Justice, have generally and consistently accepted and applied the rule that the party who asserts a fact, whether the claimant or respondent, is responsible for providing proof thereof. Also, it is a generally accepted canon of evidence in civil law, common law and, in fact, most jurisdiction, that the burden of proof rests upon the party, whether complaining or defending, who asserts the affirmative of a claim or [defense]. *If that party adduces evidence sufficient to raise a presumption that what is claimed is true, the burden then shifts to the other party, who will fail unless it adduces sufficient evidence to rebut the presumption.*' See: *Marvin Feldman v Mexico, Award dated 16 December 2002* ICSID Case No. ARB(AF)/99/1 [177], citing Appellate Body Report, *United States – Measures Affecting Imports of Woven Wool Shirts and Blouses from India (US – Wool Shirts and Blouses)*, WT/DS33/AB/R, 14.

evidential burden of proof shifts towards the respondent state during the arbitral proceeding and "requires it to rebut the evidence adduced by the claimant." Otherwise, the *Apotex* tribunal continued, "the claimant would be left to prove its case from whatever incomplete documentary evidence and witness testimony the respondent state may choose to present," which would inevitably render the task an impossible one.[134]

In *Grand River*, the issue pertained to whether the claimant had submitted sufficient evidence to show that he was in like circumstances to other foreign comparators. The claimant argued that the "strategic" burden of proof has shifted to the respondent state to justify the different treatment. The tribunal declined to accept this argument because the claimant had not met his burden of proof to show that he had been treated differently in the first place.[135]

The *Mercer* tribunal followed a similar approach in this regard. It agreed with the Article 1128 NAFTA submissions by the U.S. and Mexico, both of which argued that nothing in the text of Articles 1102 and 1103 of NAFTA suggested a shift in the burden of proof, which should accordingly remain with the claimant.[136] The tribunal then emphasized the distinction between the legal and evidential burden of proof, citing the *Pulp Mills* decision by the ICJ, which held that the burden is on the party alleging specific facts to prove the existence of such facts, according to *onus probandi incumbit actori*.[137] The *Mercer* tribunal thus concluded that while the legal burden of proof remains with the claimant, the question of whether the evidential burden shifts to the respondent remains relevant.[138] As such, the tribunal dismissed the Article 1103 claim because *Mercer* failed to provide sufficient evidence that it was in like circumstances with the ostensible comparators, and the claimant accordingly never discharged its evidential burden of proof, which therefore never shifted to the respondent.[139]

The *Bayindir* case is another instance in which the tribunal dismissed an MFN claim due to the claimant's failure to meet its burden of proof. *Bayindir* submitted a press report to show that it was being treated less favorably than other contractors.[140] The tribunal determined that in order to substantiate an MFN breach, the claimant had to, as a first step, discharge its legal burden

134 *Apotex v U.S. (III)* (n 91) [8.68].
135 *Grand River v U.S.* (n 99).
136 *Mercer International v Canada* (n 76) [7.12–13].
137 *Mercer International v Canada* (n 76) [7.15], citing *Pulp Mills* (n 128) [162].
138 *Mercer International v Canada* (n 76) [7.16].
139 *Mercer International v Canada* (n 76) [7.45].
140 *Bayindir v Pakistan* (n 81) [412].

of proof with sufficient evidence showing it was "in like circumstances" with other contractors.[141] The tribunal ruled that the relevant evidence is "clearly insufficient" to support the claimant's position. At the end of its reasoning, the tribunal acknowledged that it was aware of the claimant's difficulty discharging its burden of proof, mostly when the necessary documents were not readily available to it. It also noted, however, that a shift of the burden of proof to the respondent would require a higher degree of substantiation by the claimant. Accordingly, the tribunal ruled out any violation of the MFN clause in question.[142]

Burden of proof has not been systematically explored as a concern in the MFN context. Based on the ISDS practice of *de facto* MFN treatment, however, one may safely conclude that tribunals are generally of the view that there may come a time when the evidentiary burden of proof in relation to particular points in case shift during the course of arbitral proceedings. On the one hand, the legal burden of proof remains with the claimant and does not shift, indicating that the claimant bears the overall duty to substantiate its MFN claim. On the other hand, the evidential burden of proof may shift during the proceeding. Once it does, and the respondent state fails to rebut the claimant's allegation with sufficient evidence, the tribunal will side with the claimant.[143] Finally, for the burden of proof to shift, the submitted evidence should be enough to establish a *prima facie* case that the MFN obligation in question has been violated.

This reasoning is well reflected in the *Parkerings* case. While Parkerings claimed that BP was in like circumstances with Pinus Proprius because both foreign companies were bidding for the same construction project, Lithuania argued that they were in different situations based on the contract's content and the two companies' respective statuses. The tribunal took into account evidence from both sides and ruled that BP and Pinus were not in like circumstances.[144] This relates to another concern that the *Apotex* tribunal has raised: the documents essential to proving certain claims were far more accessible to the respondent government than to the claimant.[145] Since international instruments such as ICSID Arbitration Rules do not provide an Anglo-Saxon form of automatic disclosure of all potentially relevant documents,[146]

141 *Bayindir v Pakistan* (n 81) [417].
142 *Bayindir v Pakistan* (n 81) [418].
143 *Apotex v U.S. (III)* (n 91) [8.65].
144 *Parkerings v Lithuania* (n 106) [410–430].
145 *Apotex v U.S. (III)* (n 91) [8.66].
146 ICSID Arbitration Rules (2022), available at <https://icsid.worldbank.org/resources/rules-and-regulations/convention/arbitration-rules> accessed 20 April 2022.

the crucial documents could be exclusively controlled by the respondent government not available for production to the tribunal.

2.1.4 Discriminatory Intent

One final consideration when it comes to claims of *de facto* MFN violations is the question of whether there must be discriminatory *intent* on the part of the respondent state.

States have consistently argued that the finding of an MFN violation requires proof of discrimination on the basis of nationality. In this regard, OECD has clarified that the key to determining whether a discriminatory measure applied to foreign-controlled enterprises constitutes an exception to non-discrimination is to ascertain whether the discrimination is motivated by the fact that the enterprises in question are under foreign control.[147] In *Bayindir*, Pakistan claimed that evidence of intent is necessary to prove a violation of the MFN clause. The tribunal disagreed. It held that under the wording of the MFN clause *in casu*, proof of discrimination against an investor who happens to be a foreigner is sufficient. In this regard, the tribunal agreed with the *Feldman* tribunal's reasoning regarding national treatment in terms of Article 1102 of NAFTA. The *Feldman* tribunal believed that the national treatment standard was designed to prevent discrimination based on or because of nationality. However, for that tribunal, "it [was] not self-evident ... that any departure from national treatment must be explicitly shown to be a result of the investor's nationality" but that "[r]ather, Article 1102 by its terms suggests that it is sufficient to show less favorable treatment for the foreign investor than for domestic investors in like circumstances."[148]

The tribunal also discussed this issue from an evidentiary perspective, asserting that "[r]equiring a foreign investor to prove that discrimination is based on his nationality could be an insurmountable burden to the Claimant, as that information may only be available to the government."[149] The tribunal was also concerned that if national and MFN treatment breaches were to be limited to discrimination explicitly based on nationality, it would significantly restrict the effectiveness of national treatment and MFN clauses in protecting the interests of foreign investors. Therefore, it would tend to excuse discrimination that is not ostensibly directed at foreign-owned investments.[150]

---

147 OECD (n 117).

148 *Bayindir v Pakistan* (n 81) [390], citing: *Marvin Feldman v Mexico* (n 131) [181].

149 *Bayindir v Pakistan* (n 81) [390], citing: *Marvin Feldman v Mexico* (n 131) [183].

150 *Marvin Feldman v. Mexico* (n 131) [83–84]. To this end, the tribunal referred to *Pope&Talbot* (n 82) [78–79], which shared similar concern.

NAFTA countries have taken a consistent position on this issue, albeit that tribunals have issued slightly different decisions. In *Mercer*, the tribunal rejected the claimant's submission on the irrelevance of respondent state's discriminatory intent. On the contrary, the tribunal followed the approach advocated for by Mexico and the U.S. in their Article 1128 submissions as non-disputing parties. Both submissions argued that the claimant must show the link between discrimination and nationality. Specifically, the U.S. and Mexico argued that the alleged discrimination should be "with respect to," "on the basis of," or "[have] the effect of" discriminating against foreign investors as a class with no rational or good faith policy objectives.[151]

NAFTA parties made similar submissions in *Grand River*. The U.S. contended that to establish a violation of national or MFN treatment, the claimant must show that the alleged different treatment was "on account of" or "related to" a foreign investor's nationality. The tribunal did not determine this issue because the claimant had already failed to provide sufficient evidence in relation to its allegation that it had received less favorable treatment.[152]

The *Thunderbird* tribunal adopted a different position on this issue. In relation to Article 1102 of NAFTA, the tribunal found that Thunderbird was not expected to explicitly show that the less favorable treatment it received was based on nationality because "the text of Article 1102 of the NAFTA [did] not require such showing."[153]

The issue of discriminatory intent has not been as contentious an issue as the others discussed above. Indeed, most MFN clauses do not require a motivation based on nationality behind the difference in treatment. Requiring claimants to prove discriminatory intent would be to require them to meet a significant burden of proof, as noted by the *Bayindir* tribunal.

MFN treatment is designed to guarantee non-discriminatory treatment to foreign investors and level the playing field for foreign investors of different nationalities. In this regard, *de facto* MFN violations have well demonstrated the nature of MFN treatment. First, *de facto* MFN claims are based on claimants' actual treatment in practice, which should be compared to the treatment received by other foreign investors. This application echoes the formulation and objectives of modern MFN clauses as noted above.

Second, successfully bringing a *de facto* MFN claim is heavily dependent on evidence, which is significant because it is generally accepted that the legal

151 *Mercer v Canada* (n 76) [7.8–9] and footnote 242.

152 *Mercer v Canada* (n 76) [171].

153 *International Thunderbird Gaming Corporation v The United Mexican States, Award dated 26 January 2006,* UNCITRAL Arbitration [177].

burden of proof remains with the claimant throughout an arbitration (even though the evidential burden of proof may shift during the course of proceedings). An examination of the above cases has shown that the determination of whether comparators are "in like circumstances" is a fact-specific and evidence-intense process. As a result, tribunals do not usually rely on general international law concerning treaty interpretation when they are required to determine whether a *de facto* MFN claim can be sustained – the situation is quite different when it comes to attempts by claimants to incorporate a higher standard of protection, an issue which is examined in the next section.

2.2 *Invoking an MFN Clause in Pursuit of Obtaining a Higher Standard of Protection*

This section discusses a different aspect of the application of MFN clauses; one that has generated far more controversy than that of *de facto* MFN violations: that is, the invocation of an MFN clause in pursuit of incorporating different provisions contained in third-party treaties.

The practice of incorporating substantive provisions from third treaties goes back to the case *AAPL*. The *AAPL* tribunal believed that the basic treaty between Sri Lanka and UK "[was] not a self-contained closed legal system limited to provide for substantive material rules of direct applicability, but it has to be envisaged within a wider juridical context in which rules from other sources are integrated through implied incorporation methods, or by direct reference to certain supplementary rules, whether of international law character or of domestic law nature."[154] The tribunal accordingly held that "such extension of the applicable legal system resorts clearly from Article 3.(1), Article 3.(2) [the MFN provision], and Article 4 [the "compensation for losses" clause] of the BIT."[155]

In practice, tribunals tend to allow the application of MFN clause to incorporate higher protection standards from third-party treaties.[156] However, as shown below, tribunals that have approved of this practice have not done so with a strict devotion to the text of the various MFN clauses that were at issue in those cases. Instead, they have relied largely on presumptions about MFN

154 *Asian Agricultural Products Ltd (AAPL) v Republic of Sri Lanka, Award dated 27 June 1990*, ICSID Case No. ARB/87/3 [21].

155 *AAPL v Sri Lanka* (n 154).

156 However, according to Cole, 'an MFN clause in an investment treaty should not usually be understood as giving the beneficiary of the clause access to more favorable treatment in a preexisting third-party treaty, although it can give access to preexisting nontreaty treatment', see: Cole (n 2) 573.

clauses as a tool which seeks to multilateralize, which has enabled them to incorporate brand new and unanticipated standards through applying a broad interpretive approach to MFN clauses in basic treaties.[157]

In addition, the incorporated standards are more broadly drafted and therefore are considered to provide a higher standard of protection compared to the basic treaty, which contains a similar but more restrictive provision or simply does not contain such provision. This also brings into question as to whether MFN clauses have been applied by tribunals in a way that enables abusive treaty-shopping that was unanticipated by the contracting parties when concluding the basic treaties.[158] The argument adopted here is that these presumptions in relation to the application of MFN clauses is indicative of tribunals having lost sight of the importance of the core interpretive methods of international law, especially the *ejusdem generis* principle, and has facilitated treaty-shopping and the abuse of rights accorded to foreign investors.[159] Instead, tribunals should take into account the specific text of individual MFN clauses and interpret them in accordance with the *ejusdem generis* principle.

The frequently incorporated provisions or "higher standards of protection" from third-party treaties are treaty clauses relating to fair and equitable treatment (FET), full protection and security, expropriation, and umbrella clause. They will be discussed separately below.

2.2.1 The Incorporation of Fair and Equitable Treatment (FET) Clauses

Fair and equitable treatment (FET) clauses are common in IIAs.[160] They protect foreign investors and investments from discriminatory or other unfair measures.[161] ISDS tribunals have accepted invocations of MFN clauses in basic treaties in order to incorporate FET provisions from third-party treaties. "More favorable" FET clauses are usually not formulated in accordance with

157 Efraim Chalamish, 'The Future of Bilateral Investment Treaties: A de Facto Multilateral Agreement?' (2009) 34 Brooklyn Journal of International Law 304, 323.

158 For an in-depth discussion about treaty shopping in investment regime, see: Jorun Baumgartner, *Treaty Shopping in International Investment Law* (Oxford University Press 2016).

159 Sharmin (n 118) Chapter 4.

160 Patrick Dumberry, 'Has the Fair and Equitable Treatment Standard Become a Rule of Customary International Law?' (2016) 8 Journal of International Dispute Settlement 155, 1–2. In this research, the author examined all the BITs available on UNCTAD's IIA database and found that out of all 1964 BITs, only 50 did not contain FET in any form, while 25 referred to FET in their preambles. These treaties constitute less than 5 percent of all examined BITs.

161 Dumberry (n 160). Suleimenova (n 22) 166.

the minimum standard of treatment (MST) accorded to investors under customary international law. They are therefore also referred to as "stand-alone," "autonomous," or "independent" FET clauses.[162] This subsection focuses on relevant case law dealing with claimants' attempts to incorporate a new FET standard from other treaties. It looks specifically at the interpretation of MFN clauses in basic treaties adopted by tribunals in approving such incorporation, and respondent states' opposition to such incorporation. In this regard, the analysis begins with the decisions of NAFTA tribunals, given the noticeable difference between NAFTA tribunals and non-NAFTA tribunals on this issue.

NAFTA tribunals have generally been influenced by the 2001 "Notes of Interpretation of Certain Chapter 11 Provisions" (the Notes) released by the Free Trade Commission (FTC).[163] According to the Notes, Article 1105 of NAFTA should be linked to MST under customary international law, and that such a FET standard does not require treatment in addition to or beyond that which is required by the customary international law minimum standard of treatment of aliens.[164] The first NAFTA tribunal to confront this issue was the *Pope & Talbot* tribunal, which ruled that NAFTA investors should enjoy protection in terms of the MST under Article 1105 of NAFTA in addition to a "fairness elements."[165] The tribunal questioned the restrictive application of Article 1105, which would only attach to "egregiously unfair conduct" under customary international law and would also run counter to Articles 1102 (on national treatment) and 1103 (on MFN treatment) of NAFTA. The tribunal found that even if Article 1105 provided for the restrictive version of FET as envisioned under customary international law, NAFTA investors would still be entitled to resort to Article 1103 in order to incorporate a more favorable FET clause:

> NAFTA investors and investments that would be denied access to the fairness elements untrammeled by the 'egregious' conduct threshold that

162 Patrick Dumberry, 'Shopping for a Better Deal: The Use of MFN Clauses to Get "Better" Fair and Equitable Treatment Protection' [2016] Arbitration International 1.

163 NAFTA Free Trade Commission, 'NAFTA Notes of Interpretation of Certain Chapter 11 Provisions' July 2001. A copy of which is available at: <http://www.sice.oas.org/tpd/nafta/Commission/CH11understanding_e.asp> accessed 20 April 2022.

164 Patrick Dumberry, 'The Importation of the FET Standard through MFN Clauses: An Empirical Study of BITs' (2017) 32 ICSID Review 116. See also: Patrick Dumberry, *The Fair and Equitable Treatment Standard: A Guide to NAFTA Case Law on Article 1105* (Kluwer Law International 2013).

165 *Pope & Talbot v Canada* (n 82) [110].

> Canada would graft onto Article 1105 would simply turn to Articles 1102 and 1103 for relief.[166]

However, the tribunal did not apply the incorporated FET clause to the case's facts because the claimant withdrew its Article 1103 claim and focused instead on the FET claim within the NAFTA context. After the Notes were published, the tribunal expressed its concern that the Notes could lead to the absurd result of relief denied under Article 1105 but restored under Article 1103.[167] The tribunal repeated its position in its subsequent award in 2002, emphasizing NAFTA investors' rights to enjoy the same unlimited FET as non-NAFTA investors through applying the MFN clause.[168]

In the case of *ADF*, a Canadian investor sought to invoke Article 1103 of NAFTA in order to incorporate a third-party FET clause that purportedly offered a higher standard of treatment. To this end, it invoked the U.S.-Albania and U.S.-Estonia BITs. Both treaties contain FET clauses that are not directly related to customary international law.[169] The tribunal rejected the claims brought by ADF on two grounds. First, it declined to decide that the third-party treaties contained a better, autonomous FET standard distinct from the one envisioned by NAFTA because the investor did not provide sufficient evidence in this direction.[170] Moreover, the tribunal applied Article 1108(7)(a) on MFN exceptions relating to government procurement, thereby precluding reliance on Article 1103 by ADF in order to obtain better treatment *in casu*.[171] Later, the *Mesa* tribunal agreed with the *ADF* tribunal and also applied Article 1108(7)(a) in rejecting a claim which relied on Article 1103 to incorporate supposedly better treatment from a third-party treaty.[172]

166 *Pope & Talbot v Canada* (n 82) [117].

167 *Pope & Talbot v Canada* (n 82) [118].

168 *Pope & Talbot v Government of Canada, Award in Respect of Damages dated 31 May 2002*, UNCITRAL Arbitration [9].

169 *ADF v U.S.* (n 68), *Investor's Reply to the U.S. Counter-Memorial on Competence and Liability dated 28 January 2002* [221]. In this context, Article 3(a) of the Albania – U.S. BIT (1995) provides that: "Each Party shall in no case accord treatment less favorable than that required by international law". See also: Article II(3)(a) of the Estonia – U.S. BIT (1994), available at <https://investmentpolicy.unctad.org/international-investment-agreements/treaty-files/1161/download> accessed 20 April 2022.

170 *ADF v U.S.* (n 68) [194].

171 *ADF v U.S.* (n 68) [197, 198]. For some scholars, the ADF case indicates the limited effectiveness of the MFN clause that contains explicit restrictions. See: Stephan W Schill, *The Multilateralization of International Investment Law* (Cambridge University Press 2009) 142–143.

172 *Mesa Power Group LLC v Government of Canada, Award dated 24 March 2016*, PCA Case No. 2012–17 [507].

In *Chemtura*, the claimant referred to Canadian BITs signed after the conclusion of NAFTA and argued that it was entitled to the supposedly higher FET standards in those treaties under Article 1103. Specifically, the treaties relied on by the claimant contained FET clauses which sought to mirror "international law" or "principles of international law." Canada contended that these treaties do not offer more favorable treatment than Article 1105 of NAFTA since they link FET to MST. Moreover, Article 1103 could not alter the substantive content of Article 1105.[173] The tribunal declined to accept the claimant's argument because it had failed to substantiate its claim that it had been discriminated against in any form by Canada, so its claim lacked legal merit.[174]

As to whether Article 1103 could be used to incorporate a higher FET standard than the one contained in Article 1105, the tribunal pointed out that the Canadian BITs identified by the claimant had not been shown to provide for a higher FET standard than Article 1105.[175] The tribunal further explained that it had found "no facts in the conduct of the respondent that would even come close to the type of treatment required for a breach of the FET standard."[176] On the contrary, "the records show[ed] that the respondent treated the Claimant and its investment in good faith and on an equal footing with other registrants."[177] Therefore, the tribunal would have reached the same conclusion even if a higher standard could be incorporated through reliance on Article 1103.[178]

In *Apotex*, the claimant invoked Article II(6) of the U.S.-Jamaica BIT, which obliged the contracting states to provide "effective means" to assert claims and enforce rights.[179] The claimant argued that the treatment offered by Article II(6) included judicial or adjudicative proceedings and administrative decisions by the respondent, such as the FDA's decision to impose the import alert on products manufactured at two of its production facilities. Therefore, the

173 Mexico and U.S. also agreed with Canada in their Article 1128 submissions. See: *Crompton (Chemtura) Corp v Government of Canada,* UNCITRAL Arbitration, 'U.S. Article 1128 Submission' dated 31 July 2009; 'Mexico's Article 1128 Submission dated 31 July 2009.

174 *Chemtura v Canada* (n 173), *Award dated 2 August 2010* [234].

175 Specifically, the tribunal held that 'the Claimant has not established that the FET clause of any of the treaties to which it indistinctly refers grants any additional measure of protection not afforded by Article 1105 of NAFTA.' See: *Chemtura v Canada* (n 173), *Award dated 2 August 2010* [236].

176 *Chemtura v Canada* (n 173), *Award dated 2 August 2010* [236].

177 *Chemtura v Canada* (n 173), *Award dated 2 August 2010.*

178 *Chemtura v Canada* (n 173), *Award dated 2 August 2010* [235]; Suleimenova (n 22).

179 U.S. – Jamaica BIT (1994), available at: <https://investmentpolicy.unctad.org/international-investment-agreements/treaty-files/1726/download> accessed 20 April 2022.

claimant asserted that the respondent had failed to provide it with "effective means" to challenge the import alert.[180] The *Apotex* tribunal did not comment on Article 1103's ability to incorporate a new standard of treatment from other BITs signed by the U.S. It rejected the claimant's argument and relied instead on an interpretation of Article II(6) in terms of the proper interpretive principles of international law. According to the tribunal, the plain language of Article II(6), which referred only to adjudicatory proceedings, indicated to the tribunal that it did not apply to *non-adjudicatory* proceedings such as the import alert in question.[181]

In summary, all the above NAFTA tribunals declined invocations of the MFN clause in the basic treaty in order to incorporate a higher FET standard contained in a third-party treaty. Tribunals' reasonings in these cases suggest that the importation of a higher FET standard requires two essential elements. First, a broad MFN clause in the basic treaty.[182] In this sense, NAFTA tribunals have emphasized the MFN text instead of a general presumption for an expansive MFN interpretation. Second, a stand-alone FET clause that is deemed "more favorable" than that linked to MST (unlike in *ADF* and *Chemtura*, where the third-party FET was also bound by international law and therefore could not be deemed to entail a requirement of "better treatment").[183]

The situation is more complicated in non-NAFTA cases, as will be discussed below. As case law discussed here highlights, the interpretive methods and positions adopted by non-NAFTA tribunals is divided according to whether the basic treaty in question contains FET clause.

In *MTD*, Article 3(1) of the basic treaty between Chile and Malaysia offered MFN treatment in connection with FET. It read as follows:

> Investments made by investors of either Contracting Party in the territory of the other Contracting Party shall receive treatment which is fair and equitable, and not less favourable than that accorded to investments made by investors of any third State.[184]

180 *Apotex v U.S. (III)* (n 91) [9.67].

181 *Apotex v U.S. (III)* (n 91) [9.70].

182 Some scholars also hold the same opinion. See: Dumberry (n 162) 6.

183 Dumberry (n 162).

184 Chile – Malaysia BIT (1992), a copy of which is available at: <https://investmentpolicy.unctad.org/international-investment-agreements/treaty-files/690/download> accessed 20 April 2022; *MTD Equity Sdn Bhd and MTD Chile SA v Chile, Award dated 25 May 2004,* ICSID Case No. ARB/01/7 [101].

The dispute in *MTD* involved the Chilean Ministry of Housing and Urban Development's alleged refusal to rezone an area for the claimant's use. The claimant argued that by refusing to rezone the land, which was initially for agricultural purposes, Chile breached the FET standard in Article 3(1) of the 1993 Chile-Denmark BIT and Article 3(2) of the 1994 Chile-Croatia BIT, which it sought to incorporate into the basic treaty through the MFN clause.[185] Article 3(2) of the Chile-Croatia BIT required that the contracting parties grant "necessary permits" after a foreign investment is admitted.[186] While Article 3(1) of the Chile-Denmark BIT provides that contracting parties should observe any obligation they may have entered into regarding foreign investments.[187] Such requirements, however, was absent from the FET clause in the Chile-Malaysia BIT.

The *MTD* tribunal allowed the incorporation of the higher FET standards from the third-party BITs for two reasons. First, it relied on the objective of the basic BIT, which was to "protect investments and create conditions favorable to investments" to support a broad interpretation of the MFN clause in the basic treaty.[188] It noted that invoking the MFN clause to incorporate the treaty protections from Chile-Denmark BIT and the Chile- Croatia BIT was " in consonance with this purpose."[189] Second, the tribunal also referred to the MFN exceptions therein, noting that the reference to non-BIT issues such as tax treatment and regional cooperation in the exclusion list indicated the MFN clause's broad nature. For the tribunal, the MFN clause should apply to FET clause *a contrario* since the latter was not included in the exceptions.[190]

Some scholars agree with the *MTD* tribunal's reasoning and attribute the tribunal's decision to the wording of the MFN clause in the basic treaty, which provides for MFN treatment in relation to FET.[191] However, in the case's

185 *MTD v Chile* (n 184) [197].

186 It provides that 'when a Contracting Party has admitted an investment in its territory, it shall grant the necessary permits in accordance with its laws and regulations.' See: Article 3(2) of the Chile – Croatia BIT (1994), a copy of which is available at: <https://investmentpolicy.unctad.org/international-investment-agreements/treaty-files/667/download> accessed 20 April 2022. Article 2(2) of the Chile-Malaysia BIT, however, only states that "investments of investors of either Contracting Party shall at all times be accorded fair and equitable treatment". See: Article 2(2) of the Chile-Malaysia BIT (n 184).

187 Article 3(1) of the Chile – Denmark BIT (1993), a copy of which is available at: <https://investmentpolicy.unctad.org/international-investment-agreements/treaty-files/671/download> accessed 20 April 2022.

188 *MTD v Chile* (n 184) [104].

189 *MTD v Chile* (n 184).

190 *MTD v Chile* (n 184).

191 Dumberry (n 162).

annulment proceedings, the Annulment Committee adopted an even broader understanding of MFN treatment. It found that the MFN clause, although formulated in combination with FET, "[was] not limited to attracting more [favorable] levels of treatment accorded to investments from third States only where they can be considered to fall within the scope of the fair and equitable treatment standard." On the contrary, it "attract[ed] any more [favorable] treatment extended to third State investments and [did] so unconditionally."[192] This approach is problematic because it ignores the text of the MFN clause, which was explicitly linked to FET and should have been be applied this way. By allowing a broad interpretation of the MFN clause, the Committee was actually applying the clause as a multilateralization tool, which approach runs contrary to the text of the basic treaty.

The *Paushok* tribunal dealt with a similarly worded MFN clause in the Mongolia-Russia BIT. Article 3 thereof provides as follows:

> 1. Each Contracting Party shall, in its territory, accord investments of investors of the other Contracting Party and activities associated with investments fair and equitable treatment excluding the application of measures that might impair the operation and disposal with investments.
> 2. The treatment mentioned under paragraph 1 of this Article, shall not be less favorable than treatment accorded to investments and activities associated with investments of its own investors or investors of any third state.[193]

Relying on the above provision, the claimant sought to incorporate unlimited FET and a broader standard of "non-impairment by unreasonable and discriminatory measures [of] the management, operation, maintenance, use, enjoyment, acquisition, expansion or disposal of investments" from Article 3(1) of the Denmark-Mongolia BIT and Article 2(2)(a) of the U.S.-Mongolia BIT.[194] The tribunal supported incorporating a broader FET standard through

192 *MTD v Chile, Decision on Annulment dated 16 February 2007*, ICSID Case No. ARB/01/7 [64]. Julie A Maupi, 'MFN-Based Jurisdiction in Investor-State Arbitration: Is There Any Hope for a Consistent Approach?' (2011) 14 Journal of International Economic Law 157.

193 Article 3 of the Mongolia – Russia BIT (1995). A copy of which is available at: <https://investmentpolicy.unctad.org/international-investment-agreements/treaty-files/2023/download> accessed 20 April 2022.

194 *Sergei Paushok, CJSC Golden East Company and CJSC Vostokneftegaz Company v The Government of Mongolia, Award on Jurisdiction and Liability dated 28 April 2011*, UNCITRAL Arbitration [242].

applying the MFN clause in the Mongolia-Russia BIT as a matter of principle. It stated that in the case of a third-party treaty including a higher FET standard between Mongolia and another State, investors under the Mongolia-Russia BIT are "entitled to invoke it."[195] However, the tribunal added that such an extension of substantive treatment is limited to FET and that the MFN clause could not be applied to introduce into the treaty completely new substantive standards. This position was a reflection of the *ejusdem generis* principle and was fatal when the tribunal addressed the claimant's attempt to invoke an umbrella clause in the same case.[196] Umbrella clauses are further examined in a later subsection.

The *White Industries* dispute concerned the delayed enforcement of an International Chamber of Commerce (ICC) award in favor of the claimant. However, White Industries could not collect the compensation India was ordered to pay in terms of the said award for several years. Therefore, White Industries brought a claim against India under the UNCITRAL rules based on the India-Australia BIT. It alleged that India had violated the FET standard, obligations to protect against expropriation, MFN treatment standard, and the requirement that funds be allowed to be freely transferred out of the host country under the BIT by delaying the enforcement of the ICC award.[197]

To this end, the claimant attempted to invoke the MFN clause in the India-Australia BIT to import Article 4(5) of the India-Kuwait BIT, which required the contracting parties "in accordance with its applicable laws and regulations, [to] ... provide effective means of asserting claims and enforcing rights with respect to investments."[198] The India-Australia BIT, however, did not provide for the "effective means" protection guaranteed in terms of the India-Kuwait BIT.[199] India contended that using the MFN clause to expand the content of FET under the basic treaty would not only "fundamentally subvert the carefully negotiated balance of the BIT," but also run contrary to the emphasis in the BIT on domestic law.

Concerning the first argument, the tribunal explicitly distinguished procedural and substantive treatment. It stated that India's concern related to dispute settlement provisions and that the inclusion of a higher substantive standard does not "subvert" the negotiated balance of the BIT. On the contrary,

195 *Paushok v Mongolia* (n 194) [570].

196 *Paushok v Mongolia* (n 194).

197 *White Industries Australia Limited v The Republic of India, Final Award dated 30 November 2011*, UNCITRAL Arbitration.

198 *White Industries v India* (n 197) [11.1.4].

199 Australia – India BIT (1999), available at: <https://investmentpolicy.unctad.org/international-investment-agreements/treaty-files/154/download> accessed 20 April 2022.

according to the tribunal, incorporating a foreign standard in the BIT through an MFN clause "achieve[d] exactly the result which the parties intended."[200] The *White Industries* tribunal's position was questioned by Sharmin, who asked on what basis the tribunal distinguished procedural and substantive treatment, thus allowing the incorporation of the latter but not the former.[201] Moreover, it seems that the tribunal had also assumed that the MFN clause in that case had unlimited power to multilateralize substantive benefits.[202]

As to the second argument, the tribunal explained that the reference to domestic law is not an uncommon treaty practice in BITs. It did not suggest, however, that national laws either prevail over international laws or influence the interpretation of BIT obligations.[203] Therefore, according to the tribunal, it would have been "inappropriate to read-in an exception to MFN treatment because of the references in the BIT to domestic law."[204] After adopting the "effective means" standard from the Kuwait-India BIT, the tribunal then relied on the *Chevron* award to specify the "effective means" standard concerning the enforcement of rights and asserting claims since the "effective means" provision in *Chevron* was identically worded to the one contained in Kuwait-India BIT.[205]

It is worth mentioning that the tribunal dismissed White Industries' claim that the delay in relation to the enforcement of the ICC award violated the FET clause in the basic treaty. The tribunal held that India's conduct did not constitute a "denial of justice" because the claimant had not yet exhausted local remedies. In this regard, the tribunal took the same approach as the *Chevron* tribunal in respect of whether the "effective means" standard is a "less demanding" test.[206]

---

200 *White Industries v India* (197) [11.2.4].
201 Sharmin (n 118) 124.
202 Sharmin (n 118) 124.
203 *White Industries v India* (n 197) [11.2.4]. In this regard, the tribunal quoted Stephan Schill's opinion in the following terms: 'The sole relevant factor is whether MFN treatment applies or whether it is subject to an explicit or implicit exception. Furthermore, distinguishing between specifically negotiated provisions and other provisions would introduce different classes of provisions within the same treaty period … [there is] no room for creating a specific class of 'specifically negotiated' provisions of the basic treaty that is per se immune from circumvention by more favourable treatment in third-party BITs, unless those provisions can be read as constituting an exception to MFN treatment.' See Schill (n 171) 146.
204 *White Industries v India* (n 197) [11.2.9].
205 *White Industries v India* (n 197) [11.3].
206 *White Industries v India* (n 197) [11.3.2].

Whether the reasoning in *Chevron* should have been applied in *White Industries* is questionable. Although the two "effective means" clauses share the same wording, the former is nevertheless not part of a BIT signed *by India* and therefore should not in effect bind it to a commitment it never made. In addition, by allowing the claimant to rely on a new standard from another treaty, the award also raised concerns about treaty-shopping.[207] Consequently, India did not include an MFN clause in its 2015 model BIT, ostensibly in response to the *White Industries* arbitration award.

In *Bayindir*, the basic treaty between Pakistan and Turkey did not contain a FET clause in its main text. However, it did refer to FET in the preamble, stating that "fair and equitable treatment of investment is desirable in order to maintain a stable framework for investment and maximum effective utilization of economic resources."[208] The claimant attempted to invoke the MFN clause in order to incorporate FET standards from other treaties Pakistan had concluded with *inter alia* the UK and Switzerland.

The MFN clause in Article II(2) of the Pakistan-Turkey BIT provided as follows:

> Each Party shall accord to these investments, once established, treatment no less [favorable] than that accorded in similar situations to investments of its investors or to investments of investors of any third country, whichever is the most [favorable].[209]

It was limited by the exceptions contained in Article (4), which excluded treatment from agreements relating to customs unions, REIOs, and taxation.[210]

In its 2005 decision on jurisdiction, the tribunal ruled that Pakistan was obligated to treat Turkish investments fairly and equitably in light of BITs signed between Pakistan and other states (including France, China, the United Kingdom, and the Netherlands) that contained FET clauses.[211] Pakistan contended that the incorporation of FET clauses from other BITs should not be permitted under the basic treaty since "the intention had clearly been to exclude the FET standard to the extent that Turkey and Pakistan deliberately decided not to include a FET clause in the Treaty."[212]

---

207 I Kalnina, 'White Industries v. The Republic of India: A Tale of Treaty Shopping and Second Chances' (2012) 9 Transnational Dispute Management (TDM).

208 Pakistan – Turkey BIT (1995), available at: <https://investmentpolicy.unctad.org/international-investment-agreements/treaty-files/2135/download> accessed 20 April 2022.

209 Pakistan – Turkey BIT (1995) (n 208).

210 Pakistan – Turkey BIT (1995) (n 208); *Bayindir v Pakistan* (n 81) [156].

211 *Bayindir v Pakistan* (n 81) [232].

212 *Bayindir v Pakistan* (n 81) [150].

In its final award in 2009, the tribunal agreed with Pakistan that the absence of a FET clause in the main text and a reference to FET in the preamble of the Pakistan-Turkey BIT indicated that the contracting parties had not intended for the BIT to contain a FET obligation. However, the tribunal also concluded that the ordinary meaning of the MFN clause in the basic treaty, read together with the fact that its exceptions did not contain any reference to FET, suggested that the contracting parties did not intend to exclude the possibility of incorporating a higher FET standard from another treaty through the application of the MFN clause. In the tribunal's view, its interpretation was also consistent with the preamble of the basic treaty.[213] In other words, the absence of an express FET clause in the Pakistan-Turkey BIT did not preclude the claimant from relying on the MFN clause in that BIT as the basis for incorporating an external FET standard.

The tribunal also explicitly distinguished the application of the *ejusdem generis* principle to substantive and procedural treatment. It noted that:

> Indeed, the *ejusdem generis* principle that is sometimes viewed as a bar to the operation of the MFN clause with respect to procedural rights does not come into play here and the words of the treaty are clear.[214]

However, nothing in Articles 31 and 32 of the VCLT restrict the application of the *ejusdem generis* principle to procedural issues.[215] In fact, the tribunal itself applied the *ejusdem generis* principle in its reasoning when it stated that while the preamble to the treaty does not create an operative obligation, it helps interpret the MFN clause in its context and in light of the object and purpose of the basic treaty, as required in terms of Article 31(1) of the VCLT.[216] The tribunal misrepresented the *ejusdem generis* principle, according to which contracting parties should not be bound beyond the obligations they have undertaken.[217] Therefore, the tribunal effectively applied the MFN clause based on its assumption of its multilateralizing function.[218]

Such assumption, however, lead to expansive application of MFN clauses and impose treaty obligations on contracting parties that they did not anticipate when concluding the treaty of which the MFN clause in question forms

213 *Bayindir v Pakistan* (n 81) [157].
214 *Bayindir v Pakistan* (n 81) [159].
215 Sharmin (n 118) 126.
216 *Bayindir v Pakistan* (n 81) [155].
217 International Law Commission (n 1) 30, para 11.
218 Sharmin (n 118) 126.

a part. According to Sharmin, contracting parties generally merely intend to liberalize investment regulations by including MFN clauses in their IIAs and do not intend to multilateralize a given treaty benefit at all; otherwise states would explicitly state such an intention in the wording of their MFN clauses.[219] Indeed, there is no mention in the Turkey-Pakistan BIT of any intent on the part of parties to multilateralize any obligations. In other words, the tribunal made an unwarranted assumption which ran afoul of the contracting parties' intentions.

The tribunal in *LESI* also referred to the preamble of the basic treaty. In that case, the basic BIT between Algeria and Italy did not contain a FET clause. In light of the claimant's FET claim, which was based on the MFN clause in the basic BIT, the respondent state argued that the contracting parties had deliberately decided not to include FET obligations in the basic treaty and that the MFN clause could not be used to create FET obligations where none existed.[220] The tribunal rejected this argument because, in its view, the MFN clause in the basic treaty effectively allowed investors to benefit from a higher standard of protection found in other treaties concluded by Algeria.[221]

In support of its conclusion, the tribunal relied on the generally-worded preamble to the Algeria-Italy BIT, which indicated the contracting parties' desire to "create favorable conditions for investments."[222] In the tribunal's view, reading the preamble and MFN clause together was sufficient to allow the claimant to import FET obligations from other treaties. Some scholars see the *LESI* tribunal's reliance on the preamble as unnecessary because, unlike in the Pakistan-Turkey BIT in *Bayindir*, which explicitly indicated that the fair and equitable treatment of investments was desirable, the preamble relied on by the *LESI* tribunal was too general to sustain the inference that the contracting parties had intended to permit the importation of FET obligations from other treaties through an application of the MFN clause.[223]

The *ATA* case involved the annulment by a Jordanian court of an arbitral award made in favor of ATA. The Jordanian court voided the arbitration agreement in the underlying contract between ATA and Jordanian-controlled Arab

219 Sharmin (n 118) 127.

220 *LESI, S.pA and Astaldi, S.pA v People's Democratic Republic of Algeria, Awarded dated 12 November 2008,* ICSID Case No. ARB/05/3 [146].

221 *LESI v Algeria* (n 220) [150].

222 Algeria – Italy BIT (1991), a copy of which is available at <https://investmentpolicy.unctad.org/international-investment-agreements/treaty-files/50/download> accessed 20 April 2022.

223 Dumberry (n 164) 126.

Potash Company (APC) for the construction of a dike. ATA then filed a claim with ICSID after having unsuccessfully appealed the original annulment decision. The applicable Turkey-Jordan BIT did not contain any FET obligation in its main text either.[224] Similar to the Turkey-Pakistan BIT, its preamble also indicated that FET was "desirable in order to maintain a stable framework for investment and maximum effective utilization of economic resources."[225]

Before the ICSID tribunal, the claimant argued that the setting aside of the commercial award, in particular, constituted a "denial of justice" of the FET obligation contained in the UK-Jordan BIT, which could be incorporated through the MFN clause in the basic treaty.[226] The respondent state did not object to this position.[227] As an integral part of the contract, the tribunal held that the right to arbitration constituted an "asset" under the basic treaty. In a footnote to the award, the tribunal noted that under the treaty's MFN clause, Jordan assumed the obligation to provide fair and equitable treatment as contained in UK-Jordan BIT and to accord treatment no less favorable than that required by international law as prescribed by the Spain-Jordan BIT.[228] Citing the treaty's preamble, the tribunal concluded that the Jordanian court's extinguishment of the claimant's right to arbitration was contrary to "both the letter and the spirit of the Turkey-Jordan BIT."[229]

The *ATA* tribunal's reliance on the preamble of the treaty referring to FET as being desirable in order to apply the *ejusdem generis* principle may seem sound. However, it is an abuse of the *ejusdem generis* principle because unlike an FET provision in the main text, the treaty preamble does not constitute a binding obligation. Therefore, it was inappropriate for the tribunal to use the preamble of the basic treaty to incorporate a FET standard from a third-party treaty.

The *Rumeli* case is also notable on this issue. The basic BIT between Turkey and Kazakhstan did not contain a FET clause. Before the tribunal, however, the respondent accepted that the MFN clause could be used to incorporate a FET standard from another treaty signed by Kazakhstan. Moreover, it also indicated the proper treaty for the claimant to rely on.[230] However, the respondent state

224 Jordan – Turkey BIT (1993), available at: <https://investmentpolicy.unctad.org/international-investment-agreements/treaty-files/1769/download> accessed 20 April 2022.

225 Jordan – Turkey BIT (1993) (n 224); *ATA Construction, Industrial and Trading Company v Hashemite Kingdom of Jordan, Award dated 18 May 2010*, ICSID Case No. ARB/08/2 [125].

226 *ATA v Jordan* (n 225) [73].

227 *ATA v Jordan* (n 225) [84ff].

228 *ATA v Jordan* (n 225) [125] footnote 16.

229 *ATA v Jordan* (n 225).

230 *Rumeli Telekom AS and Telsim Mobil Telekomunikasyon Hizmetleri AS v Republic of Kazakhstan, Award dated 29 July 2008*, ICSID Case No. ARB/05/16 [574].

clarified that its position was that the imported FET standard from another treaty could not go beyond the scope of the international MST.[231] Citing former tribunals in this direction, the *Rumeli* tribunal agreed that FET should not be "materially different from the minimum standard of treatment in customary international law,"[232] and proceeded to conclude that the respondent had violated the FET clause incorporated through the MFN clause.[233]

In *Tatneft*, a Russian investor claimed that a series of measures by Ukrainian governmental authorities, state courts, and affiliated parties resulted in the complete extinguishment of the claimant's investment in an oil refinery operation in the territory of Ukraine. Since the Russia-Ukraine BIT did not include a FET clause, the claimant sought to import an FET clause from the BIT between Ukraine and the UK, relying on the MFN clause in the basic treaty to do so. It alleged that Ukraine's unreasonable and unfair conduct had breached the investor's legitimate expectations.[234]

The respondent did not object to the importation of the FET clause from the UK-Ukraine BIT. It did, however, argue that the FET clause's scope encompasses "no more than a prohibition of denial of justice when applied to judicial decisions,"[235] i.e., the court conduct under dispute. The tribunal allowed the importation, stating that the FET standard encompassed at least: (a) protection against the arbitrary and unreasonable measure, discrimination, and denial of justice, (b) the right to procedural propriety and due process, and (c) the assurance of a predictable, consistent and stable legal framework.[236] In the end, Ukraine was found to have violated its FET obligations.

In *Al Warraq*, a Saudi investor filed a claim against Indonesia under UNCITRAL rules per Article 17(2) of the Agreement on the Promotion, Protection, and Guarantee of Investments among Member States of the Organization of the Islamic Conference (OIC Agreement), which came into force in 1986 and did not contain a FET clause. Article 8 of the OIC Agreement provided limited MFN treatment "within the context of economic activity."[237]

However, the tribunal ignored the explicit limitation of the MFN clause contained in the OIC Agreement. It allowed the claimant to invoke the MFN

231 *Rumeli v Kazakhstan* (n 230) [592] and [597].
232 *Rumeli v Kazakhstan* (n 230) [611].
233 *Rumeli v Kazakhstan* (n 230) [609ff].
234 *OJSC "Tatneft" v Ukraine, Award on the Merits dated 29 July 2014,* UNCITRAL Arbitration.
235 *Tatneft v Ukraine* (n 234) [393].
236 *Tatneft v Ukraine* (n 234) [394].
237 Article 8 of the OIC Investment Agreement (1981). A copy of which is available at: <https://investmentpolicy.unctad.org/international-investment-agreements/treaty-files/2399/download> accessed 20 April 2022.

clause to benefit from FET clauses in other Indonesian treaties, including the BIT between the UK and Indonesia, which entered into force in 1977.[238] In this regard, the tribunal first mentioned previous arbitral decisions that recognized "the application of most-[favored]-nation clauses to import fair and equitable treatment."[239] It then referred to the *ejusdem generis* principle and stated that the MFN clause "applie[d] to import other clauses, as long as the *ejusdem generis* rule applies."[240] This case, too, entailed a misrepresentation of the *ejusdem generis* principle, a correct application of which should consider the specific limitation of the MFN clause at issue.

In the end, it concluded that the subject matter of both treaties – the OIC Agreement and the UK-Indonesia BIT – were the same, namely the protection of foreign investment.[241] The tribunal eventually concluded that Indonesia breached its FET obligations. However, since the investment was not established following Indonesia's laws and regulations, the tribunal found the claim inadmissible based on Article 9 of the OIC Agreement and the clean-hands doctrine.[242]

Lastly, the most radical decision on this issue was rendered by the *İçkale* tribunal. The dispute arose from a rather narrowly-worded BIT that does not include FET, full protection and security, non-discrimination, or umbrella clauses. Article 2 of this treaty provides MFN treatment to established investments "in similar situations."[243] The claimant sought to rely on the MFN clause to incorporate obligations that would entitle it to the allegedly more favorable treatment enjoyed by investors in accordance with other treaties concluded by Turkmenistan, particularly in accordance with the FET clauses included in Turkmenistan BITs with Bahrain, the UK, and Egypt.[244]

Unlike previous tribunals, the *İçkale* tribunal rejected the claimant's attempt to import the FET clause and other substantive protection standards from other treaties. On this score, the tribunal focused mainly on the term "similar situation" in the text of the MFN clause. It explained that according to Articles

238 *Hesham Talaat M. Al-Warraq v The Republic of Indonesia, Final Award dated 15 December 2014,* UNCITRAL Arbitration [547].

239 *Al-Warraq v Indonesia* (238) [541].

240 *Al-Warraq v Indonesia* (238) [551].

241 *Al-Warraq v Indonesia* (238) [551].

242 *Al-Warraq v Indonesia* (238) [648].

243 Turkey – Turkmenistan BIT (1992), a copy of which is available at: <https://investmentpolicy.unctad.org/international-investment-agreements/treaty-files/4785/download> accessed 20 April 2022.

244 *İçkale İnşaat Limited Şirketi v Turkmenistan, Award dated 8 March 2016,* ICSID Case No. ARB/10/24 [314].

31 and 32 of the VCLT, the text of the MFN clause suggested that an obligation existed "only in so far as the investments of the investors of the home State and those of the investors of the third State [could] be said to be in 'a similar situation'."[245]

On the contrary, the MFN obligation did not exist for the tribunal when there was no real discrimination. For example, when an investor under the Turkey-Turkmenistan BIT was not "in a similar situation" to investors from other treaties.[246] It referred to the *effet utile* principle to explain that any term in the treaty provision should be interpreted in a manner which renders it effective. Therefore, the tribunal concluded that the application of MFN clause in the Turkey-Turkmenistan BIT had to be done within the limits of factual treatment received by foreign investors, otherwise the term "similar situation" would be rendered meaningless.[247]

The tribunal also notably rejected the claimant's reliance on the preamble of the treaty to import FET obligations. The preamble in this dispute was worded similarly to that in *Bayindir*, where the contracting parties agreed that "fair and equitable treatment of investment is desirable in order to maintain a stable framework for investment and maximum effective utilization of economic resources."[248] In the tribunal's view, while the preamble to a treaty could be used as part of the treaty context in interpreting the treaty, it nevertheless could not be used to create binding legal obligations.

İçkale was the first tribunal to adopt a restrictive approach to the application of an MFN clause to incorporate higher standards from other treaties. Comments on this award have been divided. Some scholars praise the *İçkale* approach as having opened a "new MFN debate" by emphasizing MFN clauses' actual texts instead of general assumptions in relation to the rationale of MFN treatment.[249] Others express concerns that the award was too rigorous and that it did not follow general international law on treaty interpretation.[250]

The restrictive application of the "in like circumstance" in MFN clasue has been endorces by later tribunals. For example, the tribunal in *Muhammet Cap*

245 *İçkal v Turkmenistan* (n 244) [328].
246 *İçkal v Turkmenistan* (n 244) [328].
247 *İçkal v Turkmenistan* (n 244) [328–329].
248 Turkey – Turkmenistan BIT (1992) (n 243); *İçkal v Turkmenistan* (n 244) [333].
249 Simon Batifort and J Benton Heath, 'The New Debate on the Interpretation of MFN Clauses in Investment Treaties: Putting the Brakes on Multilateralization' (2018) 111 American Journal of International Law 873, 877.
250 Stephan W Schill, 'MFN Clauses as Bilateral Commitments to Multilateralism: A Reply to Simon Batifort and J. Benton Heath' (2017) 111 American Journal of International Law 914, 931–32; Sharmin (n 155) 140.

v Turkmenistan aligned itself in its award with the reasoning of the *İçkale* tribunal.[251] It determined that the MFN provision applied only to investments that were, in fact, in a similar situation. As such, the "in like circumstances" requirement in the MFN clause under dispute indicated a "limitation of scope" that prevented tribunals from importing additional substantive standards of protection. To establish a breach of MFN treatment, the claimant should prove that the respondent adopted "actual measures" towards "actually investors" from third states in similar situations with the claimant.[252]

Given the lack of a clear definition of "treatment" in international law, *de facto* MFN violations and the application of MFN clauses to incorporate higher treaty standards are notably distinct. That is, the "treatment" in *de facto* MFN violations refers to the actual governmental measures imposed on foreign investors, while the "treatment" in the latter scenario refers to treaty provisions that are usually abstract. Therefore, while the "in like circumstances" criterion is essential for ascertaining the former, it is an impractical parameter for the latter due to the difficulty of ascertaining the circumstances of foreign investors in a holistic fashion.[253] As such, it is arguable that the tribunals in *İçkale* and *Muhammet Cap* may have employed an overly restrictive textual approach to the "in like circumstances" requirement that may exclude incorporation of more favorable substantive treaty provisions.[254] However, the *İçkale* tribunal reached the right conclusion when it did not allow the application of the MFN clause in order to incorporate a brand new treaty standard absent from the basic treaty. The tribunal's approach, which entailed a detailed textual examination instead of leaning heavily on inappropriate assumptions about the rationale of MFN clauses, should also be praised.

In general, tribunals are divided on whether to allow the importation of a FET standard in a third-party treaty through the application of an MFN clause in the basic treaty. Some tribunals have relied on the *ejusdem generis* principle and refused to incorporate a new treaty standard that is absent from the basic treaty (*Paushok*). Other tribunals, meanwhile, have relied on preambular expression and the *expressio unius est exclusio alterius* maxim to import new treaty standards (*Bayindir*). According to Sharmin, the latter practice is based on the assumption that MFN is a multilateralizing tool, which is unwarranted

251 *Muhammet Çap & Sehil Inşaat Endustri ve Ticaret Ltd. Sti. v Turkmenistan, Award dated 4 May, 2021*, ICSID Case No. ARB/12/6.

252 *Muhammet Çap v Turkmenistan* (n 251) [778–788].

253 Okezic Chukwumerije, 'Interpreting Most-Favoured-Nation Clauses in Investment Treaty Arbitrations' (2007) 8 The Journal of World Investment & Trade 597.

254 Schill (n 171) 20.

in international law.[255] For Batifort and Heath, the conventional wisdom currently applicable to the interpretation of MFN clauses in relation to the importation of treaty standards from outside of a basic treaty ignores the specific text of MFN clauses and the proper interpretive methods of international law.[256] Indeed, tribunals should defer to the treaty text and interpret MFN clauses in accordance with the interpretive methods discussed in above Chapter 2. Above all, the *ejusdem generis* principle is essential in this regard. For *de facto* MFN violations, it requires the identification of third-party investors "in like circumstances." For incorporation of higher treaty standards, it requires the inclusion of such standard in the basic treaty.

That said, the "more favorable" FET standards in this context are autonomous and stand-alone standards, which are different to those associated with the MST in customary international law.[257] Contracting states' responses in this regard have been divergent. States such as Kazakhstan in *Rumeli* and Ukraine in *Tatneft* accepted the incorporation of external FET standards through an MFN clause. India, however, took a strong position against applying the MFN clause to incorporate the "effective means" protection sought by the claimant in *White Industries*. It also completely removed the MFN clause from its new model BIT in 2015 to avoid similar decisions to the one rendered by the *White Industries* tribunal in the future.

In response to tribunals' broad interpretation of MFN clauses in this regard, states have adopted restrictive treaty terms to limit the scope of MFN clauses. For example, Article 8.7(4) of CETA provides for MFN treatment, adding that substantive obligations in other IIAs and trade agreements do not in themselves constitute "treatment," therefore excluding the possibility of applying its MFN clause to obligations pertaining to substantive treatment in third-party treaties.[258] A similar provision can also be found in Article 5.3 of the Investment Cooperation and Facilitation Agreement between the Federative Republic of Brazil and the Republic of Colombia.[259]

---

255 Sharmin (n 118) 127.

256 Batifort and Heath (n 249). See also: Pérez-Aznar (n 54) 786.

257 Dumberry (n 162); Dumberry (n 164).

258 EU – Canada FTA (CETA, 2017) Article 8.7(4). A copy of which is Available at: <https://ec.europa.eu/trade/policy/in-focus/ceta/ceta-chapter-by-chapter/> accessed 20 April 2022.

259 Brazil – Colombia BIT (2015), available at <https://investmentpolicy.unctad.org/international-investment-agreements/treaty-files/5765/download> accessed 20 April 2022. For a discussion of these treaties, see: Pérez-Aznar (n 54).

2.2.2 The Incorporation of Full Protection and Security Clauses

Full protection and security is a standard of protection often included in investment treaties. Like FET, the relationship between full protection and security and MST in customary international law, the formulation, and scope of full protection and security clauses in different treaties have caused debates in ISDS proceedings.[260] In this context, claimants have relied on MFN clauses to incorporate allegedly higher full protection and security standards from other treaties, with tribunals having reached diverging decisions in relation to whether this should be permissible.

The importation of a full protection and security standard through the application of an MFN clause has already been examined in relation to the *AAPL* case, where the tribunal confirmed the ability of the MFN clause in the basic treaty to import applicable rules from general customary international law and other specific international rules.[261]

In *AAPL*, Article 2(2) of the basic treaty provided for FET and full protection and security protection, stating that "[i]nvestments of nationals or companies of either Contracting Party shall at all times be accorded fair and equitable treatment and shall enjoy full protection and security in the territory of the other Contracting Party."[262] Concerning the respondent state's obligation to offer full protection and security, the claimant alleged that Article 2(2) went beyond the MST and constituted an autonomous and independent clause which went beyond the protection offered by customary international law.[263]

Moreover, under the heading "Compensation for Losses," Article 4 of the basic treaty contained a clause relating to "war" or "civil disturbances" according to which the state party was exempted from having to provide full protection and security and to compensate investors for losses due to the destruction of property. The claimant thus alleged that the Sri Lanka-Switzerland BIT provided a higher standard of strict liability concerning full protection and security protection since it contained no such exemption.[264]

The tribunal rejected the claimant's argument as unfounded. According to the tribunal, there existed no grounds to believe that the Sri Lanka-Switzerland

260 Sebastián Mantilla Blanco, *Full Protection and Security in International Investment Law*, vol 8 (Springer International Publishing 2019); Suleimenova (n 22).

261 *AAPL v Sri Lanka* (n 154) [22].

262 Article 2(2) of the Sri Lanka – UK BIT (1980). A copy of which is Available at: <https://investmentpolicy.unctad.org/international-investment-agreements/treaty-files/2293/download> accessed 20 April 2022.

263 *AAPL v Sri Lanka* (n 154) [26(A)(B)].

264 *AAPL v Sri Lanka* (n 154) [54(i)].

BIT adopted a stricter standard insofar as liability was concerned.[265] Ultimately, the tribunal found that since it had not been proven that the Sri Lanka-Switzerland BIT accorded more favorable full protection and security treatment, the MFN clause in the Sri Lanka-UK BIT could therefore not be justifiably invoked *in casu*. In the absence of a higher standard of liability in the basic treaty as *lex specialis*, the tribunal concluded that the general international law rules have to be applied as *lex generalis*.[266]

As with the FET standard, tribunals have tended to allow the importation of a higher full protection and security standard from third-party treaties through applying MFN clauses. It is the comparison of two full protection and security standards, i.e., whether the imported full protection and security standard is actually of a higher level or not, that they are concerned with. As noted above, the *Rumeli* tribunal allowed the claimant to rely on a more favorable FET standard in the Kazakhstan-UK BIT through an application of the MFN clause in the basic treaty. The Kazakhstan-Turkey BIT did not contain a full protection and security clause. In the same vein, then, the tribunal held that the full protection and security standard in the Kazakhstan-UK BIT could be incorporated by applying the MFN clause in the basic treaty.[267] The tribunal proceeded with its analysis on the basis that Kazakhstan owed the claimant the same full protection and security standard as it owed investors under the Kazakhstan-UK BIT and concluded that Kazakhstan had failed to meet its obligations in this regard.[268]

In *ADF*, the case was still pending when the 2001 Notes of the NAFTA Free Trade Commission (FTC) came out, which linked full protection and security and FET's content to MST in customary international law in the NAFTA context.[269] There the claimant asserted in a subsequent submission that other treaties concluded by the U.S., notably the U.S.-Albania and U.S.-Estonia BITs, did not prescribe such connections in their full protection and security clauses. Therefore, it argued that they were broader and more favorable. Accordingly, the claimant alleged that it was entitled to enjoy the full protection and security standards in the U.S.-Albania and U.S.-Estonia BITs through Article 1103 of NAFTA (on MFN).[270]

265 *AAPL v Sri Lanka* (n 154) [54].
266 *AAPL v Sri Lanka* (n 154) [54].
267 *Rumeli v Kazakhstan* (n 230) [575].
268 *Rumeli v Kazakhstan* (n 230) [668ff].
269 NAFTA Free Trade Commission (n 163).
270 *ADF v U.S.* (n 68) [75–80].

The U.S. contended that the claimant had misinterpreted the full protection and security clauses in the U.S.-Albania and U.S.-Estonia BITs. As in the case of Article 1105(1) of NAFTA, these clauses were also tied to customary international law. After considering the submissions of both sides, the tribunal rejected the claimant's argument. It explained that the claimant had not successfully established that the imported full protection and security standards were autonomous or more favorable. Even if they were more favorable *arguendo*, the claimant had not shown that the U.S. had breached such higher standards.[271]

In *Al-Warraq*, Article 2 of the OIC Agreement entitled foreign investors to "adequate protection and security."[272] The claimant semantically interpreted "adequate" as "full" and claimed that "adequate protection and security" in the OIC Agreement provided the exact same standard as "full protection and security."[273] Alternatively, even if it offered less favorable protection, the claimant invoked the MFN clause of the OIC Agreement, claiming that it enjoyed "full protection and security" as envisioned in Article 3(2) of the UK-Indonesia BIT or in other treaties concluded by Indonesia.[274] The tribunal did not side with the claimant, holding that "full protection and security" was not a higher standard than "adequate protection and security." Therefore, it did not find a violation by Indonesia of its adequate protection or full protection and security obligations.

In *CC/Devas,* the claimant relied on *White Industries* and other tribunals' reasoning to support importing a higher full protection and security standard from a third-party treaty (*in casu,* Article 3(2) of the Serbia-India BIT). The case was brought under the India-Mauritius BIT, which did not contain a full protection and security clause.[275] The claimant argued that a distinction should be drawn between the importation of a brand-new provision from importation of a more favorable standard, because the rights contained in Serbia-India BIT and India-Mauritius BIT were not "wholly distinct" from each other, among others. Both treaties dealt with the same subject matter, i.e., the treatment of foreign investments.[276]

---

271 *ADF v U.S.* (n 68) [194].

272 Article 2 of the OIC Investment Agreement (n 237).

273 *Al-Warraq v Indonesia* (n 238) [423].

274 *Al-Warraq v Indonesia* (n 238) [424].

275 India – Mauritius BIT (1998), available at: <https://investmentpolicy.unctad.org/international-investment-agreements/treaty-files/1577/download> accessed 20 April 2022.

276 *CC/Devas (Mauritius) Ltd, Devas Employees Mauritius Private Limited, and Telcom Devas Mauritius Limited v Republic of India, Award on Jurisdiction and Merits dated 25 July 2016,* PCA Case No. 2013–09 [488].

India, on the other hand, contended that such importation would "entail creating a standard that is not present in the applicable Treaty."[277] The tribunal followed the line of the claimant's argument and applied the full protection and security standard in Serbia-India BIT.[278] However, the tribunal used the standard restrictively, describing it as an "obligation of vigilance and due diligence" under customary international law.[279] In the end, the tribunal did not find a breach of full protection and security by India and rejected the claim.[280]

In *Teinver*, the basic treaty concluded between Argentina and Spain did not contain a traditional full protection and security clause. It merely stated that contracting parties should "protect within its territory the investments made in accordance with its legislation by investors of the other Party."[281] The claimant attempted to rely on Article IV (the MFN clause) in the Argentina-Spain BIT to incorporate the full protection and security guarantee in Article II(2)(a) of U.S.-Argentina BIT. The basic treaty accorded MFN treatment in the same provision as it accorded FET, stating that "[i]n all matters governed by this Agreement, such treatment shall be no less [favorable] than that accorded by each Party to investments made in its territory by investors of a third country."[282] To this end, the claimant relied on the *ejusdem generis* principle and claimed that MFN treatment should apply insofar as the more favorable third-party treaty provision is of the same type as in the basic treaty. In this regard, the U.S.-Argentina BIT addressed the same matter governed by the Spain-Argentina BIT, as both dealt with the protection of foreign investors and investments.[283]

Argentina opposed the argument, asserting instead that the application of MFN principles in the basic treaty were limited only to FET due to the use of the term "such treatment" in Article IV(2).[284] Argentina also argued that the MFN clause could not include a new full protection and security standard since the basic treaty did not contain one. According to the respondent state, such incorporation would amount to the importation of a "new guarantee or protection, different from the one contained in Article III(1) of the Treaty."[285]

277 *Devas v India* (n 276) [490].
278 *Devas v India* (n 276) [496].
279 *Devas v India* (n 276) [498, 499].
280 *Devas v India* (n 276) [500].
281 Argentina – Spain BIT (1991), a copy of which is available at:<https://investmentpolicy.unctad.org/international-investment-agreements/treaty-files/119/download> accessed 20 April 2022. *Autobuses Urbanos del Sur SA, Teinver SA and Transportes de Cercanías SA v Argentine Republic, Award dated 21 July* 2017, ICSID Case No. ARB/09/1 [879].
282 *Teinver v Argentina (n 281)* [868].
283 *Teinver v Argentina (n 281)* [882].
284 *Teinver v Argentina (n 281)* [877].
285 *Teinver v Argentina (n 281)* [879].

The tribunal rejected Argentina's arguments on both grounds. Regarding the scope of the MFN clause concerning FET, the tribunal stated that the MFN clause was not restricted to FET. It found that the ordinary meaning of the sentence "all matters governed by this Agreement" in Article IV(2) unambiguously required it to extend not only to FET but also full protection and security.[286] Specifically, the tribunal reasoned that in all matters governed by the treaty, the treatment accorded to investments had to be fair and equitable treatment according to Article IV(1). In terms of Article IV(2), it should be "no less favorable than the treatment accorded to investments made by investors of a third country." It could be used "in respect of all matters governed by the Treaty to incorporate more favorable provisions from other BITs concluded by Argentina."[287]

As for Argentina's contention that the MFN clause could not incorporate a new provision from third-party treaties, the tribunal considered the term "in all matters governed by this Agreement" to be critical. The tribunal relied on the *ejusdem generis* principle. It noted that Article III of the treaty already provided for the full protection and security standard by referring to "protection." Therefore, the tribunal believed that such provision should also be included in the "all matters" category. The claimant did not attempt to incorporate a brand new standard from other treaties but rather sought to improve the old standard.

Based on this reasoning, the tribunal concluded that the MFN clause in question could in fact be relied on in order to incorporate the full protection and security standard in the U.S.-Argentina BIT. After comparing the "protection" and "full protection" provisions in Spain-Argentina and U.S.-Argentina BITs, the tribunal observed that their differences were insignificant.[288] In the end, the tribunal concluded that "to the extent the standard of 'full protection and security' may be more favorable, the tribunal applies that standard as set out in Article II(2)(a) of the U.S.-Argentina BIT."[289]

In *Rusoro Mining*, the claimant alleged that Venezuela breached the full protection and security standard in the basic treaty (*in casu*, the Canada-Venezuela BIT) by adopting a series of regulatory measures.[290] The respondent state denied that the full protection and security standard provided for the

286 *Teinver v Argentina* (*n 281*) [880].

287 *Teinver v Argentina* (*n 281*) [881].

288 *Teinver v Argentina* (n 281) [893].

289 *Teinver v Argentina* (n 281) [897].

290 *Rusoro Mining Ltd v Bolivarian Republic of Venezuela, Award dated 22 August 2016,* ICSID Case No. ARB(AF)/12/5 198 [543].

MST as per customary international law and asserted that it should be limited to the investors' physical harms to the exclusion of legal regulations. The claimant responded that even though the basic treaty only provided for physical protection, it should enjoy "full protection and legal security" treatment as per the Uruguay-Venezuela BIT through the MFN clause in the basic treaty.[291] The tribunal did not elaborate on the issue of the MFN clause. It merely concluded that Venezuela was not violating its obligation, even assuming *arguendo* the widest possible full protection and security.[292]

Saint Gobain is another case against Venezuela that involved discussion of the full protection and security. In this case, Saint Gobain claimed that Article 3(2) of the France-Venezuela BIT on full protection and security had been breached. It construed the full protection and security standard to encompass not only physical protection but also legal guarantees.[293] Venezuela made a similar claim as in the *Rusoro* case, stating that the full protection and security standard referred "primarily, and perhaps exclusively, to the physical security of the investment."[294] The claimant sought to rely on the MFN clause to incorporate the full protection and security clause in the Uruguay-Venezuela BIT. The tribunal did not consider this issue in detail but merely concluded that the legal security claim had been considered and dismissed.[295]

As observed earlier, the conventional wisdom is for tribunals to incorporate supposedly higher full protection and security standard in third-party treaties through the application of MFN clauses. The above cases indicate that tribunals have on occasion refused to conclude that full protection and security breaches have taken place for two main reasons. Either the respondent state did not adopt measures grave enough to constitute a violation of its full protection and security obligations (even in the broadest possible scope), or the target full protection and security standard was not in fact a higher standard than the original one to which it was being compared.[296] In cases where the basic treaty did not contain a full protection and security clause, tribunals seemed less reluctant to rely on the MFN clause in the basic treaty to incorporate a new full protection and security standard in view of the *ejusdem generis* principle.

---

291 *Rusoro Mining v Venezuela* (n 290) [544].

292 *Rusoro Mining v Venezuela* (n 290) [547].

293 *Saint-Gobain Performance Plastics Europe v Bolivarian Republic of Venezuela, Decision on Liability and the Principles of Quantum dated 30 December 2016,* ICSID Case No. ARB/12/13 [545].

294 *Saint-Gobain v Venezuela* (n 293) [549].

295 *Saint-Gobain v Venezuela* (n 293) [559–560].

296 It should be noted that tribunals have not reached a consistent conclusion in relation to how to determine whether a full protection and security standard is higher than another.

In cases where the basic treaty contained a full protection and security clause, careful attention was paid to comparing the texts of the different provisions.

As in the FET-related cases above, cases relating to full protection and security clauses usually entail respondent claiming a link to MST in customary international law, mostly in relation to whether to extend full protection and security protection to legal security, which also relates to the relationship between FET and full protection and security.[297] In this sort of scenario, it is indeed hard for tribunals to recognize and import a higher full protection and security standard. First, because full protection and security clauses form part of an extended spectrum of different texts which share a similar scope: from “full protection and security,” “adequate protection and security,” and “full physical security and protection,” to “full protection and legal security.” Second, because the burden of proof for claimants is onerous.[298] Therefore, when the basic treaty only provides for “protection,” tribunals are careful to incorporate a third-party full protection and security standard to “improve the old standard.”[299] As a result, the broad interpretation of full protection and security leads the claimants to rely on the original full protection and security clause and use the MFN clause as an alternative.

To conclude, although reliance of an MFN clause is not the best option for claimants, its ability to incorporate the full protection and security standard has generally been recognized by tribunals, even in cases where basic treaties do not contain a full protection and security clause. On the other hand, in cases where basic treaties contain a full protection and security clause, tribunals are more careful to import a new full protection and security standard into a dispute. A comparison of treaty texts is necessary, but the compared full protection and security clauses are more often than not deemed to be similar in scope and, in the end, the “old” full protection and security clause tends to be applied.

2.2.3 The Incorporation of Expropriation Clauses

Investors have also invoked MFN clauses to incorporate a higher standard of treatment insofar as expropriation is concerned. In this regard, the quantum of expropriation compensation is usually debated.[300] For example, in *Garanti Koza*, the UK claimant alleged that Turkmenistan had expropriated an

297 Although none of the above cases involved a basic treaty that link full protection and security to customary international law. See: Mantilla Blanco (n 260) Chapter 15.

298 Mantilla Blanco (n 260) Chapter 13.

299 *Teinver v Argentina* (n 281).

300 Suleimenova (n 22) 203.

investment in seizing its factory and equipment, machinery, and the material therein and terminating the construction contract between Turkmenistan and the claimant.[301]

During the proceedings, the claimant attempted to incorporate Article 5 of the France-Turkmenistan BIT because it contained an additional requirement for what constituted a lawful expropriation.[302] In terms of the France-Turkmenistan BIT, expropriations should also not have violated a specific commitment of the host state.[303] At the same time, the claimant also referred to Article 6 of the United Arab Emirates-Turkmenistan BIT, which required an expropriation to "not violate any specific provision or contractual stability or expropriation contained in an investment agreement between the natural and juridical persons concerned and the party making the expropriation," and that an expropriation had to be "accomplished under due procedures of law."[304]

To this end, the claimant relied on Article 3 (MFN clause) of the basic treaty signed between the UK and Turkmenistan.[305] The tribunal found that such an attempt by the claimant raised two significant difficulties. First, it attempted to use provisions from different treaties to create a "tailor-made" treaty clause not agreed in any of the treaties entered into by the respondent. Second, the claimant failed to demonstrate that the treatment granted by the France-Turkmenistan or United Arab Emirates-Turkmenistan BITs were, *in fact,* more favorable than the treatment applied in the UK-Turkmenistan BIT.[306] The tribunal did not make any further pronouncements on this score and rejected this argument because the claimant had failed to establish an expropriation breach at all.[307]

---

301 *Garanti Koza LLP v Turkmenistan, Decision on the Objection to Jurisdiction for Lack of Consent dated 3 July 2013,* ICSID Case No. ARB/11/20 [363].

302 France – Turkmenistan BIT (1994). A copy of which is available at: <https://investmentpolicy.unctad.org/international-investment-agreements/treaty-files/1288/download> accessed 20 April 2022.

303 *Garanti Koza v Turkmenistan* (n 301) [373].

304 Turkmenistan – United Arab Emirates BIT (1998). A copy of which is available at: <https://investmentpolicy.unctad.org/international-investment-agreements/treaty-files/2359/download> accessed 20 April 2022; *Garanti Koza v Turkmenistan* (n 301) [374].

305 Turkmenistan – UK BIT (1995). A copy of which is available at: <https://investmentpolicy.unctad.org/international-investment-agreements/treaty-files/2360/download> accessed 20 April 2022.

306 *Garanti Koza v Turkmenistan* (n 301) [375].

307 *Garanti Koza v Turkmenistan* (n 301) [377].

In CME, Article 5 of the Dutch-Czech Republic BIT provided for "just compensation" to represent the investment's "genuine value."[308] In its final award, the tribunal first equated "just compensation" with "fair market value." As a supporting method, the tribunal relied on the MFN clause in the basic treaty to import a provision from the U.S.-Czech Republic BIT. This treaty required that "compensation [should] be equivalent to the fair market value of the expropriated investment immediately before the expropriation action was taken."[309]

Ian Brownlie criticized the tribunal's method in his dissenting opinion. He called the application of the MFN clause to import a substantially different formulated compensation clause from the U.S. treaty an "unattractive hypothesis."[310] He opined that "in the first place, it involves a strange view of the intention of the parties," that "[t]he express choice of a compensation clause becomes nugatory if the MFN clause applies in this form."[311] By defining amount of compensation as part of the dispute settlement process, he further argued that "[t]he presumption must be that the clause promises MFN treatment only in matters of treatment of an investment, and not to the process of dispute settlement."[312]

In *Siemens*, the tribunal found that the measures implemented by Argentina constituted an unlawful expropriation.[313] The Germany-Argentina BIT required compensation "equivalent to the value of the expropriated investment."[314] The claimant invoked the MFN clause in an attempt to benefit from the "fair market value" standard contained in the Germany-Argentina BIT. However, the tribunal found it unnecessary to apply the MFN clause in order to dispose of this issue. It reasoned that "the law applicable to the determination of compensation for a breach of such Treaty obligations is customary international law. The [Germany-Argentina BIT] itself only provides for compensation for expropriation in accordance with the terms of the Treaty."[315]

---

308 Czech Republic – Netherlands BIT (1991). A copy of which is available at: <https://investmentpolicy.unctad.org/international-investment-agreements/treaties/bit/1212/czech-republic---netherlands-bit-1991-> accessed 20 April 2022.

309 *CME Czech Republic BV v The Czech Republic, Final Award dated 14 March 2003,* UNCITRAL Arbitration [500].

310 *CME v Czech Republic* (n 309), *Dissenting Opinion by Ian Brownlie* [11].

311 *CME v Czech Republic* (n 309).

312 *CME v Czech Republic* (n 309).

313 *Siemens v Argentina* (n 10) [349].

314 Article 4(2) of the Argentina – Germany BIT (1991), a copy of which is available at: <https://investmentpolicy.unctad.org/international-investment-agreements/treaty-files/92/download> accessed 20 April 2022.

315 *Siemens v Argentina* (n 10) [349].

The *Siemens* tribunal subsequently adopted the customary international law principle elucidated in the *Factory at Chorzów* case to determine damages. In the *Factory at Chorzów* case, the Permanent Court of International Justice (PCIJ) determined that compensation for an aggrieved investor should "wipe out all the consequences of an illegal act and re-establish the situation which would, in all probability, have existed if that act had not been committed."[316] Later courts and tribunals applied this principle as customary international law codified in the Draft Articles on Responsibility of States for Internationally Wrongful Acts.[317] According to the *Siemens* tribunal, it was logical for it to understand that "if all the consequences of the illegal act need to be wiped out" as required by PCIJ in *Factory at Chorzów* case, "the value of the investment at the time of this Award be compensated in full. Otherwise, compensation would not cover all the consequences of the illegal act."[318] The tribunal thus concluded that, in addition to the value of the investment at the time of the expropriation, Siemens was entitled to "any greater value that enterprise has gained up to the date of this Award, plus any consequential damages."[319]

States make compensation promises in their treaties to varying degrees.[320] Compared to other substantive rights, whether treatment concerning

316 *Case Concerning The Factory At Chorzów (Germany v Republic of Poland), Claim for Indemnity, Merits, Judgment, PCIJ Series A No 17, 1928* 47.

317 Article 31(1) of the Draft Articles provides that: 'The responsible State is under an obligation to make full reparation for the injury caused by the internationally wrongful act.' The commentary of Article 31 refers explicitly to *Factory at Chorzów* case, declaring that 'The general principle of the consequences of the commission of an internationally wrongful act was stated by PCIJ in the *Factory at Chorzów* case.' Article 36 follows that: '1. The State responsible for an internationally wrongful act is under an obligation to compensate for the damage caused thereby, insofar as such damage is not made good by restitution. 2. The compensation shall cover any financially assessable damage including loss of profits insofar as it is established.' The commentary thereunder specifies the *Factory at Chorzów* case to articulate the role of compensation: 'the role of compensation was articulated by PCIJ in the following terms: Restitution in kind, or, if this is not possible, payment of a sum corresponding to the value which a restitution in kind would bear; the award, if need be, of damages for loss sustained which would not be covered by restitution in kind or payment in place of it – such are the principles which should serve to determine the amount of compensation due for an act contrary to international law.' See: International Law Commission, 'Draft Articles on Responsibility of States for Internationally Wrongful Acts, with Commentaries' (2001) Yearbook of the International Law Commission, Vol II, Part Two. Available at: <https://legal.un.org/ilc/texts/instruments/english/commentaries/9_6_2001.pdf> accessed 20 April.

318 *Siemens v Argentina* (n 10) [353].

319 *Siemens v Argentina* (n 10) [352].

320 Mark A Chinen, 'The Standard of Compensation for Takings' (2016) 25 Minnesota Journal of International Law 335; Irmgard Marboe, *Calculation of Compensation and Damages in*

compensation is more beneficial is easier to answer because compensation is more readily quantifiable.[321] However, there remains debate in the literature and practice on whether full compensation or appropriate compensation standard represents customary international law. Tribunals such as the one in *Siemens* assume that the full compensation doctrine forms part of customary international law and apply it when a treaty seeks to undercompensate investors' losses, rendering reference to MFN clauses unnecessary. Even if tribunals adopt the same approach, a question that follows is which technique should tribunals apply to calculate the damages.[322] Another question, alluded to by Ian Brownlie in the *CME* case, is whether "compensation" should be categorized as "treatment" that falls within the scope of MFN clauses in the first place.

2.2.4 The Incorporation of Umbrella Clauses

The umbrella clause is a treaty provision in IIAs whereby contracting parties guarantee treaty protection to foreign investors' private contractual undertakings.[323] ISDS tribunals have dealt with claims in which investors attempt to incorporate umbrella clauses from third-party treaties through MFN clauses.

In *EDF*, the dispute arose from an alleged violation of the France-Argentina BIT.[324] Article 10 of the BIT contained a specific obligation on "special commitments." It stipulated as follows:

> Investments which have been the subject of a specific commitment by one of the Contracting Parties towards investors of the other Contracting Party are governed, without prejudice to the provisions of this Agreement,

International Investment Law (Second edition, Oxford University Press 2017); Jonathan Bonnitcha and Sarah Brewin, 'Compensation Under Investment Treaties' (2020) IISD Best Practices Series.

321 Suleimenova (n 22) 203; Bonnitcha and Brewin (n 320).

322 Bonnitcha and Brewin (n 320).

323 Anthony C Sinclair, 'The Origins of the Umbrella Clause in the International Law of Investment Protection' (2014) 20 Arbitration International 411; CL Lim, 'Is the Umbrella Clause Not Just Another Treaty Clause?' in CL Lim (ed), *Alternative Visions of the International Law on Foreign Investment: Essays in Honour of Muthucumaraswamy Sornarajah* (Cambridge University Press 2016); Tarcisio Gazzini and Attila Tanzi, 'Handle with Care: Umbrella Clauses and MFN Treatment in Investment Arbitration' (2013) 14 The Journal of World Investment & Trade 978, 985; Pérez-Aznar (n 54); August Reinisch and Christoph Schreuer, *International Protection of Investments: The Substantive Standards* (1st edn, Cambridge University Press 2020); Schill (n 171) 84.

324 *EDF International SA, SAUR International SA and León Participaciones Argentinas SA v Argentine Republic, Award dated 11 June 2012*, ICSID Case No. ARB/03/23.

> by the terms of this commitment in the to the extent that it contains more favorable provisions than those provided for in this Agreement.[325]

While the BIT already contained an umbrella clause in Article 10, the claimants invoked Article 4 (MFN clause) of the basic treaty to incorporate more favorable umbrella clauses contained in Article 10(2) of the Argentina-Belgo-Luxembourg Economic Union BIT[326] and Article 7(2) of the Argentina-Germany BIT.[327] The claimants requested that the tribunal find a breach of particular commitments under the concession agreement. Argentina referred to Article 9 of the Draft Articles of the MFN clause. It argued that incorporating an umbrella clause from the above-mentioned third country treaties would be contrary to a proper application of the *ejusdem generis* principle to the MFN clause. According to Argentina, such principle prohibited "claimants from invoking substantive protections of a kind not explicitly contained in the Treaty itself."[328]

The tribunal allowed the importation of the umbrella clause through applying the MFN clause, which had the effect of elevating the dispute from Argentine administrative courts to international arbitration. In its conclusion, the tribunal found that ignoring the MFN clause, in this case, would "permit more favorable treatment to investors protected under third countries, which is exactly what the MFN clause is intended to prevent."[329] It added that "to interpret otherwise would effectively read the MFN clause out of the treaty. Such a result cannot be what the two countries intended by the treaty language."[330]

As for *the ejusdem generis* principle, the tribunal simply assumed that Article 10 was an umbrella clause, the aim of which was to grant "those rights which fall within the limits of the subject matter of the clause."[331] In the end, the tribunal

---

325 Article 10 of the Argentina – France BIT (1991), available at: <https://investmentpolicy.unctad.org/international-investment-agreements/treaty-files/91/download> accessed 20 April 2022.

326 The English translation of this provision could be found in the award of the case, which reads as: 'Each of the Contracting Parties shall respect at all times the commitments it has undertaken with respect to investors of the other Party.' See: *EDF v Argentina* (n 324) [209].

327 The English version of this provision reads as: 'Each Contracting Party shall comply with any other commitment undertaken in connection with the investments made by nationals or companies from the other Contracting Party in the former's territory.' See: *EDF v Argentina* (n 324) [210].

328 *EDF v Argentina (n 324)* [925].

329 *EDF v Argentina (n 324)* [932].

330 *EDF v Argentina (n 324)* [933].

331 *EDF v Argentina* (n 324) [934].

found breaches of both the "special commitments" covered by the imported umbrella clauses and FET.

The *EDF* tribunal's decision has been criticized. For example, Gazzini and Tanzi argue that, according to the interpretative methods of the VCLT, the contracting parties had not entered into obligations comparable to the obligations contemplated in the umbrella clause under Article 10. The authors thus believe that the *ejusdem generis* principle is not applicable in this case since Article 10 does not provide rights on the same subject-matter as those in third-party treaties. They write as follows:

> On the one hand, it (Article 10) preserves the rights already acquired by foreign investors on the basis of special agreements by excluding the application to investment or investors covered by these agreements of any disadvantageous treaty provision. On the other hand, it makes sure that foreign investors can fully rely on the treaty whenever it is for them convenient. Yet, claims under special agreements and claims under the treaty remain governed by the respective substantive provisions and settled in accordance to their respective remedies.[332]

The *Arif* case arose from the France-Moldova BIT.[333] Article 9 of the treaty provided for "special commitments" similar to Article 10 of the France-Argentina BIT. The claimant invoked the MFN clause to incorporate umbrella clauses contained in Article 2(2) of the Moldova-UK BIT,[334] as well as Article II(3)(c) of the Moldova-U.S. BIT.[335] The respondent objected that Article 9 in the basic BIT could not be regarded as an umbrella clause because it did not impose an independent obligation on the host state to comply with foreign investors'

332 Gazzini and Tanzi (n 323) 989.

333 France – Moldova BIT (1997). A copy of which is available at: <https://investmentpolicy.unctad.org/international-investment-agreements/treaty-files/1256/download> accessed 20 April 2022.

334 Which reads as: 'Each Contracting Party shall observe any obligation it may have entered into with regard to investments of nationals or companies of the other Contracting Party.' See: Moldova – UK BIT (1996). A copy of which is available at: <https://investmentpolicy.unctad.org/international-investment-agreements/treaty-files/2018/download> accessed 20 Aprl 2022.

335 Which reads as: 'Each Party shall observe any obligation it may have entered into with regard to investments.' See: Moldova – U.S. BIT (1993). A copy of which is available at: <https://investmentpolicy.unctad.org/international-investment-agreements/treaty-files/2019/download> accessed 20 April 2022.

specific commitments.[336] The respondent also argued that the MFN clause could not import umbrella clauses through third-country treaties. According to the respondent, the MFN clause could only import substantive obligations. Given that umbrella clauses were, according to the respondent, procedural in nature, they could accordingly not be incorporated through reliance on the MFN clause in question.[337]

The tribunal rightly sided with the respondent, refusing to identify Article 9 as an umbrella clause. According to the tribunal, the purpose of such clause "[was] not to guarantee the observation of obligations assumed by the Host State vis-à-vis the investor, but rather to provide investors with the right to claim the application of any rule of law more [favorable] than the provisions of the BIT."[338] However, the tribunal agreed with the claimant that the umbrella clause pertained to substantive treatment that falls within the MFN clause's scope of application. On that basis, the tribunal determined that it had jurisdiction over the claimant's allegation that "specific commitments" could be incorporated through the MFN clause. The tribunal eventually found that it was not entitled to rule on the breach of specific commitments under Moldovan domestic law since they had been annulled by Moldovan courts irrevocably.[339]

Gazzini and Tanzi commented that a proper application of the *ejusdem generis* principle, would have seen the *Arif* tribunal rejecting the incorporation of the umbrella clause through reliance on the MFN clause as there were no rights pertaining to the same subject-matter contained in both the basic and third-party treaties.[340] By allowing incorporation of the umbrella clause, the tribunal failed to apply the *ejusdem generis* principle and incorrectly interpreted the MFN clause in the basic treaty.

In *Impregilo*, the Italian claimant alleged that Pakistan had breached a treaty obligation in the Italy-Pakistan BIT by failing to perform its contractual obligations. Since the Italy-Pakistan BIT did not contain an umbrella clause, the claimant invoked the MFN clause in an attempt to import an umbrella clause from the Pakistan-Switzerland BIT. Interestingly, Pakistan did not object to such application of the MFN clause. The tribunal determined that it had no jurisdiction because Impregilo concluded the contract in relation to a dispute with the Pakistan Water and Power Development Authority and not Pakistan.

336 *Franck Charles Arif v Republic of Moldova, Award 8 April 2013*, ICSID Case No. ARB/11/23 176 [140].
337 *Arif v Moldova* [143].
338 *Arif v Moldova* [388].
339 *Arif v Moldova* [398].
340 Gazzini and Tanzi (n 323) 990.

On the basis of lack of privity of contract, the tribunal did not elaborate on how it would have interpreted and applied the MFN clause.[341] Some scholars nevertheless took the tribunal's silence as an admission of the possibility of importing umbrella clauses through reliance on an MFN clause.[342]

Impregilo brought a similar case against Argentina. This time, the dispute was brought in terms of the Argentina-Italy BIT, which did not contain an umbrella clause. As such, Impregilo attempted to import an umbrella clause from the Argentina-U.S. BIT through invocation of the MFN clause in the basic treaty. The tribunal denied jurisdiction because the contractual claims involved contracts to which Impregilo was not a party.[343] Therefore, the tribunal concluded that whether the MFN clause could be used to import a third-party umbrella clause and entitle the tribunal to determine contractual issues was "an entirely theoretical question" and considered it unnecessary to express any further opinion.[344]

In *Paushok*, the underlying treaty (the Mongolia-Russia BIT) linked MFN treatment with FET. As discussed above, the *Paushok* tribunal declined to incorporate a higher full protection and security standard through application of the MFN clause in the basic treaty. For the same reason, the tribunal rejected the claimant's attempt to incorporate an umbrella clause not present in the basic treaty. The tribunal explained that the MFN clause's ordinary meaning was clear enough to indicate that it only extended to substantive rights related to fair and equitable treatment.[345]

Last but not least, the *Teinver* tribunal took a rather remarkable position in this regard. As discussed in the subsection on full protection and security above, the *Teinver* tribunal allowed for the possibility of importing a higher standard of full protection and security from the U.S.-Argentina BIT.[346] However, the tribunal rejected the claimant's attempt to rely on the MFN clause to incorporate an umbrella clause from the same treaty.

The tribunal explained that the plain and ordinary meaning of the MFN clause, which referred to "all matters governed by this Agreement" indicated that its coverage was limited to the "various rights or forms of protection contained in the individual provisions of the Treaty."[347] As such, the tribunal

341 *Impregilo S.pA v Islamic Republic of Pakistan (II), Decision on Jurisdiction dated 22 April 2005*, ICSID Case No. ARB/03/3 [223].

342 Suleimenova (n 22) 195.

343 *Impregilo v Argentina* (n 41) [185].

344 *Impregilo v Argentina* (n 41) [186].

345 *Paushok v Mongolia* (n 194) [570].

346 *Teinver v Argentina* (n 281) [897].

347 *Teinver v Argentina* (n 281) [884].

concluded that since it was the contracting parties' intent not to include an umbrella clause, the MFN clause could not be used to import a brand new umbrella clause from a third-party treaty.

In the above cases, the tribunals were somehow silent on the idea of importing an umbrella clause via an MFN clause *per se*, nor did they take explicit positions on the interpretative principles applicable to MFN clauses, especially the *ejusdem generis* principle.[348] Two recent cases, however, reflect a more restrictive approach taken by tribunals. One is *İçkale* case already discussed above. There the tribunal rigorously interpreted the language of the MFN clause in question and decided that in order for it to find a violation of the MFN clause, there had to be legitimate comparators "in similar situations" who *actually* enjoyed the better substantive treatments asserted by the claimant.

In another case, *WNC*, the basic treaty was Czech Republic-UK BIT. Article 2(3) of the basic treaty provided for an umbrella clause in the following terms:

> Investors of one Contracting Party may conclude with the other Contracting Party specific agreements, the provisions and effect of which, unless more beneficial to the investor, shall not be at variance with this Agreement. Each Contracting Party shall, with regard to investments of investors of the other Contracting Party, observe the provisions of these specific agreements, as well as the provisions of this Agreement.[349]

The tribunal first declined to exercise jurisdiction over the claimant's allegation that there had been a breach of the umbrella clause because there were no "specific agreements" within the meaning of Article 2(3).[350] It subsequently denied the claimant's attempt to incorporate a more favorable umbrella clause from third-party treaties because the ISDS provision in the basic treaty did not include disputes brought in terms of its MFN clause.[351]

---

348 Pérez-Aznar (n 54), 789.

349 Article 2(3) of the Czech Republic – UK BIT (1992). A copy of which is available at: <https://investmentpolicy.unctad.org/international-investment-agreements/treaty-files/993/download> accessed 20 April 2022.

350 *WNC Factoring Ltd (WNC) v The Czech Republic, Award dated 22 February 2017*, PCA Case No. 2014–34 [320].

351 *WNC v Czech Republic* (n 350) [349]. Article 8(1) of the Czech Republic – UK BIT relates to the jurisdiction of the tribunal, which reads as: 'Disputes between an investor of one Contracting Party and the other Contracting Party concerning an obligation of the latter under Articles 2(3), 4, 5 and 6 of this Agreement in relation to an investment of the former which have not been amicably settled shall, after a period of four months from written notification of a claim, be submitted to arbitration under paragraph 2 below if either party to the dispute so wishes.' See Czech Republic – UK BIT (1992) (n 349).

Two elements are crucial to the above arbitral tribunals' reasonings: First, whether there is contractual privity between the claimant and the respondent state. Second, whether the wording of the MFN clause at issue is broad enough to raise the contractual claim to the international level. The recent restrictive approach adopted by the *İçkale* and *WNC* tribunals entails a cautious consideration of the specific wording of MFN clauses and treaty context. However, it is doubtful whether they will lead to other tribunals taking similar approaches because of the peculiar situations present in those cases.

2.2.5 The Incorporation of Other Substantive Treatment

Besides the above substantive provisions, claimants have also invoked MFN clauses in order to broaden the scope of BITs in respect of other provisions. The *CMS* case involved a dispute brought in terms of the Argentina-U.S. BIT and entailed an alleged breach by Argentina of its treaty obligations not to suspend/terminate the claimant's right to calculate tariffs in U.S. dollars and to make adjustments for inflation.[352] The respondent invoked a state of necessity exception as envisioned in Article XI of the treaty and under customary international law in order to sustain its claim that it should be exempt from liability.[353]

The claimant contended that the Argentine economic crisis did not fall within the concept of "essential security interests" as required by Article XI.[354] Even if it had, the claimant argued that it would still be entitled to treatment no less favorable than third-country investors under the MFN clause in the basic treaty.[355] The claimant also invoked the MFN clause in an attempt to avoid the state of necessity exception contained in Article XI, which was absent from other BITs concluded by Argentina.[356] The respondent contended that, firstly, the security interest should include economic security. Moreover, Argentina should be released from its treaty obligations under the circumstances given that the country faced a severe financial crisis and many instances of *force*

352 *CMS v Argentina* (n 20). For a summary of the case, see: <https://investmentpolicy.unctad.org/investment-dispute-settlement/cases/68/cms-v-argentina> accessed 20 April 2022.

353 *CMS v Argentina* (n 20) [99]. Article XI provides: 'This Treaty shall not preclude the application by either Party of measures necessary for the maintenance of public order, the fulfillment of its obligations with respect to the maintenance or restoration of international peace or security, or the protection of its own essential security interests.' See: Argentina – U.S. BIT (n 63).

354 *CMS v Argentina* (n 20) [340].

355 *CMS v Argentina* (n 20) [343].

356 *CMS v Argentina* (n 20) [343].

majeure. Additionally, the respondent asserted, the claimant had not been treated differently from nationals or investors from third countries.[357]

The tribunal did not find the claimant's arguments persuasive. It emphasized the *ejusdem generis* principle and reasoned that had other Article XI type clauses envisioned in third-party treaties of Argentina accorded treatment more favorable to third-state investors than to the claimant, the claimant's argument in relation to the operation of the MFN clause "might have been made."[358] The tribunal further explained that according to the *ejusdem generis* principle, the mere absence of such provision in other treaties did not allow it to ignore its existence in the basic treaty through an application of the MFN clause.[359]

Although the *CMS* tribunal correctly rejected the MFN claim, it nevertheless misrepresented the *ejusdem generis* principle. According to the tribunal, "the argument about the operation of the MFN might have been made" if the third-party BIT contained a similar provision.[360] However, as an exception contained in the basic treaty, Article XI should constrain the application of the MFN clause to incorporate supposedly more favorable treatment; it should not, as the tribunal's logic suggests is possible, be allowed to be overridden by it.[361]

3 Concluding Remarks

The above discussions indicate that the MFN clause, as a treaty provision, should be applied within the specific limitations contained in the clause itself, the basic treaty and the comparator treaty. MFN interpretation requires a detailed, treaty-by-treaty examination instead of a quick and general assumption in relation to the rationale of MFN clauses. The general assumption that MFN clauses are supposed to multilateralize investment protection is unfounded in international law and may lead to abusive treaty-shopping.[362]

Claimants have sought to rely on MFN clauses in ISDS in order to make out cases of *de facto* violation as well as in attempts to incorporate higher substantive standards contained in other treaties. The proper application of the *ejusdem generis* principle is essential in relation to both types of claims. In the

357 *CMS v Argentina* (n 20) [352].
358 *CMS v Argentina* (n 20) [377].
359 *CMS v Argentina* (n 20) [377].
360 *CMS v Argentina* (n 20) [377].
361 Schill (n 171) 144.
362 Baumgartner (n 158).

case of *de facto* violations, tribunals tend to conduct careful, factual examinations. This means, tribunals inquire whether the claimant was indeed treated "less favorably" than third-party investors that are "in like circumstances." As a result, most cases have failed due to the lack of likeness between claimants and the identified third country investors.[363]

On the other hand, the *ejusdem generis* principle has been applied differently when incorporating higher standards of treatment from other treaties through applying MFN clauses. First, it has been used to allow the incorporation of higher standards of treatment if the basic treaty and third-party treaty contain similar provisions. For Sharmin, such practice should be allowed when "it is in harmony with the intent of the IIA parties to be logically constructed from the text of the treaty in the light of its context."[364] For example, when the MFN clause at issue is linked with FET, relying on the MFN clause to incorporate more favorable FET standards from third treaties would be consistent with the *ejusdem generis* principle. Second, invoking an MFN clause in order to incorporate a brand new treaty standard would be to impose on the contracting parties obligations which they never contemplated, and this is inconsistent with the *ejusdem generis* principle.[365]

In conclusion, MFN clauses should be interpreted on a case-by-case basis in accordance with the *ejusdem generis* principle. Invoking an MFN clause to incorporate a treaty standard absent from the basic treaty is driven by the belief that the MFN clause is a tool aimed at multilateralizing investment protection, which borders on treaty-shopping that is unexpected by contracting states. Therefore, both tribunals and states should play their part in this regard. Tribunals should act more responsibly and properly when applying interpretive methods like the *ejusdem generis* principle. States, on the other hand, should draft more detailed MFN clauses in order to avoid unanticipated and unintended interpretations by tribunals.[366]

Chapters 4and 5 continue this discussion from the procedural perspective. As we will see, the application of MFN clauses in order to incorporate dispute settlement provisions has led to a greater deal of controversy.

363 In some cases, the tribunals rejected the MFN violation because the claimant failed to identify a more favorable foreign investor, for example: *Grand River v U.S.* (n 99).

364 Sharmin (n 118) 141.

365 International Law Commission (n 1) 30 [11].

366 UNCTAD's Reform Pacakge for the International Investment Regime (2018), 33–35. A copy of which is available at: <https://investmentpolicy.unctad.org/uploaded-files/document/UNCTAD_Reform_Package_2018.pdf> accessed 20 April 2022.

CHAPTER 4

Applying the MFN Clause to Avoid Procedural Preconditons

The discussion in this chapter focuses on whether the most-favored-nation (MFN) clause can successfully be invoked in order to incorporate more favorable treatment from third-party treaties compared to the procedural preconditions contained in the basic treaty. Before engaging in the relevant analysis, it is first necessary to clarify several points. The first is the distinction between the concepts of "jurisdiction" and "admissibility." Jurisdiction refers to an international court's or tribunal's ability to entertain a particular dispute. Without it, the court or tribunal in question simply does not have the power to decide the case before it and issue a binding decision. Admissibility, on the other hand, refers to a claimant's ability to be heard by a competent court or tribunal and relates to certain defects of a given claim *per se*.[1] These defects are curable. In other words, the difference between jurisdiction and admissibility is that "[j]urisdiction is an attribute of a [court or] tribunal and not of a claim, whereas admissibility is an attribute of a claim but not of a [court or] tribunal."[2]

In the context of investment arbitration, the distinction between jurisdiction and admissibility is important from the perspective of MFN clauses. An United Nations Conference on Trade and Development (UNCTAD) report categorizes cases concerning the application of MFN clauses to procedural treatment into two groups. The first group includes cases where claimants have invoked an MFN clause in an attempt to replace dispute settlement provisions with preconditions for submitting a claim to international arbitration

1 *Hochtief Aktiengesellschaft v Argentine Republic, Decision on Jurisdiction dated 24 October 2011*, ICSID Case No. ARB/07/31 278 [95].

2 *Hochtief* v Argentina (n 1)[90]. See generally: Filippo Fontanelli, *Jurisdiction and Admissibility in Investment Arbitration* (BRILL 2018); August Reinisch, 'Jurisdiction and Admissibility in International Investment Law' (2017) 16 The Law & Practice of International Courts and Tribunals 21; Michael Waibel, 'Investment Arbitration: Jurisdiction and Admissibility' [2014] University of Cambridge Faculty of Law Research Paper No. 9/2014 Available at SSRN: <https://papers.ssrn.com/sol3/papers.cfm?abstract_id=2391789> accessed 20 April 2022; Gabriel Bottini (ed), 'Admissibility in International Investment Law', *Admissibility of Shareholder Claims under Investment Treaties* (Cambridge University Press 2020); Jan Paulsson, 'Jurisdiction and Admissibility' [2005] Global Reflection on International Law, Commerce and Dispute Resolution 601.

in a basic treaty with dispute settlement provisions contained in a third-party treaty which do not contain the same preconditions. The UNCTAD report sees these claims as concerning "admissibility" requirements. The second group includes disputes where claimants have attempted to surmount the jurisdictional threshold using an MFN clause. This group of cases are seen by the UNCTAD report as concerning the "scope of jurisdiction."[3]

In his research, August Reinisch has identified the growing trend among investor-state dispute settlement (ISDS) tribunals to recognize the conceptual categorization as an important issue.[4] For Sharmin, such conceptual categorization indicates that on the issue of MFN clause application, admissibility issues are potentially less fatal than jurisdictional ones. As a result, tribunals can wield their discretion in order to bypass admissibility issues via reliance on an MFN clause, but they cannot apply an MFN clause as easily in order to overcome jurisdictional preconditions.[5]

This chapter examines the cases where an MFN clause was invoked for the first purpose, i.e., in order to avoid procedural prerequisites contained in a basic treaty. The controversial issue in this area is whether an MFN clause can be relied on in order to avoid or reduce the timeframes of requirements in basic treaties that certain domestic remedies first be pursued before a claimant becomes entitled to bring a dispute to an international tribunal. Key to resolving this issue is whether such requirements are jurisdictional in nature. An example in this regard is Article X(2) of the Argentina-Spain Bilateral Investment Treaty (BIT) reviewed below. The English version of this article reads as follows:

> 2. If the dispute cannot thus be settled within six months following the date on which the dispute has been raised by either party, it shall be submitted to the competent tribunal of the Contracting Party in whose territory the investment was made.[6]

Some observers believe that shortening a seemingly arbitrary waiting period that must be observed prior to the submission of a dispute affects the timing of

---

3 United Nations Conference on Trade and Development (ed), *Most-Favoured-Nation Treatment: A Sequel* (United Nations 2010) 66–7.

4 Reinisch (n 2) 21–43.

5 Tanjina Sharmin, *Application of Most-Favoured-Nation Clauses by Investor-State Arbitral Tribunals: Implications for the Developing Countries* (Springer 2020) 165.

6 Argentina – Spain BIT (1991), available at: <https://investmentpolicy.unctad.org/international-investment-agreements/treaty-files/119/download> accessed 20 April 2022. The original Spanish treaty text was translated into English by the Maffezini tribunal. See: *Emilio Agustín Maffezini v The Kingdom of Spain, Decision of the Tribunal on Objections to Jurisdiction dated 25 January 2000,* ICSID Case No. ARB/97/7 [19].

a host state's consent to arbitration in relation to investment disputes, but does not necessarily undermine the host state's consent as a whole.[7] This position is in sharp contrast to arguments by others that procedural preconditions in dispute settlement provisions are jurisdictional in nature.

For example, the International Law Commission (ILC) uses the term "admissibility of claims" as the title of Article 44 of its Draft Articles on State Responsibility. That provision states that "[t]he responsibility of a State may not be invoked if: (b) The claim is one to which the rule of exhaustion of local remedies applies and any available and effective remedy has not been exhausted."[8] In the International Court of Justice (ICJ) case concerning *Application of the International Convention on the Elimination of All Forms of Racial Discrimination ("CERD") (Georgia v Russian Federation)*, the Court was asked to interpret Article 22 of the CERD. That provision stipulates that "[a]ny dispute between two or more States Parties with respect to the interpretation or application of this Convention, which is not settled by negotiation or by the procedures expressly provided for in this Convention, shall, at the request of any of the parties to the dispute, be referred to the International Court of Justice for decision, unless the disputants agree to another mode of settlement." The ICJ determined that the ordinary meaning of Article 22 required the establishment of "preconditions before the seisin of the Court."[9]

Similarly, in *Democratic Republic of the Congo v Rwanda*, the ICJ explained the distinction as follows:

> The Court will however first address the DRC's argument that the objection based on non-fulfilment of the preconditions set out in the compromissory clauses, and in particular in Article 29 of the Convention, is an objection to the admissibility of its application rather than to the jurisdiction of the Court. The Court recalls in this regard that its jurisdiction is based on the consent of the parties and is confined to the extent accepted by them (see paragraph 65 above). When that consent is expressed in a compromissory clause in an international agreement, any conditions to

7 Ruth Teitelbaum, 'Who's Afraid of Maffezini? Recent Developments in the Interpretation of Most Favored Nation Clauses' (2005) 22 Journal of International Arbitration 225, 232; *Hochtief v Argentina* (n 1).

8 International Law Commission, 'Draft Articles on Responsibility of States for Internationally Wrongful Acts, with Commentaries' (2001) Yearbook of the International Law Commission, Vol II, Part Two. Available at: <https://legal.un.org/ilc/texts/instruments/english/commentaries/9_6_2001.pdf> accessed 20 April.

9 *Application of the International Convention on the Elimination of All Forms of Racial Discrimination (Georgia v Russian Federation), Judgment of 1 April 2011*, ICJ [141].

> which such consent is subject must be regarded as constituting the limits thereon. The Court accordingly considers that the examination of such conditions relates to its jurisdiction and not to the admissibility of the application.[10]

For the same reason, Professor Brigitte Stern stated in her dissenting opinion in the *Impregilo* award that there appears to be "no legal reason" to categorize the types of conditions of the State's consent as either "conditions of admissibility" or "conditions of jurisdiction."[11] She argued that, although such a distinction appears to explain tribunals' divisive decisions on applying the MFN clause on procedural treatment, there is nevertheless no principle which requires tribunals to decide whether an MFN clause applies to issues of admissibility instead of jurisdiction.[12]

1 The Discussion Started by the *Maffezini* Case

The possibility of MFN clauses including dispute settlement clauses within their scope of application was, in fact, analyzed before the *Maffezini* case. Grigera Naón, for example, argued that, depending on its wording, an MFN clause in a basic treaty could be construed so as to give access to a private investor to a more favorable dispute resolution mechanism envisaged in another international investment agreement (IIA).[13] The *Maffezini* tribunal interpreted the relevant MFN clause relatively broadly by allowing the clause to incorporate "more favorable" dispute settlement provisions from third-party treaties. After *Maffezini*, the question of whether MFN clauses could be used to import supposedly better procedural treatment has become one of the most hotly debated issues in investment arbitration.

The dispute between Mr. Maffezini and Spain concerned the discontinuance of his company's activities due to an internal financial crisis allegedly attributed to Spain. It included misinforming the claimant on the project's costs

---

10 *Case concerning Armed Activities on the Territory of the Congo (New Application: 2002) (Democratic Republic of the Congo v Rwanda), Judgment of 3 February 2006*, ICJ [91–93].

11 *Impregilo S.p.A. v Argentine Republic (I), Award Dated 21 June 2011, Concurring and Dissenting Opinion of Professor Brigitte Stern*, ICSID Case No. ARB/07/17 [83].

12 *Impregilo v Argentina (I)* (n 11), footnote 56.

13 Horacio A Grigera Naón, 'The Settlement of Investment Disputes between States and Private Parties' (2000) 1 The Journal of World Investment & Trade 59, 74.

and further entailed unauthorized bank transfers.[14] In this case, the claimant attempted to invoke the MFN clause contained in the Argentina-Spain BIT in order to avoid the 6-month waiting period during which claims could only be brought in front of Spain's domestic courts before and during which claims could not be submitted to international arbitration.

Article IV of the Argentina-Spain BIT provided that "[i]n all matters subject to this Agreement, this treatment shall not be less favorable than that extended by each Party to the investments made in its territory by investors of a third country."[15] Article X of the Argentina-Spain BIT, moreover, required disputing parties to first attempt to resolve the dispute amicably for six months before submitting their dispute to the Spanish courts. Only when no decision had been made on the merits of the dispute after 18 months from the initiation of domestic adjudication proceedings, or when both parties agreed, could the claim be submitted to international arbitration at the request of either disputing party.[16] To avoid the 6-month precondition, the claimant invoked the MFN clause in the basic treaty in an attempt to incorporate Article 10(2) of the Spain-Chile BIT, which contains no such precondition.[17]

In response to the disputing parties' respective contentions about whether the MFN clause could be invoked to import a shorter domestic adjudication period, the *Maffezini* tribunal first addressed the MFN clause's scope by referring to the *Anglo-Iranian* case. In that case, the ICJ stated that the basic treaty established the juridical link between the foreign investor's home state and a third-party treaty and conferred upon the home state the third party's rights. Otherwise, a third-party treaty that was independent and isolated from the basic treaty could not produce any legal effect between the contracting parties due to the *res inter alios acta* principle.[18] The tribunal explained that what this implied for MFN treatment was that the subject matter to which the MFN clause in the basic treaty applies should first be determined before it can be invoked to import provisions from third-party treaties.[19]

The tribunal then applied the *ejusdem generis* principle in order to examine whether dispute settlement provision falls into the same category of subject

14 *Maffezini v Spain* (n 6). For the summary of the case, see: <https://investmentpolicy.unctad.org/investment-dispute-settlement/cases/19/maffezini-v-spain> accessed 20 April 2022.

15 Argentina – Spain BIT (1991) (n 6); *Maffezini v Spain* (n 6) [38].

16 *Maffezini v Spain* (n 6) [19].

17 *Maffezini v Spain* (n 6) [1].

18 *Maffezini v Spain* (n 6) [44].

19 *Maffezini v Spain* (n 6) [45].

as that to which the clause itself related. It referred to the *Ambatielos* case where the Permanent Court of Arbitration (PCA) arbitration commission (PCA Commission) concluded as follows:

> It is true that the 'administration of justice', when viewed in isolation, is a subject-matter other than 'commerce and navigation', but this is not necessarily so when it is viewed in connection with the protection of the rights of traders. Protection of the rights of traders naturally finds a place among the matters dealt with by treaties of commerce and navigation.
>
> Therefore it cannot be said that the administration of justice, in so far as it is concerned with the protection of these rights, must necessarily be excluded from the field of application of the most-favored-nation clause, when the latter includes 'all matters relating to commerce and navigation'. The question can only be determined in accordance with the intention of the Contracting Parties as deduced from a reasonable interpretation of the treaty.[20]

The PCA Commission accepted that the MFN clause applied to issues of just administration and found that the clause complied with the *ejusdem generis* rule.[21] As such, the *Maffezini* tribunal determined that although the Argentina-Spain BIT did not expressly include a reference to dispute settlement in its MFN clause, there still existed "good reasons to conclude that today dispute settlement arrangements are inextricably related to the protection of foreign investors, as they are also related to the protection of rights of traders under treaties of commerce."[22]

A fact frequently noted by later tribunals is that the *Maffezini* case featured a broadly worded MFN clause. In fact, the MFN clause in the Argentina-Spain BIT provided for the widest scope of all MFN clauses examined in Spanish BITs. The expression "all matters subject to this Agreement" opened the possibility for tribunals to extend it to dispute settlement provision without coming into conflict with the *ejusdem generis* principle.

The *Maffezini* tribunal also referred to the drafting history of the International Center for the Settlement of Investment Disputes (ICSID) Convention which reflected the compromise of conflicting views between

20 *The Ambatielos Claim (Greece, United Kingdom of Great Britain and Northern Ireland), Arbitral Award of the Commission of Arbitration in 1956*, 107.

21 *Maffezini v Spain* (n 6) [50].

22 *Maffezini v Spain* (n 6) [54].

international arbitration and the so-called Calvo Doctrine.[23] It inferred that traders and investors had "traditionally felt that their rights and interests are better protected by recourse to international arbitration than by submission of disputes to domestic courts."[24] The tribunal further concluded that the MFN clause could import more favorable dispute settlement provisions in the following terms:

> [I]f a third-party treaty contains provisions for the settlement of disputes that are more favorable to the protection of the investor's rights and interests than those in the basic treaty, such provisions may be extended to the beneficiary of the most favored nation clauses as they are fully compatible with the ejusdem generis principle.[25]

To support this conclusion, the tribunal took into account the negotiating history of the basic treaty, as well as the state practice of Argentina and Spain. It noted that the Argentina-Spain BIT was a compromise between the two countries because, at the time of its conclusion, Argentina had required prior exhaustion of local remedies in its treaties while Spanish policy tended to allow direct submission to international arbitration.[26] Up to the conclusion of the Argentina-Spain BIT, Spain had followed a consistent pro-arbitration policy that allowed arbitration right away after several months of amicable negotiation.[27] Additionally, the Argentina-Spain BIT was the only Spanish treaty that formulated its MFN clause broadly enough to include "all matters subject to this Agreement." While all other Spanish treaties provide a narrower formulation of the MFN clause.[28]

In addition to the *ejusdem generis* principle, the tribunal believed that the operation of the MFN clause also had some crucial limits from a public policy perspective. The tribunal recognized such public policy considerations as "fundamental conditions" for the contracting states when they concluded BITs and that these could not be overridden by the MFN clause. In this regard, the tribunal listed four main restrictions as follows:

23 For a general introduction of the Calvo Doctrine, see supra Chapter 1. See also: Manuel R Garcia-Mora, 'The Calvo Clause in Latin American Constitutions and International Law' (1950) 33 Marquette Law Review 16.

24 *Maffezini v Spain* (n 6) [55].

25 *Maffezini v Spain* (n 6) [55].

26 *Maffezini v Spain* (n 6) [57].

27 *Maffezini v Spain* (n 6) [58].

28 *Maffezini v Spain* (n 6) [60].

1. [I]f one contracting party has conditioned its consent to arbitration on the exhaustion of local remedies. The operation of the MFN clause cannot bypass this requirement because such arrangement manifests a fundamental rule of international law;
2. [I]f the parties have agreed to a dispute settlement arrangement that provides a 'fork-in-the-road' clause which requires an irrevocable choice between the domestic Court and international arbitration. This cannot be bypassed by the MFN clause because it would 'upset the finality of arrangements that many countries deem important as a matter of public policy';
3. [I]f the parties agree to a particular arbitration forum like ICSID, such option cannot be replaced by MFN clause with a different system of arbitration; [and]
4. A highly institutionalized arbitration system that incorporates precise rules of procedure agreed to by contracting parties such as that of NAFTA cannot be bypassed by the MFN clause since such provision reflects the contracting parties' accurate will.[29]

In reaching this conclusion, the tribunal expressed its worries on the subtle distinction between the legitimate extension of treaty rights, which might lead to "the harmonization and enlargement of the scope of such arrangements," and disruptive treaty shopping, which could wreak havoc with respect to the policy objectives underlying specific treaty provisions.[30] Given the dispute at hand, the tribunal determined that the MFN clause could incorporate the more favorable dispute settlement provision in the Spain-Chile BIT. According to the tribunal, the requirement that claimants first resort to domestic courts, as provided by the Argentina-Spain BIT, did not constitute a fundamental issue of public policy. This was evident from the treaty's context, the negotiating history that led to its conclusion, and the subsequent treaty practice of Argentina and Spain.[31]

The *Maffezini* decision was criticized for inferring the contracting states' consent to arbitration through looking at a combination of two BITs via the MFN clause included in the basic treaty.[32] The dispute in *Maffezini* concerned

29 *Maffezini v Spain* (n 6) [63].
30 *Maffezini v Spain* (n 6) [63].
31 *Maffezini v Spain* (n 6) [64].
32 Brigitte Stern, 'ICSID Arbitration and the State's Increasingly Remote Consent: Apropos the Maffezini Case' in Steve Charnovitz, Debra P Steger and Peter Van den Bossche (eds), *Law in the Service of Human Dignity* (1st edn, Cambridge University Press 2005) 252.

an investor from a typically capital-importing state (Argentina) against a traditional capital-exporting state (Spain). It entailed a "reversal of roles" compared to the more typical investment arbitration cases where a disgruntled investor from developed countries sought to arbitrate in relation to treatment it received at the hands of a developing country (e.g., the *Siemens* case, brought against Argentina).[33] Against this backdrop, the tribunal examined Spanish treaty practice to support its conclusion that arbitration was not covered by the public policy envisaged by Spain and could not, therefore, be excluded from the scope of the MFN clause in the basic treaty. However, the various Spanish treaties with Argentina and other countries might have suggested that Spain never intended such dispute settlement arrangements to be replaced via the invocation of an MFN clause, which is a conclusion by other tribunals at later stages.[34]

Moreover, the tribunal's approach also gave rise to the question as to whether a different outcome would have been reached if a Spanish investor had brought an arbitration against Argentina. In other words, whether a tribunal would have viewed the consistent Argentine treaty practice against arbitration as a public policy consideration and refused to incorporate a third-party dispute settlement provision via the MFN clause in the basic treaty.[35] It is also not clear on what basis the tribunal came up with its non-exhaustive list of public considerations as part of its interpretation of the MFN clause in the basic treaty, especially given that the respective intentions of the contracting parties could not be inferred from the basic treaty itself.[36]

The reasoning and conclusion of *Maffezini* tribunal has led to fierce debate. A critical division has emerged among subsequent tribunals as to whether an MFN clause may be invoked in order to modify the preconditions contained in dispute settlement provisions in the basic treaty through the importation of "more favorable" preconditions (or the lack thereof) from third-party treaties. As such, in the upcoming sections, the following issues are examined: (1) the characteristics of procedural preconditions in the context of the operation of MFN clauses, and specifically whether these preconditions go to admissibility

33 *Siemens AG v The Argentine Republic, Decision on Jurisdiction dated 3 August 2004,* ICSID Case No. ARB/02/8.

34 Scott Vesel, 'Clearing a Path Through a Tangled Jurisprudence: Most-Favored-Nation Clauses and Dispute Settlement Provisions in Bilateral Investment Treaties' (2007) 32 Yale Journal of International Law 160.

35 Vesel (n 34) 157.

36 *Plama Consortium Limited v Republic of Bulgaria, Decision on Jurisdiction, 8th February 2005,* ICSID Case No. ARB/03/24 [221].

or jurisdiction; (2) the "more favorable" element in MFN clauses in view of tribunals' comparison between domestic and international legal systems. Given that most cases on this point concern Argentine treaties, these sections will be sub-divided according to the three Argentine BITs which are most often raised in MFN cases: the Argentina-Spain, Argentina-Germany, and Argentina-United Kingdom (UK) BITs.[37] For the sake of completion, other treaties will also be examined.

2 Exhaustion of Local Remedies and Dispute Settlement Provisions

This section will review the nature of temporal preconditions, first to establish its relationship with the exhaustion of local remedies requirement and then to explore whether it relates to a claim's admissibility or the jurisdiction of investment tribunals. The ultimate purpose is to discuss whether and to what extent MFN clauses in basic treaties are capable of incorporating temporal preconditions from third-party treaties.

2.1 *Exhaustion of Local Remedies?*

One of the four public policy considerations enumerated by the *Maffezini* tribunal that MFN clauses cannot be used to overcome is the need to exhaust local remedies, a rule from customary international law (ELR rule).[38] The rule requires that before resorting to diplomatic protection or instituting international proceedings, a foreign national allegedly harmed by a host state must first seek redress for the alleged harm in front of the administrative and judicial system of that state and must pursue this avenue until a final decision has been rendered.[39] In the international investment law framework, the ELR

37 Argentina – Spain BIT (1991) (n 6); Argentina – UK BIT (1990), available at <https://investmentpolicy.unctad.org/international-investment-agreements/treaty-files/126/download> accessed 20 April 2022; Argentina – Germany BIT (1991), available at: https://investmentpolicy.unctad.org/international-investment-agreements/treaty-files/92/download> accessed 20 April 2022.

38 For the customary international law nature of the Exhaustion of Local Remedy rule, see for example: M Valenti, 'The Most Favoured Nation Clause in BITs as a Basis for Jurisdiction in Foreign Investor – Host State Arbitration' (2008) 24 Arbitration International 447, 452; Martin Dietrich Brauch, 'Exhaustion of Local Remedies in International Investment Law' [2017] International Institute for Sustainable Development (IISD) 33; Chittharanjan Felix Amerasinghe, *Local Remedies in International Law* (2nd edn, Cambridge University Press 2004); Ian Brownlie, *Principles of Public International Law* (7th ed, Oxford University Press 2008).

39 Brauch (n 38) 2.

rule is absent from most modern BITs.[40] Article 26 of the ICSID Convention provides ELR as a jurisdictional precondition for states' consent to ICSID arbitration. It provides as follows:

> Consent of the parties to arbitration under this Convention shall unless otherwise stated, be deemed consent to such arbitration to the exclusion of any other remedy. A Contracting State may require the exhaustion of local administrative or judicial remedies as a condition of its consent to arbitration under this Convention.[41]

In her article commenting on the *Maffezini* decision, Professor Brigitte Stern defined the requirement in the basic treaty that only domestic courts may be approached for 18 months before international arbitration may be resorted to (the 18-month requirement) as the exhaustion of certain local remedies in Spain. She is of the view that this was an explicit condition of the consent to international arbitration by both Argentina and Spain.[42]

However, the 18-month requirement and other similar provisions are not considered a traditional requirement of the ELR rule by tribunals because it does not require the *exhaustion* of domestic remedies.[43] According to Schreuer, these requirements do not technically form part of an obligation to exhaust local remedies because "the parties are free to turn to ICSID, once the time has elapsed."[44] Moreover, the actual periods of time specified in these types of provisions are usually short and it is thus unrealistic to expect the proper exhaustion of local remedies to take place before they run their course. This makes one wonder whether the contracting parties expected a settlement to be achieved within these periods when concluding the provisions in question. Indeed, some scholars have deemed the need for prior domestic litigation as by nature constituting a mere extension of the waiting period required before international arbitration may be resorted to.[45]

In *Siemens*, the tribunal refused to consider the 18-month requirement as a version of the ELR rule under customary international law as contended for by

40 Brauch (n 38) 7.
41 ICSID Convention (1965).
42 Stern (n 32) 252.
43 F Orrego Vicuna, 'Reports of Maffezini's Demise Have Been Greatly Exaggerated' (2012) 3 Journal of International Dispute Settlement 299, 320; Valenti (n 38) 453.
44 Christoph Schreuer, *The ICSID Convention: A Commentary: A Commentary on the Convention on the Settlement of Investment Disputes between States and Nationals of Other States* (Cambridge Univ Press 2009) 393.
45 Vesel (n 34) 157.

the respondent. It explained that this procedural precondition did not require a final decision by domestic courts at any level. It merely required the passage of time or the continuance of a dispute after a court's decision and thus could not be considered an ELR requirement that constituted a jurisdictional precondition.[46] The *Plama* tribunal considered such a procedural arrangement to be curious and nonsensical. It held as follows:

> The decision in *Maffezini* is perhaps understandable. The case concerned a curious requirement that during the first 18 months, the dispute is tried in the local courts. The present Tribunal sympathizes with a tribunal that attempts to neutralize such a provision that is nonsensical from a practical point of view.[47]

The tribunal added, however, that "such exceptional circumstances should not be treated as a statement of general principle guiding future tribunals in other cases where exceptional circumstances are not present."[48]

The *Plama* tribunal was perhaps correct in describing the 18-month requirement as "curious." Indeed, the rationale behind such a precondition is far from clear, especially when it could be satisfied by the simple effluxion of time without the requirement that a domestic judgment be rendered, not to mention that the 18-month period might not even be enough for the dispute to reach a decision on the merits in domestic adjudication. In his dissenting opinion in *Hochtief*, Mr. Thomas explained that temporal preconditions are the product of compromise between state parties. He explained the legitimacy of such preconditions in the following terms:

> Bearing in mind that under Article 26, second sentence, of the ICSID Convention a Contracting State can require the exhaustion of local remedies as a condition of its consent to arbitration under the Convention, it is open to two States to agree to a limited recourse to local remedies as a condition of their consent to arbitration under their bilateral treaty. Their having made such a choice, the period selected had to be of sufficient time to permit a Contracting Party's legal system to at least have an opportunity to address the dispute. A prior recourse provision of say, 6 months would hardly permit any real opportunity for the parties to frame the issues, let alone permit a court to consider the dispute. On

46 *Siemens v Argentina* (n 33) [104].
47 *Plama v Bulgaria* (n 36) [224].
48 *Plama v Bulgaria* (n 36) [224].

> the other hand, from a claimant's perspective, a limited period of time is preferable to a requirement of full exhaustion of local remedies (and 18 months would be seen as preferable to 36 months or more).[49]

Similarly, in *ICS (I)*, the tribunal determined the 18-month precondition to be mandatory and jurisdictional. In so doing, it stated that the precondition is neither a procedural waiting period nor a traditional ELR requirement. In the words of the tribunal, it was "a choice of forum for the submission of disputes in the first instance and not merely a question of ripeness."[50] Given the apparent trend towards the strict application of procedural prerequisites in public international law, the tribunal decided that such requirement could only be satisfied by submitting the investment dispute to the Argentine courts for a period of 18 months or until a final decision is rendered, whichever event came first.[51]

2.2 *Jurisdiction or Admissibility?*

A further question relevant to the MFN clause's operation goes to the nature of temporal preconditions: do they concern the consent of contracting states to the jurisdiction of an international tribunal or court, meaning that they cannot be avoided, or are they instead related to the admissibility of a claim, meaning that it becomes a question of the discretion of a tribunal whether they can be bypassed through an application of an MFN clause? In this context, the decision of the *ICS (I)* tribunal is a good example of the line of tribunals that have considered these preconditions to be jurisdictional in nature, and thus mandatory. On the other hand, the *Maffezini* decision and proponents of the approach think of temporal preconditions as an issue of admissibility and, therefore, tend to be of the view that they can be circumvented through reliance on MFN clauses. The analysis in the following subsections will unpack these two schools of thought.

---

49 *Hochtief v Argentina* (n 1), *Separate and Dissenting Opinion of J. Christopher Thomas, Q.C.* [7]. It has also been argued that prior domestic litigation is an alternative safeguard for States. See: Orrego Vicuna (n 43) 320.

50 *ICS Inspection and Control Services Limited v The Argentine Republic (I), Award on Jurisdiction dated 10 February 2012,* PCA Case No. 2010-9 [261].

51 *ICS v Argentina* (n 50) [251].

2.2.1 Requiring Remedies to Be Pursued in Local Courts as an Issue of Admissibility

Cases arising under the Argentina-Spain BIT have resulted in relatively consistent reasoning on this issue by tribunals. The *Telefónica* case constitutes a reversal of *Maffezini* to the extent that it involved a Spanish investor bringing a claim against the Argentine government. As part of its objections to the tribunal having jurisdiction, Argentina contended that Telefónica had not seen out the 18-month period required by Article X of the Argentina-Spain BIT.[52] The tribunal agreed with the claimant that the MFN clause covered dispute settlement mechanisms in third-party treaties. According to the tribunal, in view of the broad text of the MFN clause at issue, according foreign investors direct access to arbitration was a "typical matter where the MFN treatment is relevant, traditional and recognized as applicable."[53]

In reaching its decision in this regard, the tribunal referred to the *Ambatielos* case, which entailed a similarly worded MFN clause in the 1886 Greece-UK Agreement (where the operative phrase was "all matters relating to commerce and navigation,"), and a similar claim from the Greek government (the right of access by a Greek investor to the British justice system on equal footing with nationals from other states).[54] The tribunal accordingly held that exempting the claimant from submitting the dispute to domestic courts before international arbitration pertained to the "treatment" that Argentina applied "within its territory" to Spanish investors, who sought to bring their dispute, which alleged a breach of certain substantive provisions of the BIT in respect of their investment in Argentina, before an ICSID arbitral tribunal.[55] As such, the dispute settlement requirement in question fell within the scope of the MFN clause.

The Argentina-Spain BIT was also the basis for the claim brought in the *Teinver* case, where the claimant sought to invoke the MFN clause in order to incorporate a dispute settlement provision in the Argentina-United States (U.S.) BIT. The tribunal undertook an extensive exposé on ISDS tribunals' discussions on applying MFN clauses to dispute settlement provisions. It relied on the UNCTAD jurisdiction-admissibility taxonomy discussed above and indicated that the MFN clause in the Argentina-Spain BIT was unusual on the basis

52 *Telefónica S.A. v Argentine Republic, Decision on Jurisdiction dated 25 May 2006,* ICSID Case No. ARB/03/20 [17].

53 *Telefónica v Argentina* (n 52) [100].

54 *Ambatielos claim* (n 20); *Telefónica v Argentina* (n 52).

55 *Telefónica v Argentina* (n 52) [102].

of its broad language.[56] The tribunal observed that all the tribunals that had dealt with Article IV(2) of the Argentina-Spain BIT had consistently applied the MFN clause's broad language to the Article X dispute settlement provisions.

Furthermore, cases concerning issues of jurisdiction and admissibility involved particular factual and legal circumstances that required individual examination. Specifically, the claimant *in casu* had not invoked the MFN clause in relation to jurisdictional issues, for example through seeking to replace the scope of the forum of rules applicable to the arbitration, but rather to avoid the requirement that a claim first be brought in domestic courts for a certain period, i.e., the claimant's argument related to admissibility of its claim. For this purpose, the "all matters" wording was, in the tribunal's view, unambiguously inclusive enough for the 18-month requirement to be avoided through an application of the MFN clause in the basic treaty.[57]

The approaches taken in relation to disputes arising out of the Argentina-Germany BIT have been less consistent on this issue. While the *Siemens* and *Hochtief* tribunals decided that the 18-month requirement could be avoided, the *Wintershall* and *Daimler* tribunals came to the opposite conclusion.[58] As in the case of the Argentina-Spain BIT, the Argentina-Germany BIT contained a dispute resolution provision in Article 10 that required a six-month amicable settlement period, after which the 18-month requirement kicked in. Notably, however, the wording of the MFN clause in the Argentina-Germany BIT was not as broad as that in the Argentina-Spain BIT. Specifically, it referred more restrictively only to "activity in connection with investments" instead of "all matters." The protocol to the basic BIT indicated "activity" to include "the management, utilization, use, and enjoyment of an investment."[59]

In *Siemens*, the dispute concerned the Argentine government's suspension and subsequent termination of a contract to establish migration control and personal identification systems.[60] The claimant relied on the MFN clause contained in the basic treaty and tried to circumvent the 18-month requirement, contending that such precondition was merely a rule of procedure instead of an obstacle to jurisdiction.[61] The tribunal affirmed the possibility of invoking

56 *Autobuses Urbanos Del Sur S.A., Teinver S.A. and Transportes de Cercanías S.A. v Argentine Republic, Decision on Jurisdiction Dated 21 December 2012,* ICSID Case No. ARB/09/1 [171].

57 *Teinver v Argentina* (n 56) [186].

58 *Daimler Financial Services AG v Argentine Republic, Award Dated 22 August 2012,* ICSID Case No. ARB/05/1; *Wintershall Aktiengesellschaft v Argentine Republic, Award dated 8 December 2008,* ICSID Case No. ARB/04/14 124.

59 Argentina – Germany BIT (1991) (n 37).

60 *Siemens v Argentina* (n 33).

61 *Siemens v Argentina* (n 33) [32].

the MFN clause in order to import the dispute settlement provisions in the Argentina-Chile BIT, which prescribed a shorter period of six months and also included a "fork-in-the-road" requirement.[62]

The tribunal explained that, like other investment treaties, the Argentina-Germany BIT "[had] a distinctive feature special dispute settlement mechanism not normally open to investors." Therefore, access to such mechanism constituted a part of the protection offered by the basic treaty and fell within reach of the MFN clause. The tribunal took account of the *Maffezini* case in particular. It found that although the MFN clause in the dispute before it referred only to "treatment" and was formulated more narrowly than the MFN clause at issue in *Maffezini*, the term "treatment" and the expression "activities related to the investments" were nevertheless broad enough to include dispute settlement.[63] The tribunal also concurred with the public policy considerations formulated by the *Maffezini* tribunal. It pronounced that a specific requirement consistently included in similar treaties executed by Argentina would indicate the existence of a particular policy that the Argentine government had sought to pursue over time.

To this end, the tribunal examined several treaties signed by Argentina in 1991, including the Argentina-Germany BIT (April 1991), the Argentina-Chile BIT (August 1991), the Argentina-Spain BIT (October 1991), and the Argentina-U.S. BIT (November 1991). The tribunal found that not every treaty signed by Argentina in 1991 required prior submission to local courts. It inferred that the lack of consistency among Argentinean BITs in the same year "[did] not support the argument that the institution of proceedings before the local court [was] a 'sensitive' issue of economic or foreign policy or that it [was] an essential part of the consent of the respondent to arbitration."[64]

In 2012, the tribunal in *Hochtief* adopted a similar interpretive method as the one adopted by the *Siemens* tribunal. The *Hochtief* tribunal came to the conclusion that it had jurisdiction over the claims by applying the MFN clause in the Argentina-Germany BIT. In view of the more restrictive MFN clause, the majority of the tribunal considered that dispute settlement was an aspect of the "management" of an investment and should therefore be covered by the MFN clause. The tribunal pronounced that the procedural right to enforce the substantive right was "one component of the bundles of rights and duties that

62 Argentina – Chile BIT (1991). A copy of which is available at: <https://investmentpolicy.unctad.org/international-investment-agreements/treaty-files/78/download> accessed 20 April 2022.

63 *Siemens v Argentina* (n 33) [103]. See also: Orrego Vicuna (n 43) 315.

64 *Siemens v Argentina* (n 33) [105].

make up the legal concept of what property is,"[65] and that Article 10 on dispute settlement was "a benefit conferred on investors and designed to protect their interests."[66]

The tribunal distinguished the operation of the MFN clause from jurisdictional issues.[67] It stated that to eschew the 18-month precondition via an application of the MFN clause did not allow the claimant to submit cases that could not be submitted originally under the dispute settlement provision in Article 10 of Argentina-Germany BIT.[68] In this regard, applying the MFN clause did not, for the tribunal, implicate jurisdiction in any respect. Its reasoning related to the "implicit limitation" of the MFN clause, i.e., the tribunal found that the MFN clause could not operate to create additional rights beyond those offered by the basic treaty.[69]

According to the tribunal, the Argentina-Chile BIT could not put the claimant in a position that it could not be put in via the reach of the MFN clause in the Argentina-Germany BIT. The operation of the MFN clause only enabled the claimant to utilize arbitration "more quickly and more cheaply, without first pursuing litigation in the courts of Argentina for 18 months."[70] After a decade of development in investment arbitration after *Maffezini*, the *Hochtief* tribunal rendered a more detailed, albeit similar, decision on the application of an MFN clause in relation to the 18-month and similar requirements. It was thus considered by commentators as a manifestation of the "*Maffezini* spirit."[71]

Three cases brought under the Argentina-UK BIT on the application of MFN clauses in relation to procedural preconditions are examined below, namely *National Grid*, *ICS (I)*, and *AWG*.[72] Among these cases, only the *ICS (I)* tribunal ruled out the possibility of the dispute settlement mechanism falling within the scope of the MFN clause contained in the basic treaty. Article 3 of the Argentina-UK BIT provided an MFN clause similar to that in the Argentina-Germany BIT. It accorded MFN treatment to foreign investors "as regards their

65 *Hochtief v Argentina* (n 1) [66].
66 *Hochtief v Argentina* (n 1) [68].
67 *Hochtief v Argentina* (n 1) [86].
68 *Hochtief v Argentina* (n 1) [86].
69 *Hochtief v Argentina* (n 1) [79].
70 *Hochtief v Argentina* (n 1) [85].
71 MJ Valasek and EA Menard, 'Impregilo SpA v Argentine Republic and Hochtief AG v The Argentine Republic: Making Sense of Dissents: The Jurisprudence Inconstante of the MFN Clause' (2012) 27 ICSID Review 21, 25.
72 *National Grid PLC v The Argentine Republic, Decision on Jurisdiction dated June 2006*, UNCITRAL Arbitration; *ICS v Argentina* (n 50); *AWG Group Ltd v The Argentine Republic, Decision on Jurisdiction dated 3 August 2006*, UNCITRAL Arbitration.

management, maintenance, use, enjoyment or disposal of their investments."[73] Article 8 of the same BIT contained an 18-month requirement.

Concerning these provisions, the *AWG* tribunal noted that Article 3(2) accorded MFN treatment to "the management, maintenance, use, enjoyment or disposal" of foreign investments. It determined that "the right to have recourse to international arbitration is very much related particularly to investors' maintenance of an investment." Therefore, the *AWG* tribunal decided that UK investors were entitled, in accordance with Article 3(2), to import more favorable dispute settlement provisions from the Argentina-France BIT, which did not include an 18-month requirement. In reaching this conclusion, the tribunal relied on Article 7 of the Argentina-UK BIT in particular. Article 7 provided a detailed list of issues to be excluded from MFN treatment in Article 3. Dispute settlement was not included on this list. As a result, the tribunal inferred that –

> the failure to refer among these excluded items to any matter remotely connected to dispute settlement reinforces the interpretation that the most-favored-nation clause includes dispute settlement.[74]

The tribunal also took note of subsequent UK treaty practice to support its position. After 1993, the UK had concluded BITs with *inter alia* Honduras, Albania, and Venezuela with the third paragraphs in their MFN clauses explicitly including dispute settlement as forming part of the scope of MFN treatment:

> For the avoidance of doubt it is confirmed that the treatment provided in paragraphs (1) and (2) above shall apply to the provisions of Articles 1 to 11 of this Agreement.[75]

The tribunal inferred that such paragraph was "intended to clarify what had been the United Kingdom's preexisting intention in negotiating its BITs: that

73 Argentina – UK BIT (1990) (n 37).

74 *AWG v Argentina* (n 72) [58].

75 Albania – UK BIT (1994), a copy of which is available at: <https://investmentpolicy.unctad.org/international-investment-agreements/treaty-files/38/download> accessed 20 April 2022; Honduras – UK BIT (1993), a copy of which is available at: <https://investmentpolicy.unctad.org/international-investment-agreements/treaty-files/1511/download> accessed 20 April 2022; UK – Venezuela BIT (1995), a copy of which is available at: <https://investmentpolicy.unctad.org/international-investment-agreements/treaty-files/2375/download> accessed 20 April 2022; *AWG v Argentina* (n 72) [58].

the most-favored-nation clause is to cover all the articles (i.e., Articles 1 to 11) of the treaty."[76]

The *National Grid* tribunal took the same approach as the *Maffezini* tribunal. It explained that –

> the Tribunal considers that … 'treatment' under the MFN clause of the treaty makes it possible for UK investors in Argentina to resort to arbitration without first resorting to Argentine courts, as it permitted under the U.S.-Argentina Treaty. Therefore, the Tribunal rejects this objection to its jurisdiction.[77]

The above cases show some consistent features that deserve attention. The first is how the various tribunals employed the *ejusdem generis* principle from the *Ambatielos* case and applied it in relation to broadly worded MFN clauses to extend their jurisdiction. Second, it is also interesting that a number of tribunals were happy to adopt the public policy reasoning offered by the *Maffezini* tribunal and applied it in the context of state practice. The third issue is the notable neglect of the formulation of MFN clauses and the extent to which such neglect affected the outcomes of these cases.

2.2.1.1 *The Failure by Tribunals to Properly Apply the* Ejusdem Generis *Principle*

The tribunal decisions discussed above relied on the *ejusdem generis* principle, as well as the fact that MFN clauses in question were all worded broadly enough to justify the conclusion that the MFN could be applied in such a manner as to override the 18-month requirement in dispute resolution provisions of the various basic treaties at issue. In doing so, tribunals took it for granted that "matters" or "treatment" in this context naturally included procedural and jurisdictional issues. In other words, the tribunals operated on the presumption that both substantive and procedural rights could be assimilated through an application of the relevant MFN clauses in issue.[78]

The *Ambatielos* decision is often cited as a positive example for this purpose. However, a careful reading of the *Ambatielos* decision suggests that the PCA Commission did not apply the MFN clause in order to alter a procedural provision, but rather to provide Greek nationals the same *substantive* protection

76 *AWG v Argentina* (n 72) [58].

77 *National Grid v Argentina* (n 72) [93].

78 *Impregilo v Argentina* (n 11), *Concurring and Dissenting Opinion of Professor Brigitte Stern* [34].

of the administration of justice, relying as it did on the what was dictated by "justice," "right" and "equity."[79] Douglas points out the error committed by *Maffezini* tribunal in using *Ambatielos* as support to extend the application of an MFN clause to dispute settlement provisions. He opines that the MFN clause in *Ambatielos* was not invoked in relation to jurisdiction. Instead, it was invoked to support a claim of denial of justice for the alleged prejudice suffered by the claimant, which is substantive treatment by nature.[80] Following this logic, it can be concluded that the *Ambatielos* case and the *ejusdem generis* principle have been improperly applied by the *Maffezini* tribunal and others that have taken a similar approach.

According to the *Daimler* tribunal, an application of the *ejusdem generis* principle could merely assist with delineating the treaty clauses' "outer limits" from the perspective of application. Without more, the principle alone cannot be relied on to categorically exclude international dispute settlement from the potential scope of an MFN clause, nor can it be relied on without more to substantiate a conclusion that it falls within the scope of such clause with any certainty.[81] In this sense, the tribunals following the *Maffezini* approach have presumed that procedural and substantive treatment have the same character, which in turn entails at least an implicit assumption that both types of treatment serve an investment protection function.[82] By contrast, Douglas has argued that there is a fundamental difference between substantive and procedural treatment, stating that while the former accords treaty protection in a legal instrument (treaty), the latter addresses the jurisdiction of a court or tribunal authorized to solve disputes arising out of the legal instrument. Therefore, according to Douglas, they are not *ejusdem generis*.[83]

The *Maffezini* tribunal explained the rationale of assimilating both procedural and substantive treatment. It was of the view that, "dispute settlement arrangements are inextricably related to the protection of foreign investors, as they are also related to the protection of rights of traders under treaties of commerce."[84] Therefore, it is arguable that applying the *ejusdem generis* principle on the basis that there is no real distinction between substantive and

79 *Salini Costruttori S.p.A. and Italstrade S.p.A. v Hashemite Kingdom of Jordan, Decision on Jurisdiction dated 9 November 2004,* ICSID Case No. ARB/02/13 [112].

80 Z Douglas, 'The MFN Clause in Investment Arbitration: Treaty Interpretation Off the Rails' (2011) 2 Journal of International Dispute Settlement 97, 98.

81 *Daimler v Argentina* (n 58) [215].

82 Douglas (n 80) 102–103.

83 Douglas (n 80) 102–103.

84 *Maffezini v Spain* (n 6) [54].

procedural treatment is rooted in the notion that both serve to protect investors and their investments, which is a factor to which a number of tribunals have given primacy in reaching their decisions.

In the end, whether MFN clauses in basic treaties are able to incorporate "better" procedural preconditions in third-treaties relates to contracting parties' intention as expressed in treaty texts. Tribunals should respect treaty texts as the authentic source for contracting parties' intention. They should not render interpretations that prioritize investment protection.

2.2.1.2 *Public Policy Considerations*

Employed by the *Maffezini* tribunal to draw a line between treaty-shopping and the legitimate extension of rights and benefits, the origins of the four public policy considerations were nevertheless left unidentified.[85] Among the non-exhaustive public policy considerations listed by *the Maffezini* tribunal, only the requirement to exhaust of local remedies seems to have an explicit genesis; that is, it ostensibly comes from Article 26 of the ICSID Convention. Therefore, the *Maffezini* tribunal has made it difficult for later tribunals who seek to take the same approach (albeit that they are under no obligation to do so) to identify and apply possible public policy considerations.[86] As a result, an application of these public policy factors sometimes lead to conflicting interpretations and even treaty-shopping.[87]

Tribunals that have followed the *Maffezini* approach have tended to identify public policy considerations from state practice.[88] In *Siemens*, for example, the tribunal took the view that a specific requirement consistently included in similar treaties executed by Argentina could indicate the existence of a particular policy preference. It thus announced that the 18-month requirement could not be a sensitive national policy issue because Argentina had signed contemporaneous treaties with different prescriptions on this issue. To this end, it compared three treaties signed in the same year between Argentina and Chile (August 2, 1991), the U.S. (October 3, 1991), and Spain (November 14, 1991). The tribunal observed that these treaties included different requirements on the

85 *Maffezini v Spain* (n 6) [63].

86 Jürgen Kurtz, 'The Delicate Extension of Most-Favoured-Nation Treatment to Foreign Investors: Maffezini v. Kingdom of Spain' in Todd Weiler (ed), *International investment law and arbitration: leading cases from the ICSID, NAFTA, bilateral treaties and customary international law* 546.

87 *Salini v Jordan* (n 79) [115].

88 Gabriel Egli, 'Don't Get Bit: Addressing ICSID's Inconsistent Application of Most-Favored-Nation Clauses to Dispute Resolution Provisions Comment' (2006) 34 Pepperdine Law Review 1045, 1084.

institution of domestic judicial proceedings before recourse could be had to international arbitration. The tribunal concluded that this lack of consistency among the Argentine BITs of the same year did not support the argument that the 18-month requirement was a sensitive issue of economic or foreign policy or an essential part of Argentina's consent to arbitration.[89]

In *Daimler*, however, despite the case also being brought under the Argentina-Germany BIT, the tribunal reached the opposite conclusion given more or less the same set of facts. The *Daimler* tribunal took note of Argentina's contemporary state practice at the time of the treaty's conclusion. The tribunal noted that during the period May 22, 1990 to May 17, 1994, Argentina concluded a total number of 29 treaties. Of these 29 treaties, 10 of them contained an 18-month requirement and among the 17 treaties that entered into force, 9 of them included an 18-month requirement.[90] Using the date of entry into force of treaties as a benchmark, the tribunal came to the conclusion that the claimant's expansive interpretation of the MFN clause in the Germany-Argentina BIT would not be in accordance with the *effet utile* rule, since it indicated that the 18-month requirements in Argentinean treaties concluded after the Argentina-Germany BIT would be interpreted as void *ab initio* by virtue of Article 10. As a result, Argentina had "needlessly and inexplicably included the domestic courts provision in nine subsequent treaties, including the German-Argentine BIT."[91]

That the *Siemens* tribunal refused to import the "fork-in-the-road" requirement from the Argentina-U.S. BIT is also noteworthy since such requirement is among the four public policy considerations listed by the *Maffezini* tribunal. Although this can be explained by the absence of a *stare decisis* doctrine in investment arbitration, it is curious that the *Siemens* tribunal would follow the reasoning of *Maffezini* and deviate from it at the same time. This also reveals the limited value of the public policy considerations elaborated by the *Maffezini* tribunal.

In this connection, Egli suggests that the adoption of an express policy by one of the contracting states may help resolve this issue. He believes that "the adoption of a policy to define the scope of the MFN clause within the provisions of the BIT itself demonstrates a state's public policy."[92] Moreover, Egli argues that a host state can rely on its explicit expression of public policy to oppose an expansive interpretation.[93] This requires more detailed treaty drafting in

89 *Siemens v Argentina* (n 33) [105].
90 Daimler v Argentina (n 58) [262].
91 Daimler v Argentina (n 58) [263].
92 Egli (n 88) 1083.
93 Egli (n 88) 1084.

view of expansive MFN interpretation. However, this suggestion is based on the public policy considerations proposed by the *Maffezini* tribunal, the origin and determination of which is questionable. In other words, a consistent state practice may not indicate a state's public policy consideration with any level of certainty. Additionally, BITs are the result of complicated negotiations and compromises between contracting parties. This correspondingly means that, merely looking to the texts of BITs does not necessarily reveal a state's policy intentions, as factors like power imbalances between different states, among others, also influence the treaty text. Therefore, the unilateral intention from the treaty practice of one of the contracting parties may not suffice to persuade the tribunal of the intention of both contracting parties. As a result, the value of public policy consideration in relation to MFN interpretation should remain limited.

2.2.1.3 *Neglect to Consider the Precise Formulation of Dispute Settlement Clauses*

Another aspect is the above tribunals' neglect of the precise formulation of dispute settlement clauses in basic treaties. Contrary to what the *Maffezini* tribunal expected, such a failure might do little to harmonize approaches to investment arbitration.[94] First, in the Argentina-Spain BIT, Article X(2) used the term "shall" in relation to the 18-month requirement. It is fair to reach the conclusion that by using "shall" instead of "may" or "should" in Article X(2), Argentina and Spain intended to condition their consent to arbitration on the 18-month requirement being satisfied.[95] Taking such an approach would result in different outcomes in relation to the waiting periods that the *Maffezini* approach have effectively overridden.[96]

94 Joachim Delaney, 'The Use of MFN Clauses in ICSID Arbitrations' (2009) 21 National Law School of India Review 125, 134.

95 See for example *Southern Pacific Properties (Middle East) Limited v Arab Republic of Egypt, Decision on Jurisdiction II, 27th April 1895* ICSID No. ARB/84/3 [74]. Where the tribunal stated that 'the starting point in statutory interpretation, as in the interpretation of treaties and unilateral declarations, is the ordinary or grammatical meaning of the terms used.' In this respect, the tribunal focused on the 'shall be settled' term in Article 8 of the Egyptian Investment Law and concluded that such language mandated the submission of disputes to the various methods required therein. See also: Michele Potestà, 'The Interpretation of Consent to ICSID Arbitration Contained in Domestic Investment Laws' (2011) 27 Arbitration International 149, 163.

96 The letter from Prof. Schreuer addressed to the tribunal of *Wintershall*, see: *Wintershall v Argentina* (n 58) [133–53].

When considering the negotiation period and ELR as two ends of a spectrum, the 18-month requirement in the Argentina-Spain BIT falls in the middle ground and should thus be considered mandatory. For example, according to the *ICS (I)* tribunal, the requirement in Article 8(1) is neither a mere "waiting period" nor a requirement to exhaust local remedies. It falls instead between these extremes, both in respect of its content and object and purpose.[97] Thus, it is fair to say that the use of mandatory language in a dispute settlement provision is sufficient to express the contracting states' intent that it is compulsory and constitutes a part of the states' consent to international arbitration. As such, tribunals should be required to provide stronger reasoning in relation to why they have chosen to apply an MFN clause in a manner which permits an 18-month or similar requirement to be overridden.

Additionally, the *Maffezini* tribunals failed to consider that the MFN clause in the Argentina-Spain BIT was linked to fair and equitable treatment (FET). As shown in chapter 3, such formulations indicate the contracting parties' intent to limit the scope of an MFN clause to "more favorable" FET. Therefore, extending the scope of an MFN clause to dispute settlement provisions again goes explicitly against the *ejusdem generis* principle.

In addition, the territorial restriction is also an overlooked element. Article X(2) of the Argentina-Spain BIT accords MFN treatment "in the territory" of host states. However, the *Maffezini* approach does not shed much light on the meaning of this term, which may impose essential territorial restrictions. The *Daimler* tribunal correctly pronounced that international arbitration provisions are extra-territorial by nature and thus do not qualify as a treatment "in the territory" of a host state. The territorial limitation implied by the term "in the territory" established that Germany and Argentina did not anticipate international arbitration to fall within the MFN clause's scope.[98]

Moreover, the *Daimler* tribunal considered the "in its territory" modifier as a significant restriction on the MFN clause's use of the general term "treatment," a logical corollary of which should have been, at least for the tribunal, that treatment outside the contracting parties' territory did not fall within the scope of this clause.[99] According to the tribunal, while domestic adjudication constituted an activity within the host state's territory, international arbitration took place independently outside the host state's territory and control. Therefore, it did not fulfill the territorial qualification of the MFN clause.

97 *ICS v Argentina* (n 50) [248].
98 *Daimler v Argentina* (n 58) [231].
99 *Daimler v Argentina* (n 58) [226].

Similarly, the *ICS (I)* tribunal considered that international arbitration was not an activity "inherently linked to the territory of the respondent state"; instead, "[j]ust the contrary [was] true."[100] The tribunal stated that even if the term "treatment" in the MFN clause could be construed to include substantive and procedural protections included in the dispute settlement provision, this would only have obligated host states to accord MFN treatment concerning *domestic* adjudication.[101] The tribunal concluded that the concept of extra-territorial dispute resolution is ill-fitted to the clear and ordinary meaning of the expression "treatment in its territory" in the treaty's MFN clause:

> It is difficult to see how an MFN clause containing this phrase could be applied to international arbitration proceedings without discounting the explicit territorial limitation upon the scope of the clause. This pragmatic incongruity prevents the Tribunal from presuming – in the absence of any – that the Contracting Parties to the present treaty implicitly intended to include international dispute resolution within the purview of the MFN clause. If such were their intent, it would seem strange that they should impose a territorial limitation so at variance with that aim.[102]

In this regard, the tribunal found that the movement which took an expansive approach to the interpretation of MFN clauses had been approved of primarily in ISDS case law starting from the *Maffezini* tribunal. Arbitral practice has been split since *Maffezini*, suggesting the absence of established *opinio juris*.[103] Moreover, evidence has shown that there is not yet a consistent and universal treaty practice. While the recent Germany Model BIT neither endorsed nor rejected the *Maffezini* approach, it nevertheless sustained the MFN clause's territorial limitation.[104]

---

100 *ICS v Argentina* (n 50) [306].

101 *ICS v Argentina* (n 50) [308].

102 *ICS v Argentina* (n 50) [309]. By contrast, the tribunal *in UP and C.D. (Le Cheque Dejeuner) v Hungary* disagreed with Hungary's argument that MFN clause was inapplicable to international arbitration mechanisms due to the term "in its territory". The tribunal opined that, such interpretation would give the word an 'individual meaning [...] that would be at odds with the object and purpose of the clause as a whole.' The tribunal was of the view that "territory" should be considered as a condition for treaty protection, instead of a limitation on "delocalized" arbitration. See: *UP and C.D Holding Internationale v Hungary, Decision on Jurisdiction dated 3 March 2016*, ICSID Case No.ARB/13/35.

103 *ICS v Argentina* (n 50).

104 Germany Model BIT (2018), a copy of which is available at: <https://investmentpolicy.unctad.org/international-investment-agreements/treaty-files/2865/download> accessed 20 April 2022.

It has been suggested that it would be easier for tribunals following the *Maffezini* approach if they could consider the 18-month requirement as "part of the treatment applied to the foreign investors by the Host State *within* its territory."[105] Since such treatment was imposed on Argentine investors and not Chilean investors, "discriminating among foreign investors in the host country in the sense that they are not all given the same opportunities."[106] This theory is seemingly plausible but actually misrepresents the claim. The 18-month requirement was provided as a precondition to international arbitration. In this sense, the claimants did not allege an MFN breach, they invoked an MFN clause as a treaty tool to circumvent the 18-month requirement, in an attempt to conceive of it as stand-alone protection. Therefore, the domestic and international process should be viewed together as dispute settlement *in toto,* and it would be erroneous to detach the domestic litigation requirement from the dispute settlement mechanism as a whole. It would accordingly be no more meaningful to split them into domestic and foreign components for the purposes of territorial analysis and claim that the domestic part is *per se* less favorable.

2.2.2 Requiring Remedies to Be Pursued in Local Courts as an Issue of Jurisdiction

In his dissenting opinion in *Hochtief,* Mr. Thomas believed that the 18-month requirement was both mandatory and jurisdictional in nature. He explained that the contracting parties' consent to arbitration was included only in Article 10 (the dispute settlement provision), but not in Article 3 (the MFN clause). Moreover, for a perfected arbitration agreement, the prior treaty-based consent referred to above should be accepted by the claimant as an entirety, including in relation to the attached requirements.

However, by invoking the MFN clause from the Argentina-Chile BIT, the claimant ignored the conditions attached to the respondent's offer. As a result, instead of accepting the basic BIT's standing offer, the claimant in that case made a counteroffer entailing different terms.[107] In the end, the disputing parties' consent did not match due to this particular *modus operandi.*[108] According to Mr. Thomas, the only way to resolve this type of conundrum in favor of the

105 Valenti (n 38) 463. Emphasis added.

106 Valenti (n 38).

107 *Hochtief v Argentina, Separate and Dissenting Opinion of J. Christopher Thomas, Q.C.* (n 49) [27].

108 *Hochtief v Argentina, Separate and Dissenting Opinion of J. Christopher Thomas, Q.C.* (n 49) [17–22].

claimant was for the MFN clause to have the effect of altering the terms of the original offer in Article 10 before *Hochtief* could accept it.[109]

The *Wintershall* tribunal held that the 18-month requirement in Article 10 (2) was a fundamental jurisdictional precondition instead of a procedural clause. It believed that the contracting parties' consent to international arbitration i.e., the standing offer, was premised on the submission of the entire dispute to the courts of the competent jurisdiction in the host state.[110] Therefore, such a requirement could only be bypassed by some legitimate extension of rights and benefits based on the MFN clause's explicit text.[111]

Moreover, the tribunal referred to the third public policy exception specified by the *Maffezini* tribunal in relation to application of MFN clauses, which excluded a particular arbitration forum from the MFN clause's scope.[112] It explained that even allowing for the possibility of applying the MFN clause to dispute settlement, the claimant's assertion could not be supported since it attempted to replace the dispute settlement provision in the Argentina-Germany BIT with the strikingly different system of arbitration contained in the Argentina-U.S. BIT.[113]

The *Daimler* tribunal sided with the *Wintershall* tribunal on the mandatory and jurisdictional character of the 18-month requirement.[114] On this basis, the tribunal proceeded to answer the question as to when an aggrieved claimant may invoke an MFN clause. It stated in clear terms that –

> a claimant wishing to raise an MFN claim under the German-Argentine BIT – whether on procedural or substantive grounds – lacks standing to do so until it has fulfilled the domestic courts proviso ... since the Claimant has not yet satisfied the necessary condition precedent to Argentina's consent to international arbitration, its MFN arguments are not yet properly before the Tribunal. The Tribunal is therefore presently without jurisdiction to rule on any MFN-based claims unless the MFN clauses themselves supply the Tribunal with the necessary jurisdiction.[115]

109 *Hochtief v Argentina, Separate and Dissenting Opinion of J. Christopher Thomas, Q.C.* (n 49) [27].
110 *Wintershall v Argentina* (n 58) [160(2)].
111 *Wintershall v Argentina* (n 58) [172].
112 *Maffezini v Spain* (n 6) [63].
113 *Wintershall v Argentina* (n 58) [173–76].
114 *Daimler v Argentina* (n 58) [193].
115 *Daimler v Argentina* (n 58) [200].

In this regard, the tribunal found support in the ICJ's decision in *Anglo-Iranian*. It determined that the state must have consented to the particular type of dispute settlement in question before the claimant could raise any MFN claims before the designated forum.[116] According to the tribunal, the 18-month requirement was a significant impediment which might be surmounted by the content of the MFN clause in question, in particular, if it could "evince an intention ... to allow the Treaty's conditions precedent to accessing international arbitration to be altered by operation of its MFN provisions."[117] Since the MFN clause at issue failed to take a position in this regard, the tribunal was of the view that it could not alter the preconditions to state consent.

In *ICS (I)*, under the Argentina-UK BIT, the tribunal examined whether the claimant may be exempted from the procedural precondition via an application of the MFN clause in Article 3(2). It noted that the current discussion is vital due to its ability to "change the nature of international investment treaty arbitration from a scheme of bilateral relationships into a multilateral system nearing compulsory arbitration arbitral jurisdiction."[118] In this regard, the tribunal emphasized the provenance of the force of states' consent from the *pacta sunt servanda* rule in international law, the burden of proof of which falls on the claimant. Where a claimant fails to prove state consent with sufficient certainty, the tribunal would decline to exercise jurisdiction. The tribunal agreed with the respondent that –

> the MFN clause must constitute more than a mere prohibition of discrimination between investors based on their provenance: the MFN clause must also be in itself a manifestation of consent to the arbitration of investment disputes according to the rules that the MFN provision might attract from other comparator treaties.[119]

In her dissenting opinion in *Impregilo*, Professor Brigitte Stern opposed the decision of majority of the tribunal, arguing as she did that Article 8 of the Argentina-Italy BIT provided a conditional offer to arbitrate, i.e., the offer to arbitrate was conditional on the 18-month requirement.[120] She believed that such qualifying conditions and restrictions in dispute settlement provisions are jurisdictional requirements which must be fulfilled in order to sustain the

---

116 *Daimler v Argentina* (n 58) [204].
117 *Daimler v Argentina* (n 58) [204].
118 *ICS v Argentina* (n 50) [275].
119 *ICS v Argentina* (n 50) [278].
120 *Impregilo v Argentina, Concurring and Dissenting Opinion of Professor Brigitte Stern* (n 11).

conclusion that contracting states had consented to arbitration. Such consent could not be displaced through the application of an MFN clause.[121]

In other words, as long as the qualifying conditions are not fulfilled, tribunals should not conclude that consent to arbitration has been given and access to dispute settlement at the international level should be denied.[122] Stern thought that by allowing Impregilo access to the cumulative remedy of both domestic courts and arbitration, the majority of the tribunal provided it with treatment better than that accorded to investors both under the Argentina-Italy BIT and the Argentina-UK BIT.[123] In this sense, she believed that a possible ramification of *Maffezini* logic was that, the use of broadly drafted MFN clauses to unexpectedly incorporate the investor-state dispute settlement mechanism in a third-party treaty would lead to compulsory arbitration in the end:

> [S]lowly but steadily we are walking ... towards a general system of compulsory arbitration involving states for all matters relating to international investments.[124]

3 What Constitutes "More Favorable" Treatment?

Another question goes to what constitutes "more favorable" treatment. Tribunals have differed a fair deal in this regard. As mentioned in the previous chapter, this element requires an effective comparison between foreign investors from the beneficiary state and a third state.[125] Tribunals that uphold the MFN clause's ability to extend to temporal preconditions have nonetheless overlooked this element.

3.1 *The Approach Considering Domestic Court as Less Favorable*

In *Maffezini*, the tribunal did not conduct a comparison between domestic adjudication and international arbitration. The only relevant sentence is where the tribunal noted that the traders and investors have "traditionally felt that their rights and interests are better protected by recourse to international

121 *Impregilo v Argentina, Concurring and Dissenting Opinion of Professor Brigitte Stern* (n 11).
122 *Impregilo v Argentina, Concurring and Dissenting Opinion of Professor Brigitte Stern* (n 11) [80].
123 *Impregilo v Argentina, Concurring and Dissenting Opinion of Professor Brigitte Stern* (n 11) [12].
124 Stern (n 32) 259.
125 See supra Chapter 3.

arbitration than by submission of disputes to domestic courts."[126] According to the *Telefónica* tribunal, "it [was] preferable for an investor not to be obliged to submit, and pursue for 18 months, its claim before the courts of the Host State before being allowed to submit it to the specific investment arbitration ICSID," being exempted from such precondition therefore automatically constituted better treatment in the MFN context.[127]

The *Gas Natural* tribunal held that dispute settlement provisions are significant substantive incentives and protection for foreign investors. Therefore, an 18-month waiting period is a less favorable degree of protection than direct arbitration immediately after the negotiation period.[128] According to the tribunal, the claimant should have been be entitled to a more favorable dispute settlement provision, i.e., the one contained in Article VII of the Argentina-U.S. BIT. In this regard, the tribunal considered the 18-month requirement to constitute less favorable treatment due to the "perceived hazards of delays and political pressures of adjudication in national courts."[129] In the end, the tribunal concluded with an explicit proposition to include dispute settlement within the scope of the MFN clause in question:

> [A]ssurance of independent international arbitrations is an important – perhaps the most important – element in investor protection. Unless it appears clearly that the state parties to a BIT or the parties to a particular investment agreement settled on a different method for resolution of disputes that may arise, most-favored-nation provisions in BITs should be understood to be applicable to dispute settlement.[130]

In *Teinver*, the respondent argued that Article VII(2) of the Argentina-U.S. BIT was not more favorable than Article X(2) of the Argentina-Spain BIT. Therefore, there was no advantage from which the claimant could benefit. The tribunal held that Article VII(2) of the Argentina-U.S. BIT was "clearly" more favorable than Article X(2) of the Argentina-Spain BIT since the former provided the possibility to access arbitration with fewer procedural preconditions. Additionally, although Article VII(2) of the Argentina-U.S. BIT contained a "fork-in-the-road" requirement, it should have been inapplicable because the

126 *Maffezini v Spain* (n 6) [12].

127 *Telefónica v Argentina* (n 52) [103].

128 *Gas Natural SDG, S.A. v Argentine Republic, Decision of the Tribunal on Preliminary Questions on Jurisdiction dated 17 June 2005*, ICSID Case No. ARB/03/10 [31].

129 *Gas Natural v Argentina* (n 128) [29].

130 *Gas Natural v Argentina* (n 128) [49].

claimant had not selected the local court when reaching the "fork," so it had not forfeited its access to arbitration under the U.S.-Argentina BIT.[131]

The above findings of the tribunals that have adopted the *Maffezini* approach have been criticized for missing a detailed, case-by-case comparison between domestic adjudication and international arbitration before reaching a conclusion.[132] The potential defects of domestic adjudication have indeed been extensively discussed. Without differentiating each host state's individual situations, domestic adjudication has by and large been considered insufficient to cope with mass claims through the adoption of a fair and effective procedure.[133] As such, international arbitration is utilized to "keep dispute resolution out of the courts of plodding through the long corridors of national judicial bureaucracies."[134]

However, to assume that having to approach domestic courts by default puts a given investor in a less favorable position is quite a leap to make purely to render an 18-month requirement inapplicable. In his dissenting opinion in *Hochtief*, Mr. Thomas argued that a prior examination of the dispute in front of a domestic court, even if it might not result in a settlement, would enhance the prospects of success in any subsequent international claim:

> A claimant that enjoyed some success in the local courts would surely advert to that fact in support of any claimed breach of the treaty. Likewise, if the respondent demonstrated an obstructionist defensive posture in the local proceedings, that too would figure in the way in which a subsequent claim was formulated. It might lead to an additional cause of action.[135]

According to Sharmin, tribunals taking the expansive *Maffezini* approach to MFN interpretation in order to circumvent the need for domestic adjudication have ignored the need of host state, in particularly that of developing countries. This in turn has deepened these countries' doubts around the legitimacy of ISDS and has contributed to the ongoing wave of ISDS backlash.[136]

131 Teinver v Argentina (n 56) [184].

132 Kurtz (n 86) 546; Valenti (n 38) 461.

133 Orrego Vicuna (n 43) 308; *Abaclat and others v Argentina, Decision on Jurisdiction and Admissibility dated 4 August 2011*, ICSID Case No. ARB/07/5 [576–91].

134 W Michael Reisman, 'The Breakdown of the Control Mechanism in ICSID Arbitration' (1989) 1989 Duke Law Journal 739, 739,743.

135 *Hochtief v Argentina, Separate and Dissenting Opinion of J. Christopher Thomas, Q.C.* (n 49), footnote 7.

136 Sharmin (n 5) 194.

3.2 "Fork-in-the-Road" Requirements

"Fork-in-the-road" clauses are included in some investment treaties. They require investors to choose between domestic litigation and international arbitration, and such choice, once made, becomes final to the exclusion of the other option.[137] Tribunals have at times been confronted with claims to replace the original dispute settlement provision with one that entails a shorter waiting period, but also where the new provision entails a fork-in-the-road requirement. The most extreme decision in this regard is the one rendered by the *Siemens* tribunal. In that case, the tribunal applied the MFN clause to incorporate the shorter waiting period in the Argentina-Chile BIT without also importing the fork-in-the-road requirement.

According to the tribunal, as the MFN clause's name indicates, the rationale of MFN treatment lies only in according *more* favorable treatment.[138] However, the *Siemens* tribunal in fact incorporated "super-favorable" treatment that was not enjoyed by either Chilean or German investors. As argued in chapter 3 above, MFN clauses should not be viewed as a tool for multilateralizing investment protection if an intention to create such a tool is not explicitly expressed in the wording chosen for a given treaty, otherwise it will lead to abuse of rights and jeopardize the legitimacy of ISDS. However, by adopting an expansive MFN interpretation which was not contemplated by the contracting parties, the *Siemens* tribunal in fact considered the MFN clause as a pro-investor tool the aim of which was to multilateralize investment protection, which enabled unwarranted treaty-shopping via the MFN clause.

In *Hochtief*, the tribunal was opposed to the idea that access to national courts was automatically less favorable for investors when compared with access to international arbitration. The tribunal rather believed that it was always more favorable for investors to choose which to apply than to have no choice at all.[139] It rejected the argument that the MFN clause in question enabled treaty shopping which will manufacture a synthetic set of conditions to which no state's nationals would be entitled.[140] Therefore, the claimant could not avail itself to the absence of an 18-month requirement in the Argentina-Chile BIT and ignore the "fork-in-the-road" requirement in Article 10(2). The tribunal demonstrated in this regard that:

137 Rudolf Dolzer and Christoph Schreuer, *Principles of International Investment Law* (Second edition, Oxford University Press 2012) 267.

138 *Siemens v Argentina* (n 33) [120].

139 *Hochtief v Argentina* (n 1) [100].

140 *Hochtief v Argentina* (n 1) [98].

> The Claimant … must rely upon the whole scheme as set out in either Article 10 of the Argentina-Chile BIT or Article 10 of the Argentina-Germany BIT. In this case it has chosen to rely upon Article 10 of the Argentina-Chile BIT.[141]

By contrast, the *Daimler* tribunal took a different view from the *Hochtief* tribunal on the question of whether Article X of the Argentina-Chile BIT was more favorable than Article 10 of the Argentina-Germany BIT. It referred to the ILC's *Commentary on the Draft Articles on most-favored-nation clauses*, stating that "different" does not necessarily mean "less favorable," which is an interpretation that has been incorrectly adopted by prior tribunals like those in *Maffezini* and *Siemens*.[142]

The tribunal also mentioned the neglect of an essential truth in relation to the *Ambatielos* decision by tribunals. Although the PCA Commission in *Ambatielos* admitted the MFN clause's ability to cover dispute settlement provisions, it eventually found that the comparator treaties' clauses were not actually more favorable.[143] Therefore, an application of the MFN clause in question made no difference. The *Daimler* tribunal believed that the point of MFN clauses was to "ensure overall equality of treatment in the sense of creating a level playing field between foreign investors from different countries, even if this is sometimes accomplished through non-identical means."[144] To reach such equality, tribunals could not rely solely on the claimant's subjective preference about which option was more favorable.

In this regard, the tribunal conducted a comparative examination on the two dispute settlement mechanisms at issue. It noted that Article 10 of the Argentina-Germany BIT allowed the claimant to still resort to international arbitration after having spent 18 months before the domestic court if it was not satisfied at that point. By contrast, the fork-in-the-road clause under Article X of the Argentina-Chile BIT entitled investors only to one irreversible chance to get a satisfactory outcome: either in front of the domestic court or before an international tribunal. At best, Article 10 might provide a quicker or cheaper result. Therefore, Article 10 and Article X are just two procedures for dispute resolution "on an equal par with those investors."[145]

141 *Hochtief v Argentina* (n 1) [98].
142 *Daimler v Argentina* (n 58) [242].
143 *The Ambatielos Claim* (n 20) 107–110.
144 *Daimler v Argentina* (n 58) [242].
145 *Daimler v Argentina* (n 58) [250].

In *ICS (I)*, the tribunal fixated on whether the dispute settlement mechanism in Article 9 of the Argentina-Lithuania BIT was more favorable than that contained in the Argentina-UK BIT. Before reviewing the text of the two comparator articles, the tribunal pronounced that this question should be addressed with reference to an objective approach, which required that "different treatment" not necessarily be used to infer "more favorable" treatment. Such evaluation should not have been conducted in a fashion limited to particular circumstances, but instead in a general manner whereby the treatment granted would not necessarily be found to be more favorable under all circumstances.[146] Therefore, the tribunal was of the view that the above two articles should be compared as a whole instead of part-by-part, and the lack of difference in treatment could not be construed as being either more or less favorable by default.[147]

After comparing the two articles' wordings, the tribunal found that while Lithuanian investors in Argentina were subject to a shorter period of six months before domestic courts, they were nevertheless subject to a "fork-in-the-road" provision. This clause required them to make an irrevocable submission to either a domestic court or international tribunal. By contrast, UK investors in Argentina could still resort to international arbitration if they were not satisfied with results in the domestic courts after 18 months – here investors would have two bites at the proverbial apple as the tribunal noted. Therefore, unless the claimant submitted evidence on a general need for it to urgently resort to international arbitration that rendered the 18-month litigation period a "consistent disadvantage," the Lithuanian investors were not necessarily entitled to a more favorable dispute settlement mechanism compared with UK investors.[148]

Besides the *Hochtief* tribunal, the *Impregilo* tribunal also held that more choices indicated more favorable treatment for investors. It conducted a textual comparison concerning this issue.

Article 8 of the Argentina-Italy BIT provided as follows:

> 1. Any dispute regarding an investment between an investor of one of the Contracting Parties and the other Party, arising out of or relating to this Agreement, shall, to the extent possible, be settled through friendly consultation between the parties to the dispute.

146 *ICS v Argentina* (n 50) [319].
147 *ICS v Argentina* (n 50) [320].
148 *ICS v Argentina* (n 50) [325].

2. If the dispute cannot be settled amicably, it may be submitted to the competent judicial or administrative courts of the Party in whose territory the investment is made.
3. Where, after eighteen months from the date of notice of commencement of proceedings before the courts mentioned in paragraph 2 above, the dispute between an investor and one of the Contracting Parties has not been resolved, it may be referred to international arbitration.

While Article 3 (1) of the Argentina-Italy BIT, meanwhile, provided as follows:

> Each Contracting Party shall, within its own territory, accord to investments made by investors of the other Contracting Party, to the income and activities related to such investments and to all other matters regulated by this Agreement, a treatment that is no less favorable than that accorded to its own investors or investors from third-party countries.[149]

Impregilo attempted to import Article VII of the Argentina-U.S. BIT via the MFN clause in the basic treaty, which contained a "fork-in-the-road" requirement.[150] As such, the tribunal first deemed the 18-month precondition in Article 8(3) as a mandatory jurisdictional requirement that has to be satisfied before an ICSID tribunal could assert jurisdiction:

> The condition to be complied with is a double one: first bringing the dispute before the domestic courts and then waiting for 18 months before proceeding to international arbitration. This condition has not been complied with by Impregilo.[151]

However, the tribunal admitted that the MFN clause had the ability to avoid the application of such a requirement in Article 3(1). It explained that the term "treatment" and "all matters regulated by this Agreement" in Article 3(1) were both wide enough to cover the dispute settlement rules. In coming to this

149 Argentina – Italy BIT (1990). A copy of which is available at: <https://investmentpolicy.unctad.org/international-investment-agreements/treaty-files/5898/download> accessed 20 April 2022.

150 Argentina – U.S. BIT (1991), a copy of which is available at: <https://investmentpolicy.unctad.org/international-investment-agreements/treaty-files/127/download> accessed 20 April 2022.

151 *Impregilo v Argentina* (n 11) [90].

determination, the tribunal drew on the broadly-worded MFN clause in question, as well as the reasoning of the tribunals that had adopted the *Maffezini* approach.[152] However, the tribunal emphasized that the core issue was not whether domestic courts offered investors more or less favorable treatment, but whether there was a choice for investors to choose between domestic proceedings and international arbitration, as in the Argentine-U.S. BIT. In the tribunal's opinion, it was evident that a system that gives a choice should be more favorable to the investor than a system that offers no alternative.[153]

The abovementioned decisions in *Impregilo* and *Hochtief* in 2012 were considered a manifestation of the *Maffezini* spirit by commentators in that they allowed the MFN clause in the basic treaty to be applied in order to avoid the 18-month requirement, especially in the face of a broadly-worded MFN clause.[154] Indeed, despite a decade of development in investment arbitration, the two tribunals rendered a similar decision in relation to the application of MFNs on the 18-month requirement, albeit that their decisions were rooted in more detailed analyses.

3.3 *The Risk of Treaty-shopping: The Siemens Approach*

As stated above, the *Maffezini* tribunal warned about the risk of unwarranted treaty shopping when adopting an expansive interpretation of the MFN clause at issue and suggested that public policy considerations be examined in order to strike a balance. However, the *Siemens* tribunal adopted a rather adventurous approach when it came to whether the operation of the MFN clause from the basic treaty should extend to all provisions of the third-party treaty as a whole.

In *Siemens*, the Argentina-Chile BIT relied on by the claimant had a "fork-in-the-road" requirement in its dispute settlement provision. The respondent contended that if the MFN clause were to be interpreted to have extensive coverage, then it should apply to the Chile BIT as a whole and not only the provisions convenient to the claimant.[155] The tribunal rejected this argument because it would, according to the tribunal, defeat the MFN clause's purpose of harmonizing the basic and third-party treaties' benefits. It explained as follows:

> The Tribunal recognized that there may be merit in the proposition that, since a treaty has been negotiated as a package, for other treaties

152 *Impregilo v Argentina* (n 11) [108].
153 *Impregilo v Argentina* (n 11) [101].
154 Valasek and Menard (n 71) 25.
155 *Siemens v* (n 33) [119].

> to benefit from it, they also should be subject to its disadvantages. The disadvantages may have been a trade-off for the claimed advantages. However, this is not the meaning of an MFN clause. As its own name indicates, it relates only to more favorable treatment.[156]

According to Fietta, the *Siemens* tribunal's position has incurred doubt for allowing the claimant to cherry-pick the benefits from various treaties containing an MFN clause without considering any counterbalance to these benefits in different treaties.[157] As a result, the decision of the *Siemens* tribunal has effectively led to a situation with a potentially infinite number of permutations and combinations of dispute resolution possibilities that different investors can draw on to best fit their individual circumstances.[158] The *Plama* tribunal also observed that entitling foreign investors to pick and choose provisions from various BITs can result in a host state facing a large number of permutations of potential dispute settlement provisions without knowing which will apply in which circumstances. According to the tribunal, "such a chaotic situation – actually counterproductive to harmonization – cannot be the presumed intent of Contracting Parties."[159]

In his article "Clearing a Path Through a Tangled Jurisprudence: Most-Favored-Nation Clauses and Dispute Settlement Provisions in Bilateral Investment Treaties," Vesel rightly points out that –

> [i]f claimants are allowed to borrow a filing deadline from one treaty, an evidentiary rule from another, and a statute of limitations from a third, the result will be chaotic and unworkable.[160]

As a result, the MFN clause in *Siemens* enabled German investors to enjoy the benefits of a provision the obligations contained in which Argentina had never agreed to with any countries.[161] Through its interpretation, the tribunal allowed German investors to enjoy the amalgamation of different dispute settlement mechanisms accorded by Argentina, i.e., a dispute settlement procedure in

156 *Siemens v* (n 33) [120].

157 Stephen Fietta, 'Most Favoured Nation Treatment and Dispute Resolution under Bilateral Investment Treaties: A Turning Point?' (2005) 8 International Arbitration Law Review 131, 135.

158 Fietta (n 157).

159 *Plama v Bulgaria* (n 36) [219].

160 Vesel (n 34) 179.

161 Vesel (n 34)169.

the absence of fork-in-the-road provision *and* an 18-month requirement. Such a result goes against the very purpose of MFN clauses since the fork-in-the-road under the Argentina-Chile BIT still binds Chilean investors in Argentina. Therefore, such treatment is not "more favorable treatment," but in fact, "extra-favorable treatment," which might result in a legitimate sense of injustice on the part of host states.[162]

Another consequence is that the tribunal has opened the door to a "potentially infinite variety of dispute resolution permutations and combinations that different investors might rely upon to meet their individual circumstances,"[163] which was not intended even by the *Maffezini* tribunal.[164] Although the *Siemens* tribunal agreed with *Maffezini* tribunals statements, it nevertheless failed to explain why the "fork-in-the-road" provision in the Argentina-Chile BIT should not limit the operation of the MFN clause in the basic treaty, since it was one of the four public considerations mentioned by the *Maffezini* tribunal.[165]

Although it also took an expansive approach to MFN interpretation, the *Hochtief* tribunal adopted a more cautious approach. As mentioned above, it denied the treaty-shopping effect of the MFN clause in question, which would manufacture a synthetic set of conditions to which no state's nationals would be entitled.[166] Therefore, the claimant could not avail itself of the absence of the 18-month requirement in the Argentina-Chile BIT and ignore the "fork-in-the-road" requirement in Article 10(2). The tribunal demonstrated in this regard that the claimant had to rely on the whole scheme as set out in either Article 10 of the Argentina-Chile BIT or Article 10 of the Argentina-Germany BIT.[167]

After the decision on jurisdiction in *Siemens*, Argentina and Panama exchanged diplomatic notes in their "interpretive declaration" in relation to the 1996 BIT. The declaration clarified Argentina and Panama's mutual understanding that the MFN clause does not extend to dispute resolution clauses and that this had always been their intention.[168] The *Daimler* tribunal also took into account the inserted footnote in the negotiating history of the Central America-Dominican Republic-United States Free Trade Agreement (DR-CAFTA), the annex to the 2006 Switzerland-Colombia BIT, and an issue

162 Vesel (n 34) 169.
163 Fietta (n 157) 135.
164 Orrego Vicuna (n 43) 325.
165 *Maffezini v Spain* (n 6) [63]; Vesel (n 34) 168.
166 *Hochtief v Argentina* (n 1) [98].
167 *Hochtief v Argentina* (n 1) [98].
168 *National Grid v Argentina* (n 72) [85].

paper by the European Commission (DG Trade), all of which clarify that MFN treatment was not intended to encompass dispute settlement provisions in the respective agreements.[169] Therefore, the tribunal was convinced that these treaty practices should play a confirmatory role in supporting the conclusion it reached.

4 Conclusion

The case law as discussed above shows that some ISDS tribunals have been willing to extend the scope of MFN clauses to include procedural issues based on the text of MFN clauses that are broadly worded.[170] Above all, the core issue lies in whether and to what extent MFN clauses may be relied on in order to bypass procedural preconditions. Divergent views exist in this regard. It has been argued that the dichotomy of the primary-secondary rule from general international law does not tidily fit into the scenario of investment arbitration, and that substantive and procedural rights are interrelated. For example, Orrego Vicuña argues that the distinction between substantive and procedural rights was allegedly "mysterious":

> If the State has given its consent to substantive rights of investors and these are entitled to benefit from the MFN clause where more [favorable] substantive treatment is found in treaties with third States, it is difficult to understand why this would not be equally available to the means of enforcing such rights.[171]

Accordingly, for Vicuña and others similarly minded, the 18-month requirement should serve as an admissibility obstacle that can be overcome by an application of an MFN clause.

The opposing view has a number of prongs. First, it points out that procedural and substantive treatment are not necessarily interrelated. MFN clauses extend only to substantive rights – to the exclusion of procedural rights – because the procedural rights relate to the conditions for contracting states' consent to international arbitration, i.e., *ratione voluntatis* that cannot be

169 *Daimler v Argentina* (n 58) [273–75].

170 W Shen, 'The Good, the Bad or the Ugly? A Critique of the Decision on Jurisdiction and Competence in Tza Yap Shum v. The Republic of Peru' (2011) 10 Chinese Journal of International Law 55, 87.

171 Orrego Vicuna (n 43) 303, citing Shen (n 170) 86–87.

bypassed by the application of an MFN clause without explicit treaty language permitting exactly as such.[172]

The view taken in this book is that MFN clauses do not *ipso facto* apply to procedural preconditions in dispute settlement provisions since the dispute settlement provisions cannot merely be assumed to go to the admissibility of claims as opposed to the jurisdiction of tribunals.

Secondly, as argued in chapter 3, the limitations contained in the texts of specific MFN clause should be taken into account. Therefore, tribunals should conduct a detailed textual examination of the respective clauses in each case. In this regard, such examination should entail a proper, good faith application of Articles 31 and 32 of the Vienna Convention on the Law of Treaties by tribunals. Specifically, when a 18-month or similar requirement is drafted using mandatory terms like "shall," it most probably indicates the contracting parties' intention to condition their consent to arbitration on the procedural precondition. In this scenario, it is appropriate to consider such procedural precondition as going to jurisdiction, not admissibility.

Furthermore, the good faith principle requires tribunals to adopt responsible interpretations of MFN clauses instead of allowing MFN clauses to apply to procedural issues on the basis of often unfounded presumptions. It goes against the good faith principle for tribunals to allow cherry-picking by claimants of treaty terms. This will lead to results that were unlikely to be anticipated by contracting parties when they included an MFN clause in a given treaty. Worse still, a pro-investor, expansive approach to MFN clause interpretation based on the presumption that all MFN clauses are intended to multilateralize investment protection will raise legitimate doubts on the part of states in relation to the objectivity of ISDS tribunals and the legitimacy of ISDS mechanisms.

172 *Impregilo v Argentina* (n 11), *Concurring and Dissenting Opinion of Professor Brigitte Stern.*

CHAPTER 5

Applying the MFN Clause to Avoid Jurisdictional Obstacles

This chapter examines the interpretation of most-favored-nation (MFN) clauses in cases where claimants invoked an MFN clause in order to avoid jurisdictional obstacles to their bringing a claim in terms of a basic treaty. In investor-state dispute settlement (ISDS) practice, claimants have regularly sought to have MFN clauses applied to procedural issues, including in order to circumvent preconditions contained in dispute settlement provisions in a basic treaty, to broaden the definition of "investor" or "investment" contained in the basic treaty, to import a "more favorable" ISDS mechanism from third-party treaties, and to have the basic treaty be applied retroactively. Most of these claims have been rejected by tribunals when claimants sought to extend a tribunal's jurisdiction via the application of an MFN clause in a basic treaty, with only few exceptions.[1] As such, this chapter discusses the relevant case law under two distinct headings: cases where tribunals refused to establish jurisdiction via an application of the MFN clause in question, and those three cases where tribunals exceptionally went in the other direction.

To better reveal the role of the MFN clause in establishing jurisdiction, it is first necessary to look at the nature of state consent to arbitration. State consent is a fundamental principle in general international law that emanates from a cornerstone of the international legal order: the presumption of equality among sovereign states. The basic idea is that states are bound only insofar as they agree to be bound, or obligated only to the degree to which they agree to be obligated.[2] Therefore, investment tribunals should generally only have jurisdiction to the extent that states have explicitly consented to them having jurisdiction.[3] In the context of this book, the question is whether MFN clauses

1 See, in particular: *RosInvest Co UK Ltd v Russia, Award on Jurisdiction dated October 2007*, SCC Case No. 079/2005; *Venezuela US, SRL v Bolivarian Republic of Venezuela, Interim Award on Jurisdiction dated 26 July 2016*, PCA Case No. 2013–34; *Garanti Koza LLP v Turkmenistan, Decision on the Objection to Jurisdiction for Lack of Consent dated 3 July 2013*, ICSID Case No. ARB/11/20 271.

2 *SS Lotus (France v Turkey), Judgment No 9, PCIJ Series A No 10, 7 September 1927* [18–19].

3 See, for example 'Report of The Executive Directors of the International Bank for Reconstruction and Development on the Convention on the Settlement of Investment Disputes Between States and Nationals of Other States'. Para 23 of which defines consent of

DOI:10.1163/9789004517899_007

could be interpreted so as to expand limited state consent to international arbitration, or even to manufacture consent when none is present. Tribunals have rendered diverging decisions on this issue. Prior to turning to the main focus of this chapter as alluded to above in parts two and three, the first part examines the issue of state consent. Part four entails a detailed case study on the issue of whether MFN clauses should ever be applied in a manner which entitles investment tribunals to claim jurisdiction where otherwise none exists, concluding as it does that MFN clauses should not be interpreted in pursuit of such an end. To expand or manufacture the jurisdiction of tribunals via the application of an MFN clause would require rather specific and explicit treaty language from the contracting parties allowing for this to be done.[4]

1 State Consent in Investment Arbitration

Investment treaties are of a hybrid nature. They are concluded by sovereign states for the benefit of non-sovereign third parties, i.e., investors and their investments. State parties confer treaty rights and owe treaty obligations to foreign investors, while investors tend to bear no corresponding obligations.[5] This asymmetry in duties is reflected in dispute settlement clauses in international investment agreements (IIAs), through which binding treaty obligations are enforced through the international arbitration between private investors and host states. Such dispute settlement mechanisms have been considered an offshoot of the contract-based dispute settlement mechanism in private international law.[6] Giorgio Sacerdoti accordingly defines investment arbitration as

the parties as 'the cornerstone of the jurisdiction of the Centre'. Bernard Hanotiau, 'Consent to Arbitration: Do We Share a Common Vision?' (2011) 27 Arbitration International 539, 539.

4 In this regard, Banifatemi has argued that 'the question of the applicability of a most-favoured-nation clause to dispute settlement arrangements is chiefly determined by the language of the clause.' See: Yas Banifatemi, 'The Emerging Jurisprudence on the Most-Favoured-Nation Treatment in Investment Arbitration,' in Andrea K Bjorklund, Ian A. Laird, Sergey Ripinsky (eds), *Investment Treaty Law: Current Issues III* (BIICL, 2009) 241.

5 Zachary Douglas, 'The Hybrid Foundations of Investment Treaty Arbitration' (2004) 74 British Yearbook of International Law 151; Ascensio Hervé, 'Abuse of Process in International Investment Arbitration' (2014) 13 Chinese Journal of International Law 763; Andrea K Bjorklund, 'Private Rights and Public International Law: Why Competition Among International Economic Law Tribunals Is Not Working' (2008) 59 Hastings Law Journal 64, 126.

6 Mara Valenti, 'The Scope of an Investment Treaty Dispute Resolution Clause: It Is Not Just a Question of Interpretation' (2013) 29 Arbitration International 243, 261; Bjorklund (n 5) 112; Ascensio (n 5) 766; Campbell McLachlan, 'Investment Treaties and General International Law' (2008) 57 The International and Comparative Law Quarterly 361, 372.

"arbitration of a private law character, but guaranteed by an international procedure sanctioned by a treaty."[7]

State consent to international arbitration has to be given in writing.[8] Modern investment arbitration are usually based on bilateral investment treaties (BITs), which are one of the three ways whereby states give prior consent or a standing offer to arbitrate through the IIA itself. An investment agreement will be "perfected" when eligible foreign investors accept the standing offer and consent by instituting the arbitration.[9] This is the so-called "arbitration without privity" mechanism.[10] The other two ways are to give consent through national legislation and to conclude contracts with compromissory clauses.[11]

State consent to international adjudication in IIAs instead of through the enactment of domestic legislation has been considered a derogation from state sovereignty.[12] According to Huiping Chen, the consent to International Centre on the Settlement of Investment Disputes (ICSID) or other forms of international arbitration in BITs reflects a state's sovereignty, and such consent

---

7 Sacerdoti Giorgio, 'Bilateral Treaties and Multilateral Instruments on Investment Protection (Vol 269),' in: Collected Courses of the Hague Academy of International Law 423.

8 Article 25(1) of the ICSID Convention (1965).

9 See, for example, Valenti (n 6) 244; Georges R Delamue, 'ICSID Arbitration Proceedings: Practical Aspects' (1985) 5 Pace Law Review 28, 567; Rudolf Dolzer, *Bilateral Investment Treaties* (M Nijhoff 1995) 131–32; Christoph Schreuer, *Consent to Arbitration* (Oxford University Press 2008); Andrea Marco Steingruber, *Consent in International Arbitration* (1st ed, Oxford University Press 2012) 196–212.

10 Jan Paulsson, 'Arbitration Without Privity' (1995) 10 ICSID Review – Foreign Investment Law Journal 232. About the consideration of a balanced power allocation between foreign investors and Host States, see: Y Andreeva, 'Interpreting Consent to Arbitration as a Unilateral Act of State: A Case Against Conventions' (2011) 27 Arbitration International 129, 134. See also: James Crawford, 'The ILC's Articles on Responsibility of States for Internationally Wrongful Acts: A Retrospect' (2002) 96 American Journal of International Law 874, 887 ('a standard bilateral or regional investment treaty is an interstate agreement, to which individual investors are not privy.'); Michael Waibel, 'Investment Arbitration: Jurisdiction and Admissibility' [2014] University of Cambridge Faculty of Law Research Paper No. 9/2014. Available at SSRN: <https://papers.ssrn.com/sol3/papers.cfm?abstract_id=2391789> accessed 20 April 2022.

11 Michael Waibel, 'International Investment Law and Treaty Interpretation' in Rainer Hofmann and Christian J Tams (eds), *International Investment Law and General International Law* (Nomos Verlagsgesellschaft mbH & Co KG 2011) 13–15; Rudolf Dolzer and Christoph Schreuer, *Principles of International Investment Law* (Second edition, Oxford University Press 2012) 238–53; Michele Potestà, 'The Interpretation of Consent to ICSID Arbitration Contained in Domestic Investment Laws' (2011) 27 Arbitration International 149, 152.

12 *Amco Asia Corporation and others v Republic of Indonesia, Decision on Jurisdiction dated 25 September 1983*, ICSID Case No. ARB/81/1 [393, 397].

"is a restriction to one country's sovereignty."[13] In her dissenting opinion in *Impregilo*, Professor Brigitte Stern distinguished international legal orders from national legal orders. She pointed out that most rights cannot be enforced using international adjudication except when states exceptionally consent to be bound by the decisions of international adjudicatory bodies.[14]

Similarly, in *Garanti*, the dissenting arbitrator stressed the "fundamental legal safeguard governing the issue of consent before international courts and tribunals," that is, a State's established consent to jurisdiction in international adjudication.[15] In other words, the default principle in international law is that international courts and tribunals do not have jurisdiction over the conduct of states unless those states have explicitly consented to the jurisdiction of the relevant adjudicatory body.[16]

The ICSID Convention provides a general framework for investment arbitration. The Convention's preamble clearly states that no contracting state shall be deemed to be under any obligation to submit any particular dispute to arbitration by the mere fact of its ratification, acceptance, or approval of the Convention. Article 25 of the ICSID Convention about the jurisdiction of ICSID, moreover, prescribes that state consent to international arbitration should be given in writing and in explicit language.[17]

The conventional wisdom among arbitral tribunals is to construe the requirement of state consent neither restrictively nor extensively.[18] For example, the *Amco Asia* tribunal stated the following in relation to its interpretation of state consent:

> In the first place, like any other conventions, a convention to arbitrate is not to be construed restrictively, nor, as a matter of fact, broadly or liberally. It is to be construed in a way which leads to find out and to respect

13 Chen Huiping, 'The Expansion of Jurisdiction by ICSID Tribunals: Approaches, Reasons and Damages' (2011) 12 The Journal of World Investment & Trade 671, 686.

14 *Impregilo S.p.A. v Argentine Republic (I), Award Dated 21 June 2011, Concurring and Dissenting Opinion of Professor Brigitte Stern* [45].

15 *Garanti Koza LLP v Turkmenistan, Decision on the Objection to Jurisdiction for Lack of Consent Dated 3 July 2013, Dissenting Opinion by Laurence Boisson de Chazournes*, ICSID Case No. ARB/11/20 [5].

16 Eric De Brabandere, 'Importing Consent to ICSID Arbitration? A Critical Appraisal of Garanti Koza v. Turkmenistan' (2014) 5 Investment Treaty News (ITN), IISD. A copy of which is available at: <https://www.iisd.org/system/files/publications/iisd_itn_may_2014_en.pdf> accessed 20 April 2022.

17 ICSID Convenetion (n 8); Waibel (n 11) 4.

18 Potestà (n 11) 165.

> the common will of the parties: such a method of interpretation is but the application of the fundamental principle *pacta sunt servanda*, a principle common, indeed, to all systems of internal law and to international law.[19]

Similarly, in *Southern Pacific Properties*, the tribunal noted that –

> jurisdictional instruments are to be interpreted neither restrictively not expansively, but rather objectively and in good faith, and jurisdiction will be found to exist if – but only if – the force of the arguments militating in favor of it is preponderant.[20]

By contrast, there are also those who seek to construct state consent restrictively. This school of thought addresses the hybrid nature of investment law, holding that state consent should be considered as a unilateral act by sovereigns – like states' unilateral consent to the jurisdiction of the International Court of Justice (ICJ). Therefore, state consent should be examined in light of interpretive methods in general international law other than the Vienna Convention on the Law of Treaties (VCLT).[21] For example, Rule 7 of the 2006 International Law Commission (ILC) Guiding Principles on Unilateral Acts of States (ILC Guiding Principles) has been relied on as a codification of the canons of interpretation in relation to unilateral state acts. The rule provides as follows:

> A unilateral declaration entails obligations for the formulating State only if it is stated in clear and specific terms. In the case of doubt as to the scope of the obligations resulting from such a declaration, such obligations must be interpreted in a restrictive manner. In interpreting the content of such obligations, weight shall be given first and foremost to the text of the declaration, together with the context and the circumstances in which it was formulated.[22]

19 *Amco v Indonesia* (n 12).

20 *Southern Pacific Properties (Middle East) Limited v Arab Republic of Egypt, Decision on Jurisdiction II, 27th April 1895*, ICSID Case No. ARB/84/3 [63].

21 Andreeva (n 10) 140.

22 'Guiding Principles Applicable to Unilateral Declarations of States Capable of Creating Legal Obligations with Commentaries' (2006) II Yearbook of the International Law Commission 14, para 7.

The ILC's commentary on Rule 7 of the ILC Guiding Principles refers to opinions of the ICJ. In the *Nuclear Tests* cases, for example, the ICJ held that a unilateral declaration might have the effect of creating legal obligations for the state making the declaration only if it is stated in clear and specific terms. Such declaration limits the freedom of action of states and calls for a restrictive interpretation.[23] In the *Frontier Dispute,* the ICJ determined that the interpreter must proceed with great caution in deciding the legal effects of a unilateral declaration, in particular when it has no specific addressee.[24]

According to the ICJ, the above interpretation methods in general international law are distinct from those contained in the VCLT. For the ICJ, the VCLT "may only apply analogously to the extent compatible with the *sui generis* character of the unilateral acceptance of the Court's jurisdiction."[25] However, the different canons are similar in that both give priority to the text of a given treaty or legal instrument. In this regard, the ICJ has actually applied Article 31(2) of the VCLT by analogy. For example, in the *Frontier Dispute* case, the ICJ declared that "to assess the intentions of the author of a unilateral act, account must be taken of all the circumstances in which the act occurred."[26]

The ambiguity left by varying approaches to the expression of state consent in investment law is detrimental to its consistency and should thus be discouraged.[27] In his separate opinion in *Thunderbird,* the late Professor Thomas Wälde opined that an ambiguous treaty text should be construed against a government agency if an investor "did and could reasonably have confidence in the assurance ... as a reasonable businessman in the position of the investor would do in the particular circumstances."[28] In the context of the operation of MFN clauses, the above discussion boils down to one question, namely whether MFN clause can serve as the basis for an adjudicatory body claiming jurisdiction.

---

23 *Nuclear Tests (Australia v France), Judgment of 20 December 1974,* ICJ [47].

24 *Frontier Dispute (Burkina Faso v Republic of Mali), Judgment of 22 December 1986,* ICJ [39].

25 *Fisheries Jurisdiction (Spain v Canada), Judgment of 4 December 1998* (ICJ) [46].

26 *Frontier Dispute* (n 24) 574 [40].

27 Potestà (n 11) 168.

28 *International Thunderbird Gaming Corporation v The United Mexican States, Separate Opinion of Mr. Thomas Wälde dated December 2005,* UNCITRAL Arbitration [47].

2 Cases Where Tribunals Refused to Establish Jurisdiction via the Application of an MFN Clause

With the above question in mind, this part analyzes relevant cases where tribunals rejected claimants' attempts to establish jurisdiction through the application of an MFN clause where such jurisdiction was not conferred on the tribunal in question by the basic treaty on which the claims were based.

2.1 *Application of MFN Clause to Establish Jurisdiction Ratione Personae*

This section examines ISDS cases where claimants attempted to expand the jurisdiction of a tribunal through an attempt to broaden the definition of "investment" in the basic treaty via reliance on the MFN clause therein to incorporate a more favorable definition from a third-party treaty. These cases relate to tribunals' *ratione personae* jurisdiction afforded by basic treaties, i.e., jurisdiction by virtue of who qualifies as a beneficiary under the treaties. The discussion is divided into two subsections. The first subsection deals with cases where claimants sought to construe the definition of "investment" in treaty provisions in such a way that would broaden the scope of a given tribunal through incorporating a broader definition from a third-party treaty. The second subsection focuses on cases where claimants interpreted the legality or admission requirement in the basic treaty as "treatment" and invoked an MFN clause in an attempt to eschew their application *in casu*.

2.1.1 Broadening the Definition of "Investment"

In *Yaung Chi Oo,* the dispute arose under the Association of Southeast Asian Nations (ASEAN) Investment Agreement of 1987 (1987 ASEAN Agreement). In 1993, a Singaporean claimant signed a joint venture agreement with the Myanmar Ministry of Foodstuff Industries (MFI) and State Industrial Organization (the 1993 Agreement). The 1993 Agreement established a brewery company (YCO), and disputes arising from the 1993 Agreement were subject to arbitration pursuant to the 1944 Arbitration Act of Myanmar.[29]

Subsequently, in 1997, Myanmar was admitted as an ASEAN member. Per its Protocol of Admission, Myanmar acceded to several ASEAN treaties, including the 1987 ASEAN Agreement and the Jakarta Protocol of September 12, 1996 (the ASEAN Protocol). Later in 1998, Myanmar became a party to the Framework Agreement for the ASEAN Investment Area of October 7, 1998 (ASEAN

29 *Yaung Chi OO Trading Pte Ltd. v Government of the Union of Myanmar, Award dated 31 March 2003,* ASEAN Case No. ARB/01/1, 42 540 [4].

Framework Agreement). The ASEAN Framework Agreement came into force on June 21, 1999.[30]

A series of conflicts took place, including the alleged seizure of the investor's property by armed agents of the Burmese (Myanmar) government and the freezing of certain investor bank accounts. After botched negotiations to solve the dispute, the claimant filed an arbitration under Article X of the ASEAN Agreement.

The respondent objected to the tribunal's jurisdiction based on Article I(2) of the 1987 ASEAN Agreement, which provided that –

> the term 'company' of a Contracting Party shall mean a corporation, partnership or business association, incorporated or continued under the laws in force in the territory of any Contracting Party wherein the place of effective management is situated.[31]

As such, the respondent argued that the 1987 ASEAN Agreement was inapplicable to the claimant's investment at dispute because there was no effective management of YCO in Singapore throughout the duration of the investment as required by the ASEAN Agreement.

The claimant first sought to establish jurisdiction based on the less restrictive definition of "investment" contained in the ASEAN Framework Agreement. The tribunal rejected this attempt because of the distinct and separate definitions of investment in the ASEAN Agreement and ASEAN Framework Agreement: there was no intention on the part of ASEAN members to substitute, merge or fuse one with the other.[32] The tribunal held that the two agreements were "clearly intended to operate separately" and that the definition of "investment" in the ASEAN Framework Agreement "should not [have been] ... interpreted as applying *de novo* the provisions of the []ASEAN Agreement, including Article X, to ASEAN investments."[33]

The claimant then turned to the MFN clause in Article 8 of the ASEAN Framework Agreement in an attempt to incorporate the "investment" definition in Article IX of the Myanmar-Philippines BIT. The tribunal did not accept this attempt because Article IX of the Myanmar-Philippines BIT provided for

30 *Yaung Chi v Myanmar* (n 29) [6].

31 ASEAN Agreement for the Promotion and Protection of Investments (1987). A copy of which is available at: <https://investmentpolicy.unctad.org/international-investment-agreements/treaty-files/5554/download> accessed 20 April 2022.

32 *Yaung Chi v Myanmar* (n 29) [82].

33 *Yaung Chi v Myanmar* (n 29) [82].

arbitration under United Nations Commission on International Trade Law (UNCITRAL) Rules, which entailed a different appointing authority from the one designated in Article X of the ASEAN Agreement. The tribunal therefore denied the possibility of establishing jurisdiction through Article 8 of the ASEAN Framework Agreement.[34]

In *Société Générale*, the claimant was a company constituted in France. It indirectly controlled a Cayman company (DREH), which in turn owned 50% of a Dominican company (EDE). The respondent objected the tribunal's jurisdiction because Société Générale did not qualify as a beneficiary under the BIT's definition of "investment." The claimant relied on *inter alia* the MFN clause in Article 4 of the France-Dominican BIT and a broader definition of "investment" from the Dominican Republic-Central America Free Trade Agreement (CAFTA-DR), which included the phrase "expectation of gain or profit."[35]

Although the *Société Générale* tribunal ultimately accepted that it had jurisdiction for other reasons, it denied the claimant's invocation of the MFN clause to establish jurisdiction. The tribunal explained that it was within the discretion of each treaty to define its own beneficiaries. In contrast, MFN clauses in treaties could only be applied to treatment extended to protected investments, not the definition of what a protected investment itself constituted.[36]

The same issue was addressed by the tribunal in *HICEE*, a dispute which involved legislation introduced by Slovakia which forbade health insurance companies from distribute profits and limited their permissible administrative expenses. It allegedly caused loss to two Slovakian health insurance companies, Dôvera and Apollo. These two companies were subsidiaries of another Slovakian entity that was in turn wholly owned by HICEE, a Dutch company.[37] HICEE claimed that Slovakia's legislative measures taken in respect of the health insurance market deprived it of profits from its shareholdings in Dôvera and Apollo and led to the devaluation of its investment.

---

34 *Yaung Chi v Myanmar* (n 29) [83].

35 *Société Générale in respect of DR Energy Holdings Limited and Empresa Distribuidora de Electricidad del Este, S.A. v The Dominican Republic, Award on Preliminary Objections to Jurisdiction dated 19 September 2008*, LCIA Case No. UN 7927. See further: Article 4 of the Dominican Republic – France BIT (1999), a copy of which is available at: <https://investmentpolicy.unctad.org/international-investment-agreements/treaty-files/1043/download> accessed 20 April 2022.

36 *Société Générale v Dominican Republic* (n 35) [41].

37 For a summary of the dispute, see UNCTAD IIA Navigator, <https://investmentpolicy.unctad.org/investment-dispute-settlement/cases/318/hicee-v-slovakia> accessed 20 April 2022.

Article 1 of the Netherlands-Slovakia BIT defined "investment" so as to "comprise every kind of asset invested either directly or through an investor of a third State."[38] The disputing parties disagreed on whether the BIT accorded protection to HICEE since it owned Dôvera and Apollo indirectly through its Slovakian subsidiary. HICEE relied on the MFN clause in Article 3(2) and 3(5) of the BIT in its attempt to import a broader definition of "investment" from other Slovakian BITs.[39] The MFN clause at issue was connected to fair and equitable treatment (FET) and full protection and security. It promised that existing or future more favorable treatment introduced by way of domestic law or international agreement stemming from the relationship between the Netherlands and Slovakia shall prevail over the treatment contemplated in terms of the Netherlands-Slovakia BIT.[40]

Slovakia contended that such an application would violate the basic logic of MFN clauses, which only saw MFN clauses cover substantive protection contained in a treaty and was not intended to act as a gateway for the importation of definitions such as "investors" or "investment."[41] Additionally, Slovakia argued that Article 3(2) restricted the scope of MFN treatment merely to FET treatment and full protection and security to the exclusion of the definition of "investment," and that Article 3(5) referred to more favorable treatment contained in domestic law and future international agreements *between Netherlands and Slovakia*, both of which, according to Slovakia, constituted important limitations to the scope of the MFN clause in question.[42] The tribunal agreed with the respondent, holding that the MFN clause should be interpreted according to its own terms, and that it was fallacious to presume that a general approach existed when it came to determine the scope of a particular MFN clause. It stated as follows:

> The clear purpose of Article 3(2), as of Article 3(5), is to broaden the scope of the substantive protection granted to the eligible investments of

38 Netherlands – Slovakia BIT (1991). A copy of which is Available at: <https://investmentpolicy.unctad.org/international-investment-agreements/treaty-files/2080/download> accessed 20 April 2022.

39 *HICEE BV v The Slovak Republic, Partial Award dated 23 May 2011*, PCA Case No. 2009–11 [91–3].

40 Article 3(2) and 3(5) of Netherlands – Slovakia BIT (1991) (n 38).

41 *HICEE B.V. v Slovakia* (n 39) [90].

42 *HICEE B.V. v Slovakia* (n 39) [90].

> eligible investors; it cannot legitimately be used to broaden the definition of the investors or the investments themselves.[43]

In the end, the tribunal denied that it had jurisdiction because the claimant's investment was not covered under the Netherlands-Slovakia BIT.[44]

A recent case in a similar vein is the *Heemsen* case, where the two claimants have the dual nationalities of both Germany and Venezuela and thus did not satisfy the jurisdiction *ratione personae* in the Germany-Venezuela BIT. As such, the claimants invoked the MFN clause in an attempt to incorporate a less onerous nationality standard from other Venezuelan BITs.[45] The tribunal did not allow the claimant's attempt to stand, stating that according to the text of the MFN clause in the basic treaty it only applied to treatment concerning the investors' activities related to their investments, and that a BIT's dispute settlement provision should not be considered as an "activity" in this sense. The tribunal further clarified that MFN clauses should not apply to jurisdictional issues in principle. It held that the MFN clause in question only applied to the merits component of the treaty, i.e., in relation to substantive treatment. While the definition of "investor" and "investment," as well as the dispute settlement forum are specified by the contracting parties and are related to jurisdiction and should accordingly not have been altered by the MFN clause.[46]

---

43 *HICEE B.V. v Slovakia* (n 39) [149]. For more discussion supporting the case-by-case examination of MFN clauses instead of a general perception of MFN standard, see: M Valenti, 'The Most Favoured Nation Clause in BITs as a Basis for Jurisdiction in Foreign Investor – Host State Arbitration' (2008) 24 Arbitration International 447, 459; McNair Lord, *The Law of Treaties* (Oxford University Press 1986) 285.

44 *HICEE B.V. v Slovakia* (n 39) [150].

45 The claimants relied on the case *Venezuela US, S.R.L. v Bolivarian Republic of Venezuela, Interim Award on Jurisdiction dated 26 July 2016,* PCA Case No. 2013–34. In this case the tribunal allowed for applying MFN to extend jurisdictional scope. More analysis on the *Venezuela US* case will be conducted below.

46 *Enrique Heemsen and Jorge Heemsen v Bolivarian Republic of Venezuela, award on Jurisdiction dated 29 October 2019,* PCA Case No. 2017–18 [408]. The original award was in Spanish, translated by International Arbitration Reporter, see: 'Analysis: Heemsen v. Venezuela Tribunal Refused to Find Jurisdiction on the Basis of an MFN Clause, and Held That German – Venezuela BIT Does Not Cover Dual Nationals with Citizenship of the Host State' (*Investment Arbitration Reporter*, 22 November 2019) <https://www.iareporter.com/articles/analysis-heemsen-v-venezuela-tribunal-refused-to-find-jurisdiction-on-the-basis-of-an-mfn-clause-and-held-that-german-venezuela-bit-does-not-cover-dual-nationals-with-citizenship-of-the-host-state/> accessed 20 April 2022.

2.1.2 Avoiding Legality Requirements

In *Vannessa Ventures,* the dispute was based on the Canada-Venezuela BIT, Article 1(f) of which contained a legality requirement.[47] The respondent challenged the tribunal's jurisdiction based on the absence of a lawful investment as required by Article 1(f). In view of this, the claimant relied on the MFN clause in the Canada-Venezuela BIT and attempted to incorporate the more favorable treatment offered by the Venezuela-United Kingdom (UK) BIT, Article 1(a) of which did not contain a legality requirement for foreign investment. The tribunal rejected this attempt because Article 1(f) of the basic treaty served as an indispensable limitation of the scope of application of the MFN clause. As a result, the MFN clause could not be applied to expand the category of investments to which the Canada-Venezuela BIT applied.[48]

The tribunal in *Metal-Tech* was confronted with a similar situation. Article 1(1) of the Israel-Uzbekistan BIT contained a legality requirement under which foreign investment should be "implemented in accordance with the laws and regulations of the Contracting Party in whose territory the investment is made."[49] In that case, the dispute arose from the Uzbek government's alleged decisions to expropriate the claimant's investment in violation of the Israel-Uzbekistan BIT.[50] Uzbekistan objected to the tribunal's jurisdiction because the claimant had allegedly been involved in corruption, as well as the making of fraudulent and material misrepresentations in order to obtain approval for its investment, which meant that it unlawfully implemented its investment in violation of the basic treaty.[51]

In light of the legality requirement, Metal-Tech sought to invoke the MFN clause in Article 3 of the Israel-Uzbekistan BIT in order to incorporate the broader definition of "investment" contained in Article 1(1) of the

---

47 *Vannessa Ventures Ltd v Bolivarian Republic of Venezuela,* ICSID Case No. ARB(AF)/04/6. Article 1(f) of the Canada – Venezuela BIT (1996) reads as: '"investment" means any kind of asset owned or controlled by an investor of one Contracting Party either directly or indirectly, including through an investor of a third State, in the territory of the other Contracting Party in accordance with the latter's laws.' See: Canada – Venezuela BIT (1996) <https://investmentpolicy.unctad.org/international-investment-agreements/treaty-files/644/download> accessed 20 April 2022.

48 *Vannessa Ventures v Venezuela* (n 47) [133].

49 Article 1(1) of the Israel – Uzbekistan BIT (1994). A copy of which is available at: <https://investmentpolicy.unctad.org/international-investment-agreements/treaty-files/4998/download> accessed 20 April 2022.

50 *Metal-Tech Ltd v Republic of Uzbekistan, Award dated 4 October 2013,* ICSID Case No. ARB/10/3 [107].

51 *Metal-Tech v Uzbekistan* (n 50) [110].

Greece-Uzbekistan BIT, which did not contain a legality requirement.[52] Acknowledging that the definition of "investment" did not constitute "treatment" for purposes of the MFN clause, the claimant relied on Article 7(c) of the Israel-Uzbekistan BIT, which provided for exceptions to the MFN clause. Article 7 of the basic treaty read as follows:

> The provisions of this Agreement relative to the grant of treatment not less [favorable] than that accorded to the investors of either Contracting Party or of any third state shall not be construed so as to oblige one Contracting Party to extend to the investors of the other the benefit of any treatment, preference or privilege resulting from: ... (c) the definitions of "investment" (Article 1, paragraph 1) and 'reinvestment' (Article 1, paragraph 2) and the provisions of Article 6 contained in Agreements entered into by the State of Israel prior to January 1, 1992.[53]

The claimant alleged that the inclusion of the term "investment" in Article 7(c) indicated that the contracting parties' intention was for the term "treatment" in Article 3(2) to include a more favorable definition of the term "investment."[54]

The tribunal refused to construe "investment" as used in Article 1(1) as constituting "treatment" for the purpose of applying the MFN clause. According to the tribunal, an investor must be entitled to the protection of a particular treaty in order to submit a claim in terms of that treaty. For the tribunal, the definition of a term could not be seen as a form of treatment. It merely established the baseline for determining whether a certain category of persons was entitled to MFN treatment.[55]

As for the Article 7(c) exception, the tribunal relied on the interpretation principles included in Article 31(1) of the VCLT. It took into account the ordinary meaning of "investment," the context of Article 7 in general, and the particular context surrounding Article 7(c). The tribunal was of the view that "investment" as referred to in Article 7(c) should not be seen as an independent concept, a proposition argued for by Metal-Tech, and should be understood

52 Article 1 of the Greece – Uzbekistan BIT (1997). A copy of which is available at: <https://investmentpolicy.unctad.org/international-investment-agreements/treaty-files/1484/download> accessed 20 April 2022.

53 Article 7 of the Israel – Uzbekistan BIT (1994) (n 49). A copy of which is available at: <https://investmentpolicy.unctad.org/international-investment-agreements/treaty-files/4998/download> accessed 20 April 2022.

54 *Metal-Tech v Uzbekistan* (n 50) [134].

55 *Metal-Tech v Uzbekistan* (n 50) [145–153].

in the context of repatriation and reinvestment as per the basic treaty.[56] The tribunal also applied Article 32 of the VCLT. It confirmed its interpretation by looking at Israel's treaty practice, which showed that several Israeli BITs explicitly limited their understanding of "investment" to the context of repatriation.[57] In the end, the tribunal rejected the argument that it had jurisdiction due to the lack of the existence of a legal investment pursuant to the laws and regulations of Uzbekistan, which was a jurisdictional precondition by virtue of Article 1(1) of the basic treaty.[58]

In *Rafat Ali Rizvi*, the claimant attempted to rely on the MFN clause in the Indonesia-UK BIT to overcome an admission provision. The Indonesia-UK BIT did not contain a legality requirement in Article 1(1) in its definition of "investment." However, it included an admission requirement in Article 2(1) on the BIT's scope. It provided that the BIT only covered UK investments in Indonesia's territory that had been admitted under the Foreign Capital Investment Law of Indonesia (FCIL).[59] The claimant distinguished between legality and admission requirements. It argued that while legality requirements constituted a jurisdictional issue, admission requirements went instead to the validity of an "investment" and constituted "treatment."[60] The tribunal disagreed. It considered that both legality and admission requirements were *conditio sine qua non* for the application of the UK-Indonesia BIT to UK investments in the territory of Indonesia, and that they both entailed a jurisdictional dimension. Therefore, an investment would not be protected by the BIT if it failed to satisfy either requirement.[61]

In conclusion, all the above efforts to avoid jurisdictional prerequisites through incorporating less restrictive definitions via MFN clauses failed. Tribunals have been consistent in considering the prerequisites necessary for a BIT to apply in the first place as a starting point before applying an MFN clause. In other words, the definition of "treatment" generally requires that investors qualify *ratione personae* for investment protection before being entitled to MFN treatment. Such conditions must be met before the treaty in question can

56 *Metal-Tech v Uzbekistan* (n 50) [151–152].

57 *Metal-Tech v Uzbekistan* (n 50) [159–160].

58 *Metal-Tech v Uzbekistan* (n 50) [372].

59 Indonesia – UK BIT (1976). A copy of which is available at: <https://investmentpolicy.unctad.org/international-investment-agreements/treaty-files/1646/download> accessed 20 April 2022.

60 *Rafat Ali Rizvi v Republic of Indonesia, Award dated 17 July 2013*, ICSID Case No. ARB/11/13 [204–206].

61 *Rafat v Indonesia* (n 60) [233].

even be applied and they cannot be replaced via the treaty's MFN clause before it can be shown that the MFN clause applies in the first place.[62]

2.2 *Bypassing Limitations Contained in Dispute Settlement Provisions*

This section concerns cases that dealt with claimants' attempt to invoke MFN clauses to incorporate a less restrictive ISDS mechanism in a third-party treaty. Many of the basic treaties in question involved limited dispute settlement provisions that only permitted claims to be submitted to international arbitration in relation to compensation for expropriation. In this regard, the following ISDS cases will examined in chronological order: *Plama, Berschader, Telenor, Renta 4, Shum, Austrian Airlines, EURAM, ST-AD, Sanum (I)*, and *Beijing Urban Construction.*[63]

Tribunals have notably declined to find jurisdiction via the application of an MFN clause in all the above cases, which shows tribunal's reluctance towards MFN application for this purpose. Furthermore, the examination below also reveals the limited assistance of the VCLT in the face of a broadly-drafted MFN clause. As such, tribunals have adopted circumstantial evidence to discern contracting parties' intentions. Therefore, the role of tribunals' presumptions cannot be overlooked. It is arguable that when applying interpretive methods does not lead to a specific answer, other significant parameters in international investment law should be given due consideration. These include in particular the basic principle of state sovereignty and the fundamental role of state

62 *Impregilo v Argentina, Concurring and Dissenting Opinion of Professor Brigitte Stern* (n 14); Stephan W Schill, 'Maffezini v. Plama: Reflections on the Jurisprudential Schism in the Application of Most-Favored-Nation Clauses to Matters of Dispute Settlement' in Meg Kinnear and others (eds), *Building international investment law: the first 50 years of ICSID* (Alphen aan den Rijn: Wolters Kluwer 2016); F Orrego Vicuna, 'Reports of Maffezini's Demise Have Been Greatly Exaggerated' (2012) 3 Journal of International Dispute Settlement 299; Banifatemi (n 4) 250.

63 *Plama Consortium Limited v Republic of Bulgaria, Decision on Jurisdiction dated 8th February 2005*, ICSID Case No. ARB/03/24; *Telenor Mobile Communications AS v Republic of Hungary, Award dated 13 September 2006*, ICSID Case No. ARB/04/15; *Quasar de Valores SICAV SA, Orgor de Valores SICAV SA, GBI 9000 SICAV SA and ALOS 34 SL v The Russian Federation, Award on Preliminary Objections dated 20 March 2009*, SCC Case No. 24/2007; *Tza Yap Shum v Republic of Peru, Decision on Jurisdiction and Competence dated 19 June 2009* 82, ICSID Case No. ARB/07/6; *Austrian Airlines v The Slovak Republic, Final Award dated 9 October 2009*, UNCITRAL Arbitration; *European American Investment Bank AG v The Slovak Republic, Award on Jurisdiction dated 22 October 2012*, PCA Case No. 2010–17; *ST-AD GmbH v The Republic of Bulgaria, Award on Jurisdiction dated 18 July 2013*, PCA Case No. 2011–06; *Sanum Investments v Lao People's Democratic Republic (I), Award on Jurisdiction dated 13 December 2013*, PCA Case No. 2013–13; *Beijing Urban Construction Group Co Ltd v Republic of Yemen, Decision on Jurisdiction dated 31 May 2017*, ICSID Case No. ARB/14/30.

consent in international law, the good faith principle, and the re-balancing efforts of states in their continuing quest to recalibrate the scales when it comes to state interest and investor protection in IIAs.

In *Plama*, the dispute was about certain Bulgarian authorities' alleged expropriation that supposedly damaged the Cypriote claimant's oil refinery, as well as the authorities' unreasonable hesitation when it came to adopting adequate corrective measures.[64] According to Article 4 of the 1987 Cyprus-Bulgaria BIT, the legality of expropriation should have been resolved in terms of the domestic laws of the host state, while disputes concerning the amount of expropriation could be presented to an *ad hoc* international tribunal after three months of failed negotiations.[65]

The claimant alleged that the Bulgarian government had breached its substantive obligations in the Energy Charter Treaty (ECT), to which both Bulgaria and Cyprus were treaty members. Alternatively, the claimant contended that Bulgaria had consented to ICSID arbitration in the 1987 Bulgaria-Cyprus BIT through the MFN clause contained therein.[66] The MFN clause provided that "[e]ach Contracting Party [should] apply to the investments in its territory by investors of the other Contracting Party a treatment which [were] not less favorable than that accorded to investments by investors of third states."[67]

According to the claimant, the MFN clause should have applied to all aspects of treatment, which included the dispute settlement mechanism. To this end, the claimant relied *inter alia* on the Bulgaria-Finland BIT, which allowed for the legality of expropriation to be settled by ICSID arbitration.[68]

---

64 *Plama v Bulgaria* (n 63).

65 Article 4 of the Cyprus – Bulgaria BIT (1987), a copy of which is available at: <https://investmentpolicy.unctad.org/international-investment-agreements/treaty-files/522/download> accessed 20 April 2022; *Plama v Bulgaria* (n 63) [26].

66 *Plama v Bulgaria* (n 63) [183].

67 Article 3(1) of the Cyprus – Bulgaria BIT(1987) (n 65).

68 It provides that: 'If such a dispute cannot be settled within three months from the date either party to the dispute requested amicable settlement, the investor concerned may submit the dispute to the competent court of the Contracting Party in whose territory the investment was made or alternatively to the International Center for Settlement of Investment Disputes (ICSID) set up by the "Convention on Settlement of Investment Disputes between States and Nationals of other States," done at Washington, March 18, 1965 in case both Contracting Parties are parties to the Convention or to an ad-hoc arbitral tribunal to be established under the Arbitration Rules of the United Nations Commission on International Trade Law (UNCITRAL).' See: Article 8(1) of the Bulgaria – Finland BIT (1997), available at: <https://investmentpolicy.unctad.org/international-investment-agreements/treaty-files/527/download> accessed 20 April 2022.

The *Plama* tribunal refused to find that it had jurisdiction based on the MFN clause in the Bulgaria-Cyprus BIT.[69] In reaching this conclusion, the tribunal initially focused its examination on the interpretation of the MFN clause pursuant to Articles 31 and 32 of the VCLT. It started from the ordinary meaning of the word "treatment" as contained in the MFN clause of the basic treaty. The tribunal noted that the text did not clarify whether "treatment" included dispute settlement provisions in third-party treaties to which Bulgaria was a contracting party.

The tribunal then turned to consider the exceptions to the MFN clause in Article 3(2). It provided that "[t]his treatment shall not be applied to the privileges which either Contracting Party accords to investors from third countries in virtue of their participation in economic communities and unions, a customs union or a free trade area."[70] The tribunal acknowledged that according to the principle *expressio unius est exclusio alterius*, all other matters, including dispute settlement, might fall within the scope of the MFN provision in Article 3(1). However, the tribunal also pointed out that the word "privilege" as contained in Article 3(2) could have been deemed as referring to substantive protection. Therefore, it could be argued with equal force that Article 3(2) indicated that Article 3(1) provided only for the incorporation of substantive protection from third-party BITs.[71]

The tribunal also denied the relevance of the context since the context alone was not persuasive evidence of the contracting parties' intention in this regard. Moreover, the tribunal noted that no evidence had been presented in relation to the BIT's negotiating history in relation to this matter.[72]

In the end, the tribunal considered the object and purpose of the treaty. The preamble of the Bulgaria-Cyprus BIT provided that the contracting parties had as their objective "the creation of [favorable] conditions for investments by investors of one Contracting Party in the territory of the other Contracting Party."[73] In this connection, the claimant relied on documents including the Executive Directors' report on the ICSID Convention of 1965,[74] and UNCTAD's

69 *Plama v Bulgaria* (n 63) [187].

70 Article 3(2) of the Cyprus – Bulgaria BIT (1987) (n 65).

71 *Plama v Bulgaria* (n 63) [191].

72 *Plama v Bulgaria* (n 63) [192].

73 Cyprus – Bulgaria BIT (1987) (n 65); The tribunal also considered the title of the treaty, which refers to 'mutual encouragement and protection of investments'; *Plama v Bulgaria* (n 63) [193].

74 Which declares that 'the creation of an institution designed to facilitate the settlement of disputes between States and foreign investors can be a major step toward promoting an atmosphere of mutual confidence and thus stimulating a larger flow of private

study "Bilateral Investment Treaties in the Mid-1990s."[75] Both contained language indicating that the promotion and protection of foreign investment was their objectives. The tribunal found the above statements insufficient to conclude that the contracting parties intended to include dispute settlement mechanisms within the MFN clause's scope. In this regard, the tribunal also quoted Sir Ian Sinclair's caveat on the harm of undue emphasis on the treaty's purpose.[76]

After finding that the treaty text did not provide clarity as to the contracting parties' intention, the tribunal turned to examine the evidence concerning the circumstance in which the treaty was concluded. It firstly examined the social circumstances of Bulgaria during the Bulgaria-Cyprus BIT's conclusion in 1987. It observed that at the time the treaty was concluded, Bulgaria was under a communist regime that favored bilateral investment treaties with limited protections for foreign investors and limited access to dispute resolution mechanisms.[77] Additionally, the tribunal also referred to the failed subsequent negotiations between Bulgaria and Cyprus, but with a rather peculiar inference in this regard. It noted the revision on the dispute settlement clause in the negotiation, and inferred that Bulgaria and Cyprus did not consider that the MFN provision extended to dispute settlement provisions in other BITs.[78] However, as Vesel points out, the mere fact that negotiations on the dispute settlement provision occurred does not permit one to draw any specific inferences about the parties' beliefs as to the scope and meaning of an *existing* MFN clause.[79]

That said, the tribunal referred to the fundamental prerequisite for arbitration in domestic and international law, i.e., agreement between the parties to arbitrate. According to the tribunal, this should be based on the "clear and unambiguous" consent from the contracting states.[80] The tribunal stated that an agreement to refer a matter to arbitration reached by way of incorporation via the application of an MFN clause would bring doubts as to the parties' clear and unambiguous intentions.[81] In this regard, the tribunal compared

---

international capital in those countries which wish to attract it.' See: *Plama v Bulgaria* (n 63).

75 Kenneth J Vandevelde and others, 'Bilateral Investment Treaties in the Mid-1990s.' (United Nations 1998) UNCTAD/ITE/IIT/7; *Plama v Bulgaria* (n 63) [193].

76 *Plama v Bulgaria* (n 63) [193].

77 *Plama v Bulgaria* (n 63) [195].

78 *Plama v Bulgaria* (n 63) [195].

79 Scott Vesel, 'Clearing a Path Through a Tangled Jurisprudence: Most-Favored-Nation Clauses and Dispute Settlement Provisions in Bilateral Investment Treaties' (2007) 32 Yale Journal of International Law 176.

80 *Plama v Bulgaria* (n 63) [198].

81 *Plama v Bulgaria* (n 63) [199].

the broad MFN clause in the basic treaty with those contained in the North Atlantic Free Trade Agreement (NAFTA) and the agreement establishing the Free Trade Areas of the Americas (FTAA), both of which provided narrowly-worded MFN clauses that excluded dispute settlement from their respective scopes.[82] According to the tribunal, an intention to incorporate dispute settlement provisions must be clearly and unambiguously expressed. If such intention is lacking in an MFN provision, one cannot reason *a contrario* that the dispute resolution provisions must be deemed to be incorporated.[83]

Due to their markedly different positions on the application of the MFN clause to dispute settlement provisions, the decisions of the *Plama* and *Maffezini* tribunals are often compared. However, the *Plama* and *Maffezini* tribunals were actually confronted with distinct attempts to apply the MFN clause to incorporate a more favorable dispute settlement mechanism: the former concerned jurisdiction; the latter procedural preconditions.[84]

Nevertheless, the *Plama* tribunal did refer to prior cases, and *Maffezini* in particular. It is worth noting that the *Plama* tribunal denied the relevance of the *Ambatielos* case because it related to substantive protection in the face of denial of justice in domestic courts, instead of the incorporation of dispute resolution provisions from another treaty.[85] In its analysis on *Maffezini*, the *Plama* tribunal did not agree with the *Maffezini* tribunal's statement that the application of an MFN clause to dispute settlement arrangements would lead to the harmonization in relation to the enlargement of the scope of investment treaties.[86] The *Plama* tribunal expressed its concern that instead leading to harmonization, the application of an MFN clause to incorporate dispute settlement provisions would lead to treaty-shopping. As a result, a host state might be confronted with many unpredictable permutations of dispute settlement provisions from various BITs.[87]

In light of this risk, the tribunal questioned the source of the public policy considerations proposed by the *Maffezini* tribunal, finding that the public policy considerations in fact mitigated much of the weight of the *Maffezini* tribunal's preceding observations about the application of MFN clauses to

82 *Plama v Bulgaria* (n 63) [202].

83 *Plama v Bulgaria* (n 63) [203].

84 Tanjina Sharmin, *Application of Most-Favoured-Nation Clauses by Investor-State Arbitral Tribunals: Implications for the Developing Countries* (Springer 2020) Chapter 5.

85 *Plama v Bulgaria* (n 63) [215].

86 *Emilio Agustín Maffezini v The Kingdom of Spain, Decision of the Tribunal on Objections to Jurisdiction dated 25 January 2000*, ICSID Case No. ARB/97/7 [62].

87 *Plama v Bulgaria* (n 63) [219].

procedural treatment. As such, the *Plama* tribunal decided to simplify the *Maffezini* tribunal's theory and boiled it down to its own statement that "an MFN provision in a basic treaty does not incorporate by reference dispute settlement provisions in whole or in part set forth in another treaty, unless the MFN provision in the basic treaty *leaves no doubt* that the Contracting Parties intended to incorporate them."[88]

That said, the *Plama* tribunal nevertheless sympathized with the reasoning of the *Maffezini* tribunal, recognizing that –

> [t]he decision in *Maffezini* is perhaps understandable. The case concerned a curious requirement that during the first 18 months the dispute be tried in the local courts. The present Tribunal sympathizes with a tribunal that attempts to neutralize such a provision that is nonsensical from a practical point of view. However, such exceptional circumstances should not be treated as a statement of general principle guiding future tribunal in other cases where exceptional circumstances are not present.[89]

However, the *Plama* tribunal did not clarify what exactly about an 18-month requirement would be curious, nonsensical, or exceptional.[90] Its reason might relate to the fact that there are only a small number of treaties that require a certain period during which domestic adjudication must be attempted before resorting to international arbitration (that is, after a six-month cooling-off period had elapsed), among which most of them were to be found in Argentine BITs.[91] For Schreuer, these time periods appear to be "a half-hearted revival of the local remedies rule" without any useful purpose because they are usually too short to yield a meaningful result.[92] Therefore, Schreuer considers them as "a costly ritual that serves no purpose except to delay arbitration."[93]

The unusually sweeping term "clear and unambiguous" of the *Plama* tribunal has nevertheless been criticized for being overly strict and for substantially narrowing MFN clauses' scope of application. This principle's origin has also been challenged, with criticism that it would be an "obvious travesty" in

88 *Plama v Bulgaria* (n 63) [223].

89 *Plama v Bulgaria* (n 63) [224].

90 *Daimler Financial Services AG v Argentine Republic, Award Dated 22 August 2012,* ICSID Case No. ARB/05/1 [196].

91 Christer Söderlund and Elena Burova, 'Is There Such a Thing as Admissibility in Investment Arbitration?' (2018) 33 ICSID Review – Foreign Investment Law Journal 7.

92 Christoph Schreuer, 'Calvo's Grandchildren: The Return of Local Remedies in Investment Arbitration' (2005) 4 The Law & Practice of International Courts and Tribunals 1, 4.

93 Schreuer (n 92) 5.

relation to treaty interpretation for a tribunal to disregard the parties' shared intention and substitute arbitrary assumptions of its own.[94]

By contrast, proponents argue that the *Plama* tribunal correctly addressed the essence of state consent. In her dissenting opinion in *Impregilo*, Professor Stern opined as follows:

> It is one thing to use a restrictive interpretation to find a consent, which is certainly not warranted and which ... the *Plama* tribunal does not seem to have done. And a different thing to consider that any given consent to arbitration must be clear and certain, which cannot be contested. Who would argue that an uncertain and ambiguous consent to arbitration is sufficient to confer jurisdiction to an arbitral tribunal?[95]

It has also been suggested that *Plama* and *Maffezini* adopted opposite presumptions in respect of the relationship between rule and exception in front of the similarly broadly formulated MFN clauses. This difference could be explained by the diverse epistemic represented by the two tribunals.[96] On the one hand, the *Maffezini* tribunal grounded its approach in public international law. This assumption is reinforced by an article addressing the influence of the *Maffezini* case by its presiding arbitrator, the late Francisco Orrego Vicuña, where he defended the *Maffezini* decision from a perspective of public international law in the following terms:

> ... international law is moving forward to grant the individual a readily available right to access international dispute settlement mechanism. *Maffezini* well reflects this evolving trend ... While a number of State privileges are still within the ambit of international law and there is good reason to justify their subsistence in the light of the fact that the State is a central actor of the international legal system, it is not difficult to realize

94 Myres S McDougal and others, *The Interpretation of International Agreements and World Public Order: Principles of Content and Procedure* (M Nijhoff Publishers 1994); In this regard, Vesel appraised that 'the *plama* tribunal rooted their assumption much more in the arbitrators' pragmatic concerns than in an attempt to discern the parties' actual intent as embodied in the words they used.' See: Vesel (n 79) 179–80.

95 *Impregilo S.p.A. v Argentina* (n 14), *Concurring and Dissenting Opinion of Professor Brigitte Stern* [95]. See also: Valenti (n 43) 464.

96 Schill (n 62) 9. According to Banifatemi, 'An analysis of the diverging views and the positions taken by each arbitral tribunal in relation to the decisions of other tribunals shows the extent to which this idea reflects ones' underlying philosophy of investment arbitration in general.' See: Banifatemi (n 4) 250.

> that States are not any longer the only actors … *Maffezini* conclusion is 'hardly surprising in a world characterized by globalization.' Ideally, the enactment of a single and universal standard of treatment of investors … would to a meaningful extent diminish discrepancies among treaties, just as it would narrow down the differences between domestic and international standards.[97]

On the other hand, the *Plama* tribunal rooted its reasoning in the rationales of commercial arbitration, which suggest that the severability of a compromissory agreement is a key parameter.[98] Based on this presumption, the *Plama* tribunal limited itself to a strict ascertainment of whether an agreement to arbitrate could be said to exist in clear and unambiguous terms.

It has been argued that the core issue in front of the *Plama* tribunal was not whether the agreement to arbitrate was provided "clearly and unambiguously" or whether the MFN clause could fairly cover dispute settlement provisions as such. The real issue the *Plama* tribunal failed to answer is whether, in the absence of Bulgaria's consent to the dispute at hand, the MFN clause could be viewed as a proxy for the contracting parties' consent to jurisdiction.[99] In other words, it failed to express an explicit view on whether the MFN clause in question could serve as a manifestation of state consent to investment arbitration itself.[100]

In a research paper concerning the jurisprudential schism that exists in relation to the application of MFN clauses to dispute settlement issues, Schill frames the same doctrinal issue confronted by *Plama* and *Maffezini* as "whether an investor can benefit, by means of an MFN clause, from less onerous, quicker, or wider consent to international arbitration offered under the host state's third-country BITs."[101] In the case of *Plama*, Bulgaria had given its limited standing offer to arbitrate in the international arena merely in relation to compensation for expropriation. By bringing this case to an investment tribunal, the Cyprus investor accepted and sought to alter the content of Bulgaria's standing offer through an application of the MFN clause in the basic treaty.

Should MFN clauses be applied this way? This question is not about the substantive-procedural treatment dichotomy or the existence of an agreement to arbitrate.[102] Rather, it is a question that goes to interpreting MFN clauses

97 Orrego Vicuna (n 62) 327.
98 Schill (n 62) 9.
99 Vesel (n 79) 181.
100 Banifatemi (n 4) 270.
101 Schill (n 62) 8.
102 Sharmin (n 84) 256; Banifatemi (n 4) 268.

through a proper application of the interpretative methods of general international law as part of a good faith attempt to ascertain contracting parties' intention on jurisdictional issues. This book takes the view that in *Plama,* state consent to any kind of international arbitration was only contained in the dispute settlement provision that formed part of the basic treaty (the Bulgaria-Cyprus BIT). To apply the MFN clause as a means to extend a tribunal's jurisdiction flies in the face of the intention of contracting parties.

Given that state consent emanates from their sovereignty, this sort of improper application renders the fundamental principle of state sovereignty meaningless in this realm of international law. In addition, expanding their jurisdiction through an application of an MFN clause without clear treaty language authorizing such an exercise amounts to an abuse of tribunals' *kompetenz-kompetenz* discretion. Such an approach risks annulment, especially given that instruments like Article 52(2) of the ICSID Convention explicitly allow for the possibility of annulling a tribunal's decision on the basis that it acted *ultra vires*.[103] Therefore, an MFN clause should not be used to extend the jurisdiction of a tribunal unless its text very clearly permits such an extension.

In *Berschader,* the dispute, which was administered by the Arbitration Institute of the Stockholm Chamber of Commerce (SCC), concerned late payment to Belgian investors under a construction contract to rehabilitate the Russian Supreme Court building.[104] Like the Bulgaria-Cyprus BIT, Article 10 of the Belgium/Luxembourg-Union of Soviet Socialist Republics (USSR) BIT also restricted the claims that could be referred to international arbitration to those concerning the amount payable or mode of payment in relation to an expropriation.[105]

As such, the claimant sought to incorporate a broader arbitration provision than the one contained in the basic treaty by relying on the MFN clause in attempt to import from the Norway-Russia or Denmark-Russia BITs. Article 2 of the basic treaty guaranteed that a broad set of measures would be covered by the MFN clause, that is the MFN clause's scope included treatment concerning

---

103 Christoph Schreuer, *The ICSID Convention: A Commentary: A Commentary on the Convention on the Settlement of Investment Disputes between States and Nationals of Other States* (Cambridge Univ Press 2009) 524.

104 *Vladimir Berschader and Michael Berschader v Russian Federation, Decision on Jurisdiction, 21st April 2006*, SCC Case No. 080/2004. For the summary of the case, see: <https://investmentpolicy.unctad.org/investment-dispute-settlement/cases/155/berschader-v-russia> accessed 20 April 2022.

105 Belgium/Luxembourg – USSR BIT (1989) A copy of which is available at: <https://investmentpolicy.unctad.org/international-investment-agreements/treaty-files/4695/download> accessed 20 April 2022; *Berschader v Russia* (n 104) [151].

"all matters covered by the Treaty, in particular Article 4 (fair and equitable treatment), 5 (non-compensation) and 6 (free transfer of funds)."[106] In furtherance of its aims, the claimant relied on the expansive interpretations of the MFN clauses rendered by the *Maffezini, Siemens,* and *Gas Natural* tribunals.

The *Berschader* tribunal refused to confirm that it had jurisdiction over the matter on the basis of an application of the MFN clause in the basic treaty. It stated that the question as to whether the contracting parties to the treaty intended for the MFN provision to allow for the incorporation of dispute settlement provisions in other treaties should, ultimately, only be answered through a detailed analysis of the text and the negotiating history of the relevant treaty, as well as other relevant elements if available.[107] Therefore, the tribunal started with the text of the MFN clause.

In this regard, it referred mainly to the *Plama* tribunal's pronouncement that an arbitration clause in a BIT should be clear and unambiguous in order for it to be relied on to incorporate dispute settlement provisions from third-party treaties. Nevertheless, the *Berschader* tribunal found that this approach was questionable because it indicated that dispute settlement provisions should be construed differently from other provisions. Additionally, in many jurisdictions, including Sweden, the approach taken to the existence of an agreement to arbitrate tended to be neutral, or even one that employed a wide, as opposed to restrictive, interpretation.[108] According to the tribunal, it was therefore inappropriate to presume that agreements to arbitrate had the characteristics ascribed to the by the *Plama* tribunal.

The tribunal nonetheless shared the concerns of the *Plama* tribunal in that it was of the view that incorporation through the application of an MFN clauses would cause certain doubts.[109] A such, it discussed the divergent case law in relation to the application of MFNs clause to dispute settlement provisions and its ramification on treaty drafting.[110] The tribunal denied the general presumption of the *Maffezini* School in relation to contracting parties' intention to allow for the application of MFN clauses to dispute settlement mechanisms.[111] It stated that –

106 *Berschader v Russia* (n 104) [160].
107 *Berschader v Russia* (n 104) [175].
108 *Berschader v Russia* (n 104) [177].
109 *Berschader v Russia* (n 104) [178].
110 *Berschader v Russia* (n 104) [179].
111 *Berschader v Russia* (n 104) [180].

> the present Tribunal will apply the principle that an MFN provision in a BIT will only incorporate by reference an arbitration clause from another BIT where the terms of the original BIT clearly and unambiguously so provide or where it can otherwise be clearly inferred that this was the intention of the contracting parties.[112]

It is accordingly important to note that the *Berschader* tribunal actually adopted a similar "clear and unambiguous" principle as the *Plama* tribunal, but from a different perspective. While the *Plama* tribunal held that the agreement to arbitrate should be clearly and unambiguously included in a treaty, the *Berschader* tribunal disagreed and was of the view that it is instead the uncertain relationship between MFN clauses and procedural provisions that leads to the need for the principle. Therefore, although the *Berschader* tribunal's position was viewed by commentators as amounting to substantially the same approach as that taken by the *Plama* tribunal,[113] it nevertheless correctly revealed the essence of the question, i.e., whether MFN clauses can serve as a basis for consent to arbitrate and be interpreted to modify a specific offer on the part of a contracting party to arbitrate. In this sense, the tribunal stated its position as follows:

> [T]he Tribunal does not derive the requirement for clarity and lack of ambiguity involved in this test from any general principle to the effect that arbitration clauses should be interpreted more restrictively than other agreements. Nevertheless, this test is warranted … by the particular problems … which are posed by the construction of the scope of MFN provisions in BITs.[114]

Having settled on this principle, the tribunal turned to deal with the claimant's argument that the "all matters covered by the present Treaty" phrase contained in the MFN clause meant that it extended to all matters, including dispute settlement. In this connection, the tribunal firstly declared that such language could not be considered as having an unambiguous meaning.[115] After assuming that the MFN clause applied to other treaty clauses including *inter*

112 *Berschader v Russia* (n 104) [181].

113 *Berschader v Russia* (n 104). Todd Weiler observed in his dissenting opinion of the award, that the *Berschader* tribunal was 'really not that different from that of the *Plama* tribunal' in this regard. See: *Berschader v Russia* (n 104), *Dissenting Opinion by Todd Weiler* [9].

114 *Berschader v Russia* (n 104) [182].

115 *Berschader v Russia* (n 104) [184].

alia definitions (Article 1), subrogation by insurers (Article 7), and the relations between contracting parties (Article 9 and 11), the tribunal concluded that the claimant's argument either could not be correct or, at best, remained theoretical.[116] The tribunal concluded that the expression "all matters covered by the present Treaty" could not be interpreted literally, and that one could not with certainty rely on it to extend the scope of an MFN clause to include dispute settlement.[117] Instead, the explicit inclusion of several substantive provisions in Article 2 rather indicated that the contracting parties were aware of the ambiguity of "all matters covered by the present Treaty." Additionally, the tribunal observed that Article 10 was not included in the list of substantive provisions contained in Article 2. At this point, the tribunal declared that the MFN clause's ordinary meaning was of no assistance.

Professor Todd Weiler questioned this approach in his dissenting opinion. He noted that despite explicit references in Article 2 to other articles, its application was not restricted to those articles alone. According to Weiler, the provision merely envisaged a non-exhaustive list of substantive rights that are "particularly" covered by MFN obligation. In other words, for Weiler, the fact that certain treaty provisions did not fall within the scope of the MFN clause did not mean that the MFN clause could not be relied on in order to obtain more favorable treatment in relation to dispute settlement.[118]

Similarly, Professor Orrego Vicuña disagreed, stating that "the treaty says what it says and it is the exceptions that ought to be spelled out. If a treaty provides for the application of the MFN clause to all matters governed by such a treaty, it is not possible to say that this means that it does not apply to all matters except if specifically included, as the *Berschader* case wrongly concluded."[119]

The tribunal further engaged the arguments relating to whether dispute settlement provisions constituted an essential form of investment protection and whether this implicated an application of the *ejusdem generis* principle, and whether a refusal by a tribunal to extend the scope of an MFN clause to dispute settlement provisions would run afoul of the object and purpose of BITs. The

116 *Berschader v Russia* (n 104) [187–191].

117 *Berschader v Russia* (n 104) [192].

118 *Berschader v Russia* (n 104), *Dissenting Opinion of Todd Weiler* [22]. It was commented by Prof.Vicuna that 'the treaty says what it says and it is the exception that ought to be spelled out. If a treaty provides for the application of MFN clause to all matters governed by such a treaty, it is not possible to say that this means that it does not apply to all matters except if specifically included, as the Berschader case wrongly concluded.' See: Orrego Vicuna (n 62) 314.

119 Orrego Vicuna (n 62) 314; *Berschader v Russia* (n 104), *Dissenting Opinion of Todd Weiler*.

tribunal rejected both arguments for being of too general a nature. It acknowledged that such views might provide strong support for the conclusion that an MFN provision is generally capable of incorporating a dispute resolution clause and that such incorporation would typically advance the purpose of a BIT.[120] However, the tribunal determined that such arguments offered little or no guidance in determining the contracting parties' intention in specific cases.

As to whether the right to bring claims to international arbitration was an essential part of investment protection and therefore must be covered by the MFN clause, given the inadequacy of preparatory works tendered to clarify the contracting parties' intention, the tribunal decided to take account of factual circumstances. It first examined contemporary jurisprudence from 1989 when the basic treaty was concluded. The tribunal observed that at the time of the treaty's conclusion, there was no generally accepted approach to the question of whether an MFN provision encompassed arbitration clauses.[121] Since it has not been clearly addressed in the jurisprudence, the tribunal inferred that contracting parties simply did not contemplate the possibility that the MFN clause in Article 2 could incorporate treatment more favorable than that contained in the arbitration provision in Article 10.[122] Otherwise, according to the tribunal, the contracting parties would have included Article 10 within the scope of Article 2 for clarification "in view of the highly uncertain state of the law."[123]

Finally, the tribunal conducted a detailed review of the intention of the USSR as a contracting party. It examined treaties signed between the USSR and Turkey, South Korea, Switzerland, Spain, China, Austria, and Italy, amongst others. It found that they all removed reference to expropriation from their arbitration provisions.[124] The tribunal thus noted that when signing the BIT with Belgium-Luxembourg, the USSR, out of its firm position on state sovereignty, pursued a somewhat consistent policy that it never consented to arbitration concerning whether expropriation had in fact occurred.[125] The tribunal concluded that the USSR had not intended for the MFN provision in Article 2 to cover dispute settlement issues in the specific treaty at dispute.[126] In the end, the tribunal emphasized that the MFN clause could only incorporate an

120 *Berschader v Russia* (n 104) [197].

121 *Berschader v Russia* (n 104) [200].

122 *Berschader v Russia* (n 104) [202].

123 *Berschader v Russia* (n 104) [202].

124 *Berschader v Russia* (n 104) [204]. For a brief review of the USSR treaty policy, see: Noah Rubins and Azizjon Nazarov, 'Investment Treaties and the Russian Federation: Baiting the Bear?' (2008) 9 Business Law International 100.

125 *Berschader v Russia* (n 104) [203].

126 *Berschader v Russia* (n 104) [204].

arbitration clause from another BIT when the terms of the basic BIT *clearly and unambiguously* allow for this or when it could otherwise clearly be inferred that this was the intention of the contracting parties.[127]

The tribunal's concluding remarks about the interpretive methods it applied are interesting. As in *Plama*, it determined that examining the treaty text in light of the VCLT principles led to an inconclusive interpretation. The "ordinary meaning" element was not capable of leading to a clear meaning of Article 2, and the object and purpose of the BIT was a general statement that could not contribute to the interpretation. As such, the tribunal pointed out that the treaty text and "other relevant facts" would help reach a reasonable interpretation in relation to what intentions of the contract parties were at the time of the conclusion of the basic treaty. Its reliance on "other relevant facts," i.e., the factual circumstances around the conclusion of the treaty, and especially the previous treaty practice of the USSR, is seemingly an application of Article 32 of the VCLT on supplementary means of interpretation. For the sake of convenience, the text of Article 32 is reproduced here. It provides as follows:

> Recourse may be had to supplementary means of interpretation, including the preparatory work of the treaty and the circumstances of its conclusion.[128]

According to Mbengue, the relevance of the circumstances in Article 32 depends on their ability to illustrate the intentions of the contracting parties.[129] In *EC – Chicken Cuts*, the World Trade Organization's Appellate Body noted on the "circumstances of conclusion" in Article 32 that –

> [a]n 'event, act or instrument' may be relevant as supplementary means of interpretation ... when it helps to discern what the common intention of the parties were at the time of the conclusion with respect to the treaty or specific provision ... not only 'multilateral' sources, but also 'unilateral' acts, instruments, or statements of individual negotiating parties may be useful in ascertaining 'the reality of the situation which the parties wish to regulate by means of the treaty' and, ultimately, for discerning the common intentions of the parties.[130]

---

127 *Berschader v Russia* (n 104) [206].

128 Article 32 of the Vienna Convention on the Law of Treaties (1969).

129 Makane Moïse Mbengue, 'Rules of Interpretation (Article 32 of the Vienna Convention on the Law of Treaties)' (2016) 31 ICSID Review 388, 392.

130 Appellate Body Report, *European Communities – Customs Classification of Frozen Boneless Chicken Cuts* (*EC-Chicken Cuts*), WT/DS269/AB/R; WT/DS286/AB/R [289].

The Appellate Body continued to establish objective factors that may help to clarify the relevance of a specific circumstance for treaty interpretation in the following terms:

> [W]e can conceive of a number of objective factors that may be useful in determining the degree of relevance of particular circumstances for interpreting a specific treaty provision. These include the type of event, document, or instrument and its legal nature; temporal relation of the circumstance to the conclusion of the treaty; actual knowledge or mere access to a published act or instrument; subject matter of the document, instrument, or event in relation to the treaty provision to be interpreted; and whether or how it was used or influenced the negotiations of the treaty.[131]

In light of the approach taken in *EC – Chicken Cuts* by the Appellate Body, the consideration of USSR treaty practice seemingly fell into the category of circumstances of conclusion. This approach was, however, countered by Professor Todd Weiler in his dissenting opinion for being irrelevant. He argued as follows:

> What the Contracting Parties might have agreed upon in later situations with other partners says nothing conclusive about what the terms of the instant Treaty actually mean.[132]

According to Weiler, in view of the subsequent practice of the USSR where it concluded agreements with other Organisation for Economic Co-operation and Development members, including France and Canada, that made greater concessions towards investment liberalization and dispute settlement, USSR treaty practice should have strengthened the case that Article 2 should be interpreted as illustrating an intention to include dispute settlement within its scope, not weakened it. More importantly, he argued that the very fact that the respondent entered into a great number of agreements after it signed the Belgium/Luxembourg-USSR BIT actually indicated that its partners in this treaty were "first-movers" for whom a broad and remedial MFN provision would be crucially important.[133]

---

131 *EC-Chicken Cuts* (n 130) [291].

132 *Berschader v Russia* (n 104), *Dissenting Opinion of Todd Weiler* [24].

133 *Berschader v Russia* (n 104), *Dissenting Opinion of Todd Weiler.*

As provided for by Article 32 of the VCLT, reliance on factual circumstances should be done in order to confirm the meaning resulting from an application of Article 31 of the VCLT or determine the meaning when the interpretation from Article 31 leaves the meaning ambiguous or obscure or leads to a result that is manifestly absurd or unreasonable.[134] Due to the generality of the above elements, they cannot provide decisive clarity, but only offer support to the tribunals' reasoning, as in the *Plama* case.[135] As in *Plama*, the *Berschader* tribunal chose to rely on the factual circumstances to support its presumption about the MFN clause rather than backing its interpretation through reliance on the interpretive methods of the VCLT.

The decision of *Telenor* came later in the same year as *Berschader*. The *Telenor* dispute was about a series of measures adopted by Hungary concerning telecommunications service providers that allegedly affected the operation of a concession agreement which entitled the claimant to provide public mobile radiotelephone services. The agreement was concluded between the Norwegian claimant's wholly-owned subsidiary and the Hungarian Minister of Transport, Communications, and Water Management.[136] Article XI of the Norway-Hungary BIT provided for ICSID arbitration, but only in relation to the amount and consequence of compensation and repatriation.[137] Article IV of the same treaty provided for MFN treatment to be accorded to foreign investments, except in relation to treatment accorded by a customs union, free trade agreement, or taxation agreement.[138] The claimant invoked the MFN clause in an attempt to enlarge the scope of Article IV so as to include disputes concerning the breach of FET in Article III. However, the claimant failed to identify any specific, more favorable dispute settlement clauses to support its position, and only referred to the decisions in *Maffezini* and *Siemens*.[139]

After examining the decisions in *Maffezini*, *Siemens*, *Gas Natural*, *Plama*, and *Salini*, the *Telenor* tribunal "wholeheartedly" endorsed the analysis and statement of principle established by the *Plama* tribunal and declined to exercise jurisdiction over the claim alleging a breach of the FET clause in the basic treaty.[140]

---

134 Article 32 of the Vienna Convention on the Law of Treaties (1969) (n 128).

135 Tarcisio Gazzini, *Interpretation of International Investment Treaties* (First Edition, Hart Publishing 2016) 368.

136 *Telenor v Hungary* (n 63).

137 Article XI of the Norway – Hungary BIT (1991).

138 Article IV of the Norway – Hungary BIT (1991) (n 137).

139 *Telenor v Hungary* (n 63) [85].

140 *Telenor v Hungary* (n 63) [90].

The tribunal presented four main reasons for its decision. First, according to the interpretive principle set out in Article 31(1) of the VCLT, the text of the MFN clause before the tribunal did not show an intention on the part of the contracting parties to extend its scope to dispute settlement mechanisms, as had been done in some other BITs.[141]

The tribunal then referred to the *Plama* tribunal, indicating that it shared its concerns around treaty shopping in view of the broad interpretation of MFN clauses. Moreover, an expansive interpretation may, according to the tribunal, have rendered the meaning of treaties uncertain and unstable since the operative limitation in the basic BIT might at some point be replaced by a broader dispute settlement mechanism from third-party treaties.[142]

Finally, the tribunal relied on the treaty practice of the contracting states with other countries. It stated that a broad interpretation of MFN clauses was usually rendered from the perspective of investor protection being the overarching purpose of BITs. However, according to the tribunal, contracting states' intention should instead be the guiding principle when it came to the interpretation of MFN clauses.[143] Therefore, instead of relying on the inferential extension of the scope the MFN clause, the tribunal referred to the fact that both Norway and Hungary had entered into other BITs that subjected *all* disputes to arbitration. As such, the tribunal asserted that it would be fair to assume that, in relation to the current BIT, Norway and Hungary shared a common intention to limit the jurisdiction of the arbitral tribunal to the specified categories enumerated in the treaty.[144] Therefore, according to the tribunal, extending the MFN clause to cover dispute settlement would "subvert the parties' intention to the basic treaty."[145]

The tribunal drew on additional materials for support in this regard. Specifically, it adopted as relevant the respondent's submission that on the part of Norway, among the 15 publicly available Norwegian BITs, the one with Hungary was the *only one* that specified the categories of disputes subject to ICSID arbitration, while the other 14 all allowed for "all disputes" or "any disputes" to be referred to ICSID arbitration. On the other hand, about half of the BITs concluded by Hungary limited consent to ICSID arbitration to expropriation issues. The tribunal also conducted its own research and found that in 22 Hungarian BITs, seven of them applied arbitration to expropriation or

141 *Telenor v Hungary* (n 63) [92].
142 *Telenor v Hungary* (n 63) [94].
143 *Telenor v Hungary* (n 63) [95].
144 *Telenor v Hungary* (n 63) [95].
145 *Telenor v Hungary* (n 63) [95].

nationalization issues, 13 allowed submissions of any legal dispute to arbitration and only two (including the one with Norway) consented to arbitration with specified categories additional to expropriation or nationalization, such as compensation for losses due to war.[146]

In the end, the tribunal concluded with certainty that "in the present case the MFN clause cannot be used to extend the Tribunal's jurisdiction to categories of claim other than expropriation, for this would subvert the common intention of Hungary and Norway in entering into the BIT in question."[147]

It is, however, questionable how the *Telenor* tribunal came to its conclusion. Although the tribunal relied on the VCLT at the beginning of its reasoning, it nevertheless assumed that the ordinary meaning of the MFN clause covered substantive rights to the exclusion of procedural treatment. Its treaty-shopping and uncertainty concerns were not robust either since they pertained to these as results of, instead of as reasons for, a broad interpretation of the MFN clause. The last limb of its reasoning also merits attention. Instead of relying on the interpretive principles embodied in the VCLT, the tribunal accorded much weight to each contracting party's treaty practice with other countries and inferred the contracting parties' intention with reference to other treaties. Such practice also seems to be an application of Article 32 of the VCLT, which allows for reliance on sources including *inter alia* "the circumstances of conclusion" of the BIT at issue.

In the *Renta 4* case, the dispute arising out of the Russia-Spain BIT was related to the *Yukos* case.[148] In the current case, the Spanish investor alleged that a series of governmental actions taken by Russia eliminated all value of its American Depositary Receipts in Yukos and, therefore, constituted an expropriation in violation of Article 6 of the Russia-Spain BIT.[149] Article 10 of the basic treaty provided for a restrictive dispute settlement procedure that only related to the amount or method of payment of the compensation.[150] Russia argued that Article 10 did not encompass all issues relating to expropriation. Since there was still disagreement as to whether any of the criticized measures were expropriatory, the dispute had to be resolved in a proper forum before

146 *Telenor v Hungary* (n 63) [96].

147 *Telenor v Hungary* (n 63) [100].

148 *Yukos Universal Limited (Isle of Man) v The Russian Federation*, PCA Case No. 2005-04/AA227.

149 *Renta 4 v Russia* (n 63).

150 Russian Federation – Spain BIT (1990), a copy of which is available at: <https://investmentpolicy.unctad.org/international-investment-agreements/treaty-files/2225/download> accessed 20 April 2022.

matters of quantum could go to international arbitration as provided for in Article 10.[151]

The claimant argued that the MFN clause contained in Article 5(2) would allow it to bring the case to an international tribunal even if Article 10 did not.[152] Article 5(2) accorded MFN treatment with reference to the FET obligation contained in Article 5(1). The claimant sought to invoke the MFN clause in order to broaden the scope of matters that could be brought before an international tribunal through incorporating the more favorable treatment allegedly accorded by Article 8(1) of the Denmark-Russia BIT, which allowed for any dispute between a foreign investor and its host state in connection with an investment to be brought to international arbitration.[153] Russia argued that its consent to arbitration could not be inferred from Article 5(2) of the basic treaty, which should not, according to Russia, have impacted the consent it had given in terms of Article 10.

After a lengthy examination of ICJ cases, including its decisions in *Rights of US Nationals in Morocco, Anglo-Iranian,* and *Ambatielos*, the tribunal observed that a general statement on an MFN clause is insufficient with respect to a particular case. Instead, the core issue should be the text of that specific MFN clause.[154] The tribunal also noted the limited normative applicability of the above cases, because the relevant statements in those matters were made *obiter dicta* instead of *ratio decidendi*. It means that although they may be persuasive, they are still *a priori* of less weight.[155]

The tribunal was of the view that its duty was to discover the meaning of treaty provisions, not create it. It rebuffed the proposition that access to different types of dispute resolution mechanisms through an application of an MFN clause might lead to forum shopping, since the extension of particular commitments was, for the tribunal at least, the rationale of MFN clauses. In this regard, it warned about the danger of purposive readings of treaty texts. According to the tribunal, purposive readings rely on speculations and risk encroaching on the essential policy considerations that contracting parties look to give effect to through the conclusion of treaties. Therefore, the tribunal stated that one should be careful when using the expression "forum shopping" for the sake of purposive speculation. The derogatory use of the term "forum

151 *Renta 4 v Russia* (n 63) [20].
152 *Renta 4 v Russia* (n 63) [69].
153 *Renta 4 v Russia* (n 63) [69].
154 *Renta 4 v Russia* (n 63) [90].
155 *Renta 4 v Russia* (n 63) [91].

shopping" was, for the tribunal, only an assertion of opinions, and could easily be adopted or rejected.[156]

The tribunal also questioned the primary/secondary rules dichotomy, which it merged with the procedural/substantive treatment discussion in relation to the scope of MFN clauses. It noted that there were no normative rules about the primary/secondary rule distinction. This classification was introduced by the ILC in its work on state responsibility.[157] There was no authority or dominant view about whether MFN clauses should be limited to "primary" obligations.[158] The tribunal opined that access to international arbitration has undoubtedly been a fundamental and constant desideratum of investment protection. Therefore, it should have been a "weighty factor" in considering the object and purpose of BITs in the tribunal's eyes.[159] In this regard, the tribunal concluded as follows:

> There is no textual basis or legal rule to say that 'treatment' does not encompass the Host State 's acceptance of international arbitration … The investor's gateway to MFN treatment is the status of protected investor and ownership of a qualifying investment in terms of the BIT as the 'basic treaty.' This is the position the Claimants here seek to establish under the Spanish BIT. There is nothing unsound about the general proposition they seek to vindicate.[160]

The tribunal endorsed the approach adopted in *Ambatielos*, which eschewed the question of whether MFN clauses could incorporate dispute settlement mechanisms under the procedural/substantive dichotomy and instead focused on the *ejusdem generis* principle. Following the *ejusdem generis* principle, the *Renta 4* tribunal examined the text of the MFN clause in the Spanish-Russia BIT. Paragraph (1) of the clause provided for FET, and paragraph (2), which provided for MFN treatment, referred to the FET clause in paragraph (1). The tribunal stated that such restrictive terms were different from the more generic "all matters covered by this Agreement" phrasing adopted by MFN clauses in other treaties. On the contrary, the MFN clause at issue was restricted to the right to enjoy a no less favorable level of FET.[161]

156 *Renta 4 v Russia* (n 63) [92].
157 *Renta 4 v Russia* (n 63) [99].
158 *Renta 4 v Russia* (n 63) [99].
159 *Renta 4 v Russia* (n 63) [100].
160 *Renta 4 v Russia* (n 63) [101].
161 *Renta 4 v Russia* (n 63) [105].

After determining that FET does not include access to international arbitration, the tribunal undertook a verbatim examination of the MFN clause's wording. It determined that subparagraph (1) of Article 5(2) explicitly and plainly referred to FET. Additionally, subparagraph (2) of Article 5(2) referred back to FET to the exclusion of international arbitration by referring to treatment "accorded by either Party in respect of investments made within its territory by investors of any third state." So far, the remaining question is mostly posed by subparagraph (3) of the same article, which proceeds to state that MFN treatment shall not include privileges from *inter alia* taxation agreements and free trade areas, none of which are FET issues. As such, the claimant argued that the term "treatment" contained in subparagraph (3) did not refer to FET but rather to "treatment" in generic terms. Furthermore, since subparagraph (3) referred to "treatment under this article," it could fairly be inferred that "treatment" in Article 5 was not limited to FET, and should therefore be read so as to include international arbitration within its scope.[162]

The tribunal noted that if MFN treatment were limited to the FET clause, subparagraph (3) would be unnecessary and that such an interpretation would go against the *effet utile* principle. Therefore, it seemed to the tribunal that the MFN clause should be understood in a broad sense to include investor-state arbitration. Thus, the tribunal had to choose between the "explicit stipulation," which led to a restrictive reading of the MFN clause, and the "revelation by grammatical deconstruction," which led to a broad reading of the MFN clause.[163] As such, the tribunal admitted that it "naturally prefer[red] the former."[164] As for why the contracting parties included subparagraph (3) while anticipating "treatment" in other subparagraphs of the same article to be limited to FET, the tribunal gave its understanding as follows:

> The drafters were conscious of the ramification of the MFN promise. They were determined to ensure that it would not encroach on their freedom to extend special privileges in the context of regional integration or other arrangements envisaged in Subparagraph 3. Such exceptions to MFN clauses are commonplace in BIT practice. This may have led to a reflexive insertion of the clause in the Spanish BIT. A searching exegetical endeavor would have revealed that this was unnecessary in this particular instance. The drafters may not have realized this. Or they may not have wished to rely on others – including trade representatives or

162 *Renta 4 v Russia* (n 63) [107].
163 *Renta 4 v Russia* (n 63) [117].
164 *Renta 4 v Russia* (n 63) [117].

> tribunals – to reach the same recondite conclusion. Either way the attribution to Subparagraph 3 of sophisticated implications simply cannot dislodge the qualifying adjective 'fair and equitable' in Subparagraph 1. Even less can it undermine the unambiguous reference in Subparagraph 2 to 'treatment referred to in paragraph 1 above'.[165]

The *Renta 4* tribunal rightly applied the *ejusdem generis* principle in *Ambatielos* without making any specific assumptions in order to interpret and apply the MFN clause. Its decision was primarily based on the reference to FET in the text of the MFN clause itself. As the tribunal noted, general propositions do not act as a laser beam pointing to a clear answer.[166] To move from broad purposive considerations to a specific determination of what had been agreed required analysis of the specific features of the case and instruments at hand.[167] Therefore, it was conceivable that the tribunal might come to an opposite conclusion given a differently worded MFN clause.

The investor-appointed arbitrator, Charles N. Brower, did not agree with the majority of the tribunal. In his dissenting opinion, he argued that the authentic treaty text of Russian and Spanish suggested that the MFN clause referred in generic terms to "treatment" instead of FET. In this regard, the arbitrator stated that a state that did not provide foreign investors access to international arbitration procedures would necessarily deny that investor FET when a dispute arose.[168] Even if the tribunal majority was correct to restrict the scope of the MFN clause to FET, dispute settlement mechanisms would still fall within the broader concept of "treatment" of foreign investors and investments.[169]

In this sense, the arbitrator considered it undeniable that a wider choice of dispute settlement issues, i.e., additional causes of action that could be pleaded and decided by international arbitration tribunals, was to be considered more favorable than a limited scope of arbitration. The arbitrator's approach, which essentially treated state consent to arbitration as a form of FET, is questionable.[170] As argued above, state consent relates to sovereignty and is the very basis of tribunals' jurisdiction. FET, meanwhile, is a type of substantive treatment that relates to whether a claimant was treated in a just fashion in domestic adjudication, not a sovereign state's promise to submit to international

165 *Renta 4 v Russia* (n 63) [117].
166 *Renta 4 v Russia* (n 63) [102].
167 *Renta 4 v Russia* (n 63) [102].
168 *Renta 4 v Russia* (n 63) *Separate Opinion of Charles N. Brower* [23].
169 *Renta 4 v Russia* (n 63) *Separate Opinion of Charles N. Brower* [20].
170 *Renta 4 v Russia* (n 63) *Separate Opinion of Charles N. Brower* [23].

arbitration in relation to a particular dispute. Therefore, the absence of state consent to international arbitration in relation to several issues does not amount to a claimant not being able to access "dispute settlement procedures at all" and will not "necessarily … deny [a] … (foreign) investor any FET when a dispute arises."[171]

In *Tza Yap Shum*, the dispute concerned the seizure of the claimant's enterprise's bank account due to a tax debt and other alleged actions undertaken by the Peruvian tax authorities that resulted in the claimant being substantively deprived of his investment.[172] Peru challenged the tribunal's jurisdiction in response to the Chinese investor Tza Yap Shum's claims, including in relation to *inter alia* expropriation, FET, and free transfer of profits. It argued that Article 8(3) of the China-Peru BIT only permitted disputes to be submitted in relation to the amount to be awarded in relation to an expropriation to international arbitration and that all other matters had to be resolved by virtue of other means.[173]

In China-Peru BIT, ICSID tribunals established under the China-Peru BIT may assert jurisdiction under two specific circumstances. First, only after local courts have determined that the investment in question was indeed expropriated and, if the dispute did involve compensation, the investor would then be able to submit a claim to international arbitration in relation to the amount of compensation to be awarded for the expropriation in question. Second, when the tribunal has jurisdiction in relation to other matters such as FET breaches, provided that the disputing parties agreed to the tribunal having jurisdiction.[174]

As such, the claimant argued that the tribunal's jurisdiction could be broadened through an application of the MFN clause in Article 3.2 of the BIT to allow it to hear matters including FET breaches. For this purpose, the claimant sought to incorporate Article 12 of the Peru-Colombia BIT, which provided more favorable treatment by allowing "any controversy of a legal nature" to be submitted to international arbitration.[175]

Article 3 of the China-Peru BIT guaranteed fairly typical MFN treatment linked with FET as follows:

171 *Renta 4 v Russia* (n 63), *Separate Opinion of Charles N. Brower* [23].

172 *Tza Yap Shum v Peru* (n 63).

173 China – Peru BIT (1994). A copy of which is available at: <https://investmentpolicy.unctad.org/international-investment-agreements/treaty-files/767/download> accessed 20 April 2022; *Tza Yap Shum v Peru* (n 63) [129].

174 *Tza Yap Shum v Peru* (n 63) [129].

175 *Tza Yap Shum v Peru* (n 63) [191].

1. Investments and activities related to investments of any of the contracting parties shall enjoy fair treatment and equitable, as well as protection in the territory of the other Party Contractor.
2. The treatment and protection mentioned in paragraph 1 of this article will not be less favorable than those agreed to investments of investors of a third State and activities related to such investments.

Considering that the MFN clause at issue is linked to FET, the tribunal questioned whether the "treatment" of foreign investors in Article 3 of the Peru-China BIT could be interpreted to include procedural treatment in the event of an alleged FET violation. To this end, the tribunal relied on the interpretive principles in Articles 31 and 32 of the VCLT. It concluded that the wordings of Articles 3(1) and 3(2), considering their ordinary meaning, the context, and the object and purpose of the BIT, did not seem to restrict the scope of the word "treatment" to matters of substantive business such as exploitation and investment management.[176] Moreover, the tribunal did not find any evidence suggesting that the contracting parties had intended for the term "treatment" in the MFN clause to bear a special meaning. Therefore, the tribunal believed that the wording of the MFN clause made it possible for a broader interpretation to include more favorable procedural protections (potentially including arbitration before ICSID) for alleged violations of the FET standard.[177]

Having concluded that the MFN clause potentially extended to procedural treatment, the tribunal turned to examine Article 8 in the treaty. It noted that Article 8(3) permitted "[a]ny dispute regarding other matters between an investor of Any Contracting Party and the other Contracting Party [to] be submitted to the Center if the parties to the dispute so agree."[178]

The tribunal understood that the text of Article 8 reflected the contracting parties' common intention on two fundamental points. First of all, they agreed to submit disputes in relation to expropriation to international arbitration before ICSID. Second, they specifically considered the possibility of submitting other types of disputes to ICSID arbitration on the assumption of agreement between the disputing parties.[179] As such, the tribunal determined

176 *Tza Yap Shum v Peru* (n 63) [213].

177 Before reaching this conclusion the tribunal also considered the testimonies from negotiating representatives from both Contracting Parties. The tribunal however did not deem such testimonies 'to be a convincing manifestation of a common agreement on the subject, or the intention of the Contracting Parties with respect to the scope of this MFN clause.' See: *Tza Yap Shum v Peru* (n 63) [213].

178 Article 8 of the China – Peru BIT (1994) (n 173).

179 *Tza Yap Shum v Peru* (n 63) [216].

that since the contracting parties provided explicitly for the possibility of submitting "other matters" to ICSID arbitration in their BIT, the specific language of Article 8(3) had to prevail over the general language of the MFN clause of Article 3. Therefore, the arguments of the claimant had to be rejected.[180] To this end, the tribunal sided with the restrictive approach of the *Plama* tribunal. As in *Plama*, the tribunal also required there to be "clear and unambiguous" consent on the part of state parties contained in the MFN clause. Since the MFN clause in dispute did not contain such consent, the contracting parties could not be presumed to have consented to the MFN clause having the effect of agreeing to ICSID jurisdiction.[181]

It is curious how the tribunal perceived the interplay between Article 3 and Article 8(3). It seems that after determining that the MFN clause was linked to the FET clause, the tribunal could have examined whether FET included procedural issues, as the *Renta 4* tribunal did. Instead, the tribunal decided to specify a hierarchy between Article 3 and Article 8(3).[182]

The order in which rules of law are to be applied is not included as part of the interpretation method in the VCLT. According to the ILC, *lex specialis derogat lege generali* applies in the event of two conflicting rules. It suggests that "if a matter is being regulated by a general standard as well as a more specific rule, then the latter should take precedence over the former."[183] However,

180 *Tza Yap Shum v Peru* (n 63) [216].

181 W Shen, 'The Good, the Bad or the Ugly? A Critique of the Decision on Jurisdiction and Competence in Tza Yap Shum v. The Republic of Peru' (2011) 10 Chinese Journal of International Law 55, 86.

182 Although the tribunal refused to build its jurisdiction on FET and free transfer breaches via MFN clause, it nevertheless affirmed its jurisdiction on the determination of expropriation and continued to render an award thereupon. It established its jurisdiction by a broad interpretation of the term "involving" in Article 8(3) and was criticized by some Chinese scholars as "unreasonable and unacceptable". See: An Chen, 'Queries to the Recent ICSID Decision on Jurisdiction Upon the Case of Tza Yap Shum v. Republic of Peru: Should China–Peru BIT 1994 Be Applied to Hong Kong SAR Under the "One Country, Two Systems" Policy?' in An Chen (ed), *The Voice from China: An CHEN on International Economic Law* (Springer Berlin Heidelberg 2013). Nils Eliasson, 'Investor-State Arbitration and Chinese Investors Recent Developments in Light of the Decision on Jurisdiction in the Case Mr. Tza Yap Shum v. the Republic of Peru' (2009) 2 Contemporary Asia Arbitration Journal 347. See also: Guiguo Wang, 'Consent in Investor-State Arbitration: A Critical Analysis' (2014) 13 Chinese Journal of International Law 335, 349–53.

183 International Law Commission, *Fragmentation of International Law: Difficulties Arising from the Diversification and Expansion of International Law: Report of the Study Group of the International Law Commission, Finalized by Martti Koskenniemi*, United Nations General Assembly A/CN.4/L.682 (2006), 256, 35. A copy of which is available at: <https://legal.un.org/ilc/documentation/english/a_cn4_l682.pdf> accessed 20 April 2022.

the fact that Article 3 is open to the possibility of being interpreted as including procedural issues does not make it a general standard to regulate procedural treatment. Even assuming that the MFN clause can be considered as a general standard for procedural issues, it still does not regulate the same matter as Article 8(3) does. Because Article 8(3), by its text, regulates the foundation for ICSID arbitration, i.e., the state consent, which is different from other procedural matters.

Additionally, the tribunal's failure to apply the same textual examination to the scope of "dispute" in Article 8(3) as it did in Article 3 is confusing.[184] According to Shen, although the tribunal drew on the specific wording of Article 8 to reject the extension via the MFN clause, it nonetheless did not give the same weight in its reasoning on the scope of "dispute," which was based on the notion of state consent. As a result, the tribunal failed to answer the question as to whether the MFN clause could conceivably extend to jurisdictional issues. This makes one wonder whether the tribunal would have established that it had jurisdiction via the MFN clause in the absence of Article 8(3). A better understanding would be that Article 8(3) explicitly limited the contracting parties' state consent to expropriation issues while leaving the possibility of including broader issues through future expressions of consent based on the compromissory clause between the disputing parties.

In *Austrian Airlines*, the dispute concerned the Slovakian government's alleged debt to a Slovakian airline invested in by the Austrian claimant.[185] The claimant filed an international arbitration claim asserting breaches by Slovakia, including in relation to indirect expropriation, FET, full protection and security, and an umbrella clause. Slovakia objected to the tribunal asserting jurisdiction due to the inclusion in the basic BIT of a restrictive dispute settlement provision which excluded the above types of claims. As such, the claimant attempted to establish that the tribunal had jurisdiction by relying on the MFN clause in the treaty.

The respondent contended that the MFN clause could not operate to replace the dispute settlement system agreed by the contracting states in the basic treaty. It argued that such operation would be in conflict with the plain text of Article 3 since there was nothing in Article 3 that indicated its extension to dispute settlement. In this regard, the respondent drew on the *ejusdem generis* principle, arguing that the contracting parties would not have narrowed the scope of Article 8 during their negotiations if they "had at the same

184 Shen (n 181) 86.
185 *Austrian Airlines v Slovakia* (n 63).

time intended that dispute settlement be covered by the MFN clause."[186] The respondent also observed that the treaty practice of Slovakia concerning dispute settlement clauses in later treaties did not support the claimant's assertion that Slovakia subsequently consented to broaden the available dispute resolution mechanisms.[187]

The tribunal took the view that the dispute settlement provisions should not be strictly interpreted since there was no principle of either restrictive or extensive interpretation of an agreement to arbitrate in international law.[188] In this regard, the tribunal cited Judge Rosalyn Higgins for the position of the Permanent Court of International Justice (PCIJ) and ICJ in the following terms:

> [T]here is no rule that requires a restrictive interpretation of compromissory clauses. But equally, there is no evidence that the various exercises of jurisdiction by the two Courts really indicate a jurisdictional presumption in [favor] of the plaintiff ... The Court has no judicial policy of being either liberal or strict in deciding the scope of compromissory clauses: they are judicial decisions like any other.[189]

As such, the tribunal was determined to interpret the MFN clause "neither restrictively nor expansively but rather objectively and in good faith,"[190] following the interpretation rules of Articles 31 and 32 of the VCLT. It firstly examined the text of MFN treatment in Article 3(1), noting that Article 3(1) did not specify whether it applied to procedural issues. The term "treatment" in this article did not indicate the distinction between substantive and procedural issues. Therefore, the plain language neither affirmed nor ruled out such possibility.[191]

The tribunal then turned to the context of Article 3(1), i.e., Article 3(2) on MFN exceptions and Article 8 on dispute settlement. It noted that according to the *expressio unius* principle, the fact that the exceptions enumerated in Article 3(2) did not include procedural issues indicated that contracting parties did not intend to exclude other topics such as procedural treatment. It could also be argued that Article 3(2) exceptions pertained to substantive

186 *Austrian Airlines v Slovakia* (n 63) [111].
187 *Austrian Airlines v Slovakia* (n 63) [111].
188 *Austrian Airlines v Slovakia* (n 63) [119].
189 *Austrian Airlines v Slovakia* (n 63) [120]. Citing: *Oil Platforms (Islamic Republic of Iran v United States of America), Judgment on Preliminary Objections dated 12 December 1996, Separate Opinion by Judge Higgins* (ICJ) 857 [35].
190 *Austrian Airlines v Slovakia* (n 63) [121].
191 *Austrian Airlines v Slovakia* (n 63) [126].

treatment, and that Article 3(1) should thus be construed to have been limited to substantive matters.[192] Given the *expressio unius* principle's supplementary character, the tribunal determined that the exceptions in Article 3(2) did not lead to a specific answer which would resolve the dispute at issue and that it should therefore proceed with caution.

The tribunal then turned to Article 8 in search of clarification. It first examined the objective meaning of Article 8 as supported by the negotiating history of the treaty, which showed the contracting parties' intention to limit arbitral jurisdiction to the amount and payment of expropriation compensation, to the exclusion of whether a given alleged expropriation was legal.[193] The tribunal also drew on the contemporary treaty practice of the Slovak Republic in this connection and found that Czechoslovakia indeed concluded treaties containing broader dispute settlement provisions. As was the case with the *Tza Yap Shum* tribunal, the tribunal concluded that the manifest, specific intention to restrict dispute settlement as contained in Article 8 of the Austria-Slovakia BIT should prevail over the general, unspecific intent expressed in the MFN clause.[194] It stated that as follows:

> As a result of these contextual considerations, the specific intent expressed in Article 8, 4(4) and 4(5) informs the scope of the general intent expressed in Article 3(1), with the result that the former prevails over the latter. In other words, the restrictive dispute settlement mechanism for expropriation claims set out in Article 8, 4(4), and 4(5) constitutes an exception to the scope of Article 3(1). Hence, the MFN clause does not apply to the settlement of disputes over the legality of expropriations.[195]

The tribunal also relied on other propositions to support its conclusion. First, Article 8 did not confine itself to the amount and conditions of payment for expropriation compensation. It also subjected disputes on transfer obligations under Article 5 to arbitration. The tribunal saw it as an indication of the contracting parties' intent to deliberately limit the scope of Article 8.

The second factor was the *travaux préparatoires* of the treaty. In 1988, a draft of Article 8(1) noted the differences between a contracting state and an investor from another contracting state "regarding an investment" without

---

192 *Austrian Airlines v Slovakia* (n 63) [129].
193 *Austrian Airlines v Slovakia* (n 63) [132].
194 *Austrian Airlines v Slovakia* (n 63) [135].
195 *Austrian Airlines v Slovakia* (n 63) [135].

any limitation.[196] This draft was subsequently replaced by a more restrictive one relating to disputes "regarding an investment concerning the amount or modality of compensation," which was identical to the final version. According to the tribunal, such evolution in relation to the wording of the clause was a clear confirmation of the contracting parties' intent to limit the scope of matters in relation to which arbitration claims could be brought.

In conclusion, the tribunal stated that the claimant's attempt to incorporate a broader scope of jurisdiction through Article 3(1) "could only succeed if Article 3(1) were to be read as a neutral MFN clause independently from the context."[197] However, the tribunal determined that the Article 3(1) was not a neutral MFN clause. Given the express treaty limitations on arbitration, the general intention demonstrated in the MFN clause was inadequate to displace the limitations.[198]

The *EURAM* case was also based on the Austria-Slovakia BIT. The dispute concerned legislative measures introduced by Slovakia which allegedly reversed a previous push to liberalize the Slovak health insurance market, which prompted the claimant to invest in Slovakia's health insurance sector.[199] The claimant alleged that Slovakia had breached its indirect expropriation and FET obligations, including in relation to denial of justice and transfer of funds.

In this case, the respondent, in similar manner as in *Austria Airlines*, argued that the tribunal lacked jurisdiction since the dispute at issue did not concern the amount or conditions of payment in relation to compensation due for an expropriation, but rather that the "more fundamental question whether there [had] been an expropriation" was at issue.[200] The claimant invoked the MFN clause in response, arguing that even if the tribunal declined its jurisdiction due to the limited scope of Article 8, it could still establish jurisdiction through an application of the MFN clause in Article 3.[201]

The *EURAM* tribunal started from the neutrality of the MFN clause at issue. In this connection, it first noted the lack of *jurisprudence constante* on interpreting MFN clauses. It further noted the inconsistency of tribunals' interpretations on this issue. The tribunal attributed it to the different treaty language adopted by different BITs, and different or even conflicting presumptions adopted by tribunals.[202] The tribunal then rejected both parties' submissions

196 *Austrian Airlines v Slovakia* (n 63) [137].
197 *Austrian Airlines v Slovakia* (n 63) [138].
198 *Austrian Airlines v Slovakia* (n 63) [139].
199 *EURAM Bank v Slovakia* (n 63).
200 *EURAM Bank v Slovakia* (n 63) [343].
201 *EURAM Bank v Slovakia* (n 63) [345].
202 *EURAM Bank v Slovakia* (n 63) [437].

in relation to whether the MFN clause in question should be interpreted broadly or restrictively. According to the tribunal –

> the object and purpose of the BIT does not require either a broad or a restrictive approach to the interpretation of its provision for arbitration. Nor does the Tribunal accept that there is any general principle of international law that the acceptance by a State of the jurisdiction of an international court or tribunal must be restrictively construed.[203]

The tribunal proceeded to examine the various ways for contracting parties to express consent to arbitration, noting that there was no general principle that precluded an MFN clause from determining the extent of consent to arbitration. It concluded that because of the neutrality of Article 3(1), "there [was] no express provision that the guarantee of most [favored] nation treatment [was] intended to apply to investor-state arbitration but nor [was] there an express provision excluding that possibility."[204]

Having reached this conclusion, the tribunal went on to analyze the difference between substantive provisions and arbitration clauses, holding that only an arbitration clause could create or enable the creation of a direct relationship between a host state and an investor.[205] The tribunal explained that Article 8 of the Austria-Slovakia BIT had a dual character, as it not only established the treaty obligation of the contracting parties, but also acted as a gateway through which the investor had to pass in order to enter into an arbitration agreement necessary for the jurisdiction to the tribunal.[206] Therefore, the tribunal deemed that applying an MFN clause to alter the scope of an arbitration provision was an essentially distinct matter from applying it to other treaty provisions which did not have the same dual character.[207]

To support its conclusion, the tribunal applied the *ejusdem generis* principle as follows:

> If a BIT has no provision for investor-State arbitration, there is no offer of arbitration and thus no scope for the creation of an arbitration agreement. Even if that BIT contains a broadly worded MFN clause, that clause cannot substitute for the arbitration provision and make it possible for

203 EURAM *Bank v Slovakia* (n 63) [439].
204 EURAM *Bank v Slovakia* (n 63) [444].
205 EURAM *Bank v Slovakia* (n 63) [445].
206 EURAM *Bank v Slovakia* (n 63) [445,446].
207 EURAM *Bank v Slovakia* (n 63) [445,446].

> an investor successfully to bring arbitration proceedings against a State Party to the BIT, no matter what provisions for arbitration that State Party might have agreed to include in its other BITs. By contrast, if a BIT contains no provision on fair and equitable treatment, an investor may nonetheless be able to derive from the MFN clause contained in that BIT a right to be accorded such treatment by one of the States Parties, provided that there is at least one other BIT concluded by that State which contains a provision for fair and equitable treatment.[208]

Although the tribunal rightly cited the *ejusdem generis* principle as part of its reasoning supporting its refusal to extend the MFN clause to Article 8, the above statement was nevertheless an obvious misapplication of the *ejusdem generis* principle, because a claimant cannot rely on an MFN clause to incorporate a brand-new FET clause from a third-party treaty if the basic treaty does not contain one. Therefore, this example does not support the tribunal's conclusions pertaining to the difference between substantive treatment and arbitration provisions.

Although misapplying the *ejusdem generis* principle, the tribunal adopted a position that resembled the position taken by the *Plama* tribunal. It stated that to widen its jurisdiction beyond the scope of Article 8 would be a transformation of the arbitration provision that requires "clear indications" to permit such a transformation, i.e. that it was intended by the state parties.[209] Since there was no "clear indication," it would have been unwarranted to apply the MFN clause to transform the treaty's arbitration offer.

Following the above reasoning, the tribunal considered the text and context of the MFN clause in Article 3. In this regard, the tribunal first examined the exceptions contained in Article 3(2). It declared that these were of no assistance in this matter since they only clarified the sources for better treatment an investor could not rely on, while saying nothing about the type of rights Article 3(1) was designed to apply to.[210]

Second, the *travaux préparatoires* of Article 8 showed that there had been an alteration during negotiations from the original unrestricted version to the final limited one. The tribunal was of the view that this suggested a deliberate decision to narrow the scope of investor-state arbitration.[211]

---

208 *EURAM Bank v Slovakia* (n 63) [447].
209 *EURAM Bank v Slovakia* (n 63) [450].
210 *EURAM Bank v Slovakia* (n 63) [453].
211 *EURAM Bank v Slovakia* (n 63) [454].

Third, the tribunal considered the ordinary meaning of the term "treatment" contained in Article 3(1). According to the tribunal, the term "treatment" was "more apposite to cover substantive standards of treatment than to apply to the provision for investor-state arbitration, given what [had] already been said above regarding the special character of that provision."[212]

Fourth, the tribunal looked at the context of Article 3. The tribunal explained that Article 3(1) was located among the group of substantive provisions, including FET (Article 2(1)), expropriation (Article 4), and rights to transfer (Article 5). Failure to comply with Article 3(1) would thus constitute a substantive breach of other articles in this context. The fact that the MFN clause was located in the same category of substantive provisions indicated that it was not intended to transform the scope of the arbitration provision.[213]

Therefore, although the *EURAM* tribunal intentionally distanced itself from the *Austrian Airlines* decision, it applied a similar methodology in interpreting Article 3 by defining the MFN clause as neutral and affirming the possibility for it to be applied in relation to both substantive and procedural issues. Both tribunals also resorted to the text and context of the MFN clause with the support from the *travaux préparatoires* of the treaty, tipping the scale towards the conclusion that the MFN clause in the Austria-Slovakia BIT was not intended by the contracting parties to extend to the consent to arbitrate.

In the more recent case of *ST-AD*, the basic treaty was concluded between Bulgaria and Germany in 1986.[214] The dispute arose out of the government's alleged unlawful failure to provide restitution to a family of a specific property, including a factory and commercial buildings located on it, on a tract of land in Sofia, Bulgaria.[215]

Article 4(3) of the Bulgaria-Germany BIT provided limited access to international arbitration in relevant part. It stated as follows:

> The lawfulness of the expropriation shall, at the request of the investor, be reviewed in a properly constituted legal proceeding of the Contracting Party which has carried out the expropriation measure. In the event of disagreement over the amount of the compensation, the investor and the other Contracting Party shall hold consultations in order to determine

212 *EURAM Bank v Slovakia* (n 63) [451].

213 *EURAM Bank v Slovakia* (n 63) [452].

214 Bulgaria – Germany BIT (1986). A copy of which is available at: <https://investmentpolicy.unctad.org/international-investment-agreements/treaty-files/529/download> accessed 20 April 2022.

215 *ST-AD v Bulgaria* (n 63).

> the value of the expropriated investment. If agreement has not been reached within three months from the commencement of the consultations, the amount of the compensation shall, at the request of the investor, be reviewed either in a properly constituted proceeding of the Contracting Party that has carried out the expropriation measure, or by means of an international arbitral tribunal.[216]

Article 4(5) of the BIT provides for MFN treatment as follows:

> In matters governed by this article, the investments and investors of either Contracting Party shall enjoy treatment in the territory of the other Contracting Party that is no less [favorable] than that enjoyed by investments and investors of those third States that receive most [favorable] treatment in this respect.[217]

The claimant and respondent took opposite stances on whether Article 4(5) of the MFN clause could be applied to broaden the scope of Article 4(3). The claimant insisted that in view of the "[recognized] principle of the investor-friendly interpretation of the most [favorable] treatment clause …" and "the sustainable method of interpretation, the maxim of effectiveness," all clauses in the BIT including the arbitration provision should be broadly interpreted.[218] The respondent contended that to accept that the MFN clause in Article 4(5) could apply to consent to arbitration in Article 4(3) "would mean that an MFN clause could be used to confer on a tribunal the most expansive jurisdiction available under any of the treaties to which the state in question is a party." Such a result was viewed by the respondent as "unsustainable."[219]

Given the above submissions, the tribunal was determined to render "neither a restrictive nor an expansive interpretation" of Article 4(5).[220] To this end, it considered especially the ordinary meaning of Article 4(5), with the support from the object and purpose of Bulgaria-Germany BIT as reflected in its *travaux préparatoires*.

The tribunal started its analysis of the ordinary meaning of the text of Article 4(5) by citing Sir Gerald Fitzmaurice, who observed that –

216 Article 4(3) of the Bulgaria – Germany BIT (1986) (n 214).
217 Article 4(5) of the Bulgaria – Germany BIT (1986) (n 214).
218 *ST-AD v Bulgaria* (n 63) [381].
219 *ST-AD v Bulgaria* (n 63) [381].
220 *ST-AD v Bulgaria* (n 63) [382].

> the treaty was, after all, drafted precisely to give expression to the intentions of the parties, and must be presumed to do so. Accordingly, this intention is, *prima facie*, to be found in the text itself, and therefore the primary question is not what the parties intended by the text, but what the text itself means: whatever it clearly means on an ordinary and natural construction of its terms, such will be deemed to be what the parties intended.[221]

The tribunal noted that under Article 4(5), MFN treatment was to be rendered "in the territory of the other Contracting Party," which could not include international arbitration since it is an activity rooted overseas.[222] In this regard, the tribunal referred to the arbitration award in *Daimler*. It explained that a logical corollary of the expression "in the territory" was that treatment outside the territory of the host state did not fall within the scope of the clause. Therefore, the very concept of extra-territorial dispute resolution and a host state's consent thereto were both ill-fitted to the clear and ordinary meaning of the words "treatment in its territory" in many MFN clauses.[223]

Additionally, the tribunal applied a strict four-layered method that echoes the methods adopted by tribunals dealing with *de facto* MFN treatment as analyzed above, namely: before a tribunal can apply the MFN clause, (i) there must be a foreign investor; (ii) there must be a legitimate investment; (iii) the BIT must be applicable *ratione temporis* to the situation, and (iv) the tribunal must have jurisdiction *ratione voluntatis*, in this regard the tribunal agreed with the respondent that the condition of jurisdiction *ratione voluntatis* should not be altered or removed by the MFN provision.[224] The tribunal reasoned that the rule of *compétence-compétence* did not authorize it to use the MFN clause to "create a jurisdiction that it does not possess to begin with."[225] In other words, state consent had to be given before the tribunal could even discuss the MFN clause's scope or its applicability.

Finally, the tribunal took into account the *travaux préparatoires* pursuant to Article 32 of the VCLT. The tribunal noted that Bulgaria's original treaty draft in February 1981 did not contain an arbitration provision or an MFN clause. It was

---

221 *ST-AD v Bulgaria* (n 63) [393], citing: Fitzmaurice, G. G., 'The Law and Procedure of the International Court of Justice 1951–4: Treaty Interpretation and Other Treaty Points' (1957) 33 British Yearbook of International Law 203, 205.

222 *ST-AD v Bulgaria* (n 63) [394–395].

223 *ST-AD v Bulgaria* (n 63) [395]; *Daimler v Argentina* (n 90) [226–228, 230].

224 *ST-AD v Bulgaria* (n 63) [397].

225 *ST-AD v Bulgaria* (n 63) [398].

only in the second draft submitted by Germany in July 1981 where MFN was included while the arbitration provision was still missing. Therefore, the tribunal adopted the respondent's argument in this regard that, given that Article 4 did not contain an arbitration clause, it was clear that the new MFN provision was intended only to cover substantive protections and not dispute settlement.[226] Therefore, the tribunal concluded that it was never the intention of contracting parties to allow for MFN treatment to extend to arbitration matters given the protracted, forward-and-backward negotiations and the consequent compromise which was reflected in the carefully-drafted, limitedly-worded arbitration provision.

In *Sanum (I)*, the tribunal was established under the China-Laos BIT.[227] The dispute arose due to a series of measures by the Government of Laos, including its courts and provincial authorities, that allegedly affected the claimant's bundle of rights for the construction and operation of two hotels and casinos, among other gaming facilities in which the claimant had invested.[228]

Article 8 of the China-Laos BIT provided for *ad hoc* arbitration limited to the amount of compensation for expropriation.[229] Article 3 provided for MFN treatment linked to FET and full protection and security.[230]

The parties made arguments on whether Article 3 referred only to FET and full protection and security, or whether it also extended to all treaty protections, including international arbitration.[231] In other words, the tribunal had to decide whether the MFN clause could serve as an independent basis to extend its jurisdiction to the legality of expropriation and other substantive treatment breaches.[232] The respondent argued that MFN treatment in Article 3(2) should be limited to FET and full protection and security. The claimant, on the other hand, believed that the most natural reading of the term "protection" in Article 3(1) was one that included all of the treaty protections including dispute settlement within the scope of the MFN clause in question.[233]

The *Sanum (I)* tribunal declined to find jurisdiction through applying the MFN clause in Article 3(2). In this regard, it determined that given the limited

226 *ST-AD v Bulgaria* (n 63) [402].

227 China – Laos BIT (1993), a copy of which is available at: <https://investmentpolicy.unctad.org/international-investment-agreements/treaty-files/753/download> accessed 20 April 2022.

228 *Sanum v Laos* (n 63).

229 China – Laos BIT (1993) (n 227); *Sanum v Laos* (n 63) [323].

230 China – Laos BIT (1993) (n 227).

231 *Sanum v Laos* (n 63) [346].

232 *Sanum v Laos* (n 63) [343].

233 *Sanum v Laos* (n 63) [347].

scope of international arbitration in the basic treaty, to read into Article 3(2) a dispute settlement provision for all treaty protections would lead to –

> a substantial re-write of the Treaty and an extension of the States Parties' consent to arbitration beyond what may be assumed to have been their intention, given the limited reach of the Treaty protection and dispute settlement clauses.[234]

In *Beijing Urban Construction*, the case arose under the China-Yemen BIT concerning the alleged forced deprivation of the claimant's contract and assets on a project for constructing an airport terminal in Sana'a.[235] Article 3 of the China-Yemen BIT provided for MFN treatment similar to that in Article 3 of the above China-Laos BIT.[236] The tribunal nevertheless did not deem it necessary to examine whether MFN provisions may in principle be applicable to dispute resolution provisions in the abstract.[237] Instead, it decided to examine whether the specific wording of the MFN clause in the treaty was suitable to such application.

In this respect, the tribunal focused its analysis on the qualifying term "in its territory" in Article 3.1. It explained that even if the term "treatment" in Article 3.1 could extend to procedural measures, the qualifying reference in the same article to "treatment accorded to investors … in its territory" only referred to substantive treatment limited to the local territory by specifying a clear territorial limitation.[238] According to the tribunal, such reference had the effect of tying MFN treatment to activities that were geographically linked to foreign investment in the host state's territory and of excluding international arbitrations that would take place outside the respondent's territory.[239]

The above cases have revealed the limited guidance of the traditional interpretive methods on this issue, in particular in the face of a broadly-drafted MFN clause. As such, tribunals have had to resort to other interpretation sources to answer the question whether MFN clauses can be applied in order to broaden

234 *Sanum v Laos* (n 63) [358].

235 *Beijing Urban Construction v Yemen* (n 63).

236 China – Yemen BIT (1998), a copy of which is available at: <https://jusmundi.com/en/document/treaty/zh-zhong-hua-ren-min-gong-he-guo-zheng-fu-he-ye-men-gong-he-guo-zheng-fu-guan-yu-gu-li-he-xiang-hu-bao-hu-tou-zi-xie-ding-china-yemen-bit-1998-monday-16th-february-1998> accessed 20 April 2022.

237 *Beijing Urban Construction v Yemen* (n 63) [114].

238 *Beijing Urban Construction v Yemen* (n 63) [116].

239 *Beijing Urban Construction v Yemen* (n 63) [117–120].

tribunals' jurisdiction. These sources include circumstantial evidence around the conclusion of BITs such as state practice.

Chapter 4 argued that, although the *Ambatielos* case was frequently referred to, its logic has however been misrepresented in relation to the key point of adhering to the procedural-substantive dichotomy. Indeed, substantive and procedural treatment deal with different aspects of a treaty, but, as has been admitted by the above tribunals, there is still the possibility of MFN clauses to include procedural treatment within their scope. Therefore, the assistance of the distinction between procedural and substantive provisions is limited. As a result, the focal point should be redirected to the key role of state consent and whether MFN clauses can be applied in such a way as to give tribunals jurisdiction where they would have none under the basic treaty. Given the fundamental importance of state consent for international adjudication, it is arguable that state consent should be expressed in clear and explicit language. Therefore, it cannot be presumed that an MFN clause can be applied for this purpose unless it is included in the MFN clause with specific wording that indicates the contracting parties' intent to use it as a basis for jurisdiction.

The "natural preference" of the above *Renta 4* tribunal when choosing between "explicit stipulation" leading to a restrictive reading of MFN clauses and the "revelation by grammatical deconstruction" leading to a broad reading of MFN clauses is indicative of the notable role of tribunals' presumption in the absence of a specific answer from traditional interpretive methods. As such, tribunals should be encouraged to render responsible interpretations in good faith. This requires tribunals to give due account to the fact that we are in the Rebalancing Era as discussed in Chapter 1 and avoid rendering unexpected expansive interpretations of MFN clauses so as to properly reflect the balance between state interests and investor protection.

2.3 *Replacing Dispute Settlement Provisions in a Basic Treaty*

This section examines cases where MFN clauses were invoked in an attempt to replace the original dispute settlement mechanism in a basic treaty. To this end, the analysis below will focus on the *Salini* decision, the jurisdiction decision of which was rendered one year after *Plama*.

In *Salini*, the dispute involved the amount due to two Italian companies for their construction work in relation to the Karameh Dam in Jordan. The investment contract between Salini and Jordan provided for domestic adjudication in relation to disputes, while Article 9(3) of the Italy-Jordan BIT provided for ICSID arbitration to foreign investors.[240] However, Article 9(2) provided that "in case the investor and an entity of the Contracting Parties [had] stipulated an investment Agreement, the procedure foreseen in such investment Agreement [would] apply."[241] To have access to ICSID arbitration, the claimant alleged that Article 9(3) applied regardless of any dispute settlement clause agreed in the investment agreement, so the dispute settlement mechanism in the investment agreement should be superseded by Article 9(3).[242]

As an alternative claim, Salini also invoked the MFN clause in Article 3 of the BIT, alleging that the MFN clause should guarantee its right to a more favorable dispute settlement mechanism. To this end, the claimant referred to the *Maffezini* decision to support its argument that the MFN clause also applied to procedural rights.[243] It sought to incorporate Article IX of the U.S.-Jordan BIT and Article 6 of the Jordan-UK BIT, both of which articles entitled investors to resort to ICSID for ISDS disputes.[244]

Jordan challenged the tribunal's jurisdiction based on Article 9(2). It contended that according to Article 9(2), Jordan and Italy had agreed in the BIT to subject contractual claims to the dispute settlement provisions of the investment contract, which did not provide for ICSID arbitration. Additionally, the claimant could not invoke MFN to avail itself of more favorable dispute settlement provisions in other treaties because it did not apply to procedural rights.[245] Moreover, Jordan argued that even if the MFN clause could be applied to procedural rights as was the case in *Maffezini*, it would be subject to the overriding public policy considerations recognized by the *Maffezini* tribunal, which indicates in clear language that a dispute settlement forum specially agreed to by Contracting Parties cannot be overridden by MFN clause.[246] As a result, the MFN clause could not be used to override the clear intention of the contracting parties pertaining to jurisdiction as stipulated in Article 9(2).

The *Salini* tribunal rejected that it had jurisdiction over the contractual claims. It firstly distanced the case at hand from the circumstances of *Ambatielos* and *Maffezini*. It explained that in *Ambatielos*, Greece invoked the

240 Article 9(3) of the Italy – Jordan BIT (1996). A copy of which is available at: <https://investmentpolicy.unctad.org/international-investment-agreements/treaty-files/3379/download> accessed 20 April 2022.

241 Article 9(2) of the Italy – Jordan BIT (1996) (n 240).

242 *Salini Costruttori S.p.A. and Italstrade S.p.A. v Hashemite Kingdom of Jordan, Decision on Jurisdiction dated 9 November 2004,* ICSID Case No. ARB/02/13 [19].

243 *Maffezini v Spain* (n 86).

244 *Salini v Jordan* (n 242) [102].

245 *Salini v Jordan* (n 242) [23].

246 *Maffezini v Spain* (n 86) [63].

MFN clause not to incorporate a dispute settlement procedure, but to import substantive rights for Greek investors to be treated "in accordance with "justice," "right" and "equity.""[247] This was different from the dispute settlement claim in *Salini*. Additionally, it compared the texts of the MFN clauses in the three cases. The tribunal concluded that *Salini* was distinguishable from *Ambatielos* and *Maffezini* because the MFN clause in the Italy-Jordan BIT did not contain an "in all matters" expression like those in the Greece-UK agreement and the Spain-Argentina BIT.

Moreover, the tribunal concluded that the claimant did not submit any evidence including on any state practice by Jordan or Italy that could help establish the contracting parties' common intention as to the scope of the MFN clause. On the contrary, Article 9(2) rather expressed the contracting parties' intention to exclude the possibility of contractual disputes between a foreign investor and host state from being referred to ICSID arbitration unless the relevant contract allowed for this, which meant for the tribunal that the dispute *in casu* could only be settled pursuant to the procedures set out in the contract.[248]

The *Salini* tribunal has been criticized for reaching the correct conclusion (finding that it did not have jurisdiction) while misrepresenting the *Maffezini* and *Ambatielos* cases. It paralleled and misrepresented the intention of the MFN clause and Article 9(2), and focused on whether the MFN clause could be applied to dispute settlement procedures. However, as discussed above, the focal point was allegedly not the procedural-substantive treatment dichotomy perceived by tribunals, but the existence of Article 9(2) that already clarified the contracting parties' intention not to subject contractual claims to ICSID arbitration. According to Vesel, the decisive factor here should be the basic rule of international law that the jurisdiction of an international tribunal is based on explicit consent from disputing parties.[249] Therefore, what the *Salini* tribunal should have asked is whether the MFN clause could be applied to extend a tribunal's jurisdiction and alter, or in the case of *Salini*, manufacture the consent to ICSID jurisdiction at the behest of the contracting parties.

2.4 *Applying the Basic Treaty Retroactively*

This section discusses cases where the claimant attempted to invoke the MFN clause to broaden the scope of the basic treaty's temporal application. In this connection, the *Tecmed* and *M.C.I.* cases will be discussed.

247 *Salini v Jordan* (n 242) [112].
248 *Salini v Jordan* (n 242) [118].
249 Vesel (n 79) 172.

In *Tecmed*, the dispute arose out of the Mexico-Spain BIT involving Mexico's alleged non-renewal of a license which was essential to operate a landfill of hazardous industrial waste.[250]

The MFN clause in Article 8(1) of the Mexico-Spain BIT provided as follows:

> In the event that any legal provision of either Contracting Party, or any current or future obligation arising out of international law outside of this Agreement between the Contracting Parties results in general or special regulations that would require that the investments of investors of the other Contracting Party be accorded treatment more [favorable] than that provided for under this Agreement, such regulations shall prevail over this Agreement, to the extent that that are more [favorable].[251]

Through the MFN clause, the claimant sought to apply the basic treaty retroactively to include the respondent's conduct before the entry into force of the Mexico-Spain BIT on December 18, 1996. For this purpose, it referred to the Mexico-Austria BIT in an attempt to incorporate the more favorable treatment enjoyed by Austrian investors in this regard. The tribunal rejected the request that it apply the basic treaty retroactively and stated as follows:

> The Arbitral Tribunal … deems that matters relating to the application over time of the Agreement, which involve more the time dimension of application of its substantive provisions rather than matters of procedure or jurisdiction, due to their significance and importance, go to the core of matters that must be deemed to be specifically negotiated by the Contracting Parties. These are determining factors for their acceptance of the Agreement, as they are directly linked to the identification of the substantive protection regime applicable to the foreign investor and, particularly, to the general (national or international) legal context within which such regime operates, as well as to the access of the foreign investor to the substantive provisions of such regime. Their application cannot therefore be impaired by the principle contained in the most favored nation clause.[252]

250 *Técnicas Medioambientales Tecmed, S.A. v The United Mexican States, ICSID Case No. ARB (AF)/00/2, Award dated 29 May 2003,* ICSID Case No. ARB(AF)/00/2.

251 Article 8(1) of the Spain – Mexico BIT (2006). A copy of which is available at: <https://investmentpolicy.unctad.org/international-investment-agreements/treaty-files/5621/download> accessed 20 April 2022.

252 *Tecmed v Mexico* (n 250) [69].

However, the *Tecmed* tribunal provided rather bizarre reasoning on this score, in that it distinguished between treaty provisions that constituted decisive elements in relation to the treaty's essence and those which did not. This method presumptively constructed a hierarchy of treaty provisions that cannot be inferred from the treaty text. The *Siemens* tribunal is an example of the opposite approach. When the respondent contended that the dispute settlement clause departed from standard German BITs to support its position that this was a clause "specially negotiated and hence should be differentiated from the rest," the *Siemens* tribunal disagreed and explained that –

> [t]he acceptance of a clause from a model text does not invest this clause with either more or less legal force than other clauses which may had been more difficult to negotiate. The end result of the negotiations is an agreed text and the legal significance of each clause is not affected by how arduous was the negotiating path to arrive there … in fact, the purpose of the MFN clause is to eliminate the effect of specially negotiated provisions unless they have been excepted.[253]

The *Tecmed* tribunal's general and open-ended language about the core matters that must be considered to be specifically negotiated by the contracting parties attracted much criticism for offering limited guidance. According to Banifatemi, it should be presumed that contracting states intend no difference in the nature and drafting of different treaty provisions.[254] Therefore, the *Tecmed* tribunal's statement that the "specifically negotiated" provisions in a basic treaty were beyond the MFN clause's application and was unwarranted.

Additionally, it was also inconsistent with the purpose and normal operation of the MFN clause.[255] Specifically, the purpose of the unconditional MFN clause was to prevent two states from providing unique guarantees exclusive to others.[256] For example, the *Siemens* tribunal rejected the claimant's attempt to rely on the *Tecmed* tribunal proposition because the objective of the MFN clause was to eliminate the effect of specifically negotiated provisions unless they had been excepted.[257]

253 *Siemens A.G. v The Argentine Republic, Decision on Jurisdiction (3 August 2004)*, ICSID Case No. ARB/02/8 [106].

254 Banifatemi (n 4) 269.

255 Vesel (n 79) 163.

256 Vesel (n 79) 63.

257 *Siemens v Argentina* (n 253) [106].

Non-retroactivity is a well-established principle in international law. It has been embodied in Article 28 of the VCLT in the following terms:

> Unless a different intention appears from the treaty or is otherwise established, its provisions do not bind a party in relation to any act or fact which took place or any situation which ceased to exist before the date of the entry into force of the treaty with respect to that party.[258]

Article 28 represents the strong presumption in international law on non-retroactivity of treaties.[259] As such, the question in *Tecmed* should not have been whether MFN treatment applies to core matters concerning a specific set of substantive provisions. The problem should rather have been whether the MFN clause could be construed to establish the explicit intention of contracting parties to apply the basic treaty retroactively. Therefore, although the *Tecmed* tribunal reached the correct conclusion, it adopted somewhat problematic reasoning and therefore its decision should be of limited guidance to subsequent tribunals.[260]

Another case in this regard is *M.C.I.* The case was based on the Ecuador-U.S. BIT and concerned a series of differences between the investor and Ecuador's Electricity Institute regarding the execution of a contract concerning an electric power generation project. The disputes included the suspension of operations, non-payment of invoices, and the subsequent termination of the contract.[261] The respondent challenged the jurisdiction of the tribunal based on the idea that the Ecuador-U.S. BIT could not be applied retroactively, contending that the investment ceased to exist before the entry into force of the Ecuador-U.S. BIT, and that there was already a dispute in front of the Ecuadorian courts on the same issue before the BIT came into force.[262] As such, the claimant invoked *inter alia* the MFN clause in the basic treaty in an attempt to incorporate a more favorable time limit from Article VII of the Argentina-Ecuador BIT.[263]

---

258 Article 28 of the Vienna Convention on the Law of Treaties (1969) (n 128).

259 Vesel (n 79) 163.

260 R Dolzer and T Myers, 'After Tecmed: Most-Favored-Nation Clauses in Investment Protection Agreements' (2004) 19 ICSID Review 49.

261 *M.C.I. Power Group, L.C. and New Turbine, Inc. v Republic of Ecuador, Award dated 31 July 2007*, ICSID Case No. ARB/03/6.

262 *M.C.I. v Ecuador* (n 261) [45–54].

263 *M.C.I. v Ecuador* (n 261) [121]. Article VII of the Argentina – Ecuador BIT provides that: If the provisions of the law of either Contracting Party or obligations under international law existing at present or that are established in the future between the Contracting Parties

The respondent denied the relevance of Article VII of the Argentina-Ecuador BIT since it was of no effect retroactively. It merely stated that the rules of international law that may be established in the future between the contracting parties (Ecuador and Argentina) "[should] to the extent that they are more [favorable], prevail over this Treaty."[264] The respondent also relied on reasoning in *Tecmed* that the MFN clause "[could not] be invoked in the particular circumstances of the present case since the application of the investment treaty [went] to the core of matters that must [have been] deemed to be specifically negotiated by the Contracting Parties."[265]

The tribunal did not opine on *Tecmed*. It relied on Article 31 of the VCLT, noting that the terms in Article VII such as "either Contracting Party," "between the Contracting Parties," "an investor of one Contracting Party and the other Contracting Party," and "the other Contracting Party" explicitly referred to the two contracting parties of the Argentina-Ecuador BIT. Ultimately, the tribunal rightly rejected the possibility of applying the MFN clause and declined to exercise jurisdiction over disputes which arose before the entry into force of the Ecuador-U.S. BIT.

It is dubious whether the terms used in Article VII of the Argentina-Ecuador BIT could preclude an application of the MFN clause in the basic treaty. In a prior paragraph, the tribunal stated that "the silence of the text of the BIT with respect to its scope in relation to disputes prior to its entry into force does not alter the effects of the principle of the non-retroactivity of treaties."[266] It seems that the *M.C.I* tribunal, like the *Tecmed* tribunal, also misunderstood the core issue here, which should rather have been whether the MFN clause could replace the strong presumption of non-retroactivity in international law and extend the time dimension of dispute settlement provisions.

In both cases above, the basic treaties did not explicitly delineate the scope of the dispute settlement provision in question. The principle of non-retroactivity in international law, as embodied in Article 28 of the VCLT, has

---

in addition to this Treaty or if any Agreement between an investor of one Contracting Party and the other Contracting Party contain rules, whether general or specific entitling investments by investors of the other Contracting Party to treatment more favorable than is provided for in this Treaty, such rules shall, to the extent that they are more favorable, prevail over this Treaty. The text was originally in Spanish and translated into English by the tribunal. See: Argentina – Ecuador BIT (1994). A copy of which is available at: <https://investmentpolicy.unctad.org/international-investment-agreements/treaty-files/87/download> accessed 20 April 2022.

264 *M.C.I. v Ecuador* (n 261) [126].

265 *M.C.I. v Ecuador* (n 261) [125].

266 *M.C.I. v Ecuador* (n 261) [61].

been applied by tribunals as a strong presumption to exclude the possibility of jurisdiction in relation to conduct that occurred before a treaty's entry into force. The above tribunals' reasoning, however, was misplaced. Instead of determining whether applying the MFN clause in relation to this issue was a "core matter" of a treaty or a matter limited between two contracting parties, the actual determination they should have made goes to whether the consent of the contracting parties to refer disputes arising before the coming into force of the given BITs could be inferred through an application of the MFN clauses in question. In other words, the tribunals should have discussed whether MFN clauses could be applied to establish jurisdiction with respect to the temporal dimensions of claims. The future could bring more cases in this regard and it remains to be seen how tribunals would deal with such cases.

3 Cases Where Tribunals Established Jurisdiction via the Application of an MFN Clause

This part concerns the three cases where tribunals agreed to apply an MFN clause in relation to jurisdictional issues, i.e., *RosInvest, Garanti* and *Venezuela US.* Each case dealt with a different aspect of the operation of an MFN clause to found jurisdiction.

3.1 *Bypassing Limitations Contained in Arbitration Provisions*

In *RosInvest,* the claim concerned a series of actions taken by Russia against Yukos Oil Company, including arrests, large tax assessments and liens, and the auctioning off of Yukos main facility. These actions allegedly caused the bankruptcy of Yukos and eliminated all value of the UK claimant's 7 million shares in that company.[267] Article 8 of the UK-Russian BIT offered dispute settlement limited to the amount or payment of compensation, any other matter consequential upon an act of expropriation, or the consequences of the non-implementation, or of the incorrect implementation.[268]

In view of the Article 8 restrictions, the claimant invoked Article 3 of the UK-USSR BIT, which guaranteed MFN treatment to foreign investments and

267 *RosInvest v Russia* (n 1).

268 Article 8 of the UK – USSR BIT (1989). A copy of which is available at: <https://investmentpolicy.unctad.org/international-investment-agreements/treaty-files/2235/download> accessed 20 April 2022.

foreign investors concerning their management, maintenance, use, enjoyment or disposal or their investments.[269]

The tribunal acknowledged the ability of the MFN clause to broaden the scope of the dispute settlement provision. It provided separate reasoning in respect of paragraphs (1) and (2) of the MFN clause. Regarding paragraph (1), the tribunal stated that although the protection by an arbitration clause covering expropriation was a highly relevant aspect of expropriation as treaty treatment, it merely directly affected the procedural rights of investors as envisaged in paragraph (2) of Article 3, instead of the foreign investment itself.[270]

Concerning paragraph (2), the tribunal paid particular attention to the terms "use" and "enjoyment." According to the tribunal, expropriation jeopardized the investors' use and enjoyment of its investment. In this sense, submission to arbitration constituted a highly relevant part of the protection for the investor in case of interference with their use and enjoyment of the investment. Therefore, granting investors the procedural option of international arbitration was of obvious significance compared to the sole option of challenging such interference before the domestic court of the host state.[271]

In the tribunal's opinion, the above logic remains extant even though Article 8 of the UK-USSR BIT expressly limited jurisdiction to matters other than a finding of expropriation. Instead, the expansion of the tribunal's jurisdiction should be a normal result of the application of the MFN clause, and it was part of the nature and intent of the MFN clause that protection not recognized in one treaty be extended through the transfer of protection accorded in another treaty.[272]

According to the tribunal, an arbitration clause was of the same protective value as any substantive protection, at least in the context of expropriation. It held that if the application of the MFN clause was generally accepted in the context of substantive protection, it "[saw] no reason not to accept it in the context of procedural clauses such as arbitration clauses" and that "on the contrary, it could be argued that if it applied to substantive protection, then it should apply even more to 'only' procedural protection."[273]

In this regard, the tribunal referred to Article 7 of the UK-USSR BIT for support. Article 7 provided exceptions in respect of which the MFN clause would not apply, including treatment accorded by the formation of customs

269 Article 3 of the UK – USSR BIT (1989) (n 268).
270 *RosInvest v Russia* (n 1) [128].
271 *RosInvest v Russia* (n 1) [128].
272 *RosInvest v Russia* (n 1) [131].
273 *RosInvest v Russia* (n 1) [132].

unions, mutual economic assistance agreements, and taxation agreements.[274] According to the tribunal, submission to arbitration was an issue as important as taxation, and the absence of arbitration issues from Article 7 could not be explained by oblivion, especially given the careful drafting of the dispute settlement provision in Article 8. As such, the tribunal was of the following view:

> Had the Parties intended that the MFN-clauses should also not apply to arbitration, it would indeed have been easy to add a sub-section (c) to that effect in Article 7. The fact that this was not done … is further confirmation that the MFN-clauses in Article 3 are also applicable to submissions to arbitration in other Treaties.[275]

In the end, the tribunal referred to previous case law on point. It noted that different conclusions could be drawn based on the separate evaluation of MFN clauses' wording and dispute settlement provisions. Although the tribunal acknowledged the similarities between MFN clauses in that they for the most part allowed for a generalized interpretation, it nevertheless noted that the combination of Article 3 and Article 7 in the dispute at hand was peculiar and not identical to that in other treaties under other disputes.

Although paying lip service to the VCLT, the *RosInvest* tribunal actually acted on the basis of its presumption that expansive MFN clauses were a tool meant to multilateralize. Its logic was that, since the MFN clause covered the use and enjoyment of investors' investments, it should be recognized that expropriation as a process deprived investors of use and enjoyment of their investment. In this regard, allowing investors to broaden the scope of expropriation issues to include arbitration was an important protection covered by the MFN clause in the tribunal's view.

The problem is that the tribunal conflated the concepts of "expropriation" and "submission of expropriation issues to arbitration." While the former falls within the MFN clause's scope as substantive treatment, the latter forms part of the context of a dispute settlement mechanism that allows for claims in relation to substantive treatment and requires consent from disputing parties. In other words, it is one thing to link the submission to arbitration to protect investors concerning the "use and enjoyment" of their investment as the tribunal rightly did, but quite another thing to apply the MFN clause in order to

274 Article 7 of the UK-USSR BIT (1989) (n 268).
275 *RosInvest v Russia* (n 1) [135].

manufacture consent to a broad scope of events on behalf of the contracting parties.

Therefore, the *RosInvest* tribunal actually extended the term "use and enjoyment" of investment contained in the MFN clause to include a notion of right to arbitration. It did so without properly applying the principles in Articles 31 and 32 of the VCLT.

3.2 *Replacing the Chosen Forum for Dispute Settlement*

In the *Garanti* case, the dispute arose out of the conflicts between a UK investor and Turkmenistan concerning performance of certain construction contracts that resulted in the suspension of works and the subsequent termination of the construction contract by Turkmenistan due to *inter alia* the investor's alleged failure to complete the work on time.[276]

Article 8 of the UK-Turkmenistan BIT provided that the investor and the host state could refer their disputes to either ICSID, International Chamber of Commerce (ICC) or UNCITRAL arbitration. If the disputing parties failed to reach an agreement in this regard, Article 8 required submitting the dispute in writing to *ad hoc* UNCITRAL arbitration.[277] No agreement had been concluded between the claimant and Turkmenistan. In the end, the dispute was submitted to ICSID arbitration, through the claimant's invocation of the MFN clause in Article 3 of the UK-Turkmenistan BIT, instead of to UNCITRAL arbitration. Article 3(3) of the UK-Turkmenistan BIT provided as follows:

> For the avoidance of doubt, it is confirmed that the treatment provided for in paragraphs (1) and (2) above shall apply to the provisions of Articles 1 to 11 of this Agreement.[278]

The tribunal noted that it was the first tribunal ever called upon to interpret an MFN clause worded in the manner of Article 3(3). In this case, the claimant sought to invoke the MFN clause in Article 3 to incorporate the dispute settlement provision in the Switzerland-Turkmenistan BIT. According to the claimant, while the UK-Turkmenistan BIT allowed investors to resort only to UNCITRAL Rules except in the case of Turkmenistan consenting to ICSID arbitration in a particular instance, the Switzerland-Turkmenistan BIT provided

276 *Garanti v Turkmenistan* (n 1).

277 Article 8(2) of the Turkmenistan – UK BIT (1995), a copy of which is available at: <https://investmentpolicy.unctad.org/international-investment-agreements/treaty-files/2360/download> accessed 20 April 2022.

278 Article 3 of the Turkmenistan – UK BIT (1995) (n 277).

a more favorable arbitration provision which gave investors a free choice between ICSID arbitration and UNCITRAL arbitration.[279]

The tribunal started by examining the text of the MFN clause. It found that since Article 3(3) applied to Articles 1 to 11 of the basic treaty, the dispute settlement provision in Article 8 should also be included as a matter of course. Moreover, the inclusion of Article 8 was even mandatory due to the use of the word "shall" in Article 3(3).[280] In this connection, the tribunal referred to Article 3(3) of the UK Model BIT as a template for the MFN clause at issue. It relied on the reasoning of the *Plama* tribunal and the statement of Professor Stern in *Impregilo*, both of which cited Article 3(3) of the UK Model BIT as an example which carried express, clear, and unambiguous consent to import international arbitration provisions from third-party treaties through an MFN clause.[281]

The respondent argued that MFN clauses were designed only to improve rights already granted under the basic treaty by importing more favorable conditions for the exercise of such rights, but not to create new rights entirely.[282] Citing Professor Schreuer, the claimant contended that the use of an MFN clause to establish state consent to ICSID arbitration would simply be "a particular example of using an MFN clause to import into a treaty a right that the treaty does not otherwise provide."[283] This was because –

> [a] MFN clause [was] not a rule of interpretation that [came] into play only where the wording of the basic treaty [left] no room for doubt. It [was] intended to endow its beneficiary with rights that [were] additional to the rights contained in the basic treaty. The meaning of an MFN

279 *Garanti v Turkmenistan* (n 1) [81]. Article 8(2) of the Switzerland-Turkmenistan BIT (2008) provides that: '... If these consultations do not result in a solution within six months from the date of request for consultations, the investor may submit the dispute for settlement to: (a) the International Centre for Settlement of Investment Disputes (ICSID) provided for by the Convention on the Settlement of Investment Disputes between States and Nationals of other States, opened for signature at Washington, on 18 March 1965 (hereinafter the,,Convention of Washington"); or (b) an ad hoc-arbitral tribunal which, unless otherwise agreed upon by the parties to the dispute, shall be established under the arbitration rules of the United Nations Commission on International Trade Law (UNCITRAL).' See: Switzerland – Turkmenistan BIT (2008), available at: <https://investmentpolicy.unctad.org/international-investment-agreements/treaty-files/4834/download> accessed 20 April 2022.

280 *Garanti v Turkmenistan* (n 1) [42].

281 *Garanti v Turkmenistan* (n 1) [43–45].

282 *Garanti v Turkmenistan* (n 1) [47].

283 *Garanti v Turkmenistan* (n 1) [48].

> [was] that whoever [was] entitled to rely on it be granted rights accruing from a third party treaty even if these rights clearly [went] beyond the basic treaty.[284]

However, the tribunal deemed it unnecessary to answer this question because access to international arbitration, to the extent it was considered as a "right" of a foreign investor, had already been granted by Article 8(1) of the UK-Turkmenistan BIT. According to the tribunal, there was no need to resort to the MFN clause to create such a right.[285] Therefore, according to the tribunal, the contracting parties has already granted general consent to international arbitration in Article 8(1). It stated as follows:

> There is no need for the claimant to seek to import that consent into the UK-Turkmenistan BIT, because Article 8(1) of the UK BIT already achieves the same result.[286]

The tribunal held that the only provision more favorable in the third-party treaty between Switzerland and Turkmenistan was Article 8(2), which permitted Swiss investors to choose between ICSID and UNCITRAL arbitration. The claimant argued that such provision was more favorable than Article 8(2) of the UK-Turkmenistan BIT, which restricted dispute settlement to UNCITRAL arbitration.[287] According to the tribunal, "such an application to Article 8(2) [was] consistent with the International Law Commission's observation that the beneficiary of an MFN clause not only [had] an 'either/or' choice, but might also [have been] in a position to opt for the cumulative enjoyment of all, some, or parts of the various treatments concerned."[288]

It is notable how the tribunal decided which treaty provided a "more favorable" dispute settlement provision. After comparing ICSID and UNCITRAL arbitration features, the tribunal agreed with the respondent on the difficulty of describing ICSID arbitration as objectively more favorable to investors than UNCITRAL arbitration, since both systems had their own advantages and disadvantages.[289] Having reached this conclusion, the tribunal determined that while ICSID arbitration might not be objectively more favorable for purposes

284 *Garanti v Turkmenistan* (n 1), citing Schreuer (n 103) 248.
285 *Garanti v Turkmenistan* (n 1) [49].
286 *Garanti v Turkmenistan* (n 1) [75].
287 *Garanti v Turkmenistan* (n 1) [76].
288 *Garanti v Turkmenistan* (n 1) [76].
289 *Garanti v Turkmenistan* (n 1) [89].

of establishing jurisdiction *in casu*, it agreed with the claimant that having a choice between the two dispute settlement systems was more favorable than not having a choice.[290] To this end, the tribunal referred to a line of prior ISDS tribunals and determined that –

> where BIT 'A' provides an investor with the option of selecting, as between two different systems of arbitration, the one that appears to that investor most favorable to the presentation of the particular claim that investor wishes to pursue with regard to an investment protected by the BIT, and BIT 'B' restricts investors covered by that treaty to bringing a claim under only one of those systems of arbitration unless the State concerned agrees to the use of another system for the particular dispute, it appears to the majority of this Tribunal that investors under BIT 'A' have been accorded more favorable treatment, as regards their management, use, enjoyment, and disposal of their investments, than investors under BIT 'B.' Indeed, depending on the circumstances, investors making a claim under BIT 'B' may be said to be at a competitive disadvantage compared to investors claiming under BIT 'A'.[291]

In the end, the tribunal considered itself competent to hear the case at hand.

The above reasoning was opposed by the respondent-appointed arbitrator Laurence Boisson de Chazournes. She disagreed with the tribunal majority's problematic method of considering paragraphs (1) and (2) of Article as two separate provisions, arguing that the two should be construed as a whole. While Article 8(1) conditioned the general consent to international arbitration on a four-month waiting period, Article 8(2) specified the strict conditions under which the foreign investor could resort to one specific forum for international arbitration.[292] According to Boisson de Chazournes, the tribunal had confused the power to initiate arbitration with the consent to arbitration by pronouncing that Article 8(1) amounted to consent to international arbitration.[293] That Article 8(2) provided that the foreign investors and the contracting states "may agree to refer the dispute either to" the four listed arbitration options indicated the need for both disputing parties to agree to a particular arbitration forum.[294] Boisson de Chazournes believed that such reading was confirmed

290 *Garanti v Turkmenistan* (n 1) [90].

291 *Garanti v Turkmenistan* (n 1) [94].

292 *Garanti v Turkmenistan* (n 1), *Dissenting Opinion by Laurence Boisson de Chazournes* [19].

293 *Garanti v Turkmenistan* (n 1) [21].

294 *Garanti v Turkmenistan* (n 1) [22].

by the last sentence of Article 8(2), which designated UNCITRAL arbitration as the default forum in the absence of agreement to one of the alternative fora after four months from written notification of the claim.[295]

Additionally, Boisson de Chazournes argued that the main objective of the MFN clause was not to remedy the absence of consent, but to ensure that once consent was given, it was implemented most favorably compared to treaties signed with other states.[296] Therefore, MFN clauses could only be applied if the foreign investor and the host state were subject to a dispute settlement relationship based on one of the dispute settlement options that were provided for in Article 8(2).[297] Since the consent to ICSID arbitration was absent from the basic treaty, the tribunal could not rely on such consent to find jurisdiction via an application of the MFN clause. In other words, the MFN clause could not be applied to give the tribunal jurisdiction. In this regard, Boisson de Chazournes was of the view that the tribunal majority had failed to interpret the MFN clause in the light of its context in the basic treaty.

The *Garanti* case was exceptional by appearance because its MFN clause referred explicitly to provisions including dispute settlement provision. The tribunal's logic was that the MFN clause in the basic treaty did not function to "create" jurisdiction. It instead applied as a gateway to improve the contracting states' already given consent without conflicting with the *ejusdem generis* principle. In this case, the tribunal applied the MFN clause in order to replace the dispute settlement mechanism in the UK-Turkmenistan BIT with that in the Switzerland-Turkmenistan BIT. According to the tribunal, such interpretation was reasonable because Article 8(1) of the UK-Turkmenistan BIT had already granted consent to ICSID arbitration. Therefore, the MFN clause could not be applied to create jurisdiction. For ease of discussion, the text of Article 8(1) is reproduced here. It reads as follows:

> Disputes between a national or company of one Contracting Party and the other Contracting Party concerning an obligation of the latter under this Agreement in relation to an investment of the former which have not been amicably settled shall, after a period of four [months] from written notification of a claim, be submitted to international arbitration if the national or company concerned so wishes.

295 *Garanti v Turkmenistan* (n 1) [26].
296 *Garanti v Turkmenistan* (n 1) [61].
297 *Garanti v Turkmenistan* (n 1) [82].

The tribunal's interpretation of Article 8 seems to conflict with the wording and logic of the clause by disconnecting paragraphs (1) and (2).[298] Read as a whole, this paragraph's ordinary meaning does not suggest consent to ICSID arbitration as the tribunal believed it did. It rather indicates that Article 8(1) itself cannot constitute as standalone consent specifically to ICSID arbitration. If it does, Article 8(2) would become redundant, which would go against the *effet utile* principle.[299] On the contrary, by "shall, after a period of four [months] from written notification of a claim, be submitted to international arbitration," the clause merely conveys the contracting parties' willingness to subject disputes to potential fora for international arbitration.

Therefore, Article 8(1) needs to be read together with the paragraphs which follow it in order for the reading to be complete. Article 8(2) permits ICSID, ICC, or UNCITRAL arbitration based on case-by-case consent. At this point, the consent to any form of international arbitration was not yet accorded. If the disputing parties do not reach an agreement to refer the dispute to one of the identified fora within a period of four months (which was the case in *Garanti*), "the dispute shall at the request in writing of the national or company concerned be submitted to arbitration under the Arbitration Rules of the United Nations Commission on International Trade Law as then in force."[300] The default alternative of UNCITRAL arbitration if no agreement was reached clearly indicates that specific consent is required for ICSID arbitration, and that the contracting parties only gave consent to the default UNCITRAL arbitration.[301]

In conclusion, contrary to the tribunal's reasoning, Article 8(1) did not amount to consent to ICSID arbitration. Turkmenistan did not reach an agreement with *Garanti* to submit their disputes to ICSID arbitration as provided for by Article 8(2). In other words, there was no consent to ICSID arbitration in any form from Turkmenistan. Even if, *arguendo*, general consent had been provided, such consent could not be replaced via the application of an MFN clause for the reasons discussed above. Therefore, the tribunal incorrectly applied the *ejusdem generis* principle and manufactured Turkmenistan's consent to ICSID arbitration. As such, the tribunal stated that "more choices is more favorable than no choice."[302] However, the issue is not the "choice-no

298 Brabandere (n 16) 5.

299 Brabandere (n 16) 6.

300 Turkmenistan – UK BIT (1995) (n 277).

301 Turkmenistan – UK BIT (1995) (n 277).

302 The tribunal's decision was endorsed by a later tribunal in *Krederi v Ukraine*. Examing a similarly-worded BIT, the tribunal majority in *Krederi* decided that the consent to arbitration was already given by Ukraine in Article 8(1) of the treaty which did not specify

choice" comparison, but whether the MFN clause could be applied in such a way as to find jurisdiction by incorporating consent given elsewhere by one of the parties to investors from another contracting state, which is exactly what the tribunal did in this instance.

3.3 *Manufacturing Jurisdiction through an Application of an MFN Clause*

This section discusses the case where the claimant invoked an MFN clause to create jurisdiction for a tribunal. In *Venezuela US*, the dispute arose under Barbados-Venezuela BIT.[303] The Barbados-Venezuela BIT was signed on July 15, 1994 after Venezuela acceded to ICSID Convention, but before the ICSID Convention entered into force for Venezuela on June 1, 1995. On January 24, 2012, Venezuela notified its exit from the ICSID Convention. Its denunciation took effect from July 25, 2012.

Article 8 of the Barbados-Venezuela BIT provided the ISDS mechanism and read as follows:

> (1) Disputes between one Contracting Party and a national or company of the other Contracting Party concerning an obligation of the former under this Agreement in relation to an investment of the latter shall, at the request of the national concerned, be submitted to the International Centre for Settlement of Investment Disputes for settlement by arbitration or conciliation under the Convention on the Settlement of Investment Disputes between States and Nationals of other States, opened for signature at Washington on March 18, 1965.
> (2) As long as the Republic of Venezuela has not become a Contracting State of the Convention as mentioned in paragraph 1 of this Article, disputes as referred to in that paragraph shall be submitted to the International Centre for Settlement of Investment disputes under the Rules Governing the Additional Facility for the Administration of Proceedings by the Secretariat of the Centre (Additional Facility Rules). If for any reason the Additional Facility is not available the investor shall have the right to submit the dispute to arbitration

UNCITRAL arbitration. As a result, the tribunal majority agreed that although MFN clause could not be used to import consent, it was applicable for choosing between different arbitration systems. See: *Krederi Ltd. v Ukraine, Award dated 2 July 2018,* ICSID Case No. ARB/14/17.

303 Barbados – Venezuela BIT (1994). A copy of which is available at: <https://investmentpolicy.unctad.org/international-investment-agreements/treaty-files/288/download> accessed 20 April 2022.

under the rules of the United Nations Commission on International Trade Law (UNCITRAL).

…

(4) Each Contracting Party hereby gives its unconditional consent to the submission of disputes as referred to in paragraph 1 of this Article to international arbitration in accordance with the provisions of this Article.

The claimant attempted to submit its dispute with Venezuela to UNCITRAL arbitration under Article 8(4). The respondent objected to the jurisdiction of the tribunal *ratione voluntatis*. It denied that Article 8 in any way expressed its consent to UNCITRAL arbitration after it denounced the ICSID Convention in 2012. It argued that while Article 8(1) provided for ICSID arbitration, Article 8(2) bore a temporal limitation towards ICSID Additional Facility (AF) Rules by stating that "[a]s long as the Republic of Venezuela has not become a Contracting State of the Convention as mentioned in paragraph 1 of this Article." According to the respondent, consent to ICSID AF Rules was only suitable for Venezuela's pre-ICSID period. During this pre-ICSID time, UNCITRAL Rules came to apply "[i]f for any reason the Additional Facility [was] not available." The tribunal agreed with the respondent and refused to found jurisdiction based on Article 8.

The claimant also relied on the MFN clause in Article 3 as an alternative for establishing jurisdiction. As in the *Garanti* case, Article 3 of the basic treaty provided for MFN treatment that explicitly referred to "Articles 1 to 11 of this Agreement." As such, the claimant argued that Article 3 allowed it to take advantage of the dispute settlement provisions contained in other BITs signed by Venezuela, including those that offered a free choice between UNCITRAL arbitration and other options, or those which provided for UNCITRAL arbitration as a default dispute settlement mechanism. Citing prior cases such as *Garanti* and *Impregilo*, the claimant argued that these BITs granted more favorable treatment in that it allowed investors more choices of dispute resolution fora.[304]

The tribunal sided with the claimant and decided to apply the MFN clause to establish jurisdiction. It stated that the MFN clause could not import consent from a third-party treaty when none exists under the Barbados-Venezuela BIT.[305] In this regard, since Barbados and Venezuela had agreed *expressis verbis*

304 *Venezuela US v Venezuela* (n 1) [91].

305 For a similar proposition, the tribunal of the recent case *Doutremepuich v Mauritius* expressed that according to the *ejusdem generis* principle, MFN clauses should only apply to provisions within their own subject-matter. In view of this, the fact that the respondent

that the MFN clause should apply to provisions including Article 8 on dispute settlement provisions and conditions for resorting to international arbitration thereunder, the tribunal was of the view that it "had no other choice than to apply and enforce these provisions in accordance with their terms pursuant to the principle of *pacta sunt servanda*."[306] According to the tribunal, refusing to apply Article 3(3) to Article 8 would otherwise render Article 3(3) meaningless.[307]

The tribunal then noted that Article 3(1) dealt with investment treatment, while Article 3(2) dealt with an investor.[308] It decided that the MFN clause extended to dispute settlement provisions in Article 8 only through the operation of Article 3(2) due to the expression "the investor shall have the right to submit the dispute to arbitration" while no procedural rights attached to investments.[309]

The tribunal relied on the *ejusdem generis* principle in allowing Article 3(2) to incorporate Article 8. Following that principle, the MFN could not import consent to arbitration when there was no consent in the Barbados-Venezuela BIT in the first place.[310] In this regard, the tribunal found comfort in Article 8(4). Like the *Garanti* tribunal, it determined that Venezuela had given its unconditional consent to international arbitration in Article 8(4), which provided that "each Contracting Party hereby gives its unconditional consent to the submission of disputes as referred to in paragraph 1 of this article to international arbitration in accordance with the provisions of this article."[311]

The tribunal explained that the term "in accordance with the provisions of this Article" used in Article 8(4) indicated that the submission of disputes to international arbitration was subject to the conditions in Article 8(1) and (2), i.e., which arbitration forum should be available to investors: either ICSID, ICSID AF, or UNCITRAL arbitration. The consent in Article 8(4) was specified in three paragraphs from Article 8(1) to (3) under different conditions specified in each paragraph – and any other interpretation would deprive Article 8(4)

---

did not consent to international arbitration in the basic treaty (France – Mauritius BIT) should be considered as a fundamental reason why MFN clause cannot be applied to import consent from a third-party treaty. See: *Christian Doutremepuich and Antoine Doutremepuich v Mauritius, Award on Jurisdiction dated 23 August 2019*, PCA Case No. 2018–37.

306 *Venezuela v Venezuela* (n 1) [102].

307 *Venezuela v Venezuela* (n 1) [102].

308 *Venezuela v Venezuela* (n 1) [104].

309 *Venezuela v Venezuela* (n 1) [104].

310 *Venezuela v Venezuela* (n 1) [105].

311 Article 8(4) of the Barbados – Venezuela BIT (1994) (n 303).

of its legal effect. Based on this understanding, the tribunal determined that Article 8(2) provided for UNCITRAL arbitration under a temporal condition, i.e., for the period before Venezuela became an ICSID member if the AF was not available for any reason.[312]

Based on the above observation, the tribunal turned to an examination of Article IX of the Ecuador-Venezuela BIT, which provided as follows:

> If the dispute cannot be settled within six months of the time it was initiated by one of the Parties, it may be submitted, at the request of the investor, to:
> - The competent courts of the Contracting Party, in whose territory the investment was made; or
> - International arbitration, on the terms laid down in paragraph 3.
>
> Once an investor has submitted the dispute to the courts of the Contracting Party in question or to international arbitration, the choice of one or other of those procedures shall be final.
>
> 3. If the investor decides to have recourse to arbitration, the dispute shall be submitted to the International Centre for Settlement of Investment Disputes (ICSID) … once both States Parties to this Agreement have acceded to the Convention. Until such condition has been met, each Contracting Party agrees that the dispute shall be submitted to arbitration in accordance with the rules of the ICSID AF for the Administration of Conciliation, Arbitration and Fact-Finding Proceedings. If for any reason ICSID or its ICSID AF is not available, the dispute shall be submitted, at the request of the investor, to an ad hoc arbitral tribunal established under the Arbitration Rules of the United Nations Commission on International Trade Law (UNCITRAL).[313]

The tribunal compared the texts of Article IX and Article 8 of the Barbados-Venezuela BIT. It found that the differences between them lay in the paragraphs dealing with *ad hoc* UNCITRAL arbitration. The tribunal noted that the text of Article IX in the Ecuador-Venezuela BIT was divided into two separate paragraphs linked with a hyphen. The first paragraph allows ICSID arbitration "once both States Parties to this Agreement have acceded to the Convention," and ICSID AF arbitration "until such condition has been met." The separate

312 *Venezuela v Venezuela* (n 1) [113].

313 *Venezuela v Venezuela* (n 1) [116]. Originally in Spanish, translated into English by the tribunal.

second paragraph, starting with a hyphen in the original Spanish text, provided for UNCITRAL *ad hoc* arbitration "if for any reason ICSID or its Additional Facility [were] not available."[314]

For the tribunal, this text was distinct from that contained in Article 8(2) of the Barbados-Venezuela BIT, which provided for UNCITRAL arbitration if for any reason ICSID AF arbitration was not available, but only under the condition that "as long as ... Venezuela [had] not become a Contracting State."[315] The tribunal determined that the Article IX subjected ISDS disputes to UNCITRAL arbitration even if either ICSID or ICSID AF arbitration were available as options, while Barbadian investors could only resort to domestic adjudication when faced with the same scenario. Therefore, Ecuadorian investors had access to a more favorable dispute settlement provision through Article IX than Barbadian investors had access to through Article 8.[316] Since the MFN clause in the Barbados-Venezuela BIT applied to provisions including Article 8, the tribunal concluded that it had jurisdiction *ratione voluntatis*.[317]

Co-arbitrator Professor Marcelo Kohen vigorously opposed the majority of the *Venezuela US* tribunal's reasoning. In his dissenting opinion, he objected that there was no consent to UNCITRAL arbitration on the part of Venezuela in the Barbados-Venezuela BIT.[318] The tribunal majority imported such consent from third-party BITs, albeit stating that MFN clauses "[could not] serve the purpose of importing consent to arbitration when none [existed] under the BIT between Barbados and Venezuela."[319]

The dissenting opinion focused on two aspects concerning Article 3(2)'s ability to import dispute settlement provisions and whether Venezuela had given UNCITRAL arbitration consent. It doubted that Article 3(3) could cover Article 8. In this regard, Professor Kohen adopted a similar position as that adopted by the *Berschader* tribunal on the expression "all matters covered by the present Treaty."[320] He contended that although Article 3(3) referred to "Articles 1 to 11," the mere inclusion of Article 8 in such general terms was not enough to assume the applicability of Article 3(3) to Article 8 since not every article from the group Articles 1 to 11 was relevant for purposes of MFN treatment.[321]

314 *Venezuela v Venezuela* (n 1) [124].
315 *Venezuela v Venezuela* (n 1) [123].
316 *Venezuela v Venezuela* (n 1) [126].
317 *Venezuela v Venezuela* (n 1) [130].
318 *Venezuela v Venezuela* (n 1), *Dissenting Opinion of Marcelo G. Kohen.*
319 *Venezuela v Venezuela* (n 1) [105].
320 *Berschader v Russia* (n 104) [187–191].
321 *Venezuela v Venezuela* (n 1), *Dissenting Opinion of Marcelo G. Kohen* [11].

Therefore, the meaning of "Articles 1 to 11" should better have been understood as "the provisions of this treaty" by its context and should have been relevant to the material scope provided for in Article 3(2), i.e., the management, maintenance, use, enjoyment or disposal or foreign investments.[322] Additionally, Articles 3(1) and (2) clearly limited MFN treatment to treatment "in [the] territory" of each contracting state. In this regard, Professor Kohen agreed with the tribunals in *Berschader* and *ICS (I)*, both of which took a restrictive approach to interpreting the term "in its territory," which should have excluded international arbitration because it had a location outside the territory of the host state.[323]

Even assuming Article 3 applied to Article 8, Professor Kohen rightly pointed out that there was no jurisdiction *ratione voluntatis* because Venezuela never gave its consent to UNCITRAL arbitration. The text of Article 8(2) provided for international arbitration "as long as the Republic of Venezuela has not become a Contracting State of the Convention." Given that the Barbados-Venezuela BIT entered into force on October 31, 1995 after the ICSID Convention entered into force for Venezuela on June 1, 1995, the requirement for Article 3(2) to come into operation did not exist at the moment the BIT entered into force. Therefore, the Barbadian investors could only have resorted to ICSID arbitration.[324]

As for Article 8(4), it contained but a general offer of "unconditional consent" to international arbitration as provided for in paragraphs (1) to (3) of that article. In other words, Article 8(4) indicated that "the acceptance by the parties of arbitration in the conditions set out in Article 8 [was] otherwise unconditional" but "[n]othing else and nothing less."[325] Article 8(4) *per se* did not constitute a standing offer as construed by the majority of the tribunal.

After determining that Article 8 alone did not provide a basis for its jurisdiction in the case at hand as arbitration under the UNCITRAL Rules and that the contracting parties contemplated it for the period during which Venezuela had not yet acceded to the ICSID Convention,[326] the tribunal applied Article 8 and Article 3 cumulatively per the *ejusdem generis* principle. It considered that since MFN could not be used to import consent where there was none in the basic treaty, Article 8 could be applied for this purpose since Article 8(4) provided "unconditional consent" to international arbitration.

322 *Venezuela v Venezuela* (n 1), *Dissenting Opinion of Marcelo G. Kohen* [21].

323 *Venezuela v Venezuela* (n 1), *Dissenting Opinion of Marcelo G. Kohen* [18–20]. See also supra Chapter 4.

324 *Venezuela v Venezuela* (n 1), *Dissenting Opinion of Marcelo G. Kohen* [42].

325 *Venezuela v Venezuela* (n 1), *Dissenting Opinion of Marcelo G. Kohen* [46].

326 *Venezuela US v Venezuela* (n 1) [89].

The paradox in the tribunal's reasoning is palpable. Consent to dispute settlement in treaties is a clear-cut, yes-or-no question. Since the tribunal had already concluded that Article 8 could not provide a basis for jurisdiction, it as a matter of course could not have provided a basis for Article 3(2) to import consent from elsewhere. If it had been determined that there was no basis in the basic treaty for the tribunal to establish jurisdiction, importing consent through an application of the MFN clause would amount to manufacturing consent where none existed. Such a result would constitute an infringement of state sovereignty.[327]

4 Can Jurisdiction Be Founded on the Basis of an MFN Clause?

So far, all but three tribunals have refused to import state consent via an application of an MFN clause. It has been the general practice of tribunals not to apply an MFN clause in relation to jurisdictional issues.[328] Indeed, state consent is an essential and serious waiver of state immunity by the contracting states to expose themselves to non-domestic courts and tribunals. In other words, agreeing to international arbitration is a "potentially costly political" action for countries to take.[329] Therefore, state consent to investor-state dispute settlement should be expressed in clear and certain treaty language instead of being manufactured by application of an MFN clause.[330]

---

327 *Venezuela v Venezuela* (n 1), *Dissenting Opinion of Marcelo G. Kohen* [2]. It should be noted that in the recent case *Kimberly-Clark v Venezuela,* the tribunal was faced with a similarly worded dispute settlement clause in the Dutch – Venezuela BIT. The tribunal was of the view that, unless the MFN clause contained in the basic treaty expressly provides that it applies to dispute resolution, "a tribunal has no power to incorporate into the treaty more favorable dispute resolution terms so as to create or expand the Contracting States' consent to arbitrate." See: *Kimberly-Clark BVBA, Kimberly-Clark Dutch Holdings, B.V., Kimberly-Clark S.L.U. v Bolivarian Republic of Venezuela, Award dated November 5, 2021,* ICSID Case No. ARB(AF)/18/3).

328 Sharmin (n 84) 258.

329 Noah Rubins, 'The Arbitral Innovations of Recent U.S. Free Trade Agreements: Two Steps Forward, One Step Back' [2003] International Business Law Journal 865, 873.

330 In this regard, Blyschak argued that '…as is customary in traditional arbitration proceedings, waiver of immunity and state consent to arbitration must be concretely established with a high standard of certainty before an Investor-State tribunal accepts jurisdiction over an investment dispute'. See: Paul Michael Blyschak, 'State Consent, Investor Interests and the Future of Investment Arbitration: Reanalyzing the Jurisdiction of Investor-State Tribunals in Hard Cases.' (2009) 9 Asper Review of International Business and Trade Law 99.

In fact, to apply an MFN clause to establish jurisdiction will cause more problems than it solves. First, such practice is in conflict with the *effet utile* principle. For Sharmin, a specifically drafted dispute settlement provision in a BIT indicates that the contracting parties most likely intended not to extend the scope of arbitration via an application of the MFN clause.[331] As a result, applying an MFN clause for jurisdictional purposes would render the dispute settlement provisions "nugatory, meaningless, or without any legal effect."[332]

Additionally, the inappropriate extension of tribunals' jurisdiction may also lead to abuse of process. As mentioned in chapter 2, abuse of process is not defined in investment treaties. It is a legal concept deriving from the good faith principle to limit the abusive wielding of procedural rights.[333] Ascensio has defined the abuse of process as "a serious divergence between the exercise of a procedural right and the overall objectives of the system of adjudication concerned," which "affects the balance of interests at stake and [favors] in a disproportionate manner the beneficiary of the right."[334]

Under the *kompetenz-kompetenz* principle, a tribunal is empowered to decide its own jurisdiction. This principle is contained in Article 41(1) of the ICSID Convention and Article 23(1) of the 2013 UNCTITRAL Rules. However, tribunals have to establish their jurisdiction based on solid justifications. For example, Article 42 of the ICSID Convention provides that tribunals have to decide their jurisdiction based on "such rules of law as may be agreed by the parties."[335] According to Sharmin, Article 42 indicates that it is tribunals' duty to decide their jurisdiction based on rules of law, instead of presumption and arbitrariness. This means, in the context of interpreting MFN clauses, tribunals should responsibly examine any claims concerning jurisdiction and pay considerable deference to treaty text. When the text of an MFN clause does not extend to state consent, tribunals should not interpret it as doing so. According to the *ST-AD* tribunal, although tribunals are able to decide their own jurisdiction, this does not authorize them to create jurisdiction via an application of an MFN clause.[336]

Additionally, Article 52 of the ICSID Convention lists several grounds for annulment of awards, including when tribunal acts *ultra vires*. When tribunals

331 Sharmin (n 84) 237.

332 Sharmin (n 84) 237.

333 E De Brabandere, '"Good Faith," "Abuse of Process" and the Initiation of Investment Treaty Claims' (2012) 3 Journal of International Dispute Settlement 609.

334 Ascensio (n 5) 765.

335 Article 42 of the ICSID Convention (n 8).

336 *ST-AD v Bulgaria* (n 63) [398].

incorrectly apply an MFN clause in the manners discussed above, this constitutes an *ultra vires* act which risks being set aside. Extending jurisdiction via an application of an MFN clause is an improper use of the tribunals' *kompetenz-kompetenz* power, and constitutes an abuse of process. Worse still, in view of criticism and backlash against ISDS from scholars and states, such irresponsible practices will conceivably further jeopardize the legitimacy of international adjudication.

As a result, MFN clauses should not be interpreted in such a way as to allow tribunals to found jurisdiction unless it was explicitly expressed in the treaty that the contracting parties intended for this to be a possibility. The decisions of the above tribunals have presented some notable idiosyncrasies in cases dealing with the jurisdictional issues as discussed. Most notable among these are oversights of the interpretive principles embodied in Articles 31 and 32 of the VCLT and the failure by tribunals to properly apply the *ejusdem generis* principle. The following sections turn to these issues. The extent to which Rule 7 of the ILC Guiding Principles is a proper way out is also discussed.

4.1 *Limitation of the Traditional Interpretive Methods*

The above ISDS cases have revealed the limited assistance of the traditional interpretive methods when it comes to the issue of applying MFN clauses to incorporate dispute settlement procedures. First, treaty interpretation through Article 31 of the VCLT has yielded limited clarity. For example, the *Plama* and *Berschader* tribunals declared that they failed to discern the intention of contracting parties in relation to the MFN clauses at issue before them by applying Article 31. They accordingly turned to other methods.

This is understandable given that the term "treatment" in MFN clause is an unavoidable topic for tribunals when they start their reasonings from the position of the VCLT, the meaning of which cannot be discerned from the treaty text. As the *Tza Yap Shum* tribunal pointed out, "treatment" as used in MFN clauses is open to a broader interpretation, including one that includes procedural issues.[337] As a result, the lack of a clear, ordinary meaning of this term in treaties and the limited assistance from the VCLT require tribunals to seek evidence from other sources to discern contracting parties' intention. To this end, subsidiary interpretation methods have been selected and applied by tribunals, often based on their presumptions.

As an aspect of Article 32 of the VCLT on the supplementary means of interpretation, state practice around the conclusion of BITs is frequently relied on.

337 *Tza Yap Shum v Peru* (n 63) [213].

However, the treaty language of Article 32 has indicated its limited guidance, which is to confirm the meaning from Article 31 or to determine it when Article 31 leads to ambiguous, obscure, manifestly absurd or unreasonable results.[338] Therefore, questions could arise when tribunals rely on subsidiary materials such as contracting parties' contemporary treaty practice as the primary support for a given interpretation.

One may indeed wonder whether tribunals will reach a different or even opposite conclusion if they analyze the treaties based on different assumptions. In other words, restrictively drafted dispute settlement provisions in basic BITs could be employed to prove that basic treaties were intentionally drafted this way so that MFN clauses cannot be relied on to overturn what is stated in the basic treaty (as in *Telenor*), or it could demonstrate that contemporary state practice entailed a broader scope of issues that could be referred to dispute settlement (as in *Maffezini*).

Such problems also exist in applying interpretive methods from customary international law such as the *expressio unius est exclusio alterius* principle, which has been applied by tribunals to reach opposite results. On the one hand, some tribunals have applied *expressio unius est exclusio alterius* and construed an MFN clause's exceptions as including dispute settlement. The tribunal in *AWG* concluded as follows:

> The use of the expression 'in all matters' when coupled with a list of specific exceptions that do not include dispute resolution, leaves no doubt that dispute resolution is covered by the most-favored-nation clause.[339]

On the other hand, tribunals like the *Austrian Airlines* tribunal read *expressio unius est exclusio alterius* with doubt. It admitted that although according to the *expressio unius* principle, the fact that exceptions listed in Article 3(2) did not mention procedural issues could imply that the contracting parties did not intend to exclude such matters, it could nevertheless also be understood that the exceptions to the MFN clause referred to substantive issues only.[340]

The inability of the traditional interpretive methods to render consistent outcomes has been one of the reasons for the chaos which has ensued in relation to the interpretation of MFN clauses by tribunals. It is true that MFN

338 Article 32 of the Vienna Convention (1969) (n 128).

339 *AWG Group Ltd. v The Argentine Republic, Decision on Jurisdiction dated 3 August 2006*, UNCITRAL Arbitration [65]. See also: *RosInvest v Russia* (n 1) [135].

340 *Austrian Airlines v Slovakia* (n 63) [192]. See also: *Daimler v Argentine Republic* (n 90) [237–239].

clauses, by their text, leaves open the possibility of importing dispute settlement provisions.[341] However, the jurisdiction of international tribunals is based on the explicit consent from disputing parties, in the absence of which there should be no jurisdiction by default. Therefore, dispute settlement provisions are different from substantive provisions given the fundamental role of state consent in international law, and tribunals should restrain themselves from extending their jurisdiction unless explicitly permitted to do so in terms of the clear wording of the MFN clause in question.

4.2 The Incorrect Application of the *Ejusdem Generis* Principle

The *ejusdem generis* principle is not applied as frequently in procedural matters as it is in relation to matters concerning substantive treatment as discussed in Chapter 3. In *Plama*, the tribunal denied the relevance of the *ejusdem generis* principle in view of the limited information provided by the text of the MFN clause in dispute.[342] Additionally, the two tribunals that did apply the *ejusdem generis* principle, applied it incorrectly in order to import consent from third-party treaties (*Garanti* and *Venezuela US*). To this end, both tribunals utilized the broadly drafted MFN clauses and dispute settlement provisions that allegedly gave consent to international arbitration. Putting aside the fact that state consent was never given in these two cases, the tribunals have incorrectly applied the *ejusdem generis* principle to manufacture state consent where there was none.

In *Venezuela US*, the tribunal stated that an MFN clause could not import consent to arbitration when there was no consent in the basic treaty between Barbados and Venezuela to begin with.[343] According to Articles 9 and 10 of the ILC Draft Articles on most-favored-nation clauses, the *ejusdem generis* principle applies to "rights which fall within the limits of the subject-matter of the clause." The question here is whether state consent qualifies as a "right" in the sense of the *ejusdem generis* principle. To answer this question, it is necessary to take a look at the structure of IIAs as the basis of treatment and dispute settlement.

In IIAs, two sovereign countries conclude an investment treaty to allow foreign investors from each state to conduct commercial activities in each other's territory. For this purpose, states promise foreign investors certain levels of substantive treatment such as FET, full protection and security, free transfer, amongst other things. As a means to enforce the above rights, dispute settlement

341 Sharmin (n 84) 256.
342 *Plama v Bulgaria* (n 63) [189].
343 *Venezuela US v Venezuela* (n 1) [105].

provisions are included in investment treaties for potential conflicts between investors and host states. As analyzed above in part 1 of this chapter, IIAs entail compromise from sovereign states through consent to international tribunals, which consent constitutes a waiver of state immunity by the host state and also of the jurisdiction of its own domestic court over disputes in its own territory.[344] Given that state consent is the basis of the enforcement mechanism of IIAs to guarantee foreign investors' substantive rights, it is rather difficult to equate them with the rights they are intended to protect. Therefore, it would be an incorrect application of the *ejusdem generis* principle to apply an MFN clause in order to expand the jurisdiction of a tribunal.

4.3 *Are the ILC Guiding Principles a Way Out?*

As has been alluded to above, Rule 7 of the ILC Guiding Principles was suggested as a restrictive interpretive method for state consent to international arbitration, because given the autonomous nature of dispute settlement provisions, "in modern BITs and domestic investment law, state consent is traditionally couched in terms of a unilateral declaration, an offer to arbitrate, addressed to an undefined and unknown number of recipients" like a unilateral declaration.[345] Rule 7 requires clear and specific terms for a unilateral declaration to entail obligations for states and a restrictive interpretation of the scope of the obligations engendered by such declaration.

It might shed some light for tribunals when they encounter attempts from investors to expand the scope of their jurisdiction through reliance on MFN clauses. However, Rule 7 of the ILC Guiding Principles was designed to apply to unilateral acts of sovereign states which are binding from the moment they were made. State consent to an international arbitration agreement, meanwhile, will only become binding when investors perfect the agreement by starting the arbitration proceedings. Additionally, Rule 7 goes to the interpretation of state consent, not the MFN clause *per se*. Since MFN clauses cannot be utilized to create jurisdiction, Rule 7 of the ILC Guiding Principles therefore only offers limited guidance of assistance when interpreting MFN clauses.

5 Concluding Remarks

Interpreting MFN clauses remains an open issue, with *ad hoc* tribunals adopting diverse and sometimes conflicting positions. According to some scholars,

344 See, for example: Blyschak (n 330) 101.

345 Andreeva (n 10)138.

applying the MFN clause in order to found jurisdiction and establish state consent will permit tribunals to claim jurisdiction over types of disputes that were not contemplated by contracting states, and will wind up with compulsory adjudication against the will of sovereign states.[346] From the above discussion, it is also clear that the chaos surrounding MFN clauses stems, at least in part, from the fragmented nature of investment law. *Ad hoc* arbitral tribunals are composed of arbitrators from diverse legal backgrounds who face different treaties and take distinct positions on issues including the standard of substantive treatment, the dichotomy of admissibility and jurisdiction, and the role of state consent in the formulation of arbitration agreements, amongst other things. These elements may affect the outcome of the application of an MFN clause in an individual case. As a result, discrepancies among tribunals leads to a further fragmented and inconsistent investment legal order. In the words of Charles H. Brower II:

> *Ad hoc* tribunals share the institutional tendency of juries to produce clusters of decisions with a deficit of consistency and a surplus of arbitrary distinctions ... When combined with the discretion granted to tribunals, the growing volume of disputes, and their importance to ever broader consistencies, the use of *ad hoc* tribunals without coordinating mechanisms seems likely to provoke a crisis.[347]

Therefore, the application of MFN clauses in IIAs should be examined from the perspective of the broader context of general international law. The fundamental values which underpin international law should be given weight when it comes to treaty interpretation, including when tribunals are called on to interpret MFN clauses. This book suggests that when Articles 31 and 32 of the VCLT do not provide a clear direction on how an MFN clause should be interpreted, tribunals should take into account other key parameters, such as state consent (which forms a cornerstone of international arbitration), the good faith principle, and the desirability of consistency in international investment to reach more balanced conclusions.

---

346 According to Fox, 'There is generally no external authority which can make an order compelling the State to submit to the arbitration'. See: Hazel Fox, 'States and the Undertaking to Arbitrate' (1988) 37 The International and Comparative Law Quarterly 1.

347 Charles H Brower II, 'Mitsubishi, Investor-State Arbitration, and the Law of State Immunity' (2005) 20 American University International Law Review 907, 921, 923.

CHAPTER 6

Conclusion

The previous chapters of this book have examined how investor-state dispute settlement (ISDS) tribunals have interpreted most-favored-nation (MFN) clauses in various international investment agreements (IIAs). As a treaty-based obligation, the original objective of MFN treatment was to provide an equal footing for foreigners in international trade law. In this sense, it has become a cornerstone of the global economy, and the MFN clause has been heavily instrumental in shaping the trajectory of international economic law. The popularity of MFN clauses in international treaties, however, has ebbed and flowed during the course of history. That is to say, it has proved to be more popular in times when economies thrive and when the political situation of the day can be characterized as stable, while there has been significantly less reliance on the MFN clause during times of economic strife and military tension.[1]

In contemporary times, the MFN clause has become embroiled in a significant controversy in a world where international investment law has become quite fragmented. As discussed in Chapter 1, the development of the MFN clause in investment law went through several different stages, with each stage featuring distinct ways in which MFN clauses were drafted. In 1987, the first treaty-based investment arbitration under the United Kingdom-Sri Lanka bilateral investment treaty (BIT) affirmed the application of an MFN clause to substantive treatment obligations contained in other treaties. Since then, the number of ISDS cases brought have consistently been on the rise. In 2001, the *Maffezini* tribunal applied an MFN clause in order to incorporate better procedural treatment from a third-party treaty, which set in motion a lengthy period during which the *Maffezini* approach was both applied and rejected by a long line of tribunals.

In relation to both substantive and procedural treatment, the chapters 3 through V discussed ISDS tribunals' interpretation of the MFN clause according to the interpretive methods of international law, which were discussed in Chapter 2. Specifically, this book has studied the application of MFN clauses in relation to substantive treatment, where *de facto* MFN violations and the application of MFN clauses in pursuit of obtaining a higher standard of treatment

1 See Chapter 1 of this book.

from treaties other than the basic treaty of which the MFN clause forms a part were discussed. It has also studied the application of MFN clauses in relation to procedural treatment, including in relation to the extent to which procedural preconditions and jurisdictional issues can be overcome by applying an MFN clause in order to incorporate "more favorable" treatment from outside of the basic treaty. This exposé showed that tribunals have largely relied on their presumptions about the rationale of MFN clauses, which has led to inconsistent reasoning and outcomes on a number of issues in ISDS practice.

Given these inconsistencies, states, as treatymakers, have taken actions by employing clearer treaty language in modern BITs to fend against the possibility of expansive interpretations of MFN clauses. Countries have also adopted methods to either marginalize the MFN clause in their treaty practice or otherwise refine it. These shifts have been described as states' movement to reclaim their regulatory power on the battlefield of investment law.[2]

1 Current Drafting Trends in Relation to MFN Clauses

The current movement in IIAs has been towards the adoption of more detailed and restrictive MFN clauses. In this regard, states have adopted different methods in view of ISDS practice concerning MFN treatment or contemporary investment policies. The methods adopted can be divided into two types: the first type sees the role of the MFN clause in IIAs being attenuated; the second type has seen the refinement of MFN clauses by way of more cautious drafting.

1.1 *Marginalization of the MFN Clause*

Some countries have concluded IIAs in which the weight of the MFN clause has been attenuated. The marginalization of the MFN clause as such has been undertaken in two main ways. Some recently concluded treaties with language such as to "endeavor to" accord MFN treatment, i.e., they have taken a soft commitment approach to MFN clauses.[3] While some countries, such as India, have decided to remove the MFN clause entirely from their new IIAs.

1.1.1 Soft Commitments

Some modern IIAs have seen the MFN clause drafted not as a hardcore guarantee, but rather as a soft commitment whereby contracting parties promise

2 Tanjina Sharmin, *Application of Most-Favoured-Nation Clauses by Investor-State Arbitral Tribunals: Implications for the Developing Countries* (Springer 2020) 262.

3 Sharmin (n 2).

to make efforts to accord MFN treatment. This type of drafting can be found in both pre- and post-*Maffezini* treaties to curb the unintended expansion of the scope of MFN clauses.[4]

A post-*Maffezini* treaty practice in this regard is visible in IIAs concluded by Japan. For example, Article 88 of the 2009 Japan-Switzerland EPA provides as follows:

> If a Party accords more favourable treatment to investors of a non-Party and their investments by concluding or amending a free trade agreement, customs union or similar agreement that provides for substantial liberalisation of investment, it shall not be obliged to accord such treatment to investors of the other Party and their investments. Any such treatment accorded by a Party shall be notified to the other Party without delay and the former Party shall *endeavour to* accord to investors of the latter Party and their investments treatment no less favourable than that accorded under the concluded or amended agreement. The former Party, upon request by the latter Party, shall enter into negotiations with a view to incorporating into this Agreement treatment no less favourable than that accorded under such concluded or amended agreement.[5]

The above soft commitment allows a contracting state to retain the power to decide whether to include MFN treatment as a treaty promise towards foreign investors from the other contracting state. It also prevents tribunals from applying expansive interpretations since MFN treatment has not been granted in the basic treaty, which is left to contracting states' discretion.[6]

1.1.2 The Total Absence of an MFN Clause

Some countries have taken a more radical approach and removed the MFN clause from their IIAs. For example, after the *White Industries* tribunal decided that the MFN clause in the 1998 India-Australia BIT could be used for higher treaty standards, India adopted its 2015 Model BIT and excluded the MFN clause as a direct response to the decision of the tribunal.[7] Subsequent to 2015

4 Sharmin (n 2).

5 Article 88 of the Japan-Switzerland EPA (2009). A copy of which is available at:< https://investmentpolicy.unctad.org/international-investment-agreements/treaty-files/2592/download> accessed 20 April 2022.

6 Sharmin (n 2) 263.

7 India Model BIT (2015). A copy of which is available at: <https://investmentpolicy.unctad.org/international-investment-agreements/treaty-files/3560/download> accessed 20

Model BIT, the three IIAs signed by India with Brazil, Kyrgyzstan and Balerus all exclude MFN clause from their texts.[8] Treaties adopting similar approch include the EU-Singapore FTA (2014)[9] and ASEAN–Australia–New Zealand FTA (2009),[10] amongst others.

Abandoning the MFN clause altogether was one of the five IIA reform options proposed by the United Nations Conference on Trade and Development (UNCTAD) for states to regain regulatory authority over their MFN clauses.[11] According to UNCTAD, the MFN clause is one of the treaty provisions that is "particularly implicated in delineating the balance between investment protection and the right to regulation in the public interest."[12] Understandably, the IIAs mentioned above have decided to drop the MFN clause given the possible unintended consequences of interpretations by tribunals that apply the clause as a multilateralizing tool. However, taking such an approach also has the capacity to raise doubts.

The first such doubt goes to the extent to which systemic discrimination may occur in relation to investors from states that do not have IIAs that contain an MFN clause. Although it goes without saying that foreign investors will not be able to bring claims in relation to MFN treatment where no MFN clause exists, this issue relates to the more fundamental challenge of building a level playing field for foreign investors with various nationalities in host states. The MFN clause is included in most modern IIAs and has been the pillar of

April 2022. More examples in this regard include South Africa Model BIT (2012) and EU-Singapore FTA (2014).

8 India – Brazil BIT (2020), a copy of which is available at: <https://investmentpolicy.unctad.org/international-investment-agreements/treaty-files/5912/download> accessed 20 April 2022; India – Kyrgzstan BIT (2019), a copy of which is available at: <https://investmentpolicy.unctad.org/international-investment-agreements/treaty-files/5993/download> accessed 20 April 2022; India – Balerus BIT (2018), a copy of which is available at: <https://investmentpolicy.unctad.org/international-investment-agreements/treaty-files/5724/download> accessed 20 April 2022.

9 EU – Singapore FTA (2014), a copy of which is available at: <https://trade.ec.europa.eu/doclib/press/index.cfm?id=961> accessed 20 April 2022.

10 ASEAN–Australia–New Zealand FTA (2009), a copy of which is available at: <https://investmentpolicy.unctad.org/international-investment-agreements/treaty-files/2589/download> accessed 20 April 2022.

11 UNCTAD, UNCTAD's reform package for the International Investment Regime (2018). UNCTAD/DIAE/PCB/INF/2020/8 34. Available at: <https://investmentpolicy.unctad.org/uploaded-files/document/UNCTAD_Reform_Package_2018.pdf> accessed 20 April 2022.

12 UNCTAD, *Word Investment Report 2015: Reforming International Investment Governance* (United Nations 2015) 315, available at: <https://unctad.org/system/files/official-document/wir2015_en.pdf> accessed 20 April 2022.

non-discrimination in international economic law. It is, therefore, a rather radical step for countries to delete the MFN clause from IIAs entirely.

1.2 *Refinement of the MFN Clause*

Countries have also concluded treaties with restrictively drafted MFN clauses to prevent tribunals from extending them in unanticipated ways. Treaty practice varies in this regard, including restricting the scope of MFN obligations to *de facto* treatment, according MFN obligations only in relation to substantive provisions of the basic treaty, and explicitly cutting out dispute settlement provisions and essential policy agendas from the scope of the MFN clause. Underscoring the element of likeness has also been a prominent method. Sometimes the above methods are employed together using clear treaty language to achieve a more restrictive and unambiguous MFN clause.

1.2.1 Retraining MFN Clause from Substantive Obligations

States have entered into treaties in which the MFN clause's scope has been limited to the actual treatment accorded to investors. For example, in the 2016 Comprehensive Economic Trade Agreement between the European Union and Canada (CETA), Article 8.7.4 of its investment chapter contains a clarification as follows:

> Substantive obligations in other international investment treaties and other trade agreement do not in themselves constitute 'treatment', and thus cannot give rise to a breach of this Article, absent measures adopted or maintained by a Party pursuant to those obligations.[13]

Specifying that the MFN clause does not extend to substantive obligations in IIAs is one of the policy options provided by UNCTAD.[14] Such a formulation limits MFN treatment to only *de facto* treatment and excludes from its scope *de jure* treatment such as a higher standard of fair and equitable treatment contained in another treaty. It thus leaves the contracting parties more control over the operation of the MFN clause.[15]

13 EU – Canada FTA (CETA, 2017). A copy of which is available at: <https://ec.europa.eu/trade/policy/in-focus/ceta/ceta-chapter-by-chapter/> accessed on 20 April 2022.

14 UNCTAD (n 11).

15 Sharmin (n 2) 269.

1.2.2 Clarifying "in Like Circumstances"

Another appropriate method is for states to elaborate on the "in like circumstances" requirement. For example, in Indonesia-Australia Comprehensive Economic Partnership Agreement (CEPA) concluded in 2019, the contracting parties decided to add a footnote to clarify the term "like circumstances" in Articles 14.4 (National Treatment) and 14.5 (MFN treatment):

> For greater certainty, whether treatment is accorded in "like circumstances" under Article 14.4 or Article 14.5 depends on the totality of the circumstances, including the relevant economic or business sector or sectors concerned and whether the relevant treatment distinguishes between investors or investments on the basis of legitimate public welfare objectives or on the basis of nationality. Where treatment distinguishes between investors or investments on the basis of legitimate public welfare objectives, that treatment is not inconsistent with Article 14.4 or Article 14.5.[16]

A more specific elucidation on the likeness requirement is visible in Artifcle 6 of the 2019 BLEU (Belgium-Luxembourg Economic Union) Model BIT, where after according MFN treatment to foreign investors in like circumstances, the following clarification was provided:

> For greater certainty, a determination of whether an investment or an investor is in comparable situations for the purposes of paragraphs 1 and 2 of this Article shall be made based on an assessment of the totality of circumstances related to the investor or the investment, including:
> a) the effect of the investment on
>   (i) the local community where investment is located;
>   (ii) the environment, including effects that relate to the cumulative impact of all investments within a jurisdiction;
> b) the character of the measure, including its nature, purpose, duration and rationale; and
> c) the regulations that apply to investments or investors.[17]

16 Australia-Indonesia CEPA (2019). A copy of which is available at: <https://investmentpolicy.unctad.org/international-investment-agreements/treaty-files/5991/download> accessed 20 April 2022.

17 BLEU Model BIT (2019). A copy of which is available at: <https://investmentpolicy.unctad.org/international-investment-agreements/treaty-files/5854/download> accessed 20 April 2022. For another example, see Article 4 of the Azerbaijan – Croatia BIT (2007),

As discussed in above Chapter 3, legitimate public welfare objectives have been included as an indicator in this regard. For example, the recently concluded Australia-Indonesia Comprehensive Economic Partnership Agreement (CEPA) contains in the footnote of Article 14.4 (National Treatment) clarifying that the decision of "in like circumstances" under MFN treatment and National Treatment of the treaty:

> ... depends on the totality of the circumstances, including the relevant economic or business sector or sectors concerned and whether the relevant treatment distinguishes between investors or investments on the basis of legitimate public welfare objectives or on the basis of nationality. Where treatment distinguishes between investors or investments on the basis of *legitimate public welfare objectives*, that treatment is not inconsistent with Article 14.4 or Article 14.5.[18]

However, the definition of a legitimate public welfare objective might confuse and leave doubts for future tribunals. Moreover, treaty practice as such leaves doubts as to whether the MFN clause could still be extended to substantive treatment in addition to *de facto* treatment. As has been analyzed in Chapter 3, tribunals seldom examine whether a third-party investor is in "in like circumstances" vis-à-vis the claimant before incorporating a higher standard of substantive treatment via an MFN clause.[19] How future tribunals interpret MFN clauses like this is still open to question.

In a similar vein, with the objective to reserve contracting parties' regulatory space, the 2021 Italy Model BIT explicitly carves out essential domestic policies from the scope of the MFN clause. After providing MFN treatment to foreign investors, Article 5 of the document stipulates that:

> Subject to the requirement that such measures are not applied in a manner that would constitute arbitrary or unjustifiable discrimination between investments or between investors, paragraphs 1 and 2 shall not

a copy of which is available at: <https://investmentpolicy.unctad.org/international-investment-agreements/treaty-files/229/download> accessed 20 April 2022.

18 Australia-Indonesia CEPA (2019), a copy of which is available at: <https://investmentpolicy.unctad.org/international-investment-agreements/treaty-files/5991/download> accessed 20 April 2022.

19 In this regard, see Jürgen Kurtz, 'The Most Favoured Nation Standard and Foreign Investment: An Uneasy Fit?' (2005) 5 The Journal of World Investment & Trade 861, 874, 883.

be construed to prevent a Party from adopting or enforcing measures necessary:

(a) to protect public morals or public order;
(b) to protect human, animal or plant life or health;
(c) to ensure compliance with laws or regulations which are not inconsistent with the provisions of this Agreement including those relating to:
   (i) the prevention of deceptive and fraudulent practices or to deal with the effects of a default on contracts;
   (ii) the protection of the privacy of individuals in relation to the processing and dissemination of persona data and the protection of confidentiality of individual records and accounts;
   (iii) safety.[20]

Although the above treaty language does not serve to clarify the concept of "in like circumstances," it may nonetheless provide useful guidance to tribunals in determining whether certain government measures were taken on the basis of legitimate policy considerations and therefore should not be subject to MFN treatment and should not be considered discriminatory.

In conclusion, the above formulations set detailed elaboration on the meaning of "in like circumstances." Although the "in like circumstances" requirement is implicit in the *ejusdem generis* principle, an explicit reference of this kind serves to remind tribunals of their obligation to undertake a reasonable and proper comparison of foreign investors in proper comparative context when assessing an alleged breach.[21]

1.2.3 Excluding Investor-State Dispute Mechanism from MFN Treatment

Countries have taken different strategies to avoid application of the MFN clause to dispute settlement mechanisms. Some countries have concluded treaties whereby the MFN clause was included in the substantive chapter of a

20 Italy Model BIT (2021). A copy of which is available at: <https://investmentpolicy.unctad.org/international-investment-agreements/treaty-files/6390/download> accessed 20 April 2022.

21 Some treaties have placed direct emphasis on the *ejusdem generis* principle instead of on "in like circumstances". See, for example, Article 2.4.6 of the EU – Vietnam FTA (2019), which provides that "[t]his Article shall be interpreted in accordance with the principle of *ejusdem generis*." EU – Vietnam FTA (2019), a copy of which is available at: <https://investmentpolicy.unctad.org/international-investment-agreements/treaty-files/5868/download> accessed 20 April 2022.

purposefully fragmented treaty system. For example, the 2021 Canada Model BIT is structurally divided into several parts. Section A provides definitions, Section B substantive obligations, and Section E for ISDS. Article 6 on MFN treatment is located in Section B on substantive investment protections.[22] However, including the MFN clause in the specific section reserved for substantive treatment alone could raise doubts and allows tribunals to adopt a broad interpretation. As such, a more straightforward approach for contracting states might be to explicitly exclude dispute settlement from the scope of their MFN clauses.[23]

Additionally, as analyzed above, tribunals have adopted opposite views in relation to the expression "*expressio unius est exclusio alterius*," especially given the absence of dispute settlement issues in the exceptions to a given MFN clause. Therefore, a clear exclusion of the dispute settlement provisions from the scope of an MFN clause will undoubtedly solve the problem caused by the *expressio unius* principle.

In order to provide direct evidence of contracting parties' intention and reduce confusion, some recent IIAs have chosen to explicitly exclude dispute settlement from the scope of the MFN clause. Such provisions have been formulated by adding a paragraph at the end of the MFN clause. For example, Article 9.5.3 in the investment chapter of the Comprehensive and Progressive Agreement for Trans-Pacific Partnership (CPTPP) provides that:

> For greater certainty, the treatment referred to in this Article does not encompass international dispute resolution procedures or mechanisms, such as those included in Section B (Investor-State Dispute Settlement).[24]

A similar formulation is visible in the newly signed Regional Comprehensive Economic Partnership (RCEP), Article 10.4.3 of which provides that "[f]or greater certainty, the treatment referred to in paragraphs 1 and 2 does not

22 Canada Model BIT (2021). A copy of which is available at: <https://investmentpolicy.unctad.org/international-investment-agreements/treaty-files/6341/download> accessed 20 April 2022.

23 Sharmin (n 2) 264. An example on point is the Canada – Burkina Faso BIT (2015). Besides locating MFN claus in the substantive treatment section, Annex III (3) of the BIT explicitly cut out dispute settlement mechanism from the scope of MFN clause. A copy of the treaty is available at: <https://investmentpolicy.unctad.org/international-investment-agreements/treaty-files/3460/download> accessed 20 April 2022.

24 Comprehensive and Progressive Agreement for Trans-Pacific Partnership (CPTPP, 2018). A copy of which is available at: <https://www.dfat.gov.au/trade/agreements/in-force/cptpp/official-documents> accessed 20 April 2022.

encompass any international dispute resolution procedures or mechanisms under other existing or future international agreements."[25]

Explicit terms to exclude dispute settlement from the MFN clause's scope have also been formulated as the so-called floating footnote, a method to document the negotiating history over contracting parties' intention.[26] Such formulation is visible in the interpretive declaration in the Dominican Republic-Central America FTA (CAFTA-DR), although it was later deleted. Footnotes like this should be regarded as part of the *travaux préparatoires* of treaties and should be viewed as part of supplementary methods of interpretation.[27] Nevertheless, the subsequent deletion of such a footnote by contracting parties could be perceived by tribunals as a change of the intention of contracting parties to include dispute settlement.

Instead of striking the footnote from the final document, some treaties have included it in the MFN clause's footnote to avoid unanticipated expansive interpretations by tribunals. For example, in the 2018 Central America-Korea FTA, the contracting states inserted a footnote underneath the MFN clause. It states that "[f]or greater certainty, Article 9.4 (MFN clause) shall not apply to investor-state dispute settlement mechanisms such as those set out in Section B or that are provided for in an international treaty or trade agreement."[28]

To better illustrate contracting parties' intention, some IIAs have adopted the above formulations in combination. For example, Article 10.4 of the recently signed RCEP provides in clear language that:

---

25 Regional Comprehensive Economic Partnership (RCEP, 2020). A copy of which is available at: <https://rcepsec.org/legal-text/> accessed 20 April 2022. See also: Article 4.5 of the Hong Kong – Mexico BIT, which provides that: for greater certainty, the obligation in this Article does not encompass a requirement to extend to investors of the other Contracting Party dispute resolution procedures other than those set out in Chapter 3. Hong Kong, China SAR – Mexico BIT (2020). A copy of which is available at: <https://investmentpolicy.unctad.org/international-investment-agreements/treaty-files/6129/download> accessed 20 April 2022; Article 4 of the Italy Model BIT (2020), a copy of which is available at: <https://investmentpolicy.unctad.org/international-investment-agreements/treaty-files/6389/download> accessed 20 April 2022.

26 Andreas Ziegler, 'Most-Favoured-Nation (MFN) Treatment' in Reinisch August (ed), *Standards of Investment Protection* (Oxford University Press 2008) 82.

27 Y Radi, 'The Application of the Most-Favoured-Nation Clause to the Dispute Settlement Provisions of Bilateral Investment Treaties: Domesticating the "Trojan Horse"' (2007) 18 European Journal of International Law 757, 769.

28 South Korea – Central America FTA (2018). A copy of which is available at: <https://investmentpolicy.unctad.org/international-investment-agreements/treaty-files/5670/download> accessed 20 April 2022.

1. Each Party shall accord to investors of another Party treatment no less [favorable] than that it accords, in like circumstances, to investors of any other Party or non-Party with respect to the establishment, acquisition, expansion, management, conduct, operation, and sale or other disposition of investments in its territory.
2. Each Party shall accord to covered investments treatment no less [favorable] than that it accords, in like circumstances, to investments in its territory of investors of any other Party or non-Party with respect to the establishment, acquisition, expansion, management, conduct, operation, and sale or other disposition of investments.
3. For greater certainty, the treatment referred to in paragraphs 1 and 2 does not encompass any international dispute resolution procedures or mechanisms under other existing or future international agreements.[29]

A footnote in the clause made clear that –

> [f]or greater certainty, whether the treatment is accorded in "like circumstances" under this Article depends on the totality of the circumstances. Those include whether the relevant treatment distinguishes between investors or investments based on legitimate public welfare objectives.[30]

2 A More Balanced Approach to MFN Interpretation

In summary, there is a clear trend in the direction of narrower formulation of MFN clauses in modern IIAs. As stated in above Chapter 1, the MFN clause plays a key role in the current Rebalancing Era for states' effective investment policies. Accordingly, the MFN clause has increasingly been formulated in a more cautious, specific, and detailed manner in more recent IIAs.[31] The most effective manner in which to achieve this may be to exclude the dispute settlement mechanism from the scope of the MFN clause with direct and explicit language.

The emphasis placed on the term "in like circumstances" is helpful, but only in relation to alleged *de facto* violations of MFN obligations. Therefore, it will

---

29 RCEP (n 25).

30 RCEP (n 25).

31 See, for example, UNCTAD, 'The Changing IIA Landscape: New Treaties and Recent Policy Developments' IIA Issues Note No. 1 (2020). UNCTAD/DIAE/PCB/INF/2020/4.

be more helpful when combined with a paragraph that constrains MFN treatment to discriminatory measures that have actually taken place.

Replacing the MFN clause with a soft commitment using terms such as "endeavor to" helps to retrieve States' regulatory power, but a total omission of the MFN clause perhaps goes too far to do so.

In any event, a restrictive formulation of MFN clauses implies an effort by contracting states to exercise state power as treatymakers and to limit the discretion of tribunals in an attempt to strike a new balance between the regulatory interests of host states and the interests of foreign investors.

Overall, responsible interpretation by tribunals and courts is required. Specifically, tribunals should decide cases according to the treaty text, and interpret MFN clauses based on a proper application of the interpretive principles of international law instead of through reliance on presumptions. In this regard, a case-by-case examination of the specific texts of an MFN clause is necessary. In addition, other essential parameters should also be given due consideration by tribunals. These include the role of state consent as the foundation for the jurisdiction of international adjudication, the current Rebalancing Era that calls for a more balanced investor-state prospect, and finally, as has been emphasized throughout this book, it is essential that interpretive principles such as *ejusdem generis* be respected by tribunals.

Bibliography

Monographs and Books

Adams CK and Trent WP, *A History of the United States* (Boston: Allyn & Bacon, 1903).

Amerasinghe CF, *Local Remedies in International Law* (2nd edn, Cambridge University Press 2004).

Arthur N, *A Concise History of the Law of Nations* (1st edn, Macmillan 1947).

Bottini G (ed), 'Admissibility in International Investment Law', *Admissibility of Shareholder Claims under Investment Treaties* (Cambridge University Press 2020).

Brownlie I, *Principles of Public International Law* (7th ed, Oxford University Press 2008).

Collins D, *An Introduction to International Investment Law* (Cambridge University Press 2017).

Cheng B, *General Principles of Law as Applied by International Courts and Tribunals* (Digitally printed 1st pbk version, Cambridge University Press 2006).

Curzon G, *Multilateral Commercial Diplomacy: The General Agreement on Tariffs and Trade, and Its Impact on National Commercial Policies and Techniques* (Michael Joseph ed, 1965).

Dolzer R, *Bilateral Investment Treaties* (M Nijhoff 1995).

Dolzer R and Myers T, 'After Tecmed: Most-Favored-Nation Clauses in Investment Protection Agreements' (2004) 19 ICSID Review 49.

Dolzer R and Schreuer C, *Principles of International Investment Law* (Second edition, Oxford University Press 2012).

Dugan CF and others, *Investor-State Arbitration* (Oxford University Press 2012).

Fellmeth AX and Horwitz M, *Guide to Latin in International Law* (Oxford University Press 2009).

Fontanelli F, *Jurisdiction and Admissibility in Investment Arbitration* (BRILL 2018).

Gardiner RK, *Treaty Interpretation* (Oxford University Press 2008).

Gazzini T, *Interpretation of International Investment Treaties* (First Edition, Hart Publishing 2016).

Gilpin R and Gilpin JM, *The Political Economy of International Relations* (Princeton University Press 1987).

Graham EM, *Fighting the Wrong Enemy: Antiglobal Activists and Multinational Enterprises* (Institute for International Economics 2000).

Gribnau HLM (ed), *Legal Protection against Discriminatory Tax Legislation: The Struggle for Equality in European Tax Law* (Kluwer Law International 2003).

Hanink DM, *The International Economy: A Geographical Perspective* (J Wiley 1994).

Hawkins HC, *Commercial Treaties and Agreements: Principles and Practice* (Rinehart 1951).

Hoekman BM and Kostecki MM, *The Political Economy of the World Trading System: The WTO and Beyond* (2nd edn, Oxford University Press 2001).

Jackson JH, *The World Trade Organization: Constitution and Jurisprudence* (Royal Institute of International Affairs 1998).

Jones G, *Multinationals and Global Capitalism: From the Nineteenth to the Twenty-First Century* (Oxford University Press 2005).

Jorun B, *Treaty Shopping in International Investment Law* (Oxford University Press 2016).

Lord M, *The Law of Treaties* (Oxford University Press 1986).

Mantilla Blanco S, *Full Protection and Security in International Investment Law* (Springer International Publishing 2019).

Marboe I, *Calculation of Compensation and Damages in International Investment Law* (Second edition, Oxford University Press 2017).

McDougal MS and others, *The Interpretation of International Agreements and World Public Order: Principles of Content and Procedure* (M Nijhoff Publishers 1994).

Mitchell AD, Sornarajah M and Voon T (eds), *Good Faith and International Economic Law* (First edition, Oxford University Press 2015).

Moore JB, *A Digest of International Law*, vol 5 (United States Government Printing Office 1906).

Nafziger EW, *The Economics of Developing Countries* (3rd ed, Prentice Hall 1997).

Neal L, Cameron RE and Cameron RE, *A Concise Economic History of the World: From Paleolithic Times to the Present* (5th edn, Oxford University Press 2016).

Newcombe AP and Paradell L, *Law and Practice of Investment Treaties: Standards of Treatment* (Wolters Kluwer Law & Business 2009).

Oppenheim L and others, *Oppenheim's International Law. Vol. 1: Peace* (9th ed, Longman 1996).

Reinisch A and Schreuer C, *International Protection of Investments: The Substantive Standards* (1st edn, Cambridge University Press 2020).

Roe T, Happold M and Dingemans J, *Settlement of Investment Disputes under the Energy Charter Treaty* (Cambridge University Press 2011).

Salacuse JW, *The Law of Investment Treaties* (Second edition, Oxford University Press 2015).

Sasse JP, *An Economic Analysis of Bilateral Investment Treaties* (Gabler 2011).

Schill S, *The Multilateralization of International Investment Law* (Cambridge University Press 2009).

Schreuer C, *Consent to Arbitration* (Oxford University Press 2008).

Schreuer C, *The ICSID Convention: A Commentary: A Commentary on the Convention on the Settlement of Investment Disputes between States and Nationals of Other States* (Cambridge Univ Press 2009).

Schreuer C and Weiniger M, *A Doctrine of Precedent?* (Oxford University Press 2008).

Sharmin T, *Application of Most-Favoured-Nation Clauses by Investor-State Arbitral Tribunals: Implications for the Developing Countries* (Springer 2020).

Shea DR, *The Calvo Clause* (NED-New edition, University of Minnesota Press 1955).

Sinclair SI, *The Vienna Convention on the Law of Treaties* (Melland Schill Monographs in International Law 1984).

Sornarajah M, *The International Law on Foreign Investment* (4th edn, Cambridge University Press 2017).

Steingruber AM, *Consent in International Arbitration* (1st ed, Oxford University Press 2012).

Subedi SP, *International Investment Law: Reconciling Policy and Principle* (Fourth edition, Hart Publishing 2020).

Suleimenova M, *MFN Standard as Substantive Treatment* (Nomos Verlagsgesellschaft mbH & Co KG 2019).

Synder RC, *The Most-Favored-Nation Clause: An Analysis with Particular Reference to Recent Treaty Practice and Tariffs* (King's Crown Press 1948).

Van Damme I, *Treaty Interpretation by the WTO Appellate Body* (Oxford University Press 2009).

Vandevelde KJ, *Bilateral Investment Treaties: History, Policy, and Interpretation* (Oxford University Press 2010).

Viner J, *International Economics* (Glencoe, III, Free Press 1951).

Viñuales JE and Langer MJ, 'Foreign Investment in Latin America: Between Love and Hatred' in Claude Auroi and Aline Helg, *Latin America 1810–2010* (Imperial College Press 2011).

Waibel M, 'International Investment Law and Treaty Interpretation' in Rainer Hofmann and Christian J Tams (eds), *International Investment Law and General International Law* (Nomos Verlagsgesellschaft mbH & Co KG 2011).

Wang G, *International Investment Law: A Chinese Perspective* (1st edn, Routledge 2014).

Weeramantry JR, *Treaty Interpretation in Investment Arbitration* (1st ed, Oxford University Press 2012).

Wilson RR, *US Commercial Treaties and International Law* (Hauser Press 1960).

Articles, Contributions to Compilations, Working Papers, and Reports (All Online Materials Last Accessed 20 April 2022)

Accominotti O and Flandreau M, 'Bilateral Treaties and the Most-Favored-Nation Clause: The Myth of Trade Liberalization in the Nineteenth Century' (2008) 60 World Politics 147.

Acconci P, 'Most-Favoured-Nation Treatment', *The Oxford Handbook of International Investment Law* (Peter T Muchlinski, Federico Ortino, Christoph Schreuer, Oxford University Press 2008).

Alvarez GA and Park WW, 'The New Face of Investment Arbitration: NAFTA Chapter 11' (2003) 28 Yale Journal of International Law 3.

Andreeva Y, 'Interpreting Consent to Arbitration as a Unilateral Act of State: A Case Against Conventions' (2011) 27 Arbitration International 129.

'Analysis: Heemsen v. Venezuela Tribunal Refused to Find Jurisdiction on the Basis of an MFN Clause, and Held That German-Venezuela BIT Does Not Cover Dual Nationals with Citizenship of the Host State' (*Investment Arbitration Reporter*, 22 November 2019).

Ascensio H, 'Abuse of Process in International Investment Arbitration' (2014) 13 Chinese Journal of International Law 763.

Agrawal K, 'Bilateral Investment Treaties: A Developing History' (2016) 7 Jindal Global Law Review 175.

Baldwin R, '21st Century Regionalism: Filling the Gap between 21st Century Trade and 20th Century Trade Rules' (2011) World Trade Organization, Economic Research and Statistics Division 39.

Bairoch P and Burke S, 'European Trade Policy, 1815–1914' in Peter Mathias and Sidney Pollard (eds), *The Cambridge Economic History of Europe from the Decline of the Roman Empire: The Industrial Economies: The Development of Economic and Social Policies*, vol 8 (Cambridge University Press 1989).

Banifatemi Y, 'The Emerging Jurisprudence on the Most-Favoured-Nation Treatment in Investment Arbitration,' in Andrea K Bjorklund, Ian A. Laird, Sergey Ripinsky (eds), *Investment Treaty Law: Current Issues III* (BIICL, 2009) 241.

Batifort S and Heath JB, 'The New Debate on the Interpretation of MFN Clauses in Investment Treaties: Putting the Brakes on Multilateralization' (2018) 111 American Journal of International Law 873.

Bemis SF, 'A Diplomatic History of the United States. Pp. Xii, 881.' (1936) New York: Henry Holt & Co.

Bhala R, 'The Myth About Stare Decisis and International Trade Law (Part One of a Trilogy)' 14 American University International Law Review 845.

Bianchi A, 'Textual Interpretation and (International) Law Reading: The Myth of (in) Determinacy and the Genealogy of Meaning' in Pieter HF Bekker, Rudolf Dolzer and Michael Waibel (eds), *Making Transnational Law Work in the Global Economy* (Cambridge University Press 2010).

Bjorklund AK, 'Private Rights and Public International Law: Why Competition Among International Economic Law Tribunals Is Not Working' (2008) 59 Hastings Law Journal 64.

Blyschak PM, 'State Consent, Investor Interests and the Future of Investment Arbitration: Reanalyzing the Jurisdiction of Investor-State Tribunals in Hard Cases.' (2009) 9 Asper Review of International Business and Trade Law 99.

Bonnitcha J and Brewin S, 'Compensation Under Investment Treaties' (2020) IISD Best Practices Series 44.

Brabandere ED, '"Importing" Consent to ICSID Arbitration? A Critical Appraisal of the Decision of the ICSID Arbitral Tribunal In' 8.

Brauch MD, 'Exhaustion of Local Remedies in International Investment Law' (2017) 33 International Institute for Sustainable Development.

Brower CN and Steven LA, 'Who Then Should Judge? Developing the International Rule of Law under NAFTA Chapter 11' 2 Chicago Journal of International Law 193.

Brower II CH, 'Investor-State Disputes under NAFTA: The Empire Strikes Back' (2001) 40 Colombia Journal of Transnational Law 43.

Brower II CH, 'Mitsubishi, Investor-State Arbitration, and the Law of State Immunity' (2005) 20 American University International Law Review 907.

Burgess M, 'The World Bank – the East Asian Miracle' (1995) 18 Asian Studies Review 147.

Caron DD and Shirlow E, 'Most Favoured Nation Treatment – Substantive Protection in Investment Law' (2015) King's College London Law School Research Paper No. 2015–23.

Chalamish E, 'The Future of Bilateral Investment Treaties: A de Facto Multilateral Agreement?' (2009) 34 Brooklyn Journal of International Law 304.

Chen A, 'Queries to the Recent ICSID Decision on Jurisdiction Upon the Case of Tza Yap Shum v. Republic of Peru: Should China–Peru BIT 1994 Be Applied to Hong Kong SAR Under the "One Country, Two Systems" Policy?' in An Chen (ed), *The Voice from China: An CHEN on International Economic Law* (Springer Berlin Heidelberg 2013).

Chinen MA, 'The Standard of Compensation for Takings' (2016) 25 Minnesota Journal of International Law 335.

Chukwumerije O, 'Interpreting Most-Favoured-Nation Clauses in Investment Treaty Arbitrations' (2007) 8 The Journal of World Investment & Trade 597.

Cole T, 'The Boundaries of Most Favored Nation Treatment in International Investment Law' (2012) 33 Michigan Journal of International Law 537.

Commission J, 'Precedent in Investment Treaty Arbitration-A Citation Analysis of a Developing Jurisprudence' (2007) 24 129.

Coutain B, 'The Unconditional Most-Favored-Nation Clause and the Maintenance of the Liberal Trade Regime in the Postwar 1870s' (2009) 63 International Organization 139.

Coyle JF, 'The Treaty of Friendship, Commerce and Navigation in the Modem Era' (2012) 51 Colombia Journal of Transnational Law.

Crawford J, 'The ILC's Articles on Responsibility of States for Internationally Wrongful Acts: A Retrospect' (2002) 96 American Journal of International Law 874.

Crawford J-A and Kotschwar B, 'Investment Provisions in Preferential Trade Agreements: Evolution and Current Trends' (2018) WTO Staff Working Paper ERSD-2018-14.

D'Amato A, 'Good faith',in Rudolf. Bernhardt (ed), *Encyclopedia of Public International Law* (1984) 7, 107.

De Brabandere E, '"Good Faith," "Abuse of Process" and the Initiation of Investment Treaty Claims' (2012) 3 Journal of International Dispute Settlement 609.

De Brabandere E, 'Importing Consent to ICSID Arbitration? A Critical Appraisal of Garanti Koza v. Turkmenistan' (2014) 5 Investment Treaty News (ITN), IISD.

Delamue GR, 'ICSID Arbitration Proceedings: Practical Aspects' (1985) 5 Pace Law Review 28.

Delaney J, 'The Use of MFN Clauses in ICSID Arbitrations' (2009) 21 National Law School of India Review 125.

Dolzer R and Myers T, 'After Tecmed: Most-Favored-Nation Clauses in Investment Protection Agreements' (2004) 19 ICSID Review 49.

Douglas Z, 'The Hybrid Foundations of Investment Treaty Arbitration' (2004) 74 British Yearbook of International Law 151.

Douglas Z, 'The MFN Clause in Investment Arbitration: Treaty Interpretation Off the Rails' (2011) 2 Journal of International Dispute Settlement 97.

Dumberry P, *The Fair and Equitable Treatment Standard: A Guide to NAFTA Case Law on Article 1105* (Kluwer Law International 2013).

Dumberry P, 'Has the Fair and Equitable Treatment Standard Become a Rule of Customary International Law?' (2016) 8 Journal of International Dispute Settlement 155.

Dumberry P, 'Shopping for a Better Deal: The Use of MFN Clauses to Get "Better" Fair and Equitable Treatment Protection' (2016) 1 Arbitration International.

Dumberry P, 'The Importation of the FET Standard through MFN Clauses: An Empirical Study of BITs' (2016) 32 ICSID Review – Foreign Investment Law Journal 116.

Dumberry P, 'The Importation of "Better" Fair and Equitable Treatment Standard Protection Through MFN Clauses: An Analysis of NAFTA Article 1103"' (2017) 1 Transnational Dispute Management (TDM).

Egli G, 'Don't Get Bit: Addressing ICSID's Inconsistent Application of Most-Favored-Nation Clauses to Dispute Resolution Provisions Comment' (2006) 34 Pepperdine Law Review 1045.

Eliasson N, 'Investor-State Arbitration and Chinese Investors Recent Developments in Light of the Decision on Jurisdiction in the Case Mr. Tza Yap Shum v. the Republic of Peru' (2009) 2 Contemporary Asia Arbitration Journal 347.

Fauchald OK, 'The Legal Reasoning of ICSID Tribunals – An Empirical Analysis' (2008) 19 European Journal of International Law 301.

Faya Rodriguez A, 'The Most-Favored-Nation Clause in International Investment: Agreements A Tool for Treaty Shopping?' (2008) 25 Journal of International Arbitration 89.

Fietta S, 'Most Favoured Nation Treatment and Dispute Resolution under Bilateral Investment Treaties: A Turning Point?' (2005) 8 International Arbitration Law Review 131.

Figueiredo RC de, 'Evolving Meaning: The Interpretation of Investment Treaties and Temporal Variations' (*Kluwer Arbitration Blog*, 2015).

Fitzmaurice, GG, 'The Law and Procedure of the International Court of Justice 1951–4: Treaty Interpretation and Other Treaty Points' (1957) 33 British Yearbook of International Law 203.

Foster AT, 'Some Aspects of the Commercial Treaty Program of the United States – Past and Present' (1946) 11 Law and Contemporary Problems 647.

Fox H, 'States and the Undertaking to Arbitrate' (1988) 37 The International and Comparative Law Quarterly 1.

Gaffney JP, 'Abuse of Process in Investment Treaty Arbitration' (2010) 11 Journal of World Investment & Trade 515.

Gaillard E, 'Abuse of Process in International Arbitration' (2017) 32 ICSID Review 17.

Garcia-Mora MR, 'The Calvo Clause in Latin American Constitutions and International Law' (1950) 33 Marquette Law Review 16.

Gazzini T and Tanzi A, 'Handle with Care: Umbrella Clauses and MFN Treatment in Investment Arbitration' (2013) 14 The Journal of World Investment & Trade 978.

Giorgio S, 'Bilateral Treaties and Multilateral Instruments on Investment Protection' Vol 269, in: Collected Courses of the Hague Academy of International Law.

Grigera Naón HA, 'The Settlement of Investment Disputes between States and Private Parties' (2000) 1 The Journal of World Investment & Trade 59.

Guillaume G, 'The Use of Precedent by International Judges and Arbitrators' (2011) 2 Journal of International Dispute Settlement 5.

Guzman A, 'Why LDCs Sign Treaties That Hurt Them: Explaining the Popularity of Bilateral Investment Treaties' (1998) 38 Virginia Journal of International Law 639.

Hanotiau B, 'Consent to Arbitration: Do We Share a Common Vision?' (2011) 27 Arbitration International 539.

Hornbeck SK, 'The Most-Favored-Nation Clause' (1909) 3 The American Journal of International Law 797.

Huiping C, 'The Expansion of Jurisdiction by ICSID Tribunals: Approaches, Reasons and Damages' (2011) 12 The Journal of World Investment & Trade 671.

IISD, 'IISD Best Practices Series: The Most-Favoured-Nation Clause in Investment Treaties: The Most-Favoured-Nation Clause in Investment Treaties' (2017).

International Law Commission, 'Draft Articles on Most-Favoured-Nation Clauses with Commentaries', (1978) *Yearbook of the International Law Commission*, vol II:2.

International Law Commission (ILC), *Second Report on Subsequent Agreements and Subsequent Practice in Relation to the Interpretation of Treaties*, United Nations General Assembly A/CN.4/671.

Irwin DA, 'Multilateral and Bilateral Trade Policies in the World Trading System: An Historical Perspective' in Arvind Panagariya and Jaime De Melo (eds), *New Dimensions in Regional Integration* (Cambridge University Press 1993).

Ishikawa T, 'Keeping Interpretation in Investment Treaty Arbitration 'on Track': The Role of States Parties' (2014) 11 Transnational Dispute Management (TDM) 115.

Jiménez De Aréchaga E, 'International Law in the Past Third of a Century (Volume 159) Collected Courses of the Hague Academy Intl L 1'.

Joubin-Bret A, 'Admission and Establishment in the Context of Investment Protection*' in August Reinisch (ed), *Standards of Investment Protection* (Oxford University Press 2008).

Jr HW, 'Modern Treaties of Friendship, Commerce and Navigation' (1958) 42 Minnesota Law Review. 1491.

Kalnina I, 'White Industries v. The Republic of India: A Tale of Treaty Shopping and Second Chances' (2012) 9 Transnational Dispute Management (TDM).

Kamil Yasseen M, 'L'interprétation Des Traités d'après La Convention de Vienne Sur Le Droit Des Traités (Volume 151)' (1976) Collected Courses of the Hague Academy of International Law.

Kaufmann-Kohler G, 'Arbitral Precedent: Dream, Necessity or Excuse?: The 2006 Freshfields Lecture' (2007) 23 Arbitration International 357.

Kaufmann-Kohler G, 'Interpretive Powers of the Free Trade Commission and the Rule of Law' in Emmanuel Gaillard and Frédéric Bachand (eds), *Fifteen Years of NAFTA Chapter 11 Arbitration* (JurisNet, LLC 2011).

Klabbers J, 'International Legal Histories: The Declining Importance of Travaux Préparatoires in Treaty Interpretation?' (2003) 50 Netherlands International Law Review 267.

Kline JM and Ludema RD, 'Building a Multilateral Framework for Investment: Comparing the Development of Trade and Investment Accords' (1997) 6 Transnational Corporations.

Kotzur M, 'Good Faith (Bona Fides)' (2009) Max Planck Encyclopedia of Public International Law.

Kurtz J, 'The Most Favoured Nation Standard and Foreign Investment: An Uneasy Fit?' (2005) 5 The Journal of World Investment & Trade 861.

Kurtz J, 'The Delicate Extension of Most-Favoured-Nation Treatment to Foreign Investors: Maffezini v. Kingdom of Spain' in Todd Weiler (ed), *International investment law and arbitration: leading cases from the ICSID, NAFTA, bilateral treaties and customary international law*.

Law Commission of India, 'Analysis of the 2015 Draft Model Indian Bilateral Investment Treaty' (Report No. 260, August 2015)'.

League of Nations, 'Report and Proceedings of the World Economic Conference, Vol 1 (League of Nations 1927) Document C.20.M.14.1929.II'.

Lim CL, 'Is the Umbrella Clause Not Just Another Treaty Clause?' in CL Lim (ed), *Alternative Visions of the International Law on Foreign Investment: Essays in Honour of Muthucumaraswamy Sornarajah* (Cambridge University Press 2016).

Linderfalk U, 'Is the Hierarchical Structure of Article 31 and 32 of the Vienna Convention Real or Not? Interpreting the Rules of Interpretation' (2007) 54 Netherlands International Law Review 133.

Magntorn J, 'Most Favoured Nation Clauses in EU Trade Agreements: One More Hurdle for UK Negotiators' (2018) UK Trade Policy Observatory Briefing Paper 25.

Matiation S, 'Arbitration with Two Twists: Loewen v. United States and Free Trade Commission Intervention in NAFTA Chapter 11 Disputes' (2003) University of Pennsylvania Journal of International Law 451.

Maupin JA, 'MFN-Based Jurisdiction in Investor-State Arbitration: Is There Any Hope for a Consistent Approach?' (2011) 14 Journal of International Economic Law 157.

Mbengue MM, 'Rules of Interpretation (Article 32 of the Vienna Convention on the Law of Treaties)' (2016) 31 ICSID Review 388.

McLachlan C, 'Investment Treaties and General International Law' (2008) 57 The International and Comparative Law Quarterly 361.

Merrills JG, 'Two Approaches to Treaty Interpretation' (1971) 4 The Australian Year Book of International Law 55.

Michael EC and Losari JJ, 'Which Is to Be the Master? Extra-Arbitral Interpretative Procedures for IIAs' in Jean E Kalicki and Anna Joubin-Bret (eds), *Reshaping the Investor-State Dispute Settlement System* (Brill | Nijhoff 2015).

Mortenson JD, 'The Travaux of Travaux: Is the Vienna Convention Hostile to Drafting History?' (2013) 107 The American Journal of International Law 780.

Myers DP, Charles G and Malloy WM, 'Treaties, Conventions, International Acts, Protocols and Agreements between the United States of America and Other Powers, 1776–1909.' United States Government Printing Office 1910.

Newcombe A, 'Canada's New Model Foreign Investment Protection Agreement' (2005) 1 Transnational Dispute Management, TDM.

OECD, 'National Treatment for Foreign-Controlled Enterprises, Including Adhering Country Exceptions to National Treatment'.

OECD, 'Most-Favoured-Nation Treatment in International Investment Law' (OECD 2004) OECD Working Papers on International Investment WP 2004/02.

Orrego Vicuna F, 'Reports of Maffezini's Demise Have Been Greatly Exaggerated' (2012) 3 Journal of International Dispute Settlement 299.

Paparinskis M, 'MFN Clauses and Substantive Treatment: A Law of Treaties Perspective of the "Conventional Wisdom"' (2018) 112 American Journal of International Law (Unbound) 49.

Paulsson J, 'Arbitration Without Privity' (1995) 10 ICSID Review – Foreign Investment Law Journal 232.

Paulsson J, 'Jurisdiction and Admissibility' (2005) Global Reflection on International Law, Commerce and Dispute Resolution 601.

Pauwelyn J and Elsig M, 'The Politics of Treaty Interpretation: Variations and Explanations Across International Tribunals' in Jeffery C Dunoff and Mark A Pollack (eds), *Interdisciplinary Perspectives on International Law and International Relations : The State of the Art* (New York: Cambridge University Press 2011).

Pérez-Aznar F, 'The Use of Most-Favoured-Nation Clauses to Import Substantive Treaty Provisions in International Investment Agreements' (2017) 20 Journal of International Economic Law 777.

Polanco Lazo R, 'The No of Tokyo Revisited: Or How Developed Countries Learned to Start Worrying and Love the Calvo Doctrine' (2015) 30 ICSID Review 172.

Polanco R, *The Return of the Home State to Investor-State Disputes: Bringing Back Diplomatic Protection?* (1st edn, Cambridge University Press 2019).

Potestà M, 'The Interpretation of Consent to ICSID Arbitration Contained in Domestic Investment Laws' (2011) 27 Arbitration International 149.

Radi Y, 'The Application of the Most-Favoured-Nation Clause to the Dispute Settlement Provisions of Bilateral Investment Treaties: Domesticating the "Trojan Horse"' (2007) 18 European Journal of International Law 757.

Radović R, 'Between Rights and Remedies: The Access to Investment Treaty Arbitration as a Substantive Right of Foreign Investors' (2019) 10 Journal of International Dispute Settlement 42.

Reinert S and Fredona R, 'Merchants and the Origins of Capitalism' (2017) Harvard Business School BGIE Unit Working Paper No. 18–021.

Reinhold S, 'Good Faith in International Law' (2013) 2 UCL Jurisprudence Review 40.

Reinisch A, 'Jurisdiction and Admissibility in International Investment Law' (2017) 16 The Law & Practice of International Courts and Tribunals 21.

Reisman WM, 'The Breakdown of the Control Mechanism in ICSID Arbitration' (1989) 1989 Duke Law Journal 739.

Robbins J, 'The Emergence Of Positive Obligations In Bilateral Investment Treaties' (2006) 13 University of Miami International and Comparative Law Review 72.

Roberts A, 'Power and Persuasion in Investment Treaty Interpretation: The Dual Role of States' 104 The American Journal of International Law 47.

Rubins N and Nazarov A, 'Investment Treaties and the Russian Federation: Baiting the Bear?' (2008) 9 Business Law International 100.

Rubins N, 'The Arbitral Innovations of Recent U.S. Free Trade Agreements: Two Steps Forward, One Step Back' (2003) International Business Law Journal 865.

Salacuse JW, 'BIT by BIT: The Growth of Bilateral Investment Treaties and Their Impact on Foreign Investment in Developing Countries' (1990) 24 The International Lawyer 655.

Schill SW, 'Maffezini v. Plama: Reflections on the Jurisprudential Schism in the Application of Most-Favored-Nation Clauses to Matters of Dispute Settlement' in Meg Kinnear and others (eds), *Building international investment law: the first 50 years of ICSID* (Alphen aan den Rijn: Wolters Kluwer 2016).

Schill SW, 'MFN Clauses as Bilateral Commitments to Multilateralism: A Reply to Simon Batifort and J. Benton Heath' (2017) 111 American Journal of International Law 914.

Schill SW and Bray HL, 'Good Faith Limitations on Protected Investments and Corporate Structuring' in Andrew D Mitchell, M Sornarajah and Tania Voon (eds), *Good Faith and International Economic Law* (Oxford University Press 2015).

Schreuer C, 'Calvo's Grandchildren: The Return of Local Remedies in Investment Arbitration' (2005) 4 The Law & Practice of International Courts and Tribunals 1.

Schreuer C, 'Fair and Equitable Treatment in Arbitral Practice' (2005) 6 The Journal of World Investment & Trade 32.

Schreuer C, 'Diversity And Harmonization Of Treaty Interpretation In Investment Arbitration' in Malgosia Fitzmaurice, Olufemi Elias and Panos Merkouris (eds), *Treaty Interpretation and the Vienna Convention on the Law of Treaties: 30 Years on* (Brill | Nijhoff 2010).

Schwarzenberger G, 'The Most-Favoured-Nation Standard in British State Practice' (1945) 22 British Yearbook on International Law 96.

Setser VG, 'Did Americans Originate the Conditional Most-Favored-Nation Clause?' (1933) 5 The Journal of Modern History 319.

Shen W, 'The Good, the Bad or the Ugly? A Critique of the Decision on Jurisdiction and Competence in Tza Yap Shum v. The Republic of Peru' (2011) 10 Chinese Journal of International Law 55.

Shenkin TS, 'Trade-Related Investment Measures in Bilateral Investment Treaties and the Gatt: Moving Toward a Multilateral Investment Treaty Comment' (1993) 55 University of Pittsburgh Law Review 541.

Sinclair AC, 'The Origins of the Umbrella Clause in the International Law of Investment Protection' (2014) 20 Arbitration International 411.

Smith RF, 'Latin America, The United States and the European Powers, 1830–1930' in Leslie Bethell (ed), *The Cambridge History of Latin America: Volume 4: c.1870 to 1930*, vol 4 (Cambridge University Press 1986).

Söderlund C and Burova E, 'Is There Such a Thing as Admissibility in Investment Arbitration?' (2018) 33 ICSID Review – Foreign Investment Law Journal.

Sohn LB and Baxter RR, 'Responsibility of States for Injuries to the Economic Interests of Aliens: II. Draft Convention on the International Responsibility of States for Injuries to Aliens' (1961) 55 American Journal of International Law 545.

Stefan K, 'The International Law Commission and role of subsequent practice as a means of interpretation under Articles 31 and 32 VCLT' (2018) Zoom-in 46 Questions of International Law Journal 5–18.

Stern B, 'ICSID Arbitration and the State's Increasingly Remote Consent: Apropos the Maffezini Case' in Steve Charnovitz, Debra P Steger and Peter Van den Bossche (eds), *Law in the Service of Human Dignity* (1st edn, Cambridge University Press 2005).

Teitelbaum R, 'Who's Afraid of Maffezini? Recent Developments in the Interpretation of Most Favored Nation Clauses' (2005) 22 Journal of International Arbitration 225.

Thomas JC, 'Investor-State Arbitration under NAFTA Chapter 11' (2000) 37 Canadian Yearbook of international Law/Annuaire canadien de droit international 99.

Thulasidhass P, 'Most-Favoured-Nation Treatment in International Investment Law: Ascertaining the Limits through Interpretative Principles' (2015) 7 Amsterdam Law Forum 3.

Titi C, 'The Timing of Treaty Party Interpretations' (2020) *EJIL: Talk!*.

Titi C, The Right to Regulate in International Investment Law (Revisited), *International and Comparative Law Research Center* 2022.

Titi C, 'The Evolution of Substantive Investment Protections in Recent Trade and Investment Treaties' (2018) Inter-American Development Bank (IDB) & International Centre for Trade and Sustainable Development (ICTSD) – RTA Exchange Think Piece.

Tschofen F, 'Multilateral Approaches to the Treatment of Foreign Investment' (1992) 7 ICSID Review – Foreign Investment Law Journal 384.

UNCTAD, 'International Investment Instruments: A Compendium' vol XIV UNCTAD/DITE/4 (1996).

UNCTAD, 'World Investment Report 2005: Transnational Corporations and the Internationalization of R&D' (United Nations 2005).

UNCTAD, 'World Investment Report 2010: Investing in a Low-Carbon Economy' (United Nations 2010).

UNCTAD, Word Investment Report 2015: Reforming International Investment Governance (United Nations 2015).

UNCTAD, 1 IIA Issues Note: Taking Stock of IIA Reform, UNCTAD/WEB/DIAE/PCB/2016/1 (2016).

UNCTAD (ed), *Most-Favoured-Nation Treatment: A Sequel* (United Nations 2010).

UNCTAD, 'Recent Developments in International Investment Agreements' IIA Monitor No. 2 (2005). UNCTAD/WEB/ITE/IIT/2005/1.

UNCTAD, 'The Changing IIA Landscape: New Treaties and Recent Policy Developments' IIA Issues Note No. 1, 2020. UNCTAD/DIAE/PCB/INF/2020/4.

United Nations, 'Yearbook of the International Law Commission, Documents of the Second Part of the Seventeenth Session and of the Eighteenth Session Including the Reports of the Commission to the General Assembly' (1967) Vol II A/CN.4/SER. A/1966/Add. 1.

International Court of Justice, 'Competence of Assembly Regarding Admission to the United Nations (Advisory Opinion) [1950] ICJ Rep 4'.

Ustor E, 'First Report on the Most-Favoured-Nation Clause, Special Rapporteur', Vol II Yearbook of the International Law Commission, (1969).

Valasek MJ and Menard EA, 'Impregilo SpA v Argentine Republic and Hochtief AG v The Argentine Republic: Making Sense of Dissents: The Jurisprudence Inconstante of the MFN Clause' (2012) 27 ICSID Review 21.

Valenti M, 'The Most Favoured Nation Clause in BITs as a Basis for Jurisdiction in Foreign Investor – Host State Arbitration' (2008) 24 Arbitration International 447.

Valenti M, 'The Scope of an Investment Treaty Dispute Resolution Clause: It Is Not Just a Question of Interpretation' (2013) 29 Arbitration International 243.

Van Damme I, 'Treaty Interpretation by the WTO Appellate Body'(2010) 21 The European Journal of International Law 3 620.

Vandevelde KJ, 'The BIT Program: A Fifteen-Year Appraisal' (1988) 82 Proceedings of the ASIL Annual Meeting 532.

Vandevelde KJ, 'Sustainable Liberalism and the International Investment Regime' (1998) 19 Michigan Journal of International Law 373.

Vandevelde KJ, 'A Brief History of International Investment Agreements' in Karl p. Sauvant and Lisa Sachs (eds), *The Effect of Treaties on Foreign Direct Investment: Bilateral Investment Treaties, Double Taxation Treaties, and Investment Flows* (Oxford University Press 2009).

Vandevelde KJ, 'Bilateral Investment Treaties in the Mid-1990s.' UNCTAD/ITE/IIT/7 (United Nations 1998).

Verloren van Themaat P, *The Changing Structure of International Economic Law: A Contribution of Legal History, of Comparative Law, and of General Legal Theory to the Debate on a New International Economic Order* (Nijhoff: TMC Asser Institute 1981).

Vesel S, 'Clearing a Path Through a Tangled Jurisprudence: Most-Favored-Nation Clauses and Dispute Settlement Provisions in Bilateral Investment Treaties' (2007) 32 Yale Journal of International Law.

Waibel M, 'Demystifying the Art of Interpretation' (2011) 22 European Journal of International Law 571.

Waibel M, 'Investment Arbitration: Jurisdiction and Admissibility' (2014) University of Cambridge Faculty of Law Research Paper No. 9/2014.

Wälde TW and Kolo A, 'Coverage of Taxation Under Modern Investment Treaties' in Peter Muchlinski, Ortino Federico and Christoph Schreuer (eds), *The Oxford Handbook of International Investment Law* (Oxford University Press 2008).

Wang G, 'Consent in Investor-State Arbitration: A Critical Analysis' (2014) 13 Chinese Journal of International Law 335.

Wang H and Wang L, 'China's Bilateral Investment Treaties' in Julien Chaisse, Leïla Choukroune and Sufian Jusoh (eds), *Handbook of International Investment Law and Policy* (Springer Singapore 2020).

WTO, The GATT Years: From Havana to Marrakesh: https://www.wto.org/english/thewto_e/whatis_e/tif_e/fact4_e.htm.

Yee WP, 'Protecting Parties' Reasonable Expectations: A General Principle of Good Faith' (2001) 1 Oxford University Commonwealth Law Journal 195.

Youngquist EV, 'United States Commercial Treaties: Their Role in Foreign Economic Policy' (1967) 2 Studies in L aw and Economic Development 72.

Zelikow P, Cameron MA and Tomlin BW, 'The Making of NAFTA: How the Deal Was Done' (2001) 80 Foreign Affairs 176.

Ziegler A, 'Most-Favoured-Nation (MFN) Treatment' in Reinisch August (ed), *Standards of Investment Protection* (Oxford University Press 2008).

Ziegler AR, 'Is the MFN Principle in International Investment Law Ripe for Multilateralization or Codification?' in Andrea K Bjorklund and August Reinisch (eds), *International Investment Law and Soft Law* (2012).

Table of Materials

Table of Treaties and Related Instruments

Charter of Economic Rights and Duties of States, General Assembly Resolution. 3281(Xxix), UN GAOR, 29th Sess., Supp. No. 31 (1974) 50

International Law Commission, 'Draft Articles on Responsibility of States for Internationally Wrongful Acts, with Commentaries' (2001) Yearbook of the International Law Commission, Vol II, Part Two

Agreement between the Government of the United Kingdom of Great Britain and Northern Ireland and the Government of the Republic of Albania for the Promotion and Protection of Investments (Albania – UK BIT), signed on 30 March 1994, entered into force on 30 August 1995

Treaty between the Government of the United States of America and the Government of the Republic of Albania concerning the Encouragement and Reciprocal Protection of Investment, with Annex and Protocol (Albania – U.S. BIT), signed on 11 January 1995, entered into force on 4 January 1998

Agreement between the Government of the Italian Republic and the Government of the People's Democratic Republic of Algeria on the Promotion and Protection of Investments (Algeria – Italy BIT), signed on 18 May 1991, entered into force on 26 November 1993, termined on 26 November 2013

Treaty between the Argentine Republic and the Republic of Chile on Promotion and Reciprocal Protection of Investments (Argentina-Chile BIT), signed on 2 August 1991, entry into force on 1 January 1995

Agreement between the Government of the Republic of Ecuador and the Government of the Argentine Republic to Reciprocal Promotion and Protection of Investments (Argentina – Ecuador BIT), signed on 18 February 1994, entered into force on 1 November 1995, terminated on 18 May 2018

Agreement between the Government of the Republic of France and the Government of the Republic of Argentina for the Encouragement and the Protection of Mutual Investments (Argentina-France BIT), signed on 3 July 1991, entry into force on 3 March 1993

Agreement between the Argentine Republic and the Italian Republic on Investment Promotion and Protection (Argentina – Italy BIT), signed on 22 May 1990, entered into force 14 October 1993

Agreement between the Government of the United Kingdom of Great Britain and Northern Ireland and the Government of the Republic of Argentina for the Promotion and Protection of Investments (Argentina – UK BIT), signed on 11 December 1990, entered into force on 19 February 1993

Treaty between United States of America and the Argentine Republic Concerning the Reciprocal Encouragement and Protection of Investment (Argentina-US BIT), signed on 14 November 1991, entry into force on 20 October 1994

Treaty between the Federal Republic of Germany and the Republic of Argentina on Promotion and Reciprocal Protection of Investments (Argentina-Germany BIT), signed on 9 April 1991, entry into force on 8 November 1993

Agreement between the Argentine Republic and the Kingdom of Spain on the Reciprocal Promotion and Protection of Investments (Argentina-Spain BIT), signed on 3 October 1991, entered into force on 28 September 1992

Agreement between the Government of Australia and the Government of the Republic of India on the Promotion and Protection of Investments (AustraliaIndia BIT), signed on 26 February 1999, entry into force on 4 May 2000

Australia-Indonesia Comprehensive Economic Partnership Agreement (IA-CEPA), signed on 4 March 2019, entered into force on 5 July 2020

Agreement between Australia and Uruguay on the Promotion and Protection of Investments (Australia – Uruguay BIT), signed on 3 September 2001, entered into force on 12 December 2002

Agreement between the United Mexican States and the Republic of Austria on the Promotion and Protection of Investments (Austria-Mexico BIT), signed on 29 June 1998, entered into force on 26 March 2001

Agreement between the Government of the Republic of Croatia and the Government of the Republic of Azerbaijan on the Promotion and Reciprocal Protection of Investments (Azerbaijan-Croatia BIT), signed on 2 October 2007, entered into force on 30 May 2008

Agreement between the Government of Barbados and the Government of the Republic of Venezuela for the Promotion and Protection of Investments (Barbados-Venezuela BIT), signed on 15 July 1994, entered into force on 31 October 1995

Agreement between the Governments of the Kingdom of Belgium and the Grand Duchy of Luxembourg and the Government of the Union of Soviet Socialist Republics concerning the encouragement and reciprocal protection of investments (Belgium/Luxembourg – USSR BIT), signed on 9 February 1989, entered into force on 18 August 1991

Belgium-Luxembourg Economic Union Model BIT

Cooperation and Investment Facilitation Agreement between the Federative Republic Brazil and the Republic of Colombia (Brazil – Colombia BIT), signed on 9 October 2015

Investment Cooperation and Facilitation Treaty between the Federative Republic of Brazil and the Republic of India (Brazil-India BIT), signed on 25 January 2020

Treaty concerning the Reciprocal Encouragement and Protection of Investments between the Federal Republic of Germany and Bulgaria (Germany-Bulgaria BIT), signed on 12 April 1986, entered into force on 10 March 1988, terminated on 9 June 2021

Agreement between the Government of the Republic of Finland and the Government of the Republic of Bulgaria on the Promotion and Protection of Investments (Bulgaria-Finland BIT), signed on 3 October 1997, entry into force on 16 April 1999

Agreement between the Government of Canada and the Government of Burkina Faso for the Promotion and Protection of Investments (Canada-Burkina Faso BIT), signed on 20 April 2015, entered into force on 11 October 2017

Agreement on Economic and Technical Cooperation between the Government of the Kingdom of the Netherlands and the Government of the Federal Republic of Cameroon (Cameroon-Netherlands BIT), signed on 6 July 1965, entered into force on 7 May 1966

Canada Model Foreign Investment Agreement, 2004

Canada Model Foreign Investment Protection Agreement, 2021

Agreement Between the Government of Canada and the Government of the People's Republic of China for the Promotion and Reciprocal Protection of Investments (Canada-China BIT), signed on 9 September 2012, entered into force on 1 October 2014

Agreement between Canada and the Czech Republic for the Promotion and Protection of Investments (Canada-Czech BIT), signed on 6 May 2009, entered into force on 22 January 2012

Agreement between the Government of Canada and the Government of the Republic of Venezuela for the Promotion and Protection of Investments (Canada-Venezuela BIT), signed on 1 July 1996, entered into force on 28 January 1998

Agreement between the Government of the Republic of Chile and the Government of the Republic of Croatia on the Reciprocal Promotion and Protection of Investments (Chile – Croatia BIT), signed on 28 November 1994, entered into force on 15 June 1996

Agreement between the Government of the Republic of Chile and the Government of the Kingdom of Denmark concerning the Promotion and Reciprocal Protection of Investments (Chile – Denmark BIT), signed on 28 May 1993, entered into force on 3 November 1995

Agreement between the Government of Malaysia and the Government of the Republic of Chile on Investment Promotion and Protection (Chile – Malaysia BIT), signed on 11 November 1992, entered into force on 4 August 1995

Agreement between the Government of the People's Republic of Chjna and the Government of the Lao People's Democratic Republic Concerning the Encouragement and Reciprocal Protection of Investments (China – Laos BIT), signed on 31 January 1993, entered into force on 1 June 1993

Agreement between the Government of the Republic of Peru and the Government of the People's Republic of China concerning the Encouragement and Reciprocal

Protection of Investments (China-Peru BIT), signed on 9 June 1994, entered into force on 1 February 1995

Agreement between the Government of the People's Republic of China and the Government of the Republic of Yemen on the Promotion and Reciprocal Protection of Investments (China-Yemen BIT), signed on 16 February 1998, entered into force on 10 April 2002

Agreement on encouragement and reciprocal protection of investments between the Government of the People's Republic of China and the Government of the Kingdom of the Netherlands (China-Netherlands BIT), signed on 1 February 1987, entered into force on 1 August 2004

Free Trade Agreement between the Government of New Zealand and the Government of the People's Republic of China (China-New Zealand FTA), signed on 7 April 2008, entered into force on 1 October 2008

Agreement for the Promotion and Protection of Investments between the Republic of Colombia and the Republic of India (China-India BIT), signed on 10 November 2009

Colombia – United States Trade Promotion Agreement (Colombia-U.S. TPA), signed on 22 November 2006, entered into force on 15 May 2012

Comprehensive and Progressive Agreement for Trans-Pacific Partnership (CPTPP), signed on 8 March 2018, entered into force on 30 December 2018

Convention on the Settlement of Investment Disputes between States and Nationals of Other States (ICSID Convention), entered into force on 14 October, 1966

Agreement on Economic and Technical Cooperation between the Government of the Kingdom of the Netherlands and the Government of the Republic of the Ivory Coast (Côte d'Ivoire-Netherlands BIT), signed on 26 April 1965, entered into force on 8 September 1966

Agreement between the Government of the people's Republic of Bulgaria and the Government of the Republic of Cyprus on Mutual Encouragement and Protection of Investments (Cyprus-Bulgaria BIT), signed on 18 May 1988, entered into force on 13 December 2020

Agreement between the Government of the United Kingdom of Great Britain and Northern Ireland and the Government of the Czech and Slovak Federal Republic for the Promotion and Protection of Investments with Protocol (Czech Republic – UK BIT), signed on 10 July 1990, entered into force on 26 October 1992

Dutch-U.S. Treaty of Amity and Commerce, 1782

Treaty between the United States of America and the Republic of Ecuador concerning the Encouragement and Reciprocal Protection of Investment (Ecuador – U.S. BIT), signed on 27 August 1993, entered into force on 11 May 1997, terminated on 18 May 2018

Energy Charter Treaty (ECT), 1994

Treaty Between the Government of the United States of America and the Government of the Republic of Estonia for the Encouragement and Reciprocal Protection of Investment (Estonia – U.S. BIT), signed on 19 April 1994, entered into force on 16 February 1997

Agreement between the European Union and Japan for an Economic Partnership (EU-Japan EPA), signed on 17 July 2018, entered into force on 1 February 2019

EU-Canada Comprehensive Economic and Trade Agreement (CETA), signed on 30 October 2016, came into force on September 21, 2017

European Convention on Human Rights, signed on 4 November 1950, entered into force on 3 September 1953

Investment Protection Agreement between the European Union and its Member States, of the One Part, and the Republic of Singapore, of the Other Part (EU-Singapore Free Trade Agreement), signed on 15 October 2018

Free Trade Agreement between the European Union and the Republic of Korea (EU-South Korea FTA), signed on 6 October 2010, entered into force on 1 July 2011

Investment Protection Agreement between the European Union and its Member States, of the One Part, and the Socialist Republic of Viet Nam, of the Other Part (EU-Viet Nam FTA), signed on 30 June 2019

Agreement between the Government of the French Republic and the Government of the Republic of Moldova on the Reciprocal Encouragement and Protection of Investments (France-Moldova, Republic BIT), signed on 8 September 1997, entered into force on 3 November 1999

Agreement between the Government of the French Republic and the Government of Turkmenistan on the Reciprocal Encouragement and Protection of Investments (France – Turkmenistan BIT), signed on 28 April 1994, entered into force on 2 May 1996

Free Trade Agreement between Central America, the Dominican Republic and the United States of America (CAFTA), signed on 5 August 2004, entered into force on 1 January 2009

Germany Model Foreign Investment Agreement, 2008

Treaty between the Federal Republic of Germany and the Republic of Guatemala for the Reciprocal Promotion and Protection of Capital Investments (Germany-Guatemala BIT), signed on 17 October 2003, entered into force on 29 October 2006

Agreement between the Arab Republic of Egypt and the Federal Republic of Germany concerning the Encoumgement and Reciprocal Protection of lnvestments (Germany-Egypt BIT), signed on 16 June 2005, entered into force on 22 November 2009

Agreement between the Federal Republic of Germany and the Islamic Republic of Iran on Reciprocal Promotion and Protection of Investments (Germany-Iran BIT), signed on 17 August 2002, entered into force on 23 June 2005

Agreement between the Federal Republic of Germany and the Hashemite Kingdom of Jordan concerning the Encouragement and Reciprocal Protection of Investments (Germany-Jordan BIT), signed on 13 November 2007, entered into force on 28 August 2010

Treaty between the Federal Republic of Germany and the Republic of Liberia for the promotion and reciprocal protection of investments (Germany-Liberia BIT), signed on 12 December 1961, entered into force on 22 October 1967

Aqreement Between the Federal Republic of Germany and the Federation of Malaya Concerning the Promotion and Reciprocal Protection of Investments (Germany-Malaysia BIT), signed on 22 December 1960, entered into force on 6 July 1963

Agreement between the Socialist Federative Republic of Yugoslavia and the Federal Republic of Reciprocal Protection and Pormotion of Investments (Germany-Montenegro BIT), signed on 10 July 1989, entered into force on 25 October 1990

Treaty between the Federal Republic of Germany and the Sultanate of Oman concerning the Encouragement and Reciprocal Protection of Investments (Germany-Oman BIT), signed on 30 May 2007, entered into force on 4 April 2010

Treaty between the Federal Republic of Germany and Pakistan for the Promotion and Protection of Investments (Germany-Pakistan BIT), signed on 25 November 1959, entered into force on 28 April 1962

Treaty between the Kingdom of Thailand and the Federal Republic of Germany concerning the Encouragement and Reciprocal Protection of Investments (Germany-Thailand BIT), signed on 24 June 2002, entered into force on 20 October 2004

Treaty between the Federal Republic of Germany and the Republic of Trinidad and Tobago concerning the Encouragement and Reciprocal Protection of Investments (Germany-Trinidad and Tobago BIT), signed on 8 September 2006, entered into force on 17 April 2010

Treaty between the Federal Republic of Germany and the Republic of Turkey concerning the Reciprocal Promotion and Reciprocal Protection of Investments (Germany-Turkey BIT), signed on 20 June 1962, entered into force on 16 December 1965

Agreement between the Government of the United Mexican States and the Government of the Hellenic Republic on the Promotion and Reciprocal Protection of Investments (Greece-Mexico BIT), signed on 30 November 2000, entered into force on 26 September 2002

Agreement between the Government of the Hellenic Republic and the Government of the Republic of Uzbekistan on the Promotion and Reciprocal Protection of Investments (Greece-Uzbekistan BIT), signed on 1 April 1997, entered into force on 8 May 1998

Agreement between the Government of the United IGngdom of Great Britain and Northern Ireland and the Government of the Republic of Honduras for the Promotion and Protection of Investments (Honduras-UK BIT), signed on 7 December 1993, entered into force on 8 March 1995

Agreement between the Government of the Hong Kong Special Administrative Region of the People's Republic of China and the Government of the United Mexican States for the Promotion and Reciprocal Protection of Investments (Hong Kong-Mexico BIT), signed on 23 January 2020, entered into force on 16 June 2021

Treaty between the Republic of Belarus and the Republic of India on Investments (India-Belarus BIT), signed on 24 September 2018

Bilateral Investment Treaty between the Government of the Kyrgyz Republic and the Government of the Republic of India (India-Kyrgzstan BIT), signed on 14 June 2019

Agreement between the Government of the Republic of Mauritius and the Government of the Republic of India for the Promotion and Protection of Investments (India – Mauritius BIT), signed on 4 September 1998, entered into force on 20 June 2000, terminated on 22 March 2017

Agreement between the Government of the United Kingdom of Great Britain and Northern Ireland and the Government of the Republic of Indonesia for the Promotion and Protection of Investments (Indonesia-United Kingdom BIT), signed on 27 April 1976, entered into force on 24 March 1977

Iran-Denmark Treaty of Friendship, Establishment and Commerce, 1934

Italy Model Bilateral Investment Treaty, 2021

Agreement between the Government of the State of Israel and the Government of the Republic of Uzbekistan for the Promotion and Reciprocal Protection of Investments (Israel-Uzbekistan BIT), signed on 4 July 1994, entered into force on 18 February 1997

Agreement between the Government of the Hashemite Kingdom of Jordan and the Government of the Italian Republic on the Promotion and Protection of Investments (Italy-Jordan BIT), signed on 21 July 1996, entered into force on 17 January 2000, terminated on 17 Jaunary 2015

Agreement between Japan and the People's Republic of Bangladesh concerning the Promotion and Protection of Investment (Japan-Bangladesh BIT), signed on 10 November 1998, entered into force on 25 August 1999

Agreement between Japan and the Arab Republic of Egypt concerning the Encouragement and Reciprocal Protection of Investment (Japan-Egypt BIT), signed on 28 January 1977, entered into force on 14 January 1978

Agreement between the Government of Japan and the Government of the Independent State of Papua New Guinea for the Promotion and Protection of Investment (Japan-Papua New Guinea BIT), signed on 26 April 2011, entered into force on 17 January 2014

Agreement Between the Hasihemite Kingdom of Jordan and the Republic of Turkey Concerning the Reciprocal Promotion and Protection of Investments (Jordan-Turkey BIT), signed on 2 August 1993, entered into force on 23 January 2006

Agreement on the Promotion and Reciprocal Protection of Investments between the Kingdom of Spain and the United Mexican States (Mexico-Spain BIT), signed on 23 June 1995, entered into force on 18 December 1996, terminated on 3 April 2008

Agreement between the Government of the United Kingdom of Great Britain and Northern Ireland and the Government of the Republic of Moldova for the Promotion and Protection of Investments (Moldova-United Kingdom BIT), signed on 19 March 1996, entered into force on 30 July 1998

Treaty between the United States of America and the Republic of Moldova concerning the Encouragement and Reciprocal Protection of Investment (Moldova-U.S. BIT), signed on 21 April 1993, entered into force on 26 November 1994

Agreement between the Government of the Russian Federation and the Government of Mongolia on Promotion and Mutual Protection of Investments (Mongolia-Russia BIT), signed on 29 November 1995, entered into force on 26 February 2006

Agreement on encouragement and reciprocal protection of investments between the Kingdom of the Netherlands and the Czech and Slovak Federal Republic (Netherlands-Slovakia BIT), signed on 29 April 1991, entered into force on 1 October 1992, terminated on 31 March 2021

Agreement between the Government of the Kingdom of the Netherlands and the Government of the Republic of Indonesia on Promotion and Protection of Investment (Netherlands-Indonesia BIT), signed on 6 April 1994, entered into force on 1 July 1995, terminated on 30 June 2015

Agreement between the Kingdom of the Netherlands and the Democratic Socialist Republic of Sri Lanka for the promotion and protection of investments (Netherlands-Sri Lanka BIT), signed on 26 April 1984, 1 May 1985

Convention between the Government of the Kingdom of the Netherlands and the Government of the Tunisia Republic concerning the Encouragement of Capital Investment and the Protection of Property (Netherlands-Tunisia BIT), signed on 23 May 1963, entered into force on 19 December 1964, terminated on 1 August 1999

Agreement on encouragement and reciprocal protection of investments between the Kingdom of the Netherlands and the Union of Soviet Socialist Republics (Netherlands-USSR BIT), signed on 5 October 1989, entered into forced on 20 July 1991

North American Free Trade Agreement between Canada, The United States and Mexico (NAFTA), signed on 17 December 1992, entered into force on 1 January 1994, terminated on 1 July 2020

Nijmegen Treaty concluded between the Netherlands and Sweden, 1679

Agreement on encouragement and reciprocal protection of investments between the Government of the Kingdom of the Netherlands and the Macedonian Government (North Macedonia-Netherlands BIT), signed on 7 July 1998, entered into force on 1 June 1999

Agreement between the Government of the Kingdom of Norway and the Government of the Republic of Hungary on the Promotion and Reciprocal Protection of Investments (Norway-Hungary BIT), signed on 8 April 1991, entered into force on 4 December 1992

OECD Model Tax Convention on Income and on Capital, 2017

Agreement on Promotion, Protection and Guarantee of Investments amongst the Member States of the Organization of the Islamic Conference (OIC Investment Agreement), signed on 5 June 1981, entered into force on February 1988

Agreement between the Islamic Republic of Pakistan and the Republic of Turkey concerning the Reciprocal Promotion and Protection of Investments (Pakistan-Turkey BIT), signed on 16 March 1995, entered into force on 3 September 1997

Regional Comprehensive Economic Partnership (RCEP), signed on 15 November 2020, entered into force on 1 January 2022

Agreement for the Promotion and Reciprocal Protection of Investments between Spain and the Russian Federation (Spain-Russia BIT), signed on 26 October 1990, entered into force on 28 November 1991

Free Trade Agreement between the Republic of Korea and the Republics of Central America (South Korea-Central America FTA), signed on 21 February 2018, entered into force on 1 March 2021

Agreement on the Promotion and Reciprocal Protection of Investments between the Kingdom of Spain and the United Mexican States (Spain-Mexico BIT), signed on 10 October 2006, entered into force on 3 April 2008

Agreement between the Government of the United Kingdom of Great Britain and Northern Ireland and the Government of the Democratic Socialist Republic of Sri Lanka for the Promotion and Protection of Investments (Sri Lanka-UK BIT), signed on 13 November 1980, entered into force on 18 December 1980

Slovakia Model Bilateral Investment Treaty, 2016

Statute of the International Court of Justice, 1945

Agreement on Free Trade and Economic Partnership between the Swiss Confederation and Japan (Switzerland-Japan EPA), signed on 19 February 2009, entered into force on 1 September 2009

Agreement between the Swiss Federal Council and the Government of Turkmenistan on the Promotion and Reciprocal Protection of Investments (Switzerland-Turkmenistan BIT), signed on 15 May 2008, entered into force on 2 April 2009

Treaty on investment protection and cooperation between the Swiss Confederation and the Republic of Congo-Brazzaville (Switzerland-Congo BIT), signed on 18 October 1962, entered into force on 11 July 1964

Treaty on investment protection and cooperation between the Swiss Confederation and the Republic of Côte d'Ivoire (Switzerland-Côte d'Ivoire BIT), signed on 26 June 1962, entered into force on 18 January 1962

Agreement on Trade, Investments and technical Cooperation between the Swiss Confederation and the Republic of Guinea (Switzerland-Guinea BIT), signed on 26 April 1962, entered into force on 29 July 1963

Trade, Investment and Technical Cooperation Agreement between the Swiss Confederation and the Republic of Niger (Switzerland-Niger BIT), signed on 28 March 1962, entered into force on 17 November 1962

Agreement between the Government of the Swiss Confederation and the Government of the United Republic of Tanzania on the reciprocal encouragement and protection of investments (Switzerland-Tanzania BIT), signed on 3 May 1965, entered into force on 16 September 1965, terminated on 6 April 2006

The General Treaty between France and Great Britain of 1856

The Treaty of Commerce and Navigation between France and Spain of 1861

Trans-Pacific Partnership Agreement (TPP), signed on 4 February 2016

Treaty of Amity, Commerce and Navigation concluded between Denmark and Liberia, 1860

Treaty of Commerce and Navigation entered into between the United States and Prussia 1828

Agreement between the Republic of Turkey and Turkmenistan concerning the Reciprocal Promotion and Protection of Investments (Turkey-Turkmenistan BIT), 2 May 1992, entered into force 13 March 1997

Agreement between the Government of the United Arab Emirates and the Government of Turkmenistan for the Promotion and Reciprocal Protection of Investments (Turkmenistan- United Arab Emirates BIT), signed on 9 June 1998, entered into force on 24 November 1999

Agreement between the Government of the United Kingdom of Great Britain and Northern Ireland and the Government of Turkmenistan for the Promotion and Protection of Investments (Turkmenistan-United Kingdom BIT), signed on 9 February 1995, entered into force on 9 February 1995

Agreement between the Government of the United Kingdom of Great Britain and Northern Ireland and the Government of the Republic of Venezuela for the Promotion and Proteetion of Investments (UK-Venezuela BIT) signed on 15 March 1995, entered into force on 1 August 1996

Agreement between the Government of the United Kingdom of Great Britain and Northern Ireland and the Government of the United Mexican States for the Promotion and Reciprocal Protection of Investments (UK-Mexico BIT), signed on 12 May 2006, entered into force on 25 July 2007

UK-Persia Treaty, 1857

UK-Persia Treaty, 1903

Agreement between the Government of the United Kingdom of Great Britain and Northern Ireland and the Government of the Union of Soviet Socialist Republics for the Promotion and Reciprocal Protection of Investments (UK-USSR BIT), signed on 6 April 1989, entered into force on 3 July 1991

UN Model Double Taxation Convention between Developed and Developing Countries (1999 Revision)

UNCITRAL Arbitration Rules, 2010

Free Trade Agreement between Australia and the United States of America (U.S.-Australia FTA), signed on 18 May 2004, entered into force on 1 January 2005

Free Trade Agreement Between the Government of Chile and the Government of the United States of America (U.S.-Chile FTA), signed on 6 June 2003, entered into force on 1 January 2004

Treaty between the United States of America and Jamaica concerning the Reciprocal Encouragement and Protection of Investment (U.S.-Jamaica BIT), signed on 4 February 1994, entered into force on 7 March 1997

Agreement between the United States of America and the Hashemite Kingdom of Jordan on the Establishment of a Free Trade Area (U.S.-Jordan FTA), signed on 24 November 2000, entered into force on 17 December 2001

Free Trade Agreement between the United States and the Republic of Korea (U.S.-Korea FTA), signed on 30 June 2007, entered into force on 15 March 2012

Agreement between the United States of America, the United Mexican States, and Canada (USMCA), signed on 30 November 2018, entered into force on 1 July 2020

U.S. Model Foreign Investment Agreement, 2004

The Treaty between the United States of America and the Republic of Panama concerning the Treatment and Protection of Investments (U.S.-Panama BIT), signed on 27 October 1982, entered into force on 30 May 1991

Free Trade Agreement between Singapore and the United States of America (U.S.-Singapore FTA), signed on 6 May 2003, entered into force on 1 January 2004

Vienna Convention on the Law of Treaties (VCLT), 1969

Table of Other Primary Legal Sources

NAFTA Free Trade Commission, 'NAFTA Notes of Interpretation of Certain Chapter 11 Provisions on July 31, 2001'

'The McKinley Tariff of 1890 | US House of Representatives: History, Art & Archives' <https://history.house.gov/Historical-Highlights/1851-1900/The-McKinley-Tariff-of-1890/> accessed 23 June 2021

UN General Assembly, 'Declaration on the Establishment of a New International Economic Order' (1974)

United Nations Conference on the Law of Treaties, First and Second Session, Documents of the Conference (1971) A/ CONF.39/1 L/Add.2

Table of Investor-State Dispute Settlement (ISDS) Cases

Abaclat and others v Argentina, Decision on Jurisdiction and Admissibility dated 4 August 2011, ICSID Case No. ARB/07/5

ADF *Group Inc v United States, Award dated 9 January 2003,* ICSID Case No. ARB(AF)/00/1

ADF *Group Inc v US, Investor's Reply to the US Counter-Memorial on Competence and Liability dated 28 January 2002,* ICSID Case No. ARB(AF)/00/1

Aguas del Tunari SA *v Republic of Bolivia, Decision on Jurisdiction dated 21 October 2005,* ICSID Case No. ARB/02/3

Amco Asia Corporation and others v Republic of Indonesia, Decision on Jurisdiction dated 25 September 1983, ICSID Case No. ARB/81/1

Anglo-Iranian Oil Co (United Kingdom v Iran), International Court of Justice

Apotex Holdings Inc and Apotex Inc v United States of America (III), Award dated 25 August 2014, ICSID Case No. ARB(AF)/12/1

Application of the International Convention on the Elimination of All Forms of Racial Discrimination (Georgia v Russian Federation), Judgment of 1 April 2011, International Court of Justice

Asian Agricultural Products Ltd (AAPL) v Republic of Sri Lanka, Award dated 27 June 1990, ICSID Case No. ARB/87/3

ATA *Construction, Industrial and Trading Company v Hashemite Kingdom of Jordan, Award dated 18 May 2010,* ICSID Case No. ARB/08/2

Austrian Airlines v The Slovak Republic, Final Award dated 9 October 2009, UNCITRAL Arbitration

Autobuses Urbanos del Sur SA, *Teinver* SA *and Transportes de Cercanías* SA *v Argentine Republic,* ICSID Case No. ARB/09/1

AWG *Group Ltd v The Argentine Republic, Decision on Jurisdiction dated 3 August 2006,* UNCITRAL Arbitration

Bayindir Insaat Turizm Ticaret Ve Sanayi AS *v Islamic Republic of Pakistan, Award dated 27 August 2009,* ICSID Case No. ARB/03/29

Beijing Urban Construction Group Co Ltd v Republic of Yemen, Decision on Jurisdiction dated 31 May 2017, ICSID Case No. ARB/14/30

Canadian Cattlemen v US, Award on Jurisdiction dated 28 January 2008, UNCITRAL Arbitration

Cargill, Incorporated v United Mexican States, Award dated 18 September 2009, ICSID Case No. ARB(AF)/05/2 167

Case concerning Armed Activities on the Territory of the Congo (New Application: 2002) (Democratic Republic of the Congo v Rwanda), Judgment of 3 February 2006

Case Concerning The Factory At Chorzów (Germany v Republic of Poland), Claim for Indemnity, Merits, Judgment, PCIJ *Series A No 17, 1928*

CC/Devas (Mauritius) Ltd, Devas Employees Mauritius Private Limited, and Telcom Devas Mauritius Limited v Republic of India, Award on Jurisdiction and Merits dated 25 July 2016, PCA Case No. 2013–09

CME Czech Republic BV v The Czech Republic, Final Award dated 14 March 2003, UNCITRAL Arbitration

CMS Gas Transmission Company v The Argentine Republic, Award dated 12 May 2005, ICSID Case No. ARB/01/8

Christian Doutremepuich and Antoine Doutremepuich v Mauritius, Award on Jurisdiction dated 23 August 2019, PCA Case No. 2018–37

Convial Callao SA and CCI – Compañía de Concesiones de Infraestructura SA v Republic of Peru, ICSID Case No. ARB/10/2

Crompton (Chemtura) Corp v Government of Canada, Award dated 2 August 2010, UNCITRAL Arbitration

Daimler Financial Services AG v Argentine Republic, Award Dated 22 August 2012, ICSID Case No. ARB/05/1

Deana Anthone, Neil Ayervais, Douglas Black and others v United Mexican States, Partial Award dated 19 July 2019, ICSID Case No. ARB(AF)/16/3

EDF International SA, SAUR International SA and León Participaciones Argentinas SA v Argentine Republic, Award dated 11 June 2012 ICSID Case No. ARB/03/23

Emilio Agustín Maffezini v The Kingdom of Spain, Decision of the Tribunal on Objections to Jurisdiction dated 25 January 2000, ICSID Case No. ARB/97/7

Enrique Heemsen and Jorge Heemsen v Bolivarian Republic of Venezuela, award on Jurisdiction dated 29 October 2019, PCA Case No. 2017–18

Ethyl Corporation v The Government of Canada, Award on Jurisdiction dated 24 June 1998, UNCITRAL Arbitration

European American Investment Bank AG v The Slovak Republic, Award on Jurisdiction dated 22 October 2012, PCA Case No. 2010–17

Fisheries Jurisdiction (Spain v Canada), Judgment of 4 December 1998, International Court of Justice

Franck Charles Arif v Republic of Moldova, Award 8 April 2013, ICSID Case No. ARB/11/23

Frontier Dispute (Burkina Faso v Republic of Mali), Judgment of 22 December 1986, International Court of Justice

Garanti Koza LLP v Turkmenistan, Decision on the Objection to Jurisdiction for Lack of Consent dated 3 July 2013, ICSID Case No. ARB/11/20 271

Gas Natural SDG, SA v Argentine Republic, Decision of the Tribunal on Preliminary Questions on Jurisdiction dated 17 June 2005, ICSID Case No. ARB/03/10 31

GEA Group Aktiengesellschaft v Ukraine, Award dated 31 March 2011, ICSID Case No. ARB/08/16 101

Glamis Gold, Ltd v United States, Award dated 8 June 2009, UNCITRAL Arbitration

Grand River Enterprises Six Nations, Ltd, et.al v United States of America, Award dated 12 January 2011, UNCITRAL Arbitration

Hesham Talaat M Al-Warraq v The Republic of Indonesia, Final Award dated 15 December 2014, UNCITRAL Arbitration

HICEE BV v The Slovak Republic, Partial Award dated 23 May 2011, PCA Case No. 2009–11

Hochtief Aktiengesellschaft v Argentine Republic, Decision on Jurisdiction dated 24 October 2011, ICSID Case No. ARB/07/31

İçkale İnşaat Limited Şirketi v Turkmenistan, Award dated 8 March 2016, ICSID Case No. ARB/10/24

ICS Inspection and Control Services Limited v The Argentine Republic (I), Award on Jurisdiction dated 10 February 2012, PCA Case No. 2010–9

Impregilo S.pA v Argentine Republic (I), Award dated 21 June 2011, ICSID Case No. ARB/07/17

Impregilo S.pA v Islamic Republic of Pakistan (II), Decision on Jurisdiction dated 22 April 2005, ICSID Case No. ARB/03/3

International Thunderbird Gaming Corporation v The United Mexican States, Award dated 26 January 2006, UNCITRAL Arbitration

Kimberly-Clark BVBA, Kimberly-Clark Dutch Holdings, B.V., Kimberly-Clark S.L.U. v Bolivarian Republic of Venezuela, Award dated November 5, 2021 ICSID Case No. ARB(AF)/18/3)

Krederi Ltd. v Ukraine, Award dated 2 July 2018, ICSID Case No. ARB/14/17

LESI, S.pA and Astaldi, S.pA v People's Democratic Republic of Algeria, Awarded dated 12 November 2008, ICSID Case No. ARB/05/3

Loewen Group, Inc and Raymond L Loewen v United States of America, Award dated 26 June 2003, ICSID Case No.ARB(AF)/98/3 71

Marvin Feldman v Mexico, Award dated 16 December 2002, ICSID Case No. ARB(AF)/99/1

MCI Power Group, LC and New Turbine, Inc v Republic of Ecuador, Award dated 31 July 2007, ICSID Case No. ARB/03/6

Mercer International v Canada, Award dated 6 March 2018, ICSID Case No. ARB(AF)/12/3

Merrill & Ring Forestry LP v Canada, award dated 31 March 2010, ICSID Case No. UNCT/07/1

Mesa Power Group LLC v Government of Canada, Award dated 24 March 2016, PCA Case No. 2012–17

Metal-Tech Ltd v Republic of Uzbekistan, Award dated 4 October 2013, ICSID Case No. ARB/10/3

Methanex v United States, final Award of the Tribunal on Jurisdiction and Merits dated 3 August 2005, UNCITRAL Arbitration

MNSS BV and Recupero Credito Acciaio NV v Montenegro Award on 4 May 2016, ICSID Case No. ARB(AF)/12/8

MTD Equity Sdn Bhd and MTD Chile SA v Chile, Award dated 25 May 2004, ICSID Case No. ARB/01/7

Muhammet Çap & Sehil Inşaat Endustri ve Ticaret Ltd. Sti. v Turkmenistan, Award dated 4 May 2021, ICSID Case No. ARB/12/6

National Grid PLC v The Argentine Republic, Decision on Jurisdiction dated June 2006, UNCITRAL Arbitration

Nuclear Tests (Australia v France), Judgment of 20 December 1974, International Court of Justice

Occidental Exploration and Production Company v Republic of Ecuador (1), Award dated 1 July 2004 UNCITRL, LCIA Case No. UN3467

Oil Platforms (Islamic Republic of Iran v United States of America), Judgment on Preliminary Objections dated 12 December 1996, Separate Opinion by Judge Higgins, International Court of Justice

OJSC "Tatneft" v Ukraine, Award on the Merits dated 29 July 2014, UNCITRAL Arbitration

Parkerings-Compagniet AS v Republic of Lithuania, Award dated 11 September 2007, ICSID No. ARB/05/8

Phoenix Action Ltd v Czech Republic, Award dated15 April 2009, ICSID Case No. ARB/06/5

Plama Consortium Limited v Republic of Bulgaria, Decision on Jurisdictio dated 8 February 2005, ICSID Case No. ARB/03/24

Pope & Talbot v Government of Canada, Award in Respect of Damages dated 31 May 2002, UNCITRAL Arbitration

Pope&talbot v Canada, Award on the Merits of Phase 2 dated 10 April 2001, UNCITRAL Arbitration

Pulp Mills on the River Uruguay (Argentina v Uruguay), Judgment of 20 April 2010, International Court of Justice

Quasar de Valores SICAV SA, Orgor de Valores SICAV SA, GBI 9000 SICAV SA and ALOS 34 SL v The Russian Federation, Award on Preliminary Objections dated 20 March 2009, SCC Case No. 24/2007

Rafat Ali Rizvi v Republic of Indonesia, Award dated 17 July 2013, ICSID Case No. ARB/11/13

Rights of Nationals of the United States of America in Morocco (France v United States of America), International Court of Justice

RosInvest Co UK Ltd v Russia, Award on Jurisdiction dated October 2007, SCC Case No. 079/2005

Rumeli Telekom AS and Telsim Mobil Telekomunikasyon Hizmetleri AS v Republic of Kazakhstan, Award dated 29 July 2008, ICSID Case No. ARB/05/16

Rusoro Mining Ltd v Bolivarian Republic of Venezuela, Award dated 22 August 2016, ICSID Case No. ARB(AF)/12/5

Saint-Gobain Performance Plastics Europe v Bolivarian Republic of Venezuela, Decision on Liability and the Principles of Quantum dated 30 December 2016, ICSID Case No. ARB/12/13

Salini Costruttori S.pA and Italstrade S.pA v Hashemite Kingdom of Jordan, Decision on Jurisdiction dated 9 November 2004, ICSID Case No. ARB/02/13

Sanum Investments v Lao People's Democratic Republic (I) (PCA Case No 2013–13), Award on Jurisdiction dated 13 December 2013, PCA Case No. 2013–13

SD Myers, Inc v Government of Canada, Final Award dated 30 December 2002

Sergei Paushok, CJSC Golden East Company and CJSC Vostokneftegaz Company v The Government of Mongolia, Award on Jurisdiction and Liability dated 28 April 2011, UNCITRAL Arbitration

SGS Société Générale de Surveillance SA v Philippines, Decision on Jurisdiction, 29 January 2004, ICSID Case No. ARB/02/6

Siemens AG v The Argentine Republic, Decision on Jurisdiction dated 3 August 2004, ICSID Case No. ARB/02/8

Société Générale in respect of DR Energy Holdings Limited and Empresa Distribuidora de Electricidad del Este, SA v The Dominican Republic, LCIA Case No. UN 7927

Southern Pacific Properties (Middle East) Limited v Arab Republic of Egypt, Decision on Jurisdiction II, 27th April 1985, ICSID No. ARB/84/3

SS Lotus (France v Turkey), Judgment No 9 dated 7 September 1927, PCIJ Series A No. 10

ST-AD GmbH v The Republic of Bulgaria, Award on Jurisdiction dated 18 July 2013, PCA Case No. 2011–06

Suez, Sociedad General de Aguas de Barcelona, SA and Interagua Servicios Integrales de Agua, SA v Argentine Republic, Decision on Jurisdiction dated 16 May 2006, ICSID Case No. ARB/03/17

Técnicas Medioambientales Tecmed, SA v The United Mexican States, Award dated 29 May 2003, ICSID Case No. ARB (AF)/00/2

Telefónica SA v Argentine Republic, Decision on Jurisdiction dated 25 May 2006, ICSID Case No. ARB/03/20

Telenor Mobile Communications AS v Republic of Hungary, Award dated 13 September 2016, ICSID Case No. ARB/04/15

The Ambatielos Claim (Greece, United Kingdom of Great Britain and Northern Ireland), Arbitral Award of the Commission of Arbitration in 1956, Reports of International Arbitral Awards

Tza Yap Shum v Republic of Peru, Decision on Jurisdiction and Competence dated 19 June 2009, ICSID Case No. ARB/07/6

United Parcel Service of America Inc v Government of Canada, Award on the Merits dated 24 May 2007, ICSID Case No. UNCT/02/1

UP and C.D Holding Internationale v Hungary, Decision on Jurisdiction dated 3 March 2016, ICSID Case No.ARB/13/35

Vannessa Ventures Ltd v Bolivarian Republic of Venezuela, Decision on jurisdiction dated 22 August 2008, ICSID Case No. ARB(AF)/04/6

Venezuela US, SRL v Bolivarian Republic of Venezuela, Interim Award on Jurisdiction dated 26 July 2016, PCA Case No. 2013–34

Vento Motorcycles, Inc. v United Mexican States, Award dated 6 July 2020, ICSID Case No. ARB(AF)/17/3

Vladimir Berschader and Michael Berschader v Russian Federation, Decision on Jurisdiction, 21st April 2006, SCC Case No. 080/2004

White Industries Australia Limited v The Republic of India, Final Award dated 30 November 2011, UNCITRAL Arbitration

Windstream Energy LLC v The Government of Canada, Award dated 27 September 2016, PCA Case No. 2013–22

Wintershall Aktiengesellschaft v Argentine Republic, Award dated 8 December 2008, ICSID Case No. ARB/04/14

WNC Factoring Ltd (WNC) v The Czech Republic, Award dated 22 February 2017, PCA Case No. 2014–34

Yaung Chi v Myanmar Yaung Chi OO Trading Pte Ltd v Government of the Union of Myanmar, Award dated 31 March 2003, ASEAN Case No. ARB/01/1

Yukos Universal Limited (Isle of Man) v The Russian Federation, PCA Case No. 2005-04/AA227

Table of WTO Cases

Appellate Body Report, *Chile – Price Band System and Safeguard Measures Relating to Certain Agricultural Products (Chile-Price Band System)*, WT/DS207/AB/R, AB-2002-2

Appellate Body Report, *European Communities – Conditions for the Granting of Tariff Preferences to Developing Countries (EC – Tariff Preferences)*, WT/DS246/AB/R

Appellate Body Report, *United States – Measures Affecting the Cross-Border Supply of Gambling and Betting Services (US – Gambling)*, WT/DS285/AB/R

Appellate Body Report, *United States – Import Prohibition of Certain Shrimp and Shrimp Products (US – Shrimp)*, WT/DS58/AB/R

Appellate Body Report, *Japan – Taxes on Alcoholic Beverages (Japan – Alcoholic Beverages II)*, WT/DS8/AB/R, WT/DS10/AB/R, WT/DS11/AB/R

Appellate Body report, *United States – Measures Affecting the Production and Sale of Clove Cigarettes (Clove Cigarettes)*, WT/DS406/AB/R

Appellate Body Report, *European Communities – Customs Classification of Frozen Boneless Chicken Cuts* (EC-*Chicken Cuts*), WT/DS269/AB/R; WT/DS286/AB/R

Appellate Body Report, *European Communities – Measures Affecting Asbestos and Asbestos-Containing Products* (EC – *Asbestos*), WT/DS135/AB/R

WTO Appellate Body Report, *United States – Continued Existence and Application of Zeroing Methodology* (US-Continued Zeroing),WT/DS350/AB/R

Index

www.ingramcontent.com/pod-product-compliance
Lightning Source LLC
LaVergne TN
LVHW010543300926
849162LV00002B/225